BUDGETING

Principles and Practice

By

HERMAN C. HEISER, C.P.A.

Partner of
LYBRAND, ROSS BROS. & MONTGOMERY

THE RONALD PRESS COMPANY • NEW YORK

COPYRIGHT, ©, 1959, by
THE RONALD PRESS COMPANY

All Rights Reserved

No part of this book may be reproduced
in any form without permission in writing
from the publisher.

Library of Congress Catalog Card Number: 59-7715

PRINTED IN THE UNITED STATES OF AMERICA

To
Prior Sinclair, C.P.A.

PREFACE

The complexities of modern business and the dynamic nature of our economy have made it necessary for management to develop special techniques for controlling the operation of a business enterprise. Decisions must be made quickly to adjust courses of action as external and internal forces change. Budgeting, as a management tool, has assumed a major role in the management function. While originally the budget constituted a financial document, there has been an ever increasing trend toward extending budgeting to include the planning, coordinating, and controlling of the entire operation of a business. Thus, budgeting becomes a function of the entire management team.

This book is a practical treatise on budgeting and deals with the problem of providing an effective means of communication among managerial personnel for the purpose of evaluating proposed plans of action, devising a coordinated program of operation, obtaining all requisite approvals, and directing the many activities toward the accomplishment of predetermined goals. The book is also concerned with the problem of formulating managerial policies and the control, not only of current operations, but also of future plans and policies.

For over twenty years I have specialized in the industrial management field as a corporate executive and in the management services consulting work of my firm. The use of budgeting as a management function is one of the areas in which I have had extensive experience. I believe that a sound knowledge of budgetary practice is a fundamental requirement of business managers. For this reason, this book has been written for the use of experienced managers, budget directors and their staffs, and for the professional accountant and consultant. The book has also been organized as a step-by-step presentation of budgetary procedures for the purpose of providing a text for students in colleges and universities. The underlying principles of budgeting are presented comprehensively and documented by descriptions of the budget practices of many companies. Management and accounting literature and publications contain a wealth of information about budgetary practice in the form of case studies, and it is one of the purposes of this book to assemble much of this information. In this respect the book is unique.

The plan of the book embraces two principal purposes. The first purpose is to emphasize the dual nature of budgeting—planning and coordination on the one hand, and control on the other—and to provide an over-all review of these aspects of the subject before investigating the detailed problems and procedures. The second purpose is to apply in detail the principles and procedures relating to planning, coordination, and control to various segments of the budget. Recognizing the need to demonstrate, in a work of this kind, the wide scope of budgeting and the interrelationship of the various segments of the over-all budget, the book includes a presentation of a budget in final form for a hypothetical company, and each segment of this budget is studied in relation to the over-all budget.

Following the plan described, the book is organized in three parts and appendixes.

Part I, consisting of five chapters, is devoted to an over-all review of budgeting for the purposes of planning and coordination and includes a chapter on the budget in final form.

Part II, consisting of three chapters, is devoted to a discussion of budgeting for the purpose of control, including the measurement of deviations from expected performance standards established both for planned operations and actual operations. Both parts contain numerous illustrations to provide the framework for the remaining chapters of the book.

Part III, consisting of twelve chapters, studies in detail the techniques of budgeting and controlling each of ten major categories of income and expenditure, and concludes with a discussion of budget revisions and alternative budgeting practices.

Appendix A contains supporting information and *pro forma* journal entries for the budget report presented in Part I, and Appendix B contains *pro forma* journal entries for budget variations for one month. These are included for the reader who wishes to explore further the mechanics of budget building. Appendix C contains a case study of an actual company budget for a full year's operation.

In gathering the material and writing this book, I have had invaluable assistance from Dr. Sterling K. Atkinson of Temple University and from Arno R. Kassander, C.P.A., a member of my firm's staff. I am grateful also for the contributions by other members of the staff—notably Theodore R. Pleim, C.P.A., and Lambert H. Spronck, C.P.A., for their comments, criticisms, and suggestions, and especially Margaret White Nally, C.P.A., for her work in editing the manuscript, checking the references, and verifying the accuracy of the numerous interrelated budget schedules that appear throughout the book.

I am particularly indebted to my partner, Prior Sinclair, C.P.A., at whose suggestion this work was undertaken. His book on budgeting, published in 1934, was one of the pioneer publications in the field and provided a sound foundation upon which to build this work. I am grateful to him for the opportunity to author a successor to his book and for the inspiration, encouragement, and support that he furnished.

HERMAN C. HEISER

Philadelphia, Pennsylvania
February, 1959

CONTENTS

Part I
BUDGETING FOR PLANNING AND COORDINATION

CHAPTER		PAGE
1	INTRODUCTION	3
2	PROFIT PLANNING	14
3	ORGANIZATION FOR BUDGETING	38
4	PREPARING THE BUDGET	56
5	THE BUDGET IN FINAL FORM	85

Part II
BUDGETING FOR CONTROL

6	ANALYSIS AND REPORTING OF VARIATIONS FROM BUDGET	107
7	FLEXIBLE BUDGET ALLOWANCES FOR COST CONTROL	131
8	ANALYSIS AND REPORTING OF COST VARIANCES	154

Part III
BUDGETING AND CONTROLLING TECHNIQUES

9	SALES	169
10	MARKETING AND DISTRIBUTION COSTS	194
11	INVENTORIES	220
12	DIRECT MATERIAL COST	236
13	DIRECT LABOR COST	247
14	FACTORY EXPENSE	258
15	GENERAL AND ADMINISTRATIVE EXPENSES AND OTHER ITEMS	270
16	RESEARCH AND DEVELOPMENT COSTS	285
17	CAPITAL EXPENDITURES	303
18	FINANCIAL POSITION	320
19	BUDGET REVISIONS	337
20	ALTERNATIVE BUDGETING PRACTICES	351

CONTENTS

APPENDIXES

A Supporting Information and Journal Entries for Illustrative
    Company Budget Report 371
B Illustrative Company's Budget Deviations in January . . 378
C A Case Study 381

Index 399

Part I

BUDGETING FOR PLANNING AND COORDINATION

CHAPTER 1

INTRODUCTION

	Page		Page
Definition of terms	3	**The Functions of Accounting in Budgeting**	
The Importance of Planning		Income and financial accounting	9
General	4	Provision and pricing of data	9
Long-range and short-range planning	5	Analysis of alternative actions	10
Planning involves coordination	6	Measurement of performance	10
Planning and control	7	Accounting requirements	10
The Budget		Cost data a prerequisite	12
General	8	Budgeting—one more step in use of accounting data	13

Definition of Terms. Budgeting is a much discussed topic, but seldom defined. Actually, it is the preparation *and* use of a budget. But what is a budget? Historically, it was a financial document prepared by government to relate anticipated revenues and planned expenditures of a fiscal period, as a basis for adjusting income to outgo, or vice versa. That essential purpose has not changed with the adoption of budgetary practices by nongovernmental enterprises and individuals. But the wider practice of the art has given rise to a loose terminology so that today the terms "budget" and "budgeting" do not mean the same thing to all people. Originally, the budget was understood to be a complete, over-all plan, but now one speaks of "sales budgets," "expense budgets," "capital expenditure budgets," and the like. Similarly, today one speaks of "budgeting one's time" as well as money. Specifically, is a budget a financial document, and can the term "budgeting" be applied in the absence of a complete and comprehensive matching of anticipated revenue with anticipated expenditures? Can a management, for example, claim to practice budgeting if it "budgets" only certain of the company's activities?

The foregoing questions are important for the insight which they give into the subject. Certain definitions, therefore, are in order as a means of marking out the path to be followed in the ensuing chapters, and of sharpening the reader's concepts at the outset.

BUDGET. The author thinks of the budget as an over-all "blueprint" of a comprehensive plan of operations and actions, expressed in financial terms.

BUDGETING. Budgeting is conceived to be the preparation of a budget *and* its fullest use, not only as a device for planning and coordinating, but also for control.

In the first definition it should be recognized that while the financial nature of the document is the necessary result of the fact that money is the common denominator of all business transactions, nevertheless, the document is only a financial reflection of transactions with nonmonetary things—man-hours of labor, tons of raw material, units of product, and so on. With reference to the common practice of applying the term "budget" to mere segments of the budget, as mentioned above, the author believes that this practice, while understandable, is unfortunate in that it leads to confused thinking on the subject and, consequently, in this work that usage will be avoided. As used throughout the text, the term accords with the formal definition presented above and has the connotation of a comprehensive, master plan. Detailed segments are referred to as *budget schedules*. Thus, a listing of budgeted sales is not referred to as a sales budget but as a schedule of budgeted sales.

With reference to the definition of budgeting, it should be emphasized that the term applies only where a budget is both prepared and used. This is in line with the generally accepted idea that budgeting should serve a threefold purpose of planning, coordination, and control.

THE IMPORTANCE OF PLANNING

Management's primary function is the effective use of the capital at its command. This refers not only to that portion of the capital which is invested in productive facilities, but also to that represented by the assets which comprise the circulating capital of the organization. The essence of capital management is foresight and planning, whether it concerns the initiation of the enterprise or its year-to-year and day-to-day operations.

The factor of time is of the utmost importance in all economic endeavor and particularly in modern business. Every expenditure of funds is for the purpose of producing income *in the future*. This is true whether one considers the investment in long-life assets such as buildings, machinery, and equipment; the recruitment and training of personnel; or the procurement and production of inventories. Every expenditure is in anticipation of the realization of income. The only difference is in the amount of foresight necessary since some expenditures anticipate income to be realized years ahead, while others involve much shorter periods of anticipation. But in every case the expenditure represents an *investment* based upon a prediction of things to come, the **propriety of the expenditure hinging on the correctness of the prediction.**

In addition to the anticipatory nature of all business expenditures, the complex nature of economic production further accentuates the need for planning and foresight. The decision, for example, to produce finished goods, either for immediate shipment or for inventory, entails the timely availability of facilities, trained labor force, and materials. This, then, suggests the need not only for "strategic" planning but also for "tactical" planning in considerable detail.

Business planning cannot be done in a vacuum. Plans must be formulated in terms of the conditions and forces surrounding the enterprise. Some are external and some internal; some can be controlled, while others must be accepted and met. Awareness of these forces and conditions, and sufficient insight concerning their nature, are prerequisites of good planning.

Among the external forces which determine the size and share of the market which an enterprise can obtain are the general state of business and the level of national income, the desirability of the company's product both intrinsically and by comparison with other products and services, and the intensity of the competitive efforts of other firms, not only in the immediate industry but in all the industries which compete for the customers' dollars. Some external forces are completely outside the control of the individual enterprise—as for example, the general state of business. Others, however, may be modified by the individual enterprise. Reference here is made to the powerful influence of promotional activities in creating product demand not only for the product in general but also for the company's own brand.

Some of the internal forces and conditions which must be recognized are the company's financial strength, the efficiency of its operating procedures, the fixed and variable nature of its costs, the controllability of its costs, the state of its facilities, and the time factor in its cycles of procurement, production, distribution, and income realization. All of these are subject to some degree of control in the long run, although in the short run some may have to be accepted as being temporarily unalterable.

Whether the forces be external or internal, management must be aware of them, must be able to classify them according to their controllability and to evaluate them, and must recognize their time characteristics. Planning implies a knowledge of objectives, and these can be determined only in the light of the circumstances surrounding the company's operations and markets.

Long-Range and Short-Range Planning. The studies and calculations which precede the launching of an enterprise are the clearest example of long-range planning. The proposed investment in long-life assets and the development of an organization preclude shortsightedness. They require estimates and plans projected far enough into the future to ensure a reasonable return on the investment, as well as its eventual recovery. But this type of planning should not cease with the launching of the company. It is generally recognized that no company can stand still—that it must continue to grow if it is to remain prosperous. Therefore, the same type of planning that preceded the birth of the organization must be carried on continuously as the company searches and plans for newer and larger markets and better methods of operation. Such planning is essentially long-range in nature: first, because of the time required to make and execute the plan; second, because usually it represents an investment which anticipates income realization over a long period of time; and third, because company policies—whether they relate to prices, labor relations, or some other aspect of the business—by their very nature frequently have long-run effects.

Short-range planning, on the other hand, is primarily concerned with the immediate use of the already available facilities and organization within the framework of the general long-range plan currently in effect. This type of planning is essentially tactical in nature rather than strategic and is concerned with the immediate, current problems of procurement, recruitment, production, distribution, and financing. The length of the planning period is largely controlled by the time cycles in the foregoing functions, as well as the traditional and actual necessity of annual progress and position reports; consequently, in most industries the short-range plans are prepared on the basis of the fiscal year or fraction thereof.

Whether the planning be long-range or short-range, it must go on continuously. To be successful, the management must be continually looking to the future, and even the short-range plans must be kept under constant study to ensure prompt and timely revision where the basic forecasts prove to be wrong.

Planning Involves Coordination. Business planning is analogous to the design of a product. First the general idea is conceived. Then it is drawn up in a master plan. The master plan is then supported by detailed blueprints of the component parts. Generally, there is an interplay of the several steps as the lessons learned in the preparation of one step force a modification of the others. The over-all design may be very acceptable market-wise but, when translated into detailed operating plans, may prove unworkable or uneconomic. Planning the design, therefore, not only involves the coordination of the various parts, but the coordination itself may affect the basic design.

The application of these principles to the periodic planning of operations starts with the basic idea involving the volume of business to be secured, and the profit objective. This in turn gives rise to a master plan supported by, and coordinated with, a series of detail plans. The master plan charts the major movements as to revenue and costs to achieve the objectives for the period which are stated in financial terms in the forecast balance sheet, operating statement, cash flow statement, and source and application of funds statement. These results, however, can be achieved only through many different operations closely integrated and coordinated. Sales, shipments, product completions, and raw material purchases are an example of just one of the chain of movements necessary to achieve a given volume of sales and the desired end-of-period inventories. The relation of these, in turn, to the cash position is an example of the interplay of the various parts. But in the planning of the detailed movements, obstacles may be encountered to achieving the master plan and necessitate revision. Cash requirements may be excessive, production flow may be unbalanced, inventory storage space may be unavailable, and other difficulties may be disclosed which require alterations in the plan. Above all things, the plan *must be workable*.

Just as the over-all plan comprises a master or summary plan and numerous detail plans or schedules, so the preparation of the plans calls for the cooperation of many persons in the organization. While top management sets the objectives initially, all ranks of management have a part in planning the details; and as a result of their studies top management's objectives may be modified, at least in the short run. The work of planning, therefore, starts at the top, moves through the lower ranks, and back to the top, reciprocating until a workable plan evolves. Cooperation at all stages is the essence of good planning.

Planning and Control. The foregoing discussion has been concerned with the purpose and nature of planning as it relates to future action. It should not be overlooked, however, that plans, themselves, also have an important role in controlling operations. Constant comparison of the plan with the results of its operations provides not only a measure of the amount of deviation but also the reasons therefor, and these are prime requisites as a basis for determining when and how the plans should be amended. For such comparisons to be useful, it is obvious that the plans must be in detail not only as to function but also as to time. For example, a sales plan for a year would have little utility in measuring progress in the accomplishment of the plan unless the plan establishes targets for fractions of the year. It must also be recognized that, particularly for cost control purposes, a flexible plan may be needed for those situations where operations do not conform with forecasted operations used to formulate the basic plan. This takes the form of a series of cost allowance schedules related to a series of sales volumes or levels of operation, or, in the absence of such cost schedules, a set of cost standards or formulae by which allowable costs can be determined for any foreseeable range in volume and activity within the period of the basic plan.

THE BUDGET

Bearing in mind the previous definition and the foregoing discussion of the functions of planning, coordination, and control, we see that the budget takes the form of a collection of documents. They include forecast statements of operations and financial position. These, in turn, are supported by as many detail schedules as are necessary in the circumstances to integrate and coordinate all underlying, planned transactions for the guidance of all ranks and divisions of management. In short, the budget is "the approved forecast program and all of its parts." [1]

The number of parts, particularly detail schedules, may vary, depending on the nature of the company's operations. A multiplicity of products or of processes, or both, will call for a more voluminous set of documents than a few products or a simple type of operation. The problem of coordination varies in difficulty from company to company. In some cases planning is simplified by the nature of the company's business in relation to its market. In such cases plans can be prepared easily with the expectation that they will not have to be changed during the period of the budget. In other cases, however, planning requires carefully made decisions, along with the ability to change the plan quickly as conditions change. Moreover, in many such cases, while the plan for the budget period as a whole may not have to be changed, there may be significant variations from the plan during segments of the period. This increases the importance, and the difficulty, of the control feature of budgeting. Management's purpose is not only to measure performance in line with the plan, but also to measure the efficiency of actual operations.

In the control of manufacturing expense, for example, the measure of efficiency should be conformity of actual expenses, not with the allowances established in the budget for the scheduled operations, but with allowances established for the actual operations. For this purpose, therefore, flexible expense allowances are necessary. Since these flexible allowances are part of the control procedure, the schedule of allowances is an integral part of the company's budget.

[1] Frank Z. Oles, "Comprehensive Budgetary Control," *N.A.A. Bulletin*, Section 1, Oct., 1951, p. 127.

THE FUNCTIONS OF ACCOUNTING IN BUDGETING

The functions of accounting in budgeting are as follows:

1. To equate all planned transactions in terms of
   a) Revenue, costs, and profit
   b) Financial position at end of selected periods, as shown by forecast balance sheets
   c) Sources and application of funds, as shown by funds statements
   d) Cash flow, as shown by statements of estimated cash receipts and disbursements
2. To provide some data and to price other data for use in preparation of the budget
3. To show the effect on profit and financial position of alternative courses of action
4. To report, in profit and financial terms, performance under the plan

Each of these functions is discussed in the following pages and will serve not only to show the importance of a sound accounting structure to budgeting, but also to promote fuller comprehension of the problems and requirements of an adequate budget procedure.

Income and Financial Accounting. Accounting's function in this phase of budgeting in effect is to journalize *pro forma* the transactions called for in the various detailed budget schedules. While *pro forma* entries need not actually be made, the debit and credit aspects of all transactions must be recognized in the preparation of the various budget schedules. This arises from the need for translating all transactions in terms of integrated, forecast statements of income and financial position. Recognition of the underlying *pro forma* entries is necessary to ensure the coordination of all segments of the plan of operations.

Provision and Pricing of Data. Although the sales forecast is not an accounting function, the fixing of the budgeted sales schedule is heavily dependent on accounting for knowledge of the relation of budgeted volume to net profit. Moreover, the forecast can be greatly facilitated by a well classified record of the company's past experience. Knowledge of the past sales performance by product line, territory, customer, and other categories is essential in appraising future prospects.

However, it is in the budgeting of costs and expenses that accounting plays the greatest role. The translation of production schedules into cost schedules is essentially cost accounting. Especially in the relation of volume to factory burden is accounting's role important. This calls for knowledge of the variability characteristics of different expense items. The use of standard costs is most helpful in budgeting; but whether the company's cost accounting is based on standards or historical costs, a record of past experience is invaluable in determining the margin of error or the variances from standards which may be expected under given circumstances.

Accounting determinations are also important in connection with the nonfactory costs. Variations of advertising and other selling expenses in relation to sales, the cost of administration and financing, the bad debts and cash discounts records are all important in forecasting the effect of the budgeted sales volume.

While many budget determinations are initially nonmonetary in character, they must finally be translated in financial terms. And in many cases the initial measurements, for reasons of expediency, are made in these terms. Thus, although budget decisions are not an accounting function, the provision of much of the data and the pricing of all the data point to accounting as the keystone of budgeting.

Analysis of Alternative Actions. Accounting determinations are of special significance in the review of alternative courses of action which is a part of the budget-making process. Selection of the best methods of distribution, product mix, pricing, and other functions can be made only with adequate knowledge of the comparative effects of these actions on net profit.

Measurement of Performance. Measurement of performance against the budget and the prompt reporting of deviations, as a basis for timely corrective action by management, calls for prompt recording and classification of transactions. The measurements may be in both monetary and nonmonetary terms. For the lower levels of management, quantitative data in terms of units of product, labor, material, and so forth, frequently are more useful since those are the things with which the operators are concerned. At higher management levels, however, monetary measurements become important because it is only through them that the effect of a budget deviation on profit can be measured. A deviation from the sales schedule or labor schedule may be measured in terms of units of product or man-hours, for use by one level of management; but they need a common denominator—monetary value—to measure the significance of one deviation as compared with another, for the information of higher levels of management. Thus accounting serves a twofold purpose in this connection. The first is to translate monetary budget standards into physical quantities as a basis for measuring budget deviations quantitatively. The second purpose is to translate quantitative deviations into monetary profit and loss data.

Accounting Requirements. An adequate classification of accounts is a prerequisite of successful budgeting. The provision of the data needed for estimating revenue, the determination of costs under different volumes and methods of operation, and the prompt comparison of actual operating results with the budget, all call for an account organization which goes beyond the requirements of mere financial reporting.

The first [prerequisite] . . . is a proper classification of accounts and statistics that will adequately reflect various items of volume, income, and expense. Such a classification system must not only accomplish the requirements of financial accounting, such as accurate distinctions between income, expense, capital investments, and the many other financial accounting areas with which you are all familiar in order to meet the requirements of proper statement preparation, inventory valuation, tax requirements, profit or loss determination, etc. It must also meet those requirements which operating management needs to control its business from day to day, week to week, and month to month. In order to make this important point crystal-clear, I should like to draw a distinction between the field of financial accounting and what I like to refer to as the field of control accounting. Both are very closely related and obviously need to be closely integrated with each other in order to avoid excessive accounting expense. The emphasis in each is quite different, however.

Financial accounting concerns itself primarily with recording the business transactions and summarizing them for the various purposes outlined above. In a broad way, the resulting statements obviously give management guidance and control information in their planning of the business operations. The field of control accounting, however, goes much further in providing various areas of management with data to control its operations. This area of accounting specializes in various planning, analytical, and control procedures such as budgets, cost accounting, operating analyses, product costs, costs for pricing, standard expense rates, overhead or burden allocations, break-even charts, and other devices. It emphasizes the strategic use of the mass of detailed information available in the accounting records in such a way as to furnish operating management with the detailed information it believes necessary to control operations. The classification system can be so organized that it will meet the requirements of these various control accounting uses and still meet all of the requirements in the financial accounting field. The reverse is not true, however, since some of the essentials to control accounting are not particularly requirements of financial accounting. For example, under a classification that meets the requirements of control accounting, it is essential that expense be departmentalized sufficiently so as to parallel management responsibilities as shown on the organization chart. If the classification system does not match the supervisory structure, the budgeting and accounting records will not readily reflect the responsibilities of the managers and the actual results of their operations.[2]

Detailed classifications of accounts are the essence of the account requirements for budgeting, as well as for all managerial control procedures. A total sales figure will satisfy the minimum requirements of an operating statement for financial reporting, but is not adequate for

---

[2] Arthur H. Smith, "Budget Preparation," in American Institute of Certified Public Accountants, *Accounting, Auditing, Taxes 1953* (New York: American Institute of Certified Public Accountaints, 1954), pp. 209–10.

other purposes. Detailed sales classifications as to territory, size, customer, product, salesman, and method of shipment are some of the requirements for forecasting, measuring actual performance, and fixing responsibility for performance. Too much emphasis cannot be placed on the detailed record of sales as an aid in forecasting future sales and preparing the schedule of budgeted sales. Since this is the starting point in budget determinations and controls all the other operations of the business, adequate information for accurate sales forecasts is an absolute necessity.

Cost Data a Prerequisite. Cost accounting is also a "must." Moreover, the use of standard costs, while not a prime requisite, greatly facilitates budgeting and other control procedures. Knowledge of unit product costs, for all products, is needed not only in pricing but also for facilitating the preparation of cost forecasts under varying conditions of volume and sales mix, as well as for the prompt analysis of alternative courses of action, consideration of which is an integral part of budgeting. Especially with reference to factory burden, budgeting relies heavily on accounting determinations. The determination of the burden absorption rate is a prerequisite to product costing, and the budgeting of burden items and related cash requirements constitutes a major task in budget preparation. For both these purposes, the accounts must provide detailed information of the relation of burden to production volume.

The commercial or selling expenses must also be capable of careful analysis. Not only do these expenses frequently account for a significant proportion of the total costs, but they also pose some very difficult problems in controlling the effectiveness of the expenditures. Measuring the relation of sales effort and promotional expenditures to sales results is more difficult than relating factory costs to production. Only by constant analysis of experience records can goals be established, and, again, to be useful the records must be well classified.

With reference to the other expenses of the business, the same need for detailed information exists. One example will suffice—that of budgeting the administrative clerical costs. Too frequently this item of cost is thought of as fixed. Actually, clerical effort should be subject to the same controls as any other effort, and the budget should be based on a volume-cost concept in this area as well as in the factory.

But costs and expenses are not the only subjects for analysis in budgeting. The forecasting of cash receipts, for example, involves not only a sales estimate but also knowledge of the time factor in the liquidation of the resulting receivables. Budgeting monthly cash receipts from customers involves a forecast of the payment pattern in time, together with estimates of cash discounts and bad debts. These estimates depend very largely on past experience made available through adequate records.

Budgeting—One More Step in Use of Accounting Data. It is quite apparent that good budgeting requires a high level of account organization and accounting procedure. It should also be equally apparent that the type of information called for in budgeting is important to management whether or not formal, complete budget procedure is followed. Therefore, while it is true that good budgeting presents substantial accounting and control requirements, for those companies which now have these requisites, budgeting is merely one more step—that of integrating and coordinating the various data and controls into a unified, over-all working plan.

One of the by-products of budgeting which does not lack importance is its aid in the maintenance of good internal control procedures so necessary in safeguarding the company's assets and preventing and detecting errors and fraud.

CHAPTER 2

PROFIT PLANNING

Objective and Measurements in Profit Planning	Page
Objective of profit planning	14
Measuring the profit objective	16

The Return on Investment Method	
Time as a factor in the analysis	17
Net operating profit vs. net income	20
The meaning of "capital employed"	20
Working assets	21
Fixed assets	22
The desired return on capital employed	24

Volume-Cost-Price-Profit Relationships	Page
Volume-cost-profit relationships	25
Fixed and variable costs	27
Break-even calculations	28
Required volume to earn a profit	29
Laws of costs and profits	30
Limitations of preceding analyses	31
Volume-price relationship	32

Planning Technique	
The method of differential analysis	33
The differences must be real	35
The concept of different costs for different purposes	36
Use of principles and techniques in planning	37

The purpose of this and the following three chapters is to present a bird's-eye view of budgeting as it relates to planning and coordination, in order to establish a framework for the subsequent discussions of detail problems and procedures. The dominant motive of a business enterprise is to utilize its available resources in the interest of profit maximization and the attainment of this objective involves management planning. This chapter therefore is devoted to the fundamental principles of profit planning.

The discussion falls into four parts. The first part deals with the objective of profit planning and the essential measurements. The second part discusses one of the measurements, return on investment, in more detail. The third part provides background information in the form of a résumé of the fundamental relationships of volume, cost, price, and profit. The fourth part provides a description of the technique by which the knowledge of the foregoing relationships is utilized in planning the most profitable course of action for a company.

OBJECTIVE AND MEASUREMENTS IN PROFIT PLANNING

Objective of Profit Planning. The motivating forces of business are many and varied and not always easy to define. The profit motive, obviously, is most important, but it is not necessarily the only motive.

The prestige associated with success or size, the creative urge, the competitive urge, the desire for social approval, fear of government intervention, and the urge to provide economic security for one's heirs are some of the motivating forces. With reference to a particular company, the significance of the several forces varies with the controlling personalities and the nature of their position in the company. The motives of an owner-manager, for example, may differ from those of the hired manager of an absentee-ownership company. Moreover, the motives of an elderly and well-established management may differ from those of young newcomers in the field. The inclination to "play it safe," or to be venturesome, is a factor that cannot always be explained or predicted.

Whatever the motives may be, they should be recognized and clearly defined in the early planning stages, for they determine the company's objective. Planning without an objective is sheer waste of time and effort. The objective obviously must be clear. This observation would be trite were it not for the fact that in all but the smallest organizations, sound planning necessitates enlisting the aid of all levels of management. Therefore, the objective must not only be defined; it must also be communicated. Otherwise the planning activities cannot be properly coordinated.

While a variety of business motives may and usually do exist in all companies, the profit motive is almost always dominant. Therefore, the profit motive is the basis of the type of planning discussed in this work and the ultimate objective is assumed to be profit maximization. The choice of alternatives and the final plan itself are assumed to be directed toward earning a maximum profit.

In establishing profit maximization as a goal, however, recognition must be given to the factor of time. Frequently decisions must recognize the difference between short-run and long-run effects. Thus a decision to maximize immediate profits may have an adverse effect in the long run. For example, during a period of acute shortages of goods, a company might refrain from charging all that the traffic will bear, in order to preserve customer good will for the time when business will again become truly competitive. Moreover, the allocation of scarce goods to numerous sales outlets involving higher distribution costs than would have been incurred in satisfying the full demand of just a few customers might be made to maintain the normal number of outlets necessary to future operations. Decisions of this type are a matter of high policy and not subject to precise measurement. Nevertheless, they are important. Hence, the grave importance of long-range planning within the framework of which the current period's operating plan should be made.

Measuring the Profit Objective. While profit maximization is considered to be the goal, this objective of itself is somewhat nebulous and is not a satisfactory basis for planning, unless quantitatively defined. Budgets are quantitative and therefore can define the profit objective by measurement in dollars. Moreover, profit maximization alone cannot be an ultimate objective unless the profit so maximized justifies continuance of the enterprise. As a practical matter, therefore, the profit objective must be established quantitatively. There are several ways in which this is done in practice, although they are not necessarily of equal usefulness.

A very common method of measuring profitability utilizes the ratio of profit to sales. Thus, the planned objective is to realize a profit of a certain percentage of sales. The planned sales are then determined at an amount which will permit the realization of a total profit sufficient to cover dividend requirements and to provide for some increase in retained earnings.

The prevalence of return on sales as a measure of profitability probably results from the long-established practice of analyzing profit and loss ratios and perhaps, even more so, from the traditional cost-plus method of setting prices. The method has a certain logic and generally is convenient to use. However, in recent years many progressive managements have come to realize that in order to reach sound decisions leading to maximum profit, adequate return on sales should be supplemented by an acceptable rate of return on investment. As will be pointed out hereafter, return on investment is a function of return on sales and capital investment turnover.

It is interesting to speculate that the lag in adopting a return-on-investment concept of profit measurement may well stem from the fact that accepted accounting practices do not account for all of the economic costs of doing business. Accountants years ago turned their back on the concept of interest on own investment as a cost, and they never did recognize the economists' concept of "pure profit." These decisions were based on practical considerations of great merit. Nevertheless, the result has been that management's attention too often has not been directed to the very important return on capital employed, except in a minor way in the form of the cost of interest actually paid on borrowed capital. While depreciation of tangible capital assets is accounted for, this applies to only a part of the total capital investment and, moreover, is merely a means of systematically recovering from operations the cost or other basic value of these assets. Depreciation does not provide for the economic cost of accumulating and employing the capital. Just as a mortgagee demands interest payments for the use of money loaned as well as periodic amortization of principal, a business concern should

PROFIT PLANNING

consider the economic cost of tying up capital in determining the profitableness of its operations. This is accomplished by including in the measure of profitability, provision for a rate of return on capital employed.

The value of this measure of profitability in conjunction with the ratio of profit to sales, can be readily illustrated by reference to the problem of comparing the profitability of two products. Product A, for example, may be salable at a price which will realize a profit of 20 per cent, while Product B may earn only 10 per cent of the sales price. It thus appears that A is much more desirable than B. Such would not be the case, however, if the production and distribution of A required, say, more than twice as large an investment of capital funds as the production and distribution of B. In such a case, Product B actually would earn a better return on investment than A and, consequently, would be the more desirable product. It is assumed, of course, in this example, that capital investment is an important factor in the enterprise. This normally is true of manufacturing but may not be in a service type of enterprise.

THE RETURN ON INVESTMENT METHOD

The author believes that a well-thought-out profit objective requires consideration of the rate of return on investment. Such consideration when coupled with planning adequate return on sales is typical of advanced management thinking. For these reasons the procedures to be described in this book include such considerations. As the method is of somewhat recent development, it may be helpful to introduce at this point a brief discussion of some underlying principles as well as problems peculiar to the method.

Time as a Factor in the Analysis. Time is an important factor in the analysis. It is the common element both in measuring profitability based on sales and on capital employed. Both measurements must be made for a time period. Thus, if the year's sales of Product A amount to $200,000 with the employment of $100,000 of capital, and the sales of Product B amount to $300,000 with the employment of $100,000 of capital, and the profit amounts to $20,000 on A and $30,000 on B, the measures of profitability would be computed as follows:

Percentage of Sales
  Product A: 20,000 ÷ 200,000 = 10 per cent
  Product B: 30,000 ÷ 300,000 = 10 per cent
Percentage of Capital Employed
  Product A: 20,000 ÷ 100,000 = 20 per cent
  Product B: 30,000 ÷ 100,000 = 30 per cent

Obviously in this example, while both products are equally desirable on the basis of the first measurement, they are unequal on the basis of the second.

The factor which accounts for the difference in the two products is the relationship of sales volume to capital employed. In the case of Product A, there is a turnover of capital employed of 200 per cent, whereas in the case of Product B, it is 300 per cent. The formula for measuring return on capital employed, therefore, should be stated as follows:

$$\frac{\text{Net operating profit}}{\text{Sales}} \times \frac{\text{Sales}}{\text{Capital employed}} = \text{Percentage return on capital employed}$$

In the case of Product A the computation is:

$$\frac{20{,}000}{200{,}000} \times \frac{200{,}000}{100{,}000} = 20 \text{ per cent}$$

And the computation of Product B is:

$$\frac{30{,}000}{300{,}000} \times \frac{300{,}000}{100{,}000} = 30 \text{ per cent}$$

The same profit rates on capital employed can be computed merely by reference to profits and capital employed, but in so doing

> ... we would lose sight of two important factors, the significance of costs in relation to sales income and the significance of the level of capital employed in relation to sales volume—two variables which must be kept under constant study if we are to know what is happening within our operations and where managerial effort needs to be concentrated.

The return, so defined and determined, can be improved in three ways:

1. By increasing net sales through higher prices or greater volume.
2. By decreasing costs.
3. By reducing the amount of capital employed through improvement in inventory levels, more rapid collection of accounts receivable, putting excess cash to use, and through economic control of additions to fixed capital.[1]

Figure 2–1 graphically portrays the relationship between profit on sales, profit on capital employed, and turnover of capital.

While the use of the return on investment concept as a tool to aid management in measuring the profitability of its operations has grown in acceptance, there is no general agreement as to what elements constitute the factors to be employed in its computation. It is not the author's intention to discuss all of the facets of return on investment since there have been many good articles written on the subject which readers may refer to if they are interested in pursuing the topic further. However,

---

[1] F. J. Muth, "Return on Capital Employed—Measure of Management," *N.A.A. Bulletin*, Section 1, Feb., 1954, pp. 700-701.

PROFIT PLANNING

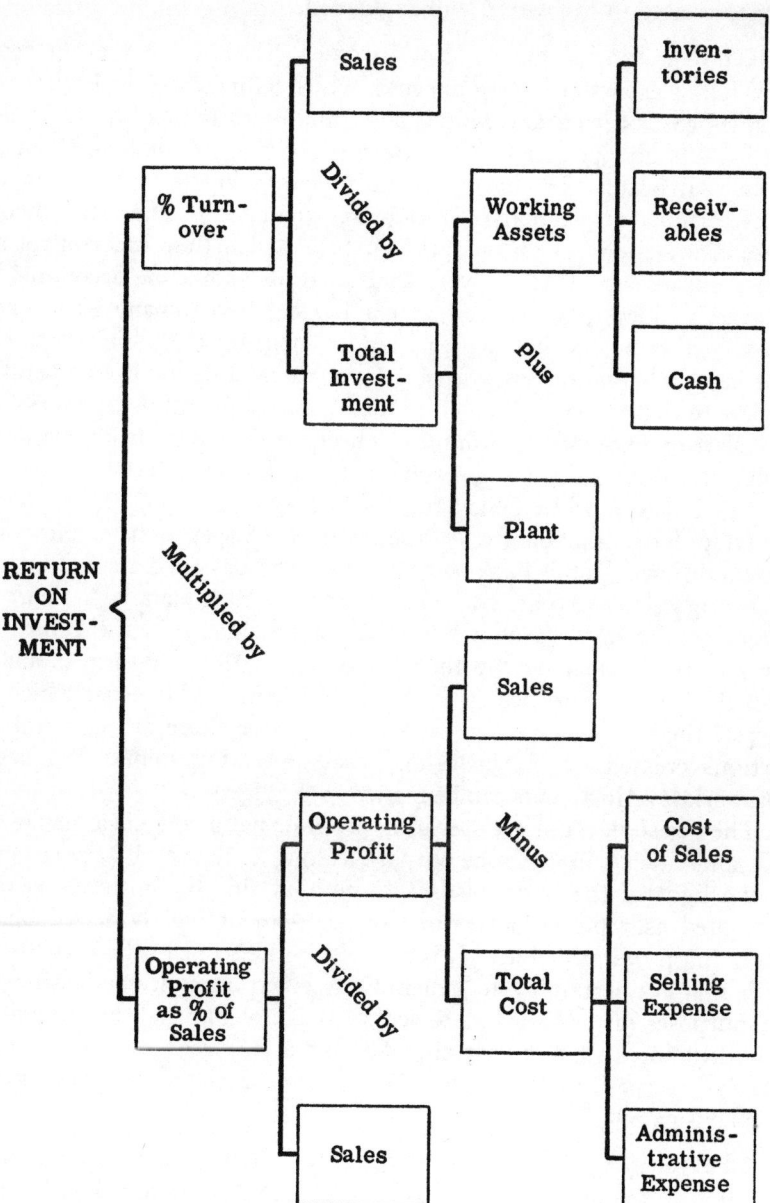

Fig. 2-1. Relationship of Factors Affecting Return on Investment

some of the areas for consideration will be discussed and some of the terms, as used in this work, will be defined.

Net Operating Profit vs. Net Income. Net operating profit represents net sales less operating expense, which as indicated in Figure 2–1, includes cost of sales and selling and administrative expenses. It does not include nonoperating income and expense items or federal income taxes. Advocates of using net operating profit in the return-on-investment formula argue that operating management is interested in only those transactions of an operating nature which they can control and that transactions of a purely financial nature should be accounted for separately since they are a responsibility of the company as a whole. They further argue that there is danger in using the all-inclusive concept because situations may arise where material items of nonoperating income or deductions will result in distortion of the ratio. Of course, the inclusion or exclusion of sales and purchase discounts from the determination of net operating profit may seriously affect comparisons among divisions when policy regarding these items vary because they are under loose control or when the diversity of operations creates varying conditions. In this book such discounts are classified among the nonoperating items as a matter of convenience in budget planning. There are others advocating use of net income (after taxes) in the return-on-investment formula on the theory that the ratio of return should be all-inclusive and thus include all items of revenue and expense which are part of the final income determination. Where there are material distortions created by the inclusion of nonoperating items, they argue, appropriate adjustments can be made.

The decision to use net operating profit or net income is a managerial one, and either will serve the purpose as long as the results are reviewed in the light of the basis used. Throughout this book, the percentage computed as representing return on investment will be based on net operating profit as defined. It is not within the scope of the book to deal with matters pertaining to generally accepted accounting classification for purposes of published statements. It is not unusual, in internal accounting statements, to classify data in a different manner to more clearly present information for the purpose of managerial guidance in decision-making.

The Meaning of "Capital Employed." Attention is called to the fact that in the foregoing discussion the term "capital employed" refers to assets. While for some purposes the relation of profits to owners' equity is a proper measure, for the purposes of managerial control the relation to investment in assets is more meaningful.

The use of the ratio of profit to owners' equity has some logical justification since it relates the profit to the owners' net investment throughout the period; and it may well be argued that, after all, management's principal concern is to satisfy the owners. One objection to the method, however, is that it may tend to promote an excessive use of borrowed funds or credit at too low a rate of return on the invested funds, but yet at a high enough rate to cover the interest costs and add something to the net profit as an additional return on owners' capital. Thus, for example, a 10 per cent return on capital of $500,000, or $50,000, may be increased to $70,000, or 14 per cent, by the simple expedient of borrowing $500,000 at 4 per cent and investing it in facilities earning 8 per cent. This increase in return to the owners may make them happy, but it tends to obscure the fact that funds have been committed to a lower rate of return than the owners would have required on their own investment. The result conceivably could be that of encouraging an uneconomic use of borrowed funds. This is not meant to condemn a possibly wise resort to borrowing as a means of pyramiding the return on owners' investment, but it suggests that *all* funds available to the management, regardless of source, should be invested economically, that is, put to work only for a fair return on the *funds used*.

Attention is called to the fact that the term "capital employed" applies not only to the tangible, fixed assets but to all assets involved in the operation under study, including the associated inventories, receivables, and working cash balance. Upon determining the items which make up the capital employed figure, there is still the problem of valuing the specific assets for the purpose of this computation.

Working Assets. Although book amounts are generally used in valuing the working assets, certain accounting practices may call for special considerations:

1. CASH. The treatment of cash will depend on the use to be made of the analysis of return on capital employed. If, for example, management attempts to compare its total operational effectiveness with that of other companies by computing rates of return for those companies from their financial statements, they must allow for the fact that at any given time a company's balance sheet may show more or less cash than the normal working requirements. Excess cash, particularly, may reflect an accumulation for some future expansion program, and this, of course, would have no bearing on the computation of the current rate of return. Moreover, in a comparison of rates of return for the several divisions within the company itself, care must be exercised to include only that cash which is normal to the division's operations.

2. RECEIVABLES. Realistic values should be used in valuing receivables, which means that the figure used should be net of the allowance for uncollectible accounts. However, if the book allowance is excessive—that is, if it includes provision for loss in excess of known or probable losses based on past experience—such excess provision should not be used in the valuation.

3. INVENTORIES. There are a number of acceptable accounting methods for valuing inventories. Some of these methods pose problems in connection with the computation of return on investment. For example, what effect does Lifo valuation of inventories have upon the computation of capital employed? Inventories valued on a Lifo basis will generally be below the actual investment in such inventories and therefore will not be a realistic valuation. If such valuation is consistently used in determining the amount of total capital employed, comparison of the company's operational effectiveness between different operating periods will present no problem. However, in comparing the company's operating effectiveness with that of other companies, or possibly other divisions, whose inventories are valued on a Fifo or average basis, allowance must be made for such differences as will result because of the method of valuing. Again, if the company operates on a divisional basis and a new division is started with a new product, the investment in inventories at the new division at current prices will make comparison with other divisions unfair.

Another example of the effect of inventory valuations on the return on investment rate is posed by the direct costing method. Proponents of direct costing argue that only the variable costs represent the investment in inventory and that fixed costs are period costs. Companies using direct costing, therefore, will show an investment in inventory which will include only the variable costs, whereas a company using an absorption costing system will show an investment in inventory based on the total of variable and fixed costs. For comparative purposes within the company, direct costing will not create any problems. As with Lifo valuations, however, due recognition will have to be given the effect of such a valuation method in comparing the rate of return on investment with other companies using an absorption costing system.

4. OTHER ASSETS. All other items of working capital should be included at their book amounts, provided, of course, such amounts are realistic.

Fixed Assets. In the case of the tangible fixed assets, another problem presents itself—namely, whether the assets should be taken at their gross book value or at the depreciated value.

The provision for depreciation and amortization presumably represents a recovery of the investment in the operations and, in the absence of losses, the gross assets will tend to increase by the amount of the funds provided. Those who favor using the depreciated value argue that this recovery must be recognized in order to avoid a duplication of assets in the balance sheet which would cause the same annual profit to result in a declining rate of return. However, this technique would measure the return against only the net capital investment in the assets originally acquired for the operations but ignores the availability of the recovered funds for *additional* investment.

To illustrate this point, assume a business starts with $1,200,000 capital, and of this it invests $1,000,000 in fixed capital assets having a ten-year life. To simplify the illustration, it will be assumed that all profits are distributed. The rates of return on capital employed using the gross asset and net asset techniques would be computed as follows:

	Start	End of First Year	End of Second Year
Working assets	$ 200,000	$ 200,000	$ 200,000
Funds provided by depreciation and amortization		100,000	200,000
Fixed assets	1,000,000	1,000,000	1,000,000
Provision for depreciation		100,000*	200,000*
Gross assets	$1,200,000	$1,300,000	$1,400,000
Net assets	$1,200,000	$1,200,000	$1,200,000
Net operating profit		$ 120,000	$ 120,000
Return on gross assets		9.2%	8.6%
Return on net assets		10%	10%

* Indicates red figures.

It can readily be seen from the foregoing illustration that the measure based on depreciated assets shows the true rate on those assets but does not disclose management's failure to keep all funds actively invested. The real significance of the analysis is that management has a constant problem of reinvestment of the depreciation funds, and the use of gross assets as the base is a measure of their performance in this regard. The implication is that management should not merely allow depreciation funds to accumulate and remain idle pending the expiration of the life of the depreciable assets and the need for replacement, but should constantly endeavor to find new uses for the funds. This implies, in turn, the need for constant expansion of the enterprise, and it is in this sense that the use of gross assets as a base is superior. It helps to measure the company's potential development and management's efforts to develop that potential.

It should be recognized, of course, that when making interdivisional comparisons, the double-counting of assets resulting from the inclusion of "depreciation cash" along with the original cost of the fixed asset can be avoided through the device of assigning to a division only the cash it actually needs to operate its current facilities. The presumption is that the investment of depreciation funds is a corporate, and not a divisional, function.

Another factor to be considered in making interdivisional comparisons of return on capital employed, particularly where facilities have been acquired at different times and at different costs by the several divisions, is the effect of these different costs on the comparisons. Obviously, a low acquisition cost or a substantial depreciation, or both, would tend to place an older plant in an advantageous position in the analysis, in spite of the fact that age tends to bring higher operating costs. For these reasons, also, there is an advantage in including depreciable assets in the computation at their gross cost. Replacement cost, which has been advanced by some as a preferable basis for stating fixed asset amounts, involves debatable questions of accounting and economics which are not within the scope of this work and hence is not discussed.

The ratio of net income to plant investment is based on the gross fixed assets figure, instead of the net amount remaining after depreciation, as a means of injecting a rough adjustment factor to provide some equalization of facility values of various divisions of a company or of comparable companies—between those with old plants built at relatively low cost and those with new plants built at high cost. By dealing with all plant values at their gross book value, the distortion of respective ratios of return on plant investment is minimized and it is felt that the relative inefficiency of the older plants is compensated adequately by their relatively lower gross value, without deduction of accrued depreciation. The use of gross plant figures does not result in truly reliable comparisons, but, unless a realistic basis for evaluation of plants on an appraisal basis is feasible, it is the most practical approach available.[2]

The Desired Return on Capital Employed. Now that the significance and the calculation of the rate of return on capital employed have been noted, the question still remains concerning the method of determining a standard of performance for the guidance of management. This question cannot be answered with precision here, but some considerations can be pointed out. Obviously, the rate of return must be sufficient to attract the necessary investment funds, but there is no precise way in which to measure a "fair" return. Presumably, each investor has some idea of the rate he thinks his funds should earn at a given time, but it is also probably true that this rate tends to change from time to time. Nevertheless, a management should have some

[2] Mark W. Cresap, Jr., "Some Guides to Long-Term Planning," *N.A.A. Bulletin*, Section 1, Jan., 1953, p. 603.

PROFIT PLANNING

standard rate in mind, below which it will not invest new funds. Aside from the investment of new funds—and they tend to accrue constantly through the mechanics of depreciation accounting—there is, as indicated above, the need to constantly evaluate the return on current investment. This serves to measure the organization's efficiency and particularly to compare divisional efficiencies. The problems are twofold: to establish a minimum desired rate, and to shift funds to the most attractive investment.

VOLUME-COST-PRICE-PROFIT RELATIONSHIPS

Volume-Cost-Profit Relationships. The most significant single factor in profit planning of the average business is the relationship between volume of business, costs, and profit. Management's problem would be very simple if all costs varied exactly with the sales. Profit would also vary in the same proportion, since the profit per unit of product sold would remain unchanged with variations in the number of units sold. But such simple situations do not exist in modern business. Actually, every business has to sell a considerable proportion of its output capacity just to break even, and profits are not realized until sales exceed this amount. The rate of profit per unit of product sold varies with the number of units sold; hence, the strong urge for increased volume.

These observations result from the fact that business costs have different degrees of variability with volume, ranging from wholly fixed costs to wholly variable costs. This fact is the basic consideration in profit planning. Its importance is illustrated by the following simplified example in which all costs are assumed to be either fixed or fully variable. It shows the relation of volume to profit, at a price.

I	II	III	IV	V	VI
			Marginal		
		Variable	Income	Fixed	Profit
No. of Units	Sales	Costs	II minus III	Costs	IV minus V
0	0	0	0	$20,000	$20,000 *
1,000	$10,000	$ 5,000	$ 5,000	20,000	15,000 *
2,000	20,000	10,000	10,000	20,000	10,000 *
3,000	30,000	15,000	15,000	20,000	5,000 *
4,000	40,000	20,000	20,000	20,000	0
5,000	50,000	25,000	25,000	20,000	5,000
6,000	60,000	30,000	30,000	20,000	10,000
7,000	70,000	35,000	35,000	20,000	15,000
8,000	80,000	40,000	40,000	20,000	20,000
9,000	90,000	45,000	45,000	20,000	25,000

* Indicates red figures.

FIG. 2-2. Volume-Cost-Profit Relationship

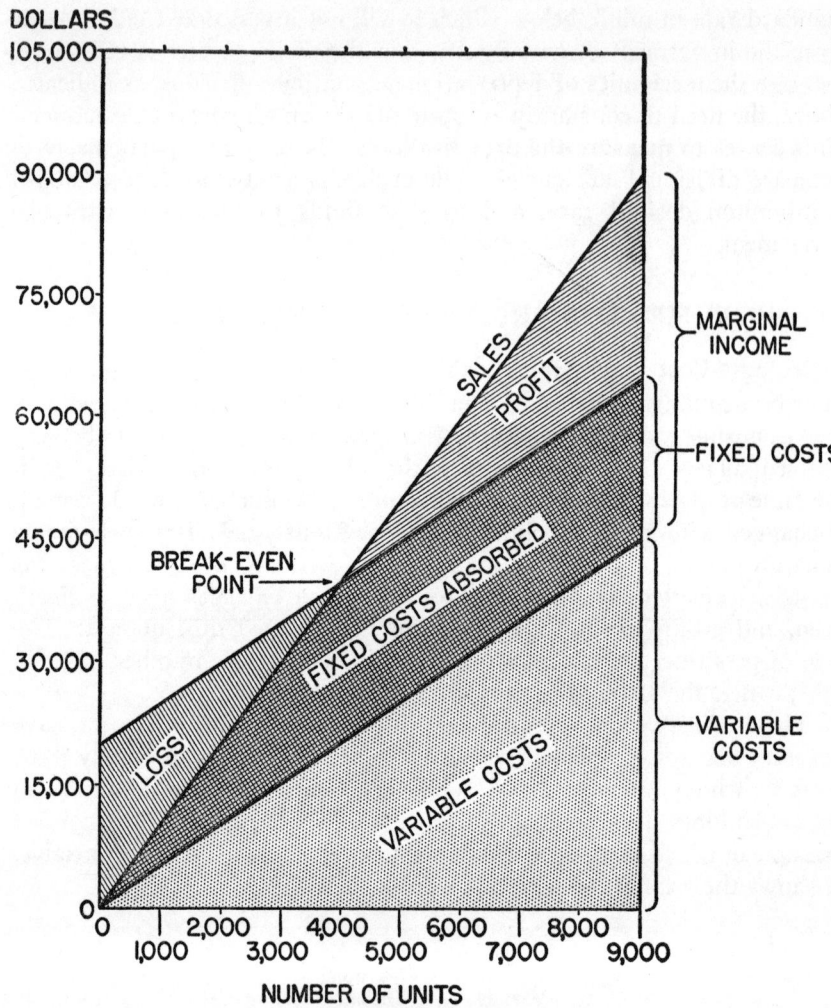

Fig. 2-3. Volume-Cost-Profit Relationship
(Break-Even Chart)

Thus, with fixed costs of $20,000 for the period, with fully variable costs of $5 per unit, and a sales price of $10 per unit, 4,000 units must be sold just to break even. This is true since, for each unit sold, the marginal income (sales less variable cost of sales) available for recovery of the fixed costs is only $5. Profit is earned by the sales in excess of the 4,000 units and increases thereafter at a much faster rate than sales since the marginal income thereafter becomes profit. Conversely, profits tend to fall at a much faster rate than sales decline as long as the basic assumptions hold true. The foregoing data are pictorially represented by a simple chart in Figure 2–3. The importance of fixed and variable costs cannot be overemphasized in profit planning. An understanding of their nature, therefore, is a prerequisite of good management.

Fixed and Variable Costs. The classification of costs as either fixed or wholly variable is partly inherent in the nature of the costs and partly a matter of managerial decision. Actually, all fixed costs are established by management decision, but they may be changed, depending on management's ability to change their nature subsequent to the original decision. A decision to incur the fixed costs of depreciation, rent (or corresponding space costs), and other fixed costs associated with plant and equipment is binding as long as the facilities are retained, and obviously their retention or disposal is not subject to ready change. Likewise, a cost commitment under a contract is presumably binding for the period of the contract.

On the other hand, management theoretically has the power to change other fixed costs at will. Managerial compensation, for example, normally can be changed if the conditions warrant it. The same may be said for many other costs which commonly are thought of as fixed. But even in these cases, however, practical considerations may militate against frequent and quick changes. For purposes of practical definition, therefore, fixed costs may be thought of as those which are expected to remain the same throughout a budgeted operating period, regardless of changes in volume, either because of legal or other practical considerations. Obviously, if the budget for the period proves to be entirely unrealistic, management may be forced to take drastic action to change the budget. But generally, fixed costs are planned to remain unchanged for the duration of the period. These costs then are fixed in total amount, but obviously the fixed costs per unit tend to vary as volume fluctuates.

Wholly variable costs, on the other hand, are those which are fixed on a unit basis and therefore vary in total as volume changes. These costs include direct materials, direct labor (to the extent that the quantity and utilization of the labor force can be regulated with volume), supplies, sales commissions, and other costs which can be made to vary with volume. It should be observed, however, that not all the variable costs are automatically variable. In the case of direct materials, it is obvious that their consumption is a direct function of production and, barring waste and inefficiency, should vary with production automatically. The same is true of sales commissions on a flat rate basis. Direct labor, on the other hand, while commonly thought of as a variable cost, is not, unless paid on the basis of a simple, direct piece-rate plan, automatically variable; and it requires managerial action to preserve the proper relationship between that cost and volume. The same is true of certain other variable costs. Their control requires managerial supervision and action.

Break-Even Calculations. Where all the costs fall into the two categories of wholly fixed and wholly variable, knowledge of the amount of fixed costs and the ratio of variable costs to sales makes possible certain simple calculations which can be very useful in planning and, particularly, in gaining insight into the important relationships between the three factors of volume, cost, and profit. The first of these calculations is the determination of the company's break-even point in sales. A simple formula is used, as follows:

$$\text{Break-even sales} = \frac{\text{Fixed costs}}{\text{Marginal income per cent}}$$

In Figure 2–2 and also in Figure 2–3, fixed costs were reported to be $20,000 for the period, and variable costs were determined to be 50 per cent of sales. Consequently, the formula calculation of the break-even point would be

$$\frac{20,000}{.50} = 40,000$$

The correctness of this break-even sales figure is confirmed by both the table and the chart. The theory of the formula is simply that if 50 per cent of each sales dollar is required to recover variable costs, the remaining 50 per cent represents the marginal income and is available for recovery of the fixed costs. The number of sales dollars, therefore, must be sufficient to provide enough fifty-cent pieces of marginal income to pay off the $20,000 of fixed costs.

On this basis it can be readily observed that, other things remaining the same, any increase in fixed costs raises the break-even sales requirement by twice that amount. On the other hand, if an increase in the fixed costs, say from $20,000 to $23,000, represented an investment in additional mechanization which served to increase the marginal income ratio from 50 per cent to 60 per cent, a new break-even point would have to be calculated as follows:

$$\frac{23,000}{.60} = 38,333$$

Thus, every time one of the factors is changed, a new calculation must be made. In the example above, the increase in fixed costs, which by itself would have raised the break-even point, is offset by a reduction in the ratio of variable costs to sales and thus makes a larger percentage of the sales dollar (that is, a larger marginal income) available for the recovery of the fixed cost.

Assuming that fixed costs remain unchanged but that variable costs change because of changes either in efficiency of utilization or in prices of the variable cost factors, the break-even point is raised or lowered depending on whether a smaller or larger percentage of the sales dollar is left for the recovery of fixed costs.

On the other hand, with no change in dollar costs, a change in sales price also affects the break-even point. Thus, in the original example where the break-even sales were $40,000 based on fixed costs of $20,000 and a variable cost ratio of 50 per cent, a 10 per cent price reduction would raise the break-even sales point because of the increase in the variable cost ratio and the corresponding decrease in the percentage of the sales dollar available for recovery of fixed cost. The variable unit cost remains the same, but the ratio of this cost to sales price changes to 5/9, or approximately 55 per cent. This leaves only 45 per cent of the sales dollar as marginal income available for the recovery of the $20,000 of fixed cost and consequently results in a new break-even sales figure of approximately $44,444 (20,000 ÷ .45).

Another calculation which is often useful in profit planning is the determination of the break-even point in terms of plant capacity. Assuming that the relationship between plant capacity and dollar sales is constant, the formula for determining the capacity at which the plant must operate to break even is

$$\frac{\text{Fixed cost} \times \text{Present \% of plant capacity}}{\text{Present sales volume} - \text{Variable costs}} = \begin{array}{c} \text{\% of plant capacity at} \\ \text{which company will} \\ \text{break even} \end{array}$$

Assuming that the present sales volume is 80 per cent of a one-shift plant capacity, and substituting dollar amounts in the formula, the computation is as follows:

$$\frac{20{,}000 \times 80\%}{48{,}000 - 24{,}000} = 66\tfrac{2}{3}\%$$

Since $48,000 represents 80 per cent of plant capacity on one-shift, 100 per cent of one-shift capacity would produce a $60,000 sales volume. At 66⅔ per cent capacity, sales volume would be $40,000, fixed costs would remain unchanged at $20,000, and variable costs would retain the same degree of variability, that is, 50 per cent of sales, or $20,000.

Required Volume To Earn a Profit. The foregoing examples are concerned only with the determination of the company's break-even point. It is more important, however, to think in terms of the sales required to earn a profit. The desired profit may be determined to be a given percentage of sales, or a fixed amount. If, again referring to the original example, management's profit goal was set at 10 per cent of sales, the profit of 10 cents per sales dollar becomes, in effect, an additional variable cost and reduces the percentage of the sales dollar available for fixed cost. The required sales to earn 10 per cent, therefore, is calculated as follows:

$$\frac{20,000}{1 - (.50 + .10)} = 50,000$$

That this is the correct amount is confirmed by the following calculation which shows a profit of $5,000, or 10 per cent:

Sales		$50,000
Less:		
Fixed cost	$20,000	
Variable costs—50%	25,000	
Total costs		45,000
Profit		$ 5,000

The correctness of the calculation can also be verified by reference to the original data in Figure 2–2 and Figure 2–3.

On the other hand, if the desired profit were not stated as a percentage of sales, but as a fixed amount of, say, $5,000, the profit would be considered in the nature of an additional fixed cost and the calculation would be

$$\frac{20,000 + 5,000}{1 - .50} = 50,000$$

Laws of Costs and Profits. The foregoing analyses give rise to the following observations which serve to define the effects of various managerial actions.

1. A change in the amount of *fixed cost* changes the break-even point of operations, but not the marginal income ratio or the progressive rate of net profit.
2. A change in the *variable cost* changes the break-even point, the marginal income ratio, and the progressive rate of net profit.
3. A change in the *selling price* has the same effect as a change in the variable cost.
4. The *marginal income ratio* is affected only by changes in selling price or variable cost.
5. A change in *both fixed and variable costs* changes to a still greater degree the break-even point, the marginal income ratio, and the progressive rate of net profit.
6. When the marginal income ratio is low—below 15 per cent—large changes in volume are required to produce any considerable change in profits. Conversely, as the volume falls below the break-even point, the accumulated losses will be at a relatively slow rate.
7. If large increases in volume are attained at a low marginal income ratio, additional working capital may be required faster than it is made

available by the marginal income. In such case, a business with inadequate working capital is likely to encounter financial difficulties.
8. When the marginal income ratio is high—above 40 per cent—large profits and an easy cash position result from comparatively small increases in volume above the break-even point. Conversely, heavy losses will result from relatively small decreases in volume below the break-even point.
9. The size of the safety margin determines to a considerable extent the soundness of the business. A high safety margin means that the business can absorb a considerable drop in sales volume before showing a loss.[3]

Limitations of Preceding Analyses. The foregoing calculations, and their variations, are very useful in approximating the effects of changes in any of the three factors of volume, cost, and profit on the over-all relationship, and in acquiring insight into the significance of the fixed and variable cost classifications. Certain cautions must be observed, however. First, it has been assumed that all the costs are either fixed, or wholly variable. In practice this may not be true and probably will not be true for the entire range of capacity operations. As significant changes in operating level occur, changes are likely to be made in certain of the fixed costs and even in the ratios of variable costs. In effect, some costs are semi-variable in nature, being a mixture of fixed and variable costs. It is the function of accounting to break this mixture down to the twofold classification as far as possible, but the fact remains that over a wide range of operating levels there is bound to be a variation in the cost relationships. Consequently, the relationship calculations tend to be more accurate when confined to smaller rather than larger variations in the operating level. If information is required for a wide range of levels, the formula calculation should give way to specific cost schedules of the flexible type, established for specific levels at intervals of, say, 10 per cent of capacity.

A second caution concerns the stability of the basic data. This is particularly true in the determination and use of break-even data. The break-even points previously calculated are valid only as long as the basic assumptions remain true. These concern the amount of fixed costs, the ratio of variable costs to sales, and the average price at which the product is to be sold. The latter two factors, particularly, are interdependent, since a change in either variable costs or price will change the variable cost ratio. This becomes especially important when one considers that total sales generally are the result of a given sales mix of products having different variable cost ratios. The average variable cost ratio used in the break-even calculation is valid only so long as the sales mix remains the same.

[3] Charles H. Gleason, "The Profit-Volume Relationship," *N.A.A. Bulletin*, Section 1, July 1, 1947, pp. 1341, 1344.

It should also be observed that as sales decrease and volume approaches the break-even point, management will strive to change the "point" by giving more attention to cost reduction and other changes which will affect the basic volume-cost-price relationships. Consequently, the basic planning data must be under constant study.

A final caution to be observed in the foregoing type of analysis concerns the effect of inventory changes on the volume-cost-price relationship. The preceding examples were all based on the assumption that production was exactly geared to sales. If some of the costs incurred are for production for stock, the cost data must be adjusted in order to make costs and sales comparable.

It is apparent that wise decisions and sound planning require a solid foundation of sales and cost data, both accurate as to amounts and adequately classified. This is one of accounting's principal contributions to budgeting, and its importance cannot be overemphasized. Subsequent chapters will be devoted to a discussion of the problems and methods of acquiring these essential data.

Volume-Price Relationship. The preceding portion of this section has been concerned with the relationship between volume, cost, and profit and its importance in profit planning. Attention now is directed to the relation between price and volume. Economists have long been concerned with the nature of price as a means of equating supply and demand and have developed numerous concepts which are useful in acquiring a broad understanding of the operations of the market place. These concepts include the elasticity of the market with respect to price or consumer income, the idea of competing products (substitute products, complementary products, and the like), demand and supply curves, and other useful ideas. From the viewpoint of the individual firm, however, two important observations may be made. The first concerns the fact that competition takes two principal forms, price competition and nonprice competition. The second concerns the apparent fact that the average firm has little accurate knowledge as to the nature of the demand curve of either its own products or those of the industry to which it belongs.

With reference to the type of competition, the decision to compete in price or in the nonprice field is extremely important. The former, in its purest sense, represents an attempt to maximize profits through increased volume gained as a result of underselling competitors. This decision assumes that price is a significant factor in the demand for its products (a condition of elastic demand), and that the nature of the industry is such that competitors either cannot or will not promptly retaliate. In general, therefore, competitive price reductions pose a serious question to management, unless an industry-wide reduction serves to tap a much larger market than was available at the earlier price scale. It should also be observed that, in view of the frequent difficulty of restoring a price cut, competitive price reductions tend to have a certain air of finality about them in the short run which makes errors of judgment very costly. On the other hand, price reductions which represent a passing on to the consumer of savings realized through improvement of methods may be very useful.

Nonprice competition covers a much wider range of actions, including various forms of advertising and promotional work, sales effort, dealer helps, improved service to customers or longer warranties, and quality changes in the product either of appearance, efficiency, or utility. This type of competition relates to the company's cost structure rather than the price situation and, since the company's cost curves are better known than its demand curves, this method of competition tends to have some advantage over price competition for the average firm. In addition, because of the numerous possibilities as to the form of nonprice competition, this method permits the exercise of management's ingenuity in devising the best of a number of alternative programs and thus automatically allows management greater freedom of selection than does mere price cutting. Effective retaliation by competitors, therefore, may be less certain, and one of the principal dangers of competitive price reduction may be partially avoided. Finally, there is not the same finality about a decision to experiment with nonprice competitive programs as there is with a price reduction. An ineffective advertising program, for example, may be susceptible to early curtailment or change and something else may be tried. This action may be accomplished more readily in many cases than restoration of a price cut which has been proved ineffective.

Regardless of the decision as to which form competition is to take, it should be based on the best available information of the effect on sales and profit of either price changes or other forms of competition. Some of the necessary data may come from the market research department, if the company has one; much comes from painstaking analyses of the company's own data relating to experience in the past. In any case, facts and more facts are the essence of sound decisions.

PLANNING TECHNIQUE

The Method of Differential Analysis. As has already been indicated, one of the basic steps in planning for profit is that of canvassing alternative methods and policies and selecting that method or policy which is most consistent with the company's profit goal. Fundamentally, this is a matter of studying comparative costs and incomes. In many cases, however, the study need not encompass a complete set of comparative data. Instead, attention need only be directed to the points of difference. This is the essence of differential analysis. A good example of this type of analysis is found in the situation where management is concerned with the advisability of going after additional sales of an existing product, either at the regular price or a special price. Thus, if the company has unused productive capacity, the only costs that need be considered for the purpose of finding the effect of the new business on profit are the additional out-of-pocket costs of producing and selling the additional volume. All other costs are expected to remain the same. On the other hand, if the additional volume requires the provision of additional capacity, other costs obviously will also change.

This use of the differential method of analysis, however, should not serve to encourage the reckless taking on of business at a special price or the pricing of a new product solely on a differential cost basis simply because the volume is already in excess of break-even requirements and fixed costs are already provided for. The practice is common and at times advantageous. It contains elements of danger, however. In the first place, ideally, every product should make its proper contribution to the total profit of the enterprise, and management's attention should always be directed to securing the best product mix. The second danger is the tendency to forget that these special pricing situations can be advantageous in increasing profit only where the present volume is above the break-even point. Of course, if the business is now operating at a loss and the only additional business available has to be taken at a price greater than the differential cost but less than the normal total cost, the special business will serve to reduce the total loss, but it cannot convert a loss position to one of profit under these circumstances.

Even where the business is already profitable, there is the added danger that the special price business unexpectedly may grow in volume to the point where it exceeds the unused capacity. This should not be allowed to happen since the result would be either a competition of the special and regular business for the productive facilities, or an expansion of capacity. The first alternative could have no other result than a reduction of total profit. The second might actually result in a loss, depending upon whether the excess of the special price over the out-of-pocket costs is sufficient to carry the additional capacity cost.

Many of the problems of differential analysis have to do with comparative methods of performing an operation, whether in the factory, the sales department, or the office. Here the analysis is one of comparative costs only. And again, the principal emphasis should be on out-of-pocket or cash costs. For example, an expenditure may be contemplated in connection with the rearrangement of a department in the factory which is designed to reduce the department's space requirements in the plant. The departmental foreman who is charged with space costs on a square-footage basis and who is cost-conscious has requested the appropriation. No other saving is expected from the change. Assuming the cost of rearrangement is significant, and that the company presently has no other use for the space to be made free, the request should be turned down. The foreman's attention to costs is commendable, but in this case the company as a whole cannot profit from the change since it would not result in any over-all cost reduction, but merely a reassignment of cost from one department to idle capacity cost.

Another example calling for careful analysis is that where management is studying a prospective change in the compensation of salesmen, from a salary-and-bonus plan to straight salary. Here the problem is not only one of determining the effect of the change on the salesmen's efforts, but also the comparative costs involved at *different* sales volumes. In many differential cost situations, it is not only necessary to make comparisons on the basis of present conditions, but also to take account of the effect of changes in the conditions themselves, to the extent that such changes may be anticipated.

The Differences Must Be Real. Some of the problems of this type are complicated, first, by the fact that the cash effect of a change may be difficult to determine because of the joint nature of many costs and, second, by the time factor, particularly in cases involving capital equipment. Thus, one of the more difficult problems of differential analysis concerns the replacement of equipment for cost reduction purposes. Not only may some of the actual operating costs of the old equipment be difficult to measure (as well as the estimated costs of the new equipment), but there are also the problems of determining the length of time to be used in depreciating the new equipment and the consideration to be given the salvage value of the old equipment as an offset to the cost of the new. The operating savings must be real—realizable through their effect on cash. Sometimes these savings may be only apparent, through cost reallocations. Actually the analysis must be in the nature of a complete study of the funds to be received and spent, starting with the salvaging of the old equipment and extending throughout the period in which the new equipment is expected to be economically productive. Moreover, the time factor must also be recognized in the determination of the comparative benefits of an immediate change against those of a change made one or two or more years hence.

The point in all these cases is that a mere comparison of a present *unit* cost and a prospective *unit* cost may not be at all indicative of the wisdom of a change of method. Consideration must be given the number of units involved, and all other relevant factors.

The Concept of Different Costs for Different Purposes. The previous examples indicate that frequently cost data are needed which differ from the normal requirements. For financial accounting purposes, the principal requirement is that costs be classified according to whether they are period costs (noninventoriable), or product costs (inventoriable). This, in turn, frequently calls for cost allocations on numerous bases, in the making of which the original cost components are merged in final cost figures and thus lose their identity.

The formal accounting processes frequently make no adequate provision for a classification of costs as to variable or fixed, short-run or long-run, and, of course, they cannot make provision for prospective costs as contrasted with current costs. Determinations of this type, therefore, fall into the category of special problems which frequently require great ingenuity in their solution. This is not a criticism of accounting. Rather it is merely recognition of the fact that the account classifications needed for one essential business purpose do not always serve the requirements of other essential purposes. A clear recognition of this fact by management, and by the accountants themselves, is necessary to an understanding of the special problems which arise at the planning stage and in the preparation of a budget, and to the devising of the means of obtaining the necessary data for planning purposes.

Cost accounting involves both analyses and syntheses. It involves breaking down the stream of costs into its elements and the grouping of these various elements into the combinations best suited to the purpose in hand. In these processes numerous bases for classification are used. These include classifications as to—

Capital and income charges.
Product costs and period costs.
Direct costs and indirect costs.
Job or project costs and process costs.
Actual costs, standard costs, and normal costs.
Fixed costs, variable costs, and semi-variable costs.
Functional costs.
Incurred costs and applied costs.
Inventory costs and over-all costs.
Sunk costs and current outlay costs.
Historical costs and expected or anticipated costs.

Different combinations of cost elements are necessary to answer properly the various questions which involve the use of cost data. A prerequisite to proper combination is a sufficiently detailed classification of costs as they arise.[4]

---

[4] "The Uses and Classifications of Costs," Research Series No. 7, *N.A.A. Bulletin*, Section 2, May 15, 1946, p. 942.

Account classifications can be defined to accomplish all the required purposes, but at a cost. The issue—and this is another example of differential costing—is between the cost of placing multiple classifications on a routine basis (thus providing much information which is needed only periodically or at infrequent intervals) and of minimizing the routine accounting, but depending on special analyses as the occasion demands.

Use of Principles and Techniques in Planning. This chapter has been devoted to a brief review of the fundamental principles of profit planning and of some of the techniques involved in assembling data for the purpose of decision-making. It is emphasized that planning in its initial stages involves a comparison and choice of alternatives. Management's first responsibility is to be alert to the alternatives. Its second responsibility is to evaluate them and make a proper choice consistent with both the long- and short-run objectives of the enterprise.

In studying alternatives, consideration must be given their practical, as opposed to their theoretical, availability. Contractual arrangements and other commitments may preclude the adoption of certain alternatives at a given time. Some decisions may be valid on a short-run basis but not for the long pull. Other decisions, though desirable, may not be consistent with the present financial position of the company. Then there is also the extremely important question of the accuracy of the estimates and calculations involved in decision-making. The difficulty inherent in some of these, and particularly in predictions and estimates of external factors, makes it evident that judgment is a very important management requisite.

In summary, it should be repeated that budgeting, which is formalized planning, is based on a continuing appraisal and reappraisal of conditions and on decision-making involving not only "yes" or "no" questions but questions of alternative choice for which adequate information must be available. The planning and budgeting must be on both a short-run and long-run basis. The plan and budget for the immediate operating period must be tailored to fit immediate conditions; but regardless of these conditions, they should serve to move the enterprise forward in a clearly charted direction and with the long-range objective in mind. This presupposes that there are an objective and long-range plans.

CHAPTER 3

ORGANIZATION FOR BUDGETING

	Page		Page
Purpose of chapter	38	**Organization for Budgetary Control**	
		Organization for control under the budget	48
		Who does the reporting?	48
Organization for Budget-Making		Who takes action?	49
Requirements	38	Accountants' part in control	51
Coordination	39		
Basic assumptions	41	**Manuals of Procedure**	
Detailed planning	42	Importance of manuals	52
Sales forecasts	42	Contents of the manual	53
Manufacturing expenses	44	Authorship	54
Capital expenditures	46	Budget forms	54
Giving the "go ahead" signal	47	Form and distribution of manual	54

Purpose of Chapter. Because so many persons are involved in the various steps in budget-making and budgetary control, the problems of coordination, lines of authority, and direction are very important.

Details of budgetary organization differ widely among companies. This is a natural result of the great variety of circumstances in which companies operate, involving differences in size, nature of budgetary problems, degree of centralization of operational control, over-all organizational setup, and personal characteristics of the management. Nevertheless, there are certain basic requirements which must be satisfied, and it is the purpose of this chapter to review them and to describe some of the methods used. The discussion follows the pattern of treating, first, the budgeting aspects and, second, the control aspects of organization, and closes with a section on the budget manual.

ORGANIZATION FOR BUDGET-MAKING

Requirements. There are essentially six steps in budget-making, as follows:

1. Specification by top management of its objectives
2. Formulation of plans and preparation of a list of assumptions by each department head
3. Amendment of plans and assumptions if necessary
4. Presentation of reworked final plans to top management for approval
5. Approval by top management
6. Giving "go ahead" signal

ORGANIZATION FOR BUDGETING

It is obvious that these steps require an organization for their orderly and timely execution.

In setting up this organization, consideration must be given the nature of the problems involved in carrying out the foregoing steps. These may be defined as follows:

1. Specification of over-all objectives and assumptions
2. Detailed planning
3. Coordination of plans
4. Provision for communication of information and authorizations

Since there is some overlapping among these steps and a considerable interaction, the ensuing discussion is broken down as follows:

1. Coordination
2. Basic assumptions
3. Detailed planning
4. Giving "go ahead" signal

Coordination. Because of the number of persons involved in preparing a budget, and the various interrelated actions and decisions, coordination becomes a problem and requires the setting up of a budget office. The budgetary system is a complicated mechanism, and a governor must be provided to ensure that it works smoothly and effectively. Some executive must be assigned this responsibility to ensure that budgeting is properly organized and carried out. This executive may be the controller or a separate coordinate executive appointed to function solely as a budget officer.

In one prominent company the prime mover in the budgetary process is the controller's office. The controller's responsibilities are described in the company's budget manual as follows:

General Responsibilities Under the Budget Plan. All forecasts and budgets are to be prepared under the direction of the Controller's Office. Specifically, the Controller's Office will:

1. Define the policies and procedures under which the budget plan is to operate.
2. Aid and advise in the preparation of forecasts and budgets; define the form and manner in which the necessary detail is to be prepared.
3. Schedule the time for submitting the required data.
4. Delegate responsibility for the preparation of certain forecast and budget data.
5. Assemble and publish forecasts and budgets.
6. Provide for the accounting for actual income and expenditures in the details necessary for the operation of the budget plan.
7. Analyze, report and interpret comparisons of actual and budget.

The Division Manager, Plant Managers and Administrative Department Heads are to be responsible for the preparation of their budgets and for submitting the required budget information to the Controller's Office according to schedule. They are also to be responsible for the execution of their respective budgets.

In another large company a different type of organization is used. Here budget administration and preparation are supervised by a separate budget department working in cooperation with a budget policy committee and a budget operations committee. The function of the first-named committee, of which the budget director is chairman, is stated in the company's manual of budget procedures as follows:

> This Committee is charged with the responsibility for the development and supervision of an overall, unified program throughout all divisions covering the budgeting of costs and expenses, and the preparation of operating and balance sheet forecasts. Its specific responsibilities include, among other things:
> 1. Approval of proposed budget and forecast policies and procedures.
> 2. Assignment of responsibilities and duties under the budget program.
> 3. Review of divisional and general staff departmental budget standards proposed for each calendar or cost year.
> 4. Review and approval of proposed forecast assumptions for use in connection with preparation of periodic forecasts.
> 5. Review of progress and performance under budget program.

The Budget Operations Committee, consisting of representatives of the budget, staff industrial engineering, and staff accounting departments, has functions defined thus:

> This Committee functions as a working group under the Budget Policy Committee, and is primarily concerned with the various questions arising out of the administration of the budget program.
> It also serves to coordinate the activities of the Budget, Staff Industrial Engineering and Staff Accounting Departments in relation to budget matters.
> Proposed new procedures or policies or changes in those currently in effect are reviewed by this Committee and submitted to the Budget Policy Committee for final approval.

The company's budget director is charged with responsibility for carrying into practice policies and procedures as established by the Budget Policy and Budget Operations Committees, and the specific duties of the Budget Department include:

> 1. Development and revision of Manual of Budget Procedures, and issuance of this, together with other appropriate instructions, to Division Managers, General Staff Department Heads, and others involved in carrying out the budget program.
> 2. Maintenance of close contacts with the Staff Industrial Engineering and Staff Accounting Departments to the end that:
>   *a*) Budget, accounting, and industrial engineering policies are fully coordinated, and
>   *b*) Responsibilities assigned under the budget program are carried out in line with approved procedures.

ORGANIZATION FOR BUDGETING

3. Cooperation with the Staff Industrial Engineering Department in the review of proposed budget standards as submitted annually by Divisions and presentation of these, with recommendations, to the Budget Policy Committee for review and to the appropriate executive officer for approval.
4. Development, in cooperation with Department Heads, of proposed budget standards for all general staff departments for each calendar year and submission of these, with recommendations to Budget Policy Committee for review and to the appropriate executive officer for approval.
5. Review of requests for interim changes in general staff department budget standards and clearance of these with the appropriate executive officer.
6. Maintenance of records covering approved general staff department budget standards and interim changes.
7. Preparation and clearance with Budget Policy Committee of Forecast Assumptions.
8. Follow-up on preparation of divisional forecasts in accordance with approved schedule.
   a) With respect to Sales Forecast Unit Data, this will be cleared with the responsible party in each division.
   b) With respect to all other phases of the divisional forecasts, this will be cleared through the Staff Industrial Accounting Department.
9. Follow-up on preparation of capital expenditure forecasts with Staff Industrial Engineering Department.
10. Checking of arithmetical accuracy of divisional forecasts and preparation of consolidated operating and balance sheet forecasts.
11. Follow-up on desirability of interim revisions of quarterly divisional forecasts.
12. Presentation of appropriate information to Budget Policy Committee and executive officers as to budgetary performance, forecasts and operating data.
13. Assistance to executive officers involved in follow-up with division managers and general staff department heads with respect to budget performance.

The foregoing excerpts from the budget manuals of two companies illustrate the importance of coordination and budget policies in budgetary procedure and different methods for attaining them.

Basic Assumptions. An important step in budgeting is the determination of the basic assumptions on which the budget plan is to be based. These basic assumptions are distinguished from the sales forecasts in that the former are much broader and deal with the fundamentals of the business situation, which, in turn, lead to the forecast of sales. The basic assumptions relating to economic forecasts, and the assumptions used by department heads and other segments of management must be reviewed for validity and compatibility. This is a top management responsibility.

Basic assumptions are often prepared by a forecasting committee which studies business conditions. This committee usually is made up of high-level executives and may include a trained economist. The assumptions prepared by such committees form the starting point in preparing the budget. The procedure used in one company is described in its budget manual as follows:

> In order that all persons engaged in preparing sales forecasts may use the same general premises covering future business conditions, the Company Economist is to prepare a summary of the economic situation. This summary is termed "Basic Assumptions" and consists of a concise written statement of the general business conditions which are most likely to prevail during the budget period for which sales forecasts are to be prepared. The basic assumptions are to be used as a guide in the preparation of all sales forecasts except in those instances where specific market conditions or other factors clearly indicate prospects other than those contained in the statement of basic assumptions. Basic assumptions are to be prepared for both the annual and mid-year sales forecasts.
>
> Upon completion of the basic assumptions, the Company Economist is to submit them to the Forecasting Committee for preliminary review. Members of the Forecasting Committee are: the Controller, the Treasurer, the Manager of Production Planning, and the Company Economist. When the basic assumptions have been accepted by the Forecasting Committee, the Controller is to submit them to the President's Office for approval. Upon approval by the President's Office, the Corporate Budgeting and Accounting Department Supervisor is to distribute copies of the basic assumptions to those engaged in preparing sales forecasts.

In the manual of the other company already cited, it is observed that the Budget Policy Committee has as one of its duties "the review and approval of proposed forecast assumptions for use in connection with preparation of periodic forecasts." In this company the assumptions are initially prepared by the budget director.

Detailed Planning. Given the organization for directing and coordinating the work of budget preparation, we are now concerned with the personnel involved in the preparation of the budget details. All departments are involved, and the question arises as to who does the work and who is responsible for it. Following are descriptions of various practices relating to certain phases of operation.

Sales Forecasts. In the first of the two companies referred to above, responsibility for the sales forecast of a division rests with the manager of the division. He in turn delegates the responsibility to the several commodity managers of the division, and the division's controller is responsible for ascertaining that the forecasts are prepared in accordance with the principles and procedures prescribed by the controller's office.

ORGANIZATION FOR BUDGETING 43

The sales forecasts prepared by the commodity managers are also required to be in line with, or reconcilable with, the statement of basic assumptions prepared for the company as a whole.

The forecasts of the commodity managers, when approved by the manager of the division, are sent to the company's forecasting committee for further review. If approved by this committee, they are transmitted by the controller's office to the president's office for approval. They are then submitted to the controller's office and form the basis for the budgetary accounting work leading to the budget in final form. Upon approval of the over-all operating plan, the approved sales forecasts are reported back to the division manager and commodity managers by the controller's office.

It should be noted that the forecasts prepared by the commodity managers of this company, with the approval of the divisional manager, cover gross sales (net of returns) and that deductions for quantity discounts, cash discounts, and other allowances are computed by the divisional controller.

In the second of the two companies referred to above, the manager of the division again is responsible for the forecasts for his division. He delegates this responsibility to the production control manager, the sales engineer, or other appropriate person who works in conjunction with representatives of the staff sales department. The production control manager's role in the forecasting of sales results from the fact that shipments, rather than orders booked, are a controlling factor in some segments of this company, and they are a function of production facilities and the production cycle.

The forecasts are made first in units of product, and responsibility for conversion to dollar sales rests with the divisional accountant. The forecast must be in line with the statement of basic assumptions approved by the budget policy committee and must finally be approved by the division's budget committee composed of representatives of the sales, production planning, manufacturing, accounting, and industrial engineering departments of the division. This committee functions in line with principles established by the company's budget department previously described.

In a third company, unit sales forecasts are prepared by field sales managers and sent to the product manager for review and approval. Conversion to dollar sales is made in the office of the product manager. In this company, while there is a formal procedure for coordinating the various phases of the budget, the responsibility for forecasting sales rests entirely on those responsible for sales. Sales supervisors prepare forecasts for the various branches or regions giving consideration to

1. Analysis of past results
2. General business conditions in their relation to the company's products
3. Local business conditions
4. Competition
5. Company policies relative to prices, advertising appropriations, sales efforts, and so forth
6. Market research

In general, it is this company's practice to rely on operating personnel rather than staff personnel for the preparation of the budget.

Manufacturing Expenses. The major problem in budgeting manufacturing expenses is the setting of budget standards for various levels of operation and the use of these data in forecasting the expenditures for a budget period. Unlike the nonmanufacturing activities, the budget data relating to production are needed for cost accounting as well as for budget purposes because of the necessity of determining standard factory expense rates which can be incorporated in product standard costs.

Commonly it is the plant manager who is responsible for the preparation of the factory's budget of expenses. The actual supervision of its preparation may, of course, be delegated, and a number of people may be involved in the work. In one company, for example, assignment of responsibilities is as follows:

1. Industrial engineers—preparation of budget schedules for indirect labor, overtime premium, shift differential, and sundry supplies
2. Plant engineer—preparation of budget schedules for maintenance and repairs
3. Power engineer—preparation of budget schedules for power costs
4. Plant controller—preparation of budget schedules for other manufacturing expenses

In this company the plant controller also acts in the place of the plant manager in coordinating all the budget work and assembling the full factory budget. He also exercises functional control over the work as a representative of the company controller's office. In this company, as in many others, the determination of usage standards for direct materials and labor is not thought of as a step in budget preparation, since it is carried out independently of the formal process of budget-making. Time study and methods analysis go on continuously and the resulting standards are, in effect, primary data which are accepted as such when the periodic job of budget-making starts. Review and analysis of the indirect expenses, however, are an integral part of budget preparation because of the lack of a fixed relationship between these expenses and various operating levels.

ORGANIZATION FOR BUDGETING

In another company, all factory budget standards are the responsibility of the chief industrial engineer, although provision is made for cooperation with the industrial accounting department in obtaining data which are primarily financial in nature. It is the industrial accountant's responsibility, under the policy direction of the budget director and budget committees, to incorporate the budget standards into the forecast operating statement for the plant or division. Final approval of this statement rests with the head of the plant or division.

In still another company, the budgeting of production, materials, labor, and expense is accomplished as follows:

Upon receipt of the sales forecasts by the various operating divisions, the operating head of each plant, in conjunction with the responsible vice-president, establishes the level of production for the budget period. The production forecast is then stated by the production planning department in terms of product, by months, with due consideration being given to the following major factors:

1. Period covered by sales forecasts.
2. Shipping requirements by months.
3. Length of the normal production cycle.
4. Time necessary to secure materials.
5. Minimum/maximum inventories, properly balanced.
6. Stability of general business conditions.

The production planning department then forwards to the plant budget supervisor for use, and to the budget department for distribution to the central operations departments and the purchasing department, properly approved copies of the production forecast.

Prior to the receipt of the production forecast, the purchasing department obtains purchase prices for the necessary raw materials and supplies by items, for use by the various plant budget departments. These costs are issued in the form of a standard material cost catalogue, revised semiannually if required by major price changes, in time for use upon receipt of the production forecast. The standard material cost catalogues are used to estimate the cost of materials, per unit, based upon standard usage rates or master formulas. Upon receiving the production forecast, the purchasing department places contracts for all necessary items, bearing in mind the following:

1. Probable requirements for the budget period, by months.
2. Quantities on hand.
3. Time required for delivery.
4. Minimum/maximum inventories, properly balanced.
5. Probable price variations and market trends.

When completed, the materials forecast is finally approved by the responsible officer for use in the cost of production forecast.

The labor forecast is developed after the sales and production forecasts have been approved. In those plants having standard costs, standard labor time allowances have been established for products, so that the standard labor hours required and cost per unit are easily ascertained. In those plants not on a standard basis, ratios and estimates based upon past experience and known changes are used to arrive at the required labor hours and unit costs. The responsibility for the preparation of the labor forecast rests with the works managers, who consider it in light of the following:

1. Length of budget period.
2. Policies of the company.
3. Variations from standard.
4. Cost per unit.
5. Recommendations of superintendents, foremen, and heads of the service departments.

When completed, this forecast is finally approved by the responsible officer for use in the cost of production forecast.

The manufacturing expense forecast is the prime responsibility of the works managers and is the result of the coordinated thinking of the heads of the many producing and service departments. Individual forecasts are established for each department based upon the approved production forecast and are tempered by experience and any known changes. The budget supervisor distributes the expenses of the service departments to the producing departments and then applies these costs to the individual products. Both the basic forecasts and their distribution are subject to the approval of the responsible department head and the works manager. After final approval by the responsible officer, this expense forecast is combined with the ones for materials and labor, for use in the cost of production forecast.[1]

Again it will be noted that, given the sales forecast, the manufacturing budget is largely a matter of internal preparation, within the manufacturing division, but coordinated through a budget office.

Capital Expenditures. The budgeting of capital expenditures provides an example of the need for company-wide coordination, since this budget schedule may involve all segments of the company. The procedure of one company, for example, provides that the chief engineer is responsible for assembling and approving, under the president, the capital expenditures and appropriations budget. Moreover, his department will counsel with all those involved in submitting projects for the capital budget. The budget manual of this company provides that on or before a specified date the chief engineer will issue instructions stating the policy which is to apply to the selection of budget projects, the information required, and the date scheduled for the submission of budget data. These instructions are to be sent to:

a) Division or operations managers
b) Division production managers
c) Research director's office
d) Company office manager
e) Manager of the insurance and real estate department
f) General purchasing agent
g) General traffic manager
h) Manager of personnel department
i) Director of advertising and promotion
j) Controller's office

[1] Frank Z. Oles, "Comprehensive Budgetary Control—A Case Study," *N.A.A. Bulletin,* Section 1, Oct., 1951, pp. 131–33.

ORGANIZATION FOR BUDGETING

Upon receipt of the instructions, the foregoing executives will, in turn, issue instructions to the plant managers and other subexecutives in their respective divisions. Detailed instructions cover all aspects of project analysis and selection. The submission of budget data follows prescribed procedures, starting with heads of subdepartments and moving upwards through the several ranks of executives to the chief engineer who, under the president and board of directors, is the final operating authority.

In another company, the executive vice-president is the chief person responsible for the capital expenditure budget. In this company recognition is also given the possibility of projects originating at the top rather than down the line. In such cases, the projects must be reviewed and considered jointly by the officer in charge of the affected division, the executive vice-president, the treasurer, and the controller.

Giving the "Go Ahead" Signal. After the management of a company has arrived at the basic assumptions and detailed forecasts have been made, attention must now be directed to the method of approving these forecasts and signaling the authorization of the entire budget as the approved plan of operations.

The approval of the various detailed forecasts must be provided for as an integral step in budget coordination. In one company all forecasts must have the final approval of the president's office and the board of directors. This company's manual provides as follows:

Approval of Forecasts and Budgets. Sales forecasts are to have the approval of the respective Division Manager, of the Forecasting Committee, and of the President's Office.
Operating budgets in connection with plant operations are to have the approval of the respective Plant Manager and the Production Manager's Office. Operating budgets in connection with Selling Division operations are to have the approval of the respective Division Manager and of the President's Office. Operating budgets for administrative departments are to have the approval of the respective Department Head, and of the President's Office.
When all forecasts and budgets are approved and assembled, they are to be presented to the President's Office and to the Board of Directors for final acceptance.

Other procedures are described in connection with the detailed forecasts just studied.

Once the over-all budget is approved, both in total and in detail, there must be a procedure for reporting the approval to all the administrative people who are to be guided by the budget in the conduct of the work under their supervision. This procedure relates, among other things, to who is to receive approved budget schedules and who is responsible for their distribution.

With reference to the first question, it is obvious that the complete budget will not be issued to those who are concerned only with segments of it, but will be issued to only a few persons in the company—the president, the treasurer, the controller, and/or the budget director. Budget schedules, likewise, will be issued only to those to whom they apply. This presents a sizable job of report preparation and distribution. Copies of each segment of the budget must be reproduced, approved, and distributed to the proper persons.

With reference to the distribution of the budget reports, it is obvious that one central office should be assigned this responsibility. Normally, distribution is the responsibility of that office, or executive, which is charged with the responsibility of coordinating and directing the work of budget preparation. In some companies, it rests with the controller (or equivalent officer); in others it rests with the budget director. It goes without saying that normally the method of distribution adheres to the company's recognized channels of communication. Thus, the chief distributing officer may be responsible only for distribution to senior administrators, the latter in turn forwarding reports to their subordinates.

ORGANIZATION FOR BUDGETARY CONTROL

Organization for Control Under the Budget. A budget is not designed to reduce the managerial function to a formula. It is a managerial tool, one purpose of which is to measure subsequent performance against the budgetary plan. The control function is a most important phase of budgetary procedure. The disclosure of the need for remedial action and the taking of remedial steps are just as important as the original drafting of the plan. To be effective, both the disclosure and the action must be organized.

The form of performance reports and the indicated actions will be discussed in detail in subsequent chapters. The organizational structure providing for reporting and appropriate action is now presented.

Who Does the Reporting? The reporting function is defined in one company's manual as follows:

> Actual performance shall be compared regularly with the established budget in each area of responsibility. Significant variations are to be analyzed, appraised, and reported.

The reporting is almost universally done by the controller's division. This is true even where there is a separate budget director's organization. The reason is obvious—the dependence on accounting records for the necessary data. Reports may come from the company controller's

ORGANIZATION FOR BUDGETING

or from a divisional controller's office, depending on the size of the company and the nature of the operations being reported. The reports are designed to measure performance by comparing actual results with the budget, either fixed or flexible, depending on circumstances.

Who Takes Action? The action function and the reporting function are not the same and, consequently, are carried out by different people. It is a generally accepted principle of management that actions must be controlled at the source. Thus, for example, costs must be controlled in the division or department which incurs them. Just as neither the budget director nor the controller creates a budget (they merely assist in its coordination), so neither of them controls performance against the budget. This is the responsibility of the head of the division or department for and by whom the budget is established.

This responsibility obviously must be delegated, in turn, to the several subordinate levels of management. Consequently, it is common practice for the performance reports of a segment of the company to be directed first to the head of that segment and then routed in detail to the appropriate subordinates—those responsible for the detail operations. It is expected that the various levels of managers in the division will take the necessary action to bring the performance of their immediate groups up to the budget standards.

It is in this area of management, however, that the principal challenge of management lies. If performance is below standard, how best can it be improved? Here is where real qualities of leadership are needed most. In many companies it is recognized that remedial action can best be determined by joint efforts. Consequently, frequent and regular staff meetings are held for the purpose of reviewing and analyzing performance. In one company such meetings are provided for as follows:

1. *Quarterly*

    At least once each quarter (preferably once each month) the division or factory manager should hold a general budget meeting which is attended by the general foremen, foremen, division industrial engineer, and controls engineer. In some cases where regular monthly meetings of the above-mentioned personnel are an established routine in a division, the budget may be discussed as a part of these meetings in lieu of instituting a separate series of conferences.

    At such a meeting, the monthly and daily budgets for various departments should be discussed, upward and downward trends in performance should be noted and general comments should be made as to what can be done to improve performance on labor and overhead items. This type of meeting should be used principally for the purpose of promoting enthusiasm for the budget. It should help to convince the foreman that the top management of the division is back of the budget and watching any improvement or retrogression in performance. Departmental charts showing operating performance are very useful for this purpose.

It should be pointed out, however, that a general meeting of this type should be confined as much as possible to general remarks, so that no offense will be taken by any member of the supervision who is singled out for criticism.

2. *Monthly*

Once a month the division industrial engineer should hold a separate informal budget meeting for each department. This meeting should include the foreman of the department, the controls engineer and any other budgetary personnel who can make a contribution to the discussion. The factory manager and/or superintendent should be informed of these meetings so that they may attend at their discretion.

Prior to the meeting, the division industrial engineer and the controls engineer should prepare an agenda of the expense items that are to be discussed. Where labor accounts are involved, trailer cards should be brought to the meeting so that a study can be made of the individuals who were included in the actual charges. For maintenance items, copies of shop orders or charges to actual shop orders may be listed so that the total maintenance cost for operating the department can be discussed in detail.

A prior investigation of this type puts the division industrial engineer and controls engineer in a favorable position to answer the general statements which are often made by the foremen.

Both the daily and monthly budget reports should be discussed at the meeting. The group should examine the items that are not only over the budget, but also those that are beating the budget. In the latter case, a decision should be made as to whether the budget standards are too loose, whether fundamental conditions have changed, or whether the item is simply one which has to be looked at on an accumulated basis.

In the instances where the foreman claims it is impossible to meet the budget, the division industrial engineer and controls engineer should be ready to suggest means whereby the budget can be met. This can often be accomplished by the introduction of a slightly different method of doing the work, by the introduction of a different grade or type of material, by increasing, shifting, consolidating or realigning responsibilities among personnel, etc.

The regular monthly meeting, such as described above, can well become the key to the success of the budget program.

3. *Daily*

The third type of meeting which appears to be essential to the successful use of budgets is conducted in a more informal way by means of daily contact between the controls engineer and the foreman of the department. (In cases where performance is satisfactory, such personal contacts need not be on a daily basis but should be made as frequently as necessary to maintain a close relationship between the controls engineer and the foreman, and to ensure that the foreman realizes that budget performance is being closely scrutinized at all times.)

One of the principal points in favor of the daily budget report is that it enables the supervisor or foreman to correct, on the following day, any condition which has led him to run over the budget on the previous day.

ORGANIZATION FOR BUDGETING

The controls engineer should carefully go over the daily report of each department and note any items which have suddenly exceeded the budget. He should find out the reason for the overage and then contact the foremen and endeavor to get them to do something about it.

It is very important that this type of frequent contact between the controls engineer and the foreman of the department be established and maintained. In the event the department is beating the budget, the controls engineer should make a point of seeing the foreman of that department and passing the comment that he is doing a good job or some similar remark that will let the foreman know that his budget performance is being watched.

4. *Emergency*

A fourth procedure which has a place in promoting the use of budgets to the fullest extent is the highly concentrated emergency type of meeting. This type of meeting should be held only in the event that there are emergency conditions which must immediately be investigated and corrected. Such meetings should be held by the top management of the division as a means of getting prompt and direct action. The meetings should be held daily until the conditions are corrected.

It is desirable that the emergency meeting include, in addition to division management, the division industrial engineer, the controls engineer, and the foremen of those departments which are showing poor performance. The usual procedure is to discuss all of the items on the daily departmental budget report which are out of line, to assign these items for investigation, and to report on the following day as to what steps were taken to correct them. This type of daily contact differs from the ordinary informal contact between the controls engineer and the foremen in that policy questions can be discussed and changed if present practices and procedures are the cause of poor performance.

Inasmuch as the emergency type of meeting ties up the top management and certain key personnel for an hour or two every day, such meetings should be discontinued at the earliest possible moment.

The question of "who takes action?" in the control phase of budgeting emphasizes the roles of the staff and the line in management. It is a universally accepted principle of management that control is a function of line management and that the staff's function is to give all possible assistance. The control of operations rests with the line management from the chief executive down to the first-line supervisors, each having responsibility for control within his respective area. It is these *people* who direct and supervise operations in accordance with the company's policies and plans. It is the function of the various staffs, on the other hand, to provide the means for planning, reporting, and interpreting the results, and to give technical assistance in achieving remedial action.

Accountants' Part in Control. Accounting is an indispensable tool in budgetary control, as well as in budgeting generally. The entire budgetary framework, particularly as it relates to monetary data, rests on the accounting system. The provision of controls and the reporting of results against the controls is an important accounting function. This is true regardless of whether this function is vested in the chief accounting officer of the company or in a coordinate control officer such as the budget director.

In this connection it should be noted that there is a considerable difference of practice among companies. In some, the maintenance of the budgetary controls is vested in the controller (or equivalent officer); in others, this function is completely separated from the office of the controller. Even in the latter case, however, it is recognized that the *accounting* for results is of necessity an accounting department function. The basic distinction between the two practices lies in who uses the accounting data for purposes of control and who determines the type of data to be recorded.

In theory, it would seem that the first practice is desirable since only in that way can the chief accounting officer direct the organization of, as well as the use of, the accounts. The second practice, however, is followed by some companies which are known for their progressive management. Conceivably, the differences may arise from the background and personality of the officers or from the scope of the responsibility. Whatever the practice may be, the function of accounting is important as a *tool* of management. It is a staff function designed to assist line management. Whether budgetary controls are administered by an accounting officer or a budget director (both using accounting data), the distinction between line and staff functions should not be ignored.

Because the function of the accountant with respect to management control involves both communication and interpretation and only a very fine line divides the latter from evaluation, the accountant's part in the control function is very delicate. Control is a responsibility of line management, but a competent, analytical control report from the accountant may make the required decision and action on the part of its recipient quite obvious. The accountant may then appear to be exercising control. This should never go beyond appearance. Control is an exclusive function of line management. The accountant does contribute to and facilitate control. Analysis of the requirements for effective control indicate clearly that these lie predominantly in his field. He may well remain content with this staff function, so essential to line action that the connection closely suggests that line and staff, working in this way, are virtually in partnership for the success of the enterprise.[2]

MANUALS OF PROCEDURE

Importance of Manuals. As companies grow in size, the need for written instructions to assist in training and in defining authority and

[2] Alwyn M. Hartogensis, "The Accountant's Place in the Control Function," *N.A.A. Bulletin,* Section 1, Dec., 1955, p. 480.

ORGANIZATION FOR BUDGETING 53

responsibility becomes obvious. The use of manuals of various kinds, thus, is common practice today. The chief functions, as they relate to managerial activities, are:

1. To place responsibility
2. To formalize systems and methods
3. To control forms and reports

Budgetary procedure is one of the activities to which these functions are directly applicable. The comprehensive nature of budgeting and budgetary control, involving all segments and ranks of management, and their importance in the operations of the company, require that manuals be prepared for the most effective use of the budgetary system. The more important advantages of such a manual are:

1. Clearly defines authority and responsibility in budget matters.
2. Promotes standardization and simplification in that presumably the best method is selected.
3. Assists in coordinating and synchronizing effort.
4. Provides a convenient reference source when questions of procedure or responsibility arise.
5. Permits better supervision in that the time of supervisors is conserved to the extent that explanations are covered in the manual.
6. Assists in the training of new employees and in transfer of duties because many phases of the job have been reduced to writing.
7. Assists in "selling" the budget by explaining the advantages of the procedure.[3]

Contents of the Manual. Budget manuals vary in form and nature depending on the size and nature of the company and also in the comprehensiveness of the budgetary procedure. In general, however, the manual should include:

1. A statement of purpose and principles
2. Definition of lines of authority and responsibility
3. Statement of duties of various personnel in preparing budget
4. Time schedules for budget preparation
5. Forms of schedules
6. Procedures for obtaining approval
7. Form and nature of performance reports
8. Procedures of budgetary control

To be useful, manuals must be prepared carefully and accurately. They must be understandable to all persons concerned, and they must accurately reflect the conditions under which each department operates. This is a large order. The style of writing and the language must be adapted to the needs of the various readers, and these may vary since

---

[3] J. Brooks Heckert and James D. Willson, *Business Budgeting and Control* (2d ed.; New York: The Ronald Press Co., 1955), p. 415.

sections of the manual will be distributed to different groups within the company.

Accuracy is particularly important. The various sections of the manual must be written with a full knowledge of the procedures and problems of the respective departments or divisions. Nothing will destroy confidence in a manual so readily as the inclusion of an instruction which does not apply, or cannot be applied. This leads to the question of who should prepare the manual.

Authorship. The manual must be based on a thorough knowledge of all problems, related procedures, and time limitations of budgeting. This requires that its preparation must be correlated closely with the preparation and use of the budgetary system. Consequently, responsibility for the drafting must be vested in the chief budget officer, be he budget director or controller, and while he may delegate much of the work, he alone must ultimately bear the responsibility for the finished product.

It goes without saying, that the same type of cooperation required in the budgetary system itself is needed in drafting the manual. Consultation with the various departments affected and trial runs are important.

Budget Forms. It was stated earlier that forms control is one of the purposes of a manual. This is just as applicable to a budgetary manual as to others. The success of the budgetary system, involving as it does a final bringing together into one master budget of all the schedules originating from all the departments of the company, depends on a uniformity of schedule preparation and a uniformity of budget reports. This is particularly important, first, because of the underlying relation of the budget to the company's chart of accounts, and, second, because of the need to ensure that the proper considerations are used in arriving at the forecasts. In all the budget manuals studied, specific instructions are given for the preparation of budgets and reports, and generally they are illustrated by sample forms.

Form and Distribution of Manual. It is obvious that certain key personnel must be provided with the complete manual, while others will receive only a section or sections of it. This, together with the need for frequent revision as policies and procedures change, largely determines the form of the manual. It should be loose-leafed, and every page should be numbered, dated, and authorized.

Needless to say, the manual should be kept up to date. This becomes a problem when it is considered that the budgetary system itself should be under constant study for the purpose of making it more useful to management. Aside from the need for reflecting these changes promptly in the manual for the guidance of personnel, the principle of timeliness has a psychological advantage in aiding to impress on all parties concerned, the idea that top management takes the budgetary system seriously. As stated earlier, budgeting must not be haphazard. It is serious business, and all must understand its significance in welding all segments of the company into a successful organization.

CHAPTER 4

PREPARING THE BUDGET

	Page
Purpose of chapter	56
The budget period	57
Steps in budget preparation	57

First Step—Specifying Objectives

The company and its operations	58
Determined objectives	59
1. Improvement of company's return on investment	59
2. Obtaining better product costs	62
3. Obtaining better relationship between sales and sales costs	64
4. Low ratio of purchase discounts taken to material costs	64
5. Improvement of inventory balance	64
6. Obtaining more uniform production schedules	64
7. Investment in capital improvements	65
Budget directives	65

Second Step—Formulation of Plans and Preparation of a List of Assumptions by Each Department Head

Integrated plans required	66
Where to begin?	66
Sales department planning	68
Sales department's decisions	70
Production department planning	72
Purchasing department planning	74
Personnel department planning	76
Engineering department planning	76
Treasury department planning	77
Planning by nonfactory departments	77
The work of the accounting department	77

Third Step—Amendment of Plans and Assumptions

Coordination of detailed plans	79
Amendments of departmental plans	79
Alterations of budget directives	81

Fourth Step—Presentation of Plan to Management

Summary of results of plan	82
Reconsideration of objectives and directives	83

Fifth Step—Approval of the Budget

General	83

Sixth Step—Issuance of the Budget

General	84

Purpose of Chapter. Budgetary planning and coordination is not a simple process. Every item on the balance sheet and income account will be affected by the operations of the forthcoming period. Consequently, in any worthwhile budgetary procedure, every transaction of the company during the budget period should be according to plan. The interrelations of the various transactions, both financial and operating, make complete planning necessary. The reciprocal relation of sales and costs and the effect of both on financial position require that plans be carefully prepared and coordinated. Moreover, the plans should be designed to accomplish specific objectives and reflect a conscious choice from among various alternative courses of action.

The planning and coordinating aspects of budgetary procedure, therefore, necessitate a number of steps and the efforts of the various segments of management. It is the purpose of this chapter to describe the necessary steps and the part that each segment of management plays in their execution. The discussion is both descriptive and illustrative in character, based on the budget-making processes of a hypothetical company. This treatment is designed to provide a comprehensive view of the over-all procedure, to serve as a framework to which subsequent discussions of detailed procedures can be fitted.

The Budget Period. The length of the budget period depends on whether the budget is for the immediate future or for long-range planning. It has already been noted in Chapter 1 that both short- and long-range planning should take place. The long-range plan is primarily strategic in nature. While it does not ignore details, it is more concerned with broad objectives and charting courses of action to attain them. Short-range planning, on the other hand, is more tactical in nature and primarily concerned with intermediate objectives realizable within an operating period. This type of planning must be in detail, and since it encompasses all the principles and procedures used in the long-range budget preparation, it is the subject of this chapter.

Since the operating period is usually a year, fiscal or calendar, the question arises as to whether budgets normally are prepared for a period of at least that long. This, obviously, is desirable since the year is the natural, basic time unit in business thinking. On the other hand, plans should not be adhered to if unrealistic. Consequently, provision should be made for periodic review, at least on a quarterly basis, and for change of plans when warranted. The sales forecast is the starting point in budgeting for most companies. Consequently, a *firm* budget plan cannot be useful for a period longer than that for which a reasonably reliable forecast can be made.

It should be recognized that special situations such as an extreme tightness in the materials market, for example, or the necessity for long-term contracting for materials may require that certain operating transactions be planned for a longer period, in spite of the increased chance of error in the sales forecast. In the present discussion, however, it is assumed that the entire budget can be keyed to the forecast. While the advantages of budgeting for a complete annual business cycle are recognized, for convenience and brevity the examples used throughout the chapter are based on a quarter.

Steps in Budget Preparation. Budget preparation is a cooperative action embracing all levels of management. Top management indicates the desired immediate objectives. Lower management levels then work out the details both to test the feasibility of the indicated objectives and to ensure coordination of all the parts. As a result of this effort, changes in the objectives may be indicated. Thus, the preparation involves not only cooperation but also an up-and-down or reciprocating adjustment of objectives and plans to achieve a realistic and workable program, as nearly as possible in line with the company's long-range plans. The basic steps are as follows:

STEP 1: Specification by top management of its objectives concerning desired volume of business, net income for the period, financial position, capital expenditures, and other factors, all tempered by analyses and forecasts of the size of the market and price and cost structures. In this step consideration is given to the alternative methods of distribution, promotion, procurement, and production.

STEP 2: Formulation of plans and preparation of a list of assumptions by each department head. This step involves the cooperation of all divisions of the business. Based upon these assumptions, the subsequent budget data are prepared reflecting the plan in terms of units of production, units of cost, and so on.

STEP 3: Amendment of plans and assumptions where detailed planning reveals the need for change.

STEP 4: Presentation of reworked final plans to top management for approval. Particular attention will be paid by top management to the end results of the budgeting, in the form of the forecast balance sheets, operating statements, source and application of funds statements, and cash flow statements.

STEP 5: Approval of summarized budget by top management based upon the premises included in the list of assumptions.

STEP 6: Issuance of budget schedules to all management levels as a "go ahead" signal and a guide to their operations during the period.

The remainder of this chapter is devoted to a discussion of how the foregoing steps are carried out in a hypothetical company. The illustration pertains to Illustrative Company, and is designed to present the comprehensive nature of budgeting, showing the nature of the decisions to be made, and by whom, and the interlocking nature of the various company functions. In order to make the discussion as realistic as possible, but at the same time keep it within reasonable bounds, certain assumptions are made. First, the company is assumed to be in the size category of less than $10,000,000 of annual sales. Second, only three products are produced and sold. Third, a three-month budget is being prepared for the first quarter of the forthcoming year.

FIRST STEP—SPECIFYING OBJECTIVES

The Company and Its Operations. Illustrative Company is a manufacturing corporation producing and selling three products, A, B, and C.

Its annual sales have been running in the neighborhood of $7,800,000. In addition to the normal service departments, the factory has three production departments, and the production sequences of the three products through the several production departments are as follows:

	Production Departments		
	1	2	3
Product A	x	x	x
Product B	x	x	x
Product C	x		x

The length of the manufacturing cycle in the first department is such that the output of this department frequently is stocked pending its transfer to succeeding departments. The company uses standard costs in the factory.[1]

The company markets its products by direct selling methods, using a staff of salesmen, supported by advertising. It maintains a typical sales administrative organization. Salesmen are paid a salary plus a commission on all sales. The company also maintains a typical administrative organization for carrying out general administrative and corporate functions. The president reports to a small board of directors of which he is a member, but he has wide latitude and extensive authority in operating the company. He is assisted by an executive committee consisting of himself, the executive vice-president, and the heads of the major divisions of the company; namely, sales, production, engineering, purchasing, personnel, treasury, and accounting.

Determined Objectives. The president of the company for some time has been dissatisfied with the company's performance and has determined that the forthcoming budget must be aimed at substantial improvement. Through study of reports and personal observation, he has formed some very definite ideas as to what must be done to improve performance and has taken up these ideas with his executive committee. Following are the principal ideas and the reaction to each by the committee:

1. IMPROVEMENT OF COMPANY'S RETURN ON INVESTMENT. The president is dissatisfied with the recent profit picture, both with respect to the ratio of net operating profit to sales and to capital employed. He insists that the ratio of net operating profit to capital employed should approach 30 per cent. At present, the rate is far below that figure. The

---

[1] The illustration would not be changed materially by the use of estimated actual rather than standard costs. The latter are used since they represent the most modern accounting procedure.

profit picture for the current quarter is presented by the controller as follows:

	Ratio of Standard Gross Profit to Sales	Ratio of Net Operating Profit to Sales	Ratio of Sales to Capital Employed (turnover)	Ratio of Net Operating Profit to Capital Employed
Total sales	24.30%	8.24%	211.26%	17.42%
Product A	35.00%	18.64%	90.90%	16.95%
Product B	24.44%	8.39%	300.00%	25.17%
Product C	18.86%	2.95%	400.00%	11.80%

It is noted that the nonmanufacturing costs (sales and administrative expenses) are approximately 16 per cent of sales in all instances. This result arises from a basic assumption in the past that the incidence of such costs is considered to be approximately proportional to the sales of the several products. The president points out that such a basic assumption may not be valid and requests that the sales manager and controller study the possibility of developing data which will measure the order-getting and order-filling costs applicable to the several products.

Since there is extensive material on the subject of accounting for nonmanufacturing costs and their assignment to products, this subject is not discussed further in this book, except to point out that in this area of cost accounting the use of periodic cost studies is frequently found just as effective and less burdensome than a complete integration of detailed distribution of nonmanufacturing costs in the accounting structure. Where such accounting integration is desired, it has been found that this field lends itself very well to the use of standard cost techniques.

Since in the present case the expenses below the standard gross profit line are considered to be approximately proportional to the sales of the several products, it is apparent that the poor over-all showing as reflected by a 17.42 per cent ratio of net operating profit to capital employed is due in part to a relatively poor ratio of standard gross profit to sales of Product C (18.86 per cent) and in part to a poor annual turnover ratio of Product A (90.90 per cent). This analysis indicates the necessity for improving the standard gross margin on Product C as well as improving the turnover ratio of Product A. Apart from the obvious solution to the problem relating to Product C of either increasing the selling price or reducing costs, a solution might be found in shifting sales from Product C to Product A (which has a 35 per cent standard gross margin rate) which would have the effect of increasing the average net operating profit rate as well as having the effect of increasing the turnover rate of Product A. It should be pointed out that the turnover rate for Product A can be improved not only by increasing the annual sales but also by reducing the amount of capital employed.

With reference to improving the standard gross margin of Product C, normally only two lines of attack are available. The first is to reduce the unit product costs, through either cost economies or increased volume. The second is to increase the sales price. The committee, both individually and as a group, has considered these two possible lines of action as a means of increasing the profitability of the product.

With reference to possible cost economies in Product C, the production manager reports that with his present facilities and the present design of the product, no substantial reduction can be made in the direct costs of production. Moreover, under present conditions of operation he sees no possibility of obtaining a significant reduction in unit product costs except through obtaining a larger sales volume, and he points out that this approach has a limited potential since the company is presently operating at a substantial percentage of the capacity available to the product. The production manager believes that substantial economies could be made, however, through either (1) substitution of materials in the product which would require less costly manufacturing, or (2) the acquisition of specific items of cost reduction equipment by the expenditure of a substantial amount of capital funds.

In connection with the possible substitution of materials in the manufacture of the product, specific suggestions have been made both by the production manager and the head of the engineering department. Two factors militate against such changes in the immediate future. One is the time required to make the changes and the other is the uncertainty concerning their effect on the marketability of the product, since the changes in reality would affect quality.

With reference to the possibility of raising the price of the product, the sales manager has stated emphatically that that possibility should not even be considered in the present state of the company's market. He had already given this possibility serious study, and the committee accepts his recommendation that this method be considered only as a last resort.

In view of the adverse circumstances surrounding the operations in this product, the committee's next consideration is the possibility of gradually shifting operations from C to the other products. This would appear to offer the greatest possibility for accomplishing an improvement in the rate of return on capital, provided additional sales of Products A and B can be effected. The sales manager believes that sales of B cannot be increased materially at present, but is optimistic concerning the growth of the market for A. It is agreed, therefore, that, without entirely abandoning C, there should be a shift in emphasis from

C to A in the forthcoming budget period. Consideration was given to the possibility of reducing the amount of capital employed in that segment of the business relating to Product A, and it was conceded that some reduction could be effected. However, it was felt that the increased sales efforts to be applied to Product A would result in increased working capital requirements represented by larger inventories and an increase in accounts receivable. It was decided, therefore, to plan on increasing the sales of Product A and at the same time minimizing any increase in capital employed.

It should be recognized that in the particular circumstances which are specified for Illustrative Company it might be difficult to determine plant investment applicable to the several products except by arithmetical allocation based on some such factor as standard machine hours or standard man-hours. Here we have a single plant consisting of several direct departments producing a limited number of products. The various products all pass through several departments; some products pass through all departments. Unless within each department there exists equipment useful only in the manufacture of a single product, it is doubtful that changing the sales mix would change the relative capital turnover with respect to plant investment.

However, in many organizations the physical association of specific plant investment with particular products is more identifiable. For this reason, the general principles involved are pointed out here even though in the circumstances which prevail in Illustrative Company significant fluctuations in relative capital employed may be restricted to the inventory categories.

2. OBTAINING BETTER PRODUCT COSTS. A problem common to most manufacturing companies is that of determining the basis for absorbing factory burden in product costs so as to determine the manufactured cost of each unit of product and to make a proper distinction between costs chargeable to the year's income and year-end inventories. The problem is important not only for the purposes of financial accounting but also for those of price policy. Since a predetermined burden absorption rate is essential in setting the burden component of the company's standard product costs, and since many of the burden costs do not vary with volume, it is necessary to establish a "normal" volume. If this volume is set too high, it may tend to cause products to be underpriced; if too low, the reverse may be true. In either case the company's year may end with substantial amounts of under- or overabsorbed burden. Some companies use the so-called "direct costing" procedure, in which burden costs which do not vary proportionately with changes in production volume are not included in the standard product costs but are treated

simply as charges against the income of the period. While this method avoids the problem of overabsorption and underabsorption of burden, it does not necessarily make the problem of unit price determination any easier in the long run.

Whether normal volume should be defined in terms of the company's ability merely to produce its products or its ability both to produce and sell is a moot question. The proponents of the first basis argue that that basis is necessary in a competitive market since customers cannot be charged with the costs of idle capacity. Proponents of the second basis argue that costs are unrealistic if unrelated to sales demand. In the case of Illustrative Company, the two parties most concerned with the problem, the sales manager and the production manager, have agreed on the capacity-to-make-and-sell concept.

Having agreed on this concept, the question still remains as to whether normal volume should be defined in terms of just one budget period or a longer period of time. This, too, is a moot question which calls for the exercise of managerial judgment. It is generally agreed in the committee that the volume selected as being normal should have some long-range significance. This latter concept presents somewhat of a problem to the sales manager in view of the changing sales picture over the past several years and the intention to obtain a different sales mix in the future. For the present, he has recommended that the burden absorption rate be based on an annual sales volume of four times the anticipated sales of the forthcoming quarter. He recognizes that the third month of that quarter, instead of the quarter as a whole, might be a better basis for annualization, in view of the fact that the planned change in sales mix will begin to have a significant effect on total sales only toward the end of the quarter. However, because of the experimental nature of the new sales plans, and also because of the presence of a seasonal factor in the annual sales, he wishes to "play it safe," pending further developments in the market. The committee has accepted this recommendation.

Since burden absorption is a direct function of production rather than sales, both the production manager and the controller have pointed out that there still remains to be defined the normal production volume, as opposed to the normal sales volume. They presume that the former will be governed by the latter, in view of the capacity-to-make-and-sell concept, but they point out that the amount of over- or underabsorption for any one month, quarter, or even for the entire year can be accurately forecast only by detailed calculations of the several departments' production equivalents of the planned sales *and* inventory changes. Since in the long run, however, production must be geared to sales, it is agreed that the normal annual volume of production is to be the production equivalent of the normal annual sales volume as previously defined. The president has assented to this conclusion, but has reminded the committee that the determination of the normal sales volume is tentative and that, while it will suffice for the forthcoming quarter, it must be re-examined in connection with the preparation of succeeding budgets.

3. OBTAINING BETTER RELATIONSHIP BETWEEN SALES AND SALES COSTS. The president is dissatisfied with the ratio of sales costs to sales and believes that the company is not expending its sales efforts as effectively as it should. He is concerned both with the form of salesmen's compensation and also with the other costs of the sales organization. It appears that proper analyses of these matters cannot now be made because of a lack of adequate detailed information, and that sales and expense statistics are not collected in a manner necessary to scientific analysis of the problems the president has presented. It is agreed that for the forthcoming quarter no changes will be made other than to provide a closer attention to sales expenses, but that the sales manager and controller shall develop a program for more adequate reporting of sales and expense statistics.

4. LOW RATIO OF PURCHASE DISCOUNTS TAKEN TO MATERIAL COSTS. The president questions the seemingly low ratio of purchase discounts taken to material costs as disclosed by the current year's operating statement. It develops that not all possible discounts have been realized, partly because of temporary cash shortages and partly because of looseness of the routines for processing and paying invoices. These are disturbing developments, and it is agreed that the routines must be improved and better observed and that the failure to realize the discounts because of poor staff work is simply inexcusable. Moreover, it is agreed that failure to realize them because of low cash balances is also evidence of poor planning. It is agreed that, as one step in the improvement of office routines, definite payment dates be established for invoices and that the terms of purchase orders hereafter be changed so as to relate the discount terms to announced payment dates.

5. IMPROVEMENT OF INVENTORY BALANCE. The president believes that the inventory policy is haphazard and that some inventories are not proportioned properly to current requirements. He is concerned not only with the present unbalance, but also with the apparent lack of inventory standards, as measured by the day's or month's requirements of direct materials, work in process, and finished product. It is agreed that such standards are to be worked out and made the basis for planning operations for the forthcoming budget period.

6. OBTAINING MORE UNIFORM PRODUCTION SCHEDULES. The president is concerned with the recent, rapid fluctuations in level of

operations in the several production departments. He believes that they are uneconomic and, in any event, not conducive to good industrial relations. At this point, however, it is obvious that leveling out production and maintaining standard inventories may be incompatible. Therefore, a compromise arrangement must be worked out in the light of the relative significance of the two objectives. It is suggested, pending working out of the detailed schedules, that flexible inventory standards be established, if necessary, to obtain a reasonably uniform level of production throughout the budget period.

7. INVESTMENT IN CAPITAL IMPROVEMENTS. For some time it has been the company's practice to make an annual investment in capital improvements, in the amount of the annual depreciation plus approximately one-third of the net income. Since the expenditures generally are planned well in advance of completion, the forthcoming quarter's budget must provide for the expenditure of $100,000 in cash, in the month of March, under a commitment previously entered into. It would appear that this amount may be high in relation to the anticipated depreciation and net income for the quarter. However, for the year as a whole, it is expected that this expenditure will not be out of line.

Budget Directives. The preceding discussion is designed to show the interplay of forces in planning, the need for coordination and integration, and the value of a group analysis of common problems as a means of arriving at carefully thought-out policies and operating decisions. The results of these deliberations need to be summarized in a formal manner not only as a matter of record for the policy-makers but also for the guidance of lower levels of management who are concerned with the execution of the policy decisions. Therefore, the following budget directives are issued by the president.

1. The sales plan for the forthcoming quarter is to be directed primarily toward an improvement in profitability by a change in sales mix, with a shift in emphasis from Product C to Product A. Desired rate of return on capital employed is 30 per cent (on an annual basis).

2. In planning sales expenses for the quarter, prior experience is to serve as the guide, but the sales manager and controller are to develop methods of achieving better control of these expenses and better statistical data to be used in the study of the effectiveness of sales effort.

3. Planned cash balances in the future must be large enough to permit the taking of all discounts, even though outside financing is entailed. Arrangements are to be made with suppliers to permit taking of discounts on specified payment dates, and invoice and payment procedures are to be improved so as to ensure the taking of all discounts.

4. Inventory standards are to be determined and used in the budget, with due allowance for a reasonably uniform level of production.

5. Production schedules in each of the production departments are to be established on a uniform level throughout the quarter, to the fullest extent practicable.

6. Approximately $100,000 must be made available for capital improvements as a result of prior commitments under the program now in effect.

SECOND STEP—FORMULATION OF PLANS AND PREPARATION OF A LIST OF ASSUMPTIONS BY EACH DEPARTMENT HEAD

Integrated Plans Required. The final budget comprises a series of detailed plans which are closely coordinated and integrated. The basic assumptions which were established by top management must be recognized by each department and, where necessary, supplemented by additional assumptions pertinent to the particular department within the over-all framework. The work of each department must be dovetailed with the others, and this requires constant consultation among the several departments' personnel engaged in budget preparation, with the budget director acting as liaison officer. The number of plans and forecasts to be prepared will vary from company to company, but complete budgetary procedure in a manufacturing company requires, as a minimum, the plans outlined in Figure 4-1. In that figure the basic plans are listed along with the departments involved in their preparation.

Where To Begin? In principle, assembling the budget involves a series of sequential steps starting with the determination of the planned sales and then fitting the plans for production, material procurement, labor recruitment, incurrence of various categories of expenses, inventory accumulation, and financing to the sales plan. In practice, however, the procedure is not so simple because of the interdependence of the several plans.

Planning sales, for example, is not simply a matter of forecasting how much can be sold at a price. It also involves the determination of the sales needed to accomplish the desired profit objective, giving effect to different prices and to costs. Can the objective be more readily achieved by securing larger volume through price reduction or by lower volume at a higher price? What is the relation between sales volume and costs? Some aspects of this question have already been noted in Chapter 2. But sales expenses, for example, particularly those in the order-getting category, do not follow the sales but precede them. It is not merely a

Plan or Forecast	Department Affected
Sales (orders and shipments)	Sales—Accounting
Inventories	
Finished goods	Sales—Production—Accounting
Work in process	Production—Accounting
Raw materials	Purchasing—Accounting
Production requirements—units	Production
Direct labor requirements	Production—Personnel
Direct material requirements	Production
Indirect manufacturing expenses	Production—Purchasing—Personnel—Accounting
Nonfactory departments' expenditures	
Executive division	
General office	
Accounting	
Purchasing	Respective Department Heads—Accounting
Industrial relations	
Sales	
Others	
Capital improvements	Engineering—Production—Sales, and others
Cost of goods manufactured	Accounting
Cost of sales	Accounting
Other income and expenses	Accounting
Prepaid expenses and accruals	Accounting
Purchases	Purchasing
Accounts payable	Accounting
Loans payable	Treasury
Payroll	Accounting
Accounts receivable	Treasury
Cash	Treasury
Profit and loss	Accounting
Balance sheet	Accounting

FIG. 4-1. Budget Plans and Forecasts and Departments Affected

matter of planning the sales and then assuming that the expenses will be in proportion thereto. Rather, it is a question of how much the management is willing to spend, and must spend, to obtain a certain sales volume. Hence, at the outset there must be a balancing of input and output factors to determine the most profitable course of action. The same type of relationship extends throughout all the budgeting operations.

Many of the relationships needed in setting the preliminary sales target to accomplish the desired objectives are already known approximately by the various members of a well-organized and experienced management team. This knowledge will serve to avoid many false starts—if it is properly communicated. This suggests the importance of cooperation, not only formal but also informal, at the very outset of the planning operation. Informal conferences and discussions of key personnel from all divisions and frequent exchanges of information are important in a smooth budgetary organization. In those companies where budgeting has been practiced over a period of time and where accounting and cost data are well organized, the probable effects of new decisions can frequently be approximated quite easily on the basis of past experience. In a new company, however, or one where budgetary procedures are being adopted for the first time, the trial and error method may have to be used, and the final budget may be the result of a process of attrition whereby the plans have to be worked and reworked a number of times before a satisfactory conclusion is reached.

Lest the foregoing discussion seem to present a too formidable picture of the budget-making process, it should be pointed out that in the average going concern the changes made in plans or methods of operation in any one operating period are generally not revolutionary in nature. Patterns of operation tend to change only gradually so that heavy reliance can be placed on past experience. Changes in price, nature of production, and operating methods at any one time tend to be minor in the aggregate. Except for unusual situations, this is necessarily true since management's freedom to make changes is restricted by the degree of organizational skill and by many forces—competitive, financial, and contractual. So it is assumed to be with the Illustrative Company. Although the president has issued a number of directives, they are primarily in the nature of sharpening the company's efforts but without making a fundamental change of direction or policy.

Admitting the interrelationship of all the various phases of the business and that no single plan is entirely independent of the others, the fact still remains that a start must be made in the preparation of the detailed schedules, and sales represent the keystone of the total plan. Consequently, the succeeding discussion of the planning work of the several departments starts with the sales department.

Sales Department Planning. Reference to Figure 4–1 indicates that the sales department is primarily concerned with the planning of sales orders and shipments, the finished goods inventories, and selling expenses. In practice there may be a substantial difference between sales orders obtained and shipments made in a given period, depending both on the length of the production cycle and the size of the company's backlog of orders. For simplicity and convenience, in the present discussion this difference is ignored, and sales and shipments are considered to be synonymous.

It has already been indicated that significant price changes are not now contemplated. Consequently, the department's principal problem is to determine how much of each product can be sold at the existing price, giving consideration to the fact that it has already been decided to

PREPARING THE BUDGET

change the sales mix. In this chapter we are not concerned with the methods of determining the sales potential (see Chapter 9), but it is emphasized that estimates must be made on as accurate a basis as possible, since all the other detailed plans and forecasts will be geared to it. While for the purposes of the forecast plan of operations, balance sheet, and other financial uses the sales plan must be measured in dollars, for production and related purposes it must also be stated in terms of units of each product. Moreover, it is not sufficient merely to set the sales goals for the budget period as a whole. Rather, they must be established for shorter periods of time—a month or less. In the current example it is assumed that they are set for the month.

The question of what can be sold, however, is not the sole determinant of the sales plan for the period. Actually the management is also interested in knowing the amount that *must* be sold in order to achieve the desired profit objectives. This is one example of the point referred to earlier, that budget preparation is a cooperative activity requiring constant referral to related activities. It is in this connection that the accounting department aids in establishing the sales plan, since it is the function of accounting to estimate the net profit to be realized from a given sales volume. If the sales department's estimate of what can be sold is not likely to yield the desired net income, consideration must be given to the possibility of raising the ceiling on sales volume by a radical change either in direction or amount of sales effort.

The sales department is also concerned with the amount of finished stock to be maintained in inventory, since the ability to fill orders promptly is an important aspect of relations with customers. This problem, too, cannot be resolved solely on the basis of one factor. Although the prompt filling of orders is important, the advantage of doing so must be weighed against the various costs of maintaining an inventory. Moreover, as previously indicated, production scheduling is also a factor to be considered. Nevertheless, the sales department normally initiates the problem by defining its minimum requirements. The ultimate decision normally involves only the degree to which these minima may be exceeded for the convenience of other divisions of the company.

The sales department is also concerned with planning and forecasting selling expenses. These fall into two principal categories—expenses of order getting and expenses of order filling. The former category, which includes such items as advertising, and salesmen's compensation and traveling expenses, in effect measures the amount and cost of sales effort and is an important factor in determining the amount of sales to be obtained. At this point, again, the accounting department cooperates with the sales department in establishing the most profitable relation, profit-wise, of sales effort and sales results.

With reference to the second category of selling expenses, the order filling costs, considerable reliance generally is placed on past experience, and here accounting information is also invaluable.

Sales Department's Decisions. The importance of the planning of sales, sales costs, and inventories of finished stock cannot be overemphasized. All three are interrelated, and the proper combination must be developed with a view to earning the desired rate of return on capital employed. Although the direction of the sales effort of Illustrative Company is to be changed relative to the several products, the type and amount of effort are tentatively expected to follow the previous pattern in the relationship of selling costs to sales. Consequently, with the controller's assistance, it is possible to estimate fairly closely the net profit to be realized from a given amount and mixture of sales, without completing all the schedules. This aids greatly in the budget preparation since it thus is possible, at the outset, to determine the sales to be used as the basis of the budget, with some assurance that the planned final results will be in line with the desired results.

The initial sales estimates, in units, are as follows:

	January	February	March	Quarter
Product A	2,000	3,000	7,000	12,000
Product B	2,000	2,000	2,000	6,000
Product C	8,000	6,000	4,000	18,000

The estimates are based on prices for the three products of $80, $90, and $35, respectively. The controller estimates that these sales will not earn the desired average rate of return on total capital employed in either January or February, but will exceed it in March as the shift from Product C to Product A becomes effective. The indicated rate for the quarter is 26.28 per cent, which is below the target rate of 30 per cent but much better than present performance.

At this point the president is consulted. In view of the substantial indicated improvement, the sales department's initial estimates are accepted as a basis for the quarter's budget, subject to confirmation by the results of the over-all budget as finally worked out in complete detail. If the final computations prove the foregoing estimate incorrect, the entire budget may have to be reworked. The process of attrition must frequently be relied on heavily in budget preparation.

Before the production department can begin to prepare its budget schedules, one other decision is required of the sales department. This concerns the amount of each product to be carried in inventory of finished goods. Giving consideration to all relevant factors, the sales department has set a month's sales (shipments) as the minimum. The number of finished product completions each month, therefore, would amount to the sum of the current month's shipments and the following month's shipments, less the inventory at the beginning of the current month. Figure 4-2 shows the preliminary computation of required monthly completions for the quarter. January 1 inventories are obtained from the supporting information in the Appendix (page 371), and the desired inventories at March 31 are based on sales estimates for April, one month beyond the current budget period, which must be made for this purpose.

The preliminary computations shown in Figure 4-2 indicate the necessary completions for the quarter but do not meet the requirements of the president's directive concerning leveling out production. This directive suggests that each month's completions should be equal—thus 6,000 of A, 2,000 of B, and 5,000 of C. However, a leveled production schedule would not provide the required minimum inventories at the end of each month as is shown in Figure 4-3.

Comparison of the desired ending inventories shown in Figure 4-2 and the ending inventories shown in Figure 4-3 indicates that a schedule of equal monthly completions will create deviations from the inventory standards in January and February. In the cases of Products A and B, the inventories will be excessive, while in the case of Product C they will amount to just half the desired amount. The plus deviations are of concern because of the inventory costs involved; the minus deviations

	Month's Shipments	Desired Inventory at End of Month	Total Requirement	Inventory at First of Month	Required Completions
Product A					
Jan.	2,000	3,000	5,000	1,000	4,000
Feb.	3,000	7,000	10,000	3,000	7,000
Mar.	7,000	7,000	14,000	7,000	7,000
Total					18,000
Product B					
Jan.	2,000	2,000	4,000	3,000	1,000
Feb.	2,000	2,000	4,000	2,000	2,000
Mar.	2,000	3,000	5,000	2,000	3,000
Total					6,000
Product C					
Jan.	8,000	6,000	14,000	6,000	8,000
Feb.	6,000	4,000	10,000	6,000	4,000
Mar.	4,000	3,000	7,000	4,000	3,000
Total					15,000

FIG. 4-2. Preliminary Computation of Finished Product Completions To Be Scheduled in Units of Product

	Inventory First of Month	Production	Total	Shipments	Inventory End of Month
Product A					
Jan.	1,000	6,000	7,000	2,000	5,000
Feb.	5,000	6,000	11,000	3,000	8,000
Mar.	8,000	6,000	14,000	7,000	7,000
Product B					
Jan.	3,000	2,000	5,000	2,000	3,000
Feb.	3,000	2,000	5,000	2,000	3,000
Mar.	3,000	2,000	5,000	2,000	3,000
Product C					
Jan.	6,000	5,000	11,000	8,000	3,000
Feb.	3,000	5,000	8,000	6,000	2,000
Mar.	2,000	5,000	7,000	4,000	3,000

Fig. 4–3. Calculation of Ending Inventories Under Level Production in Units of Product

may affect customer relations, but only in the event of the receipt of rush orders. Since the latter concern only Product C, the sales manager feels inclined to take that risk. Regarding the former, the president believes the additional inventory costs are not too high a price to pay for better industrial relations and he agrees with the contention of the production manager that level production output is conducive to higher efficiency and consequently lower production costs. It is agreed, therefore, to plan for equal monthly product completions.

Production Department Planning. This department is concerned with production schedules, the amount of work in process inventory, direct labor requirements, direct material requirements, and all items of factory burden. The starting point in this department's planning is the production schedules of the several departments. The preparation of these schedules can be quite complicated, depending on the number of products produced, the production sequences through the several departments, and the length of the production cycle in each department.

As previously indicated, the schedule of completions is not the same as the production schedule, because of work in process inventories and the practice of stocking component parts. Reference to the supporting information included in the Appendix (page 371) shows that at December 31 there are on hand 3,000 B1 parts (Product B completely processed through Department 1 and stored) and 3,000 units of Product A in process in Department 1, complete as to material A1, but only half finished as to labor and burden. The directive concerning unbalance of inventories applies to work in process and finished parts as well as finished stock. Therefore, operating management has been studying these inventory requirements, too, and has reached the following conclusions:

1. To minimize month-end inventories of work in process through improved scheduling.
2. To stop the practice of stocking part B1 since the advantages realized heretofore will no longer be present under the new scheduling procedure.
3. To begin stocking part A1 (Product A in Department 1) in the amount of one-half month's production requirements for Product A in the following department.

The foregoing inventory changes, if accomplished entirely in the first month, however, would tend partially to nullify the effect of the equalized completions schedule on the level of factory operations. Consequently, it is agreed that the changes shall be spread evenly over the quarter. The departmental operations can now be scheduled, giving effect to the planned monthly completions and the opening and desired closing inventories of work in process and finished parts. Figure 4–4 shows the computations. It will be observed that, since each product goes through a sequence of operations in the several departments, the

	Product A	Product B	Product C
Production for the quarter:			
Dept. 3			
Required completions as per Fig. 4–2........	18,000	6,000	15,000
Dept. 2			
Required for Dept. 3......................	18,000	6,000	
Dept. 1			
Required for Dept. 2......................	18,000	6,000	
Required for Dept. 3......................			15,000
Deduct:			
Product B (part B1) on hand at			
Dec. 31................................		(3,000)	
Product A (part A1) ½ finished at			
Dec. 31, equivalent to.................	(1,500)		
Add:			
Required increase in Product A1 parts....	3,000		
Required production	19,500	3,000	15,000
Monthly production (divide by 3):			
Dept. 3...................................	6,000	2,000	5,000
Dept. 2...................................	6,000	2,000	
Dept. 1...................................	6,500	1,000	5,000

Fig. 4–4. Computation of Uniform Monthly Production Requirements in Units of Product by Departments
First Quarter, 19—

calculations must also be made in sequence, but in the reverse order. It should also be noted that the calculations are in units of product rather than labor hours or machine hours, measures which would be useful in some companies. The calculations are made for the quarter and then reduced to a monthly basis since production is to be at the same rate each month.

The determination of direct labor and direct material requirements for the quarter presents no serious problems in the case of Illustrative Company. The company produces only three products and, in addition, it uses standard costs. Therefore, the determinations can be made simply by applying the quantity standards for direct labor and material to the scheduled production requirements.

In scheduling indirect manufacturing expenses (factory burden) for the quarter, the departmental organization must be recognized. Moreover, attention must be given to burden absorption as well as burden incurrence. With reference to burden absorption, it is necessary to establish departmental overhead rates based on burden allowances for normal volume, as previously defined. Since the costs of some factory departments get charged to products indirectly, by being first charged to other departments, provision must be made for the necessary expense allocations and redistributions. Thus, the problem of burden absorption concerns the cost accounting department as well as production management. The methods of budgeting factory burden are discussed in Chapter 14. Suffice it to point out here that each item of factory burden must be related to the normal volume in order to forecast the amount of burden to be absorbed at that volume.

In connection with the amount of burden expected to be incurred, the various burden items must be forecasted in relation to the scheduled production computed in Figure 4–4. To the extent that the scheduled production differs from the normal production, over- or underabsorption will be provided for in the budget for the quarter. Since the company maintains an up-to-date schedule of flexible burden allowances for various production volumes, the determination of allowances both for normal and expected volumes presents no new problem.

Purchasing Department Planning. The responsibility for scheduling purchases of direct and indirect factory materials and supplies varies among companies as between the production and the purchasing departments. In Illustrative Company, however, the responsibility lies with the purchasing department, since it is believed that this department should have the freedom to make purchases in the most economical quantities so long as the materials are available when needed.

PREPARING THE BUDGET

The immediate problem is to compute the forecasted requirements on a time basis giving effect to production requirements, desired ending inventories of materials, and the inventories on hand at the beginning of the budget period. The production requirements of direct materials are obtained from the production department and, as indicated above, can be readily computed by applying the standard material components to the scheduled production for the quarter, on a monthly basis. With reference to the desired end-of-month inventories of materials, the reader is referred to Chapter 11 for a discussion of the economics of inventory size. Suffice it to point out here that the managers of the purchasing and production departments, pursuant to the budget directive, have decided, on an experimental basis, to maintain one month's production requirements of purchased materials in inventory at all times. Thus, the desired end-of-month inventories of direct materials can readily be computed by applying the standard material components to the succeeding month's production requirements. The initial inventories of the seven types of direct materials may be obtained from the Appendix (page 371).[2] As an example of the type of computation necessary, Figure 4–5 shows the computation of the quantities of each material to be bought each month. For reasons of convenience the material requirements are not shown in feet, pounds, and so forth, but only in terms of production units. Thus, for example, one unit of Product A processed through Department 1 is deemed to require one unit of material A1.

Reference to Figure 4–5 indicates one item which needs additional explanation. This concerns the production requirements of material A1 in the three months. This requirement of 6,000 units is the difference between 6,500 and 500. The 6,500 figure represents the equivalent production of Product A in Department 1 as computed in Figure 4–4. The subtraction figure of 500 reflects the fact that in the liquidation of the 1,500 equivalent units of part A in process, over the three months of the quarter, the materials are already issued as of January 1; consequently, material requirements are 500 units less per month.

Scheduling the purchases of certain indirect materials may follow a similar procedure. The monthly requirements, however, are not obtained from the production schedule but from the expense allowance schedule for the planned production.

[2] As shown on page 59, Product A is processed through Departments 1, 2, and 3; Product B through the same departments, and Product C through only Departments 1 and 3. It is assumed that in the production of Product A, material is added in Departments 1 and 3; in Product B it is added in all three departments; and in the case of Product C in Departments 1 and 3. For convenience, the materials are designated as A1, A3, B1, etc.

	Production Requirements	Desired E.O.M. Inventory	Total	Less: Inventory 1st of Month	To Be Purchased
Jan.	(500)				
Material A1	6,500	6,000	12,000	3,000	9,000
Material A3	6,000	6,000	12,000	7,000	5,000
Material B1	1,000	1,000	2,000	1,500	500
Material B2	2,000	2,000	4,000	500	3,500
Material B3	2,000	2,000	4,000	1,000	3,000
Material C1	5,000	5,000	10,000	6,000	4,000
Material C3	5,000	5,000	10,000	4,000	6,000
Feb.	(500)				
Material A1	6,500	6,000	12,000	6,000	6,000
Material A3	6,000	6,000	12,000	6,000	6,000
Material B1	1,000	1,000	2,000	1,000	1,000
Material B2	2,000	2,000	4,000	2,000	2,000
Material B3	2,000	2,000	4,000	2,000	2,000
Material C1	5,000	5,000	10,000	5,000	5,000
Material C3	5,000	5,000	10,000	5,000	5,000
Mar.	(500)				
Material A1	6,500	7,000	13,000	6,000	7,000
Material A3	6,000	7,000	13,000	6,000	7,000
Material B1	1,000	3,000	4,000	1,000	3,000
Material B2	2,000	3,000	5,000	2,000	3,000
Material B3	2,000	3,000	5,000	2,000	3,000
Material C1	5,000	3,000	8,000	5,000	3,000
Material C3	5,000	3,000	8,000	5,000	3,000

FIG. 4-5. Computation of Monthly Purchases and Inventories of Direct Materials in Units

Personnel Department Planning. The personnel department is concerned with supplying the factory (as well as other divisions) with the required labor force to meet scheduled operational requirements. These requirements, as they relate to the factory, are obtained from the production management. The personnel department's planning function in this connection is to gear itself to recruiting and maintaining the necessary labor force, giving effect to the labor market, expected labor turnover, and other related factors. In the case of Illustrative Company, this department also carries out the company's industrial relations program. Accordingly, in preparing its schedule of expenses, provision must be made for such activities.

Engineering Department Planning. This department in Illustrative Company is concerned both with production engineering and product design and research. It must plan its expenditures for these activities. In addition, it is this department's function to evaluate proposals for capital improvements in the cost reduction category. It is, therefore, directly concerned in the preparation of the capital improvements schedule.

Treasury Department Planning. This department is concerned with the administration of cash funds and is therefore involved, together with the accounting department, in the preparation of schedules of accounts payable, loans payable, payroll, accounts receivable, and cash. Here again, the budgetary requirements of coordination and integration are well illustrated, since every one of these schedules is related to others. The cash schedule in particular is related to numerous other schedules.

Practically every item in the schedule of cash receipts and disbursements involves not only reference to data on the initiating transactions but also consideration of factors affecting the timing of the receipts and disbursements. In the case of accounts receivable, for example, the time factor must be estimated on the basis of past experience. In the case of most of the disbursements, payment dates are specified either by the terms of purchase, contractual arrangements, company policy (as in the case of stated paydays), or other factors peculiar to particular transactions.

One of the objectives of treasury department planning is to determine the need for external financing so as to ensure the presence at all times of sufficient cash to meet anticipated needs. If the cash schedule indicates the need for external financing, as it does in the case of Illustrative Company, top management must be notified of this result of the plans laid to date, and must either authorize the making of arrangements for the necessary financing, or order an alteration of the over-all plan.

Planning by Nonfactory Departments. Until now, the discussion of planning by the nonfactory departments has been primarily concerned with scheduling the transactions with which they are concerned. Nothing has been said, however, concerning the administration of each of these departments. Obviously, this cost must also be budgeted so that each of the nonfactory departments, including the accounting department, must budget its own cost of operation. In many cases, a substantial portion of these costs are not directly related to the level of the company's activity in the short run but tend to be in the nature of fixed costs, and are reviewed and analyzed only at the time the budget is under preparation.

The Work of the Accounting Department. Reference to Figure 4–1 indicates the very important part which the accounting department plays in budgeting. Their work consists of two phases. The first phase is that of supplying the other departments with basic information needed in preparing their budget schedules. In the preparation of burden allowances for the factory, for example, much of the data, to the extent that these allowances are based on past experience and not on comprehensive engineering studies, are obtained from account classifications. Even where engineering studies are used extensively in this connection, certain data still must come from the accounts, particularly those relating to costs of purchased services. Moreover, all transactions in units of labor or tangible goods must be costed. The accounting department, too, is responsible for the allocation and distribution of manufacturing expenses among the various departments and for the reallocation of service department expenses to producing departments.

In the case of other, nonfactory departments, accounting data are also important in providing data of past experience to be used as a basis for the new budget requests. Moreover, as was noted in the discussion of sales planning, this department has a very important part in selecting the basic operational pattern to be followed and this is the keystone of budget preparation.

The second phase of the planning work of the accounting department is to provide the controls necessary to ensuring the integration of all the detailed budget plans and to translate these plans into forecast profit and loss statements and balance sheets. This phase represents the bringing together of all the planned transactions so as to show their ultimate effect on net income and financial position.

In preparing the forecast profit and loss and financial statements, many of the items fall into place very readily. Sales figures, for example, come directly from the sales schedule, or if that schedule is prepared only in terms of physical quantities, the dollar sales still can readily be computed by applying the stated sales prices to the budgeted quantities. The calculation of cost of sales and finished goods inventories also presents no problem where standard costs are used. On the other hand, if some other basis of costing is used, such as first-in, first-out, or average cost, then a strictly accounting computation must be made.

The principal accounting problems in this phase of budgeting arise in connection with the estimation of accruals and prepayments, and particularly in those cases where transactions are not of a routine character. Thus, for example, the scheduling of a borrowing transaction requires that provision be made for the periodic accrual of interest on the obligation. As an example of the care with which these accrued and prepaid items must be picked up, Figure 4–6 presents a schedule of the monthly accruals and amortization charges based on the data underlying the budget shown in Figure 5–1 of the following chapter. The illustration indicates the importance of picking up all the "loose ends" of budget preparation and the importance of distinguishing between cash and noncash transactions. The data in the schedule serve not only in the

PREPARING THE BUDGET

	January	February	March
Depreciation on machinery and equipment at 1% per month	$10,000	$10,000	$ 10,000
Depreciation on buildings at ¼% per month	2,000	2,000	2,000
Real estate taxes (payable November 1)	7,100	7,100	7,100
Insurance (renewable February 1)	2,000	2,000	2,000
Interest on note			500
Interest on mortgage	1,000	1,000	950
Salesmen's commission	18,600	18,900	26,400
Provision for doubtful accounts	12,400	12,600	17,600
Income taxes (50% of net income)	13,130	20,135	49,185
	$66,230	$73,735	$115,735
Accounted for as follows:			
Included in factory burden	$18,700	$18,700	$ 18,700
Included in selling expenses	20,600	20,900	28,400
Included in general and administrative expenses	400	400	400
Included in other charges to income	26,530	33,735	68,235
	$66,230	$73,735	$115,735

Fig. 4–6. Monthly Accruals and Amortization First Quarter, 19—

preparation of the profit and loss and financial statements but also as a basis for the accounting department's own routines in the preparation of monthly entries.

THIRD STEP—AMENDMENT OF PLANS AND ASSUMPTIONS

Coordination of Detailed Plans. The foregoing discussion of the work involved in the preparation of budget plans by the several departments of Illustrative Company indicates clearly the need for a complete dovetailing of the plans. It should be quite obvious that all the plans must be prepared on the basis of common knowledge, not only of the general directives, but also of the specific plans of related departments. Figure 4–7 is designed to show graphically the need for integration of the various schedules.

Amendments of Departmental Plans. In the course of the preparation of departmental budget schedules in accordance with the budgetary directives, it frequently happens that facts are brought to light which indicate the need for modification in certain details of the planning, or for a restatement of the directives. For example, attention is called to the executive committee's discussion of the questions of inventory balance and level production. At that point it was indicated that the committee recognized that the two objectives were not necessarily com-

	Sales	Finished goods inventory	Work in process inventory	Raw materials inventory	Production requirements—units	Direct labor requirements	Direct material requirements	Indirect manufacturing expenses	Nonfactory departments expenses	Capital improvements	Cost of goods manufactured	Cost of sales	Other income and expenses	Prepaid expenses and accruals	Purchases	Accounts payable	Loans payable	Payroll	Accounts receivable	Cash	Profit and loss statements	Balance sheet
Sales					X							X							X		X	
Finished goods inventory					X						X	X										X
Work in process inventory					X																	X
Raw materials inventory					X		X															X
Production requirements—units	X	X	X	X		X	X	X			X											
Direct labor requirements					X													X				
Direct material requirements				X	X										X	X						
Indirect manufacturing expenses					X									X		X		X			X	
Nonfactory departments expenses														X		X		X			X	
Capital improvements																X		X				X
Cost of goods manufactured		X			X																	
Cost of sales	X	X																			X	
Other income and expenses														X		X	X		X	X	X	
Prepaid expenses and accruals								X	X				X				X			X		X
Purchases							X									X						
Accounts payable							X	X	X	X			X		X					X		X
Loans payable													X	X						X	X	X
Payroll						X		X	X	X										X		X
Accounts receivable	X												X							X		X
Cash													X	X		X	X	X	X			X
Profit and loss statements	X							X	X			X	X				X					X
Balance sheet		X	X	X						X				X		X	X	X	X	X	X	

FIG. 4-7. Relationship of Budget Schedules

patible, but until detailed schedules were prepared it was not possible to measure accurately the relationship between the two objectives.

In the case of Illustrative Company, the problem was complicated by the fact that, because of work in process and finished parts inventories, scheduled completions and scheduled production are not the same. Inventory standards were established, as directed, but deviations finally had to be agreed to in order to accomplish the leveling of factory operations.

Another example of the reciprocal influence of objectives and detailed plans is that already referred to concerning the financial outcome of the proposed operations. As indicated in the next chapter, the present plans require short-term financing during the budget period. This fact conceivably could be guessed but certainly could not be verified, or the amount exactly determined, prior to the preparation of the sources and applications of funds statement supported by the schedules affecting cash.

Alterations of Budget Directives. Some of the changes of the type discussed in the preceding section may not require a change in the overall plan but merely minor adjustments as among several departments. In other cases, however, a change in basic directives may be called for. These obviously require top management consideration and approval. In still other cases, a situation may arise which does not appear to be covered by the budget directives and additional directives may be requested. For example, the schedule of planned purchases of direct materials as shown in Figure 4–5 indicates that the purchasing department is to follow a close time schedule in these purchases. Upon review of the schedule, the manager of the purchasing department may feel that it does not give him sufficient freedom of action in timing his purchases to get the best possible price or method of delivery. He may request, therefore, authorization to deviate from the schedule on a time basis. In the event that a directive is issued granting him this freedom, consideration must be given by the treasury department to the effect of this deviation on the company's cash position at a given time. This consideration actually may militate against the directive's being issued. Or if it is issued, it may set certain limits to the purchasing department's discretion, and these would be recognized by the treasurer in the preparation of the cash schedules.

Throughout this chapter considerable emphasis has been placed on the formalizing of budget directives. The practice of specifying them very clearly in writing is strongly urged. This practice ensures not only a clear understanding, by all personnel concerned, of the conditions which are to control their operations, but also provides a record to be used subsequently as a basis for checking the plans and operations of the several divisions of the company. If this practice is adopted, then it follows that amendments to or additions to the budget directives should also be promulgated and made a matter of record.

FOURTH STEP—PRESENTATION OF PLAN TO MANAGEMENT

Summary of Results of Plan. When the work of preparing the budget schedules is completed, a formal report is prepared for presentation to the president. This report contains two principal sections, the narrative section and the exhibit section. The narrative section of the budget report restates the budget directives and the considerations which governed the preparation of the plans. It also comments on and summarizes the forecasted results of the plans. The exhibit section presents the schedules which reflect the plan. While all the schedules listed earlier in this chapter comprise the budget, the number to be included in the formal budget report varies with circumstances and depending on the wishes of the president. In some cases this section of the report is comprehensive and is designed to be a reference source for all actions and decisions. In other cases it is designed to give only a summarized picture of the budget and contains only a few exhibits and schedules showing the end results of the plan. In such cases the excluded schedules are still considered as supporting data but simply are not included in the budget report. The policy to be followed in this regard is determined by the local circumstances in each company. The budget report of Illustrative Company is presented in the next chapter.

Regardless of the form which the report takes, the purpose at this stage in the preparation of the budget is to present sufficient information to enable the president to evaluate the anticipated results of the forthcoming period's operations as planned. In a small or medium-sized company, the method followed in preparing the budget, involving close cooperation of top management and lower management levels, permits the end results of the plan to be fairly well known, at least approximately, prior to drafting the formal budget report. In such cases the third step (amendment of plans and assumptions) and the fourth step (presentation of plan to management) tend to merge, and the fourth step becomes somewhat of a formality.

In those companies, however, where the board of directors is separate and distinct from top operating management and where the board exercises close control of operations, the fourth step becomes truly a separate step since the presentation of the report to top operating management is merely a preliminary to presentation to the board of

PREPARING THE BUDGET

directors. In the case of Illustrative Company it is assumed that presentation to the president is the final significant step.

Study of the budget report of Illustrative Company presented in the next chapter indicates the extent to which the forecasted results of the plan meet the objectives set forth in the budget directives. As indicated there, several of the objectives are approached but not fully realized. The president and his advisors accordingly must decide now whether to accept the plan as it stands or to order a reworking of it.

Reconsideration of Objectives and Directives. In the case of Illustrative Company, it is assumed that the president accepts the plan, as modified earlier, since the results are reasonably close to his expectations and because of the degree of improvement over past experience and the expected continuance of the trend toward better results. In those cases, however, where the results are not satisfactory, consideration must be given the question of whether improvement can be attained along the lines of the original plan or whether drastic changes of direction must be made. In the case of Illustrative Company, for example, plans were laid on the premise that the principal improvement in operating results would be secured through a change in the sales mix but without a change in sales prices. If conditions warranted a reconsideration of price policy, an entirely new plan would have to be worked out, starting with a new sales forecast to which all the other schedules would be integrated. In practice, a number of alternative courses of action may be considered, each of which would call for a more or less complete reworking of plans, depending on the nature of the alternatives. In such cases, top management's final responsibility in budget preparation is that of judging the merits of the alternative plans and making a selection.

FIFTH STEP—APPROVAL OF THE BUDGET

Approval of the budget may be more or less formal, depending on the size of the company and the nature of its organization. In all but the smallest companies, however, some record should be made of the act and time of approval as a means of fixing responsibility and establishing the budget report as the basis for good budgetary control of operations under the budget.

In many companies final approval comes from the president, while in others it comes from the board of directors. Board approval seems desirable although some studies seem to indicate that this is by no means universal practice, and perhaps not even common practice. It should be noted parenthetically, however, that while the available evidence does not support the idea of presenting the budget to the board for *approval,* the practice of *reporting results* to the board, in comparison with the budget, appears to be common practice. In this connection it should also be recognized that in many companies top management is heavily represented on the board and frequently comprises the entire board membership, so that the act of approval by the board often may be only a formality. Where the practice of obtaining board approval is followed, the record of the approval appears in the minutes of the board.

SIXTH STEP—ISSUANCE OF THE BUDGET

The budget, once approved, should serve as a control document and an authorization for all the company's operations throughout the budget period. It should serve both as a "go ahead" signal and a standard of performance. This requires that all personnel who are controlled by the budget and who are responsible for the execution of detailed plans be furnished with copies of the budget schedules related to their work. Each department, therefore, will receive and constantly refer to its budget schedule as a guide to its operations. In this connection reference is again made to the question of budget approvals. The budget schedules issued to the several departments of the company should carry proper authorization.

CHAPTER 5

THE BUDGET IN FINAL FORM

	Page		Page
Purpose of chapter	85	Forecast statement of return on capital employed	96
Form of budget	85	Forecast sources and applications of funds	97
Illustration of budget	86	Forecast changes in working capital	98
Illustrative Company Budget Report First Quarter, 19—		Forecast balance sheets	99
		Section III: Schedules	100
		Forecast sales and factory cost of sales	101
Section I: Directives and conformity therewith	90	Forecast selling expenses	102
Section II: Exhibits	94	Forecast general and administrative expenses	103
Forecast operating statement	95	Forecast other income and deductions	104

Purpose of Chapter. The purpose of this chapter is to illustrate the form of the budget as it is presented to top management for final approval. It is a continuation of the budget story of Illustrative Company, begun in the preceding chapter.

The budget of the company, as reported in this chapter, serves three purposes. First, it provides top management with a summarized picture of the results to be expected from the proposed plan of operations. This aids the management in determining whether the plan is satisfactory. Second, following approval, it serves as a guide to executives and department heads responsible for individual segments of the operations. Third, it serves to measure performance, since budget deviations reflect either the organization's failure to achieve the planned standards of performance or its ability to better them. For the two last-named purposes in particular, the budget should be presented as a formal document, to serve as a record not only of the plans for the period but also of the premises, conditions, and objectives underlying the plans. The record of premises and conditions is important since any evaluation of budget deviations must consider whether a change has taken place which would invalidate the budget itself.

Form of Budget. There is no prescribed form of budget report in industrial companies. Unlike a balance sheet or an independent auditor's certificate, the budget document is designed primarily for use within the company. Consequently, its form and contents vary with companies. In some companies the document consists solely of exhibits and schedules; in others, a narrative report section is included. The author strongly favors the latter practice. He believes that the report should contain a statement of the objectives of the plan, and the premises underlying their implementation, as well as comments concerning the conformance of the plan with the objectives. This information is useful in several ways. First, it serves as a record of the reasons for planning decisions, and this record may be helpful at some later date in explaining a course of action. Second, it provides background information for an intelligent appraisal of budget deviations. But most important, in the author's opinion, the practice of including a statement of objectives in the budget report forces management to define its objectives clearly. This is a deterrent to careless and haphazard planning.

A question of form is also raised in connection with the amount of detail to be included in the budget schedules. All the schedules prepared in building the budget are integral parts of it. All are used in directing and controlling the related operations in various divisions and segments of the organization. Consequently, a complete file of them must be maintained for ready reference. Whether all of them, however, would be included in the report to top management is debatable, but in the final analysis this question generally is resolved in accordance with the wishes of top management. However, in accordance with the principle of delegation of authority and responsibility and recognizing the common difficulty in analyzing voluminous data, it is believed that the evaluation of the plan, and its subsequent use by top management in controlling operations under the plan, can best be served by including in the budget report only those forecast schedules which show the expected results under the plan. As a basis for the initial evaluation of the plan, this is all that counts. For subsequent control purposes, the president should be concerned with only *significant* deviations; lower management levels should be responsible for exercising control over the details.

Illustration of Budget. The budget of Illustrative Company, as it is presented to the president by the budget director, is shown in Figure 5-1. The budget report contains three sections. The first states the directives which governed the preparation of the budget, and comments on the extent to which the directives were achieved. The second section contains the following exhibits:

Forecast Operating Statement
Forecast Statement of Return on Capital Employed
Forecast Sources and Applications of Funds
Forecast Changes in Working Capital
Forecast Balance Sheets

THE BUDGET IN FINAL FORM

These five exhibits summarize the planned results of the period's operations. The third section contains selected schedules to supplement the exhibits.

The data appearing in the budget report are based on a complete set of assumed facts relating to Illustrative Company. Some of these facts have already been presented in the preceding chapter. Additional data are presented in Figure 5–1, and other supporting data will be shown and referred to in subsequent chapters. While the example is designed to be realistic and comprehensive, the variety of situations in practice, and considerations of size and ease of understanding, present certain limitations which make it impossible for the example to be a complete portrayal of a real situation. This must be kept in mind in studying the figure. It is merely an illustration in its entirety; however, it does serve to show all the significant steps in budget preparation.

Referring to the schedules which comprise the third section of the budget report in Figure 5–1, the account classification conforms to that of the company's operating statements. It should be pointed out, however, that an alternative practice is followed by some companies— namely, that of classifying the data by nature of responsibility as well as by type of expense. Thus, for example, general and administrative expenses might be reclassified according to whether the expenses are chargeable to the credit department, the accounting department, the treasury, or some other department.

In reviewing Figure 5–1, it should also be kept in mind that since this report is for the use of top management, many detailed schedules which are an integral part of the budget have been omitted. These schedules, however, are maintained in the budget file and are the basis of the budget instructions issued to operating management once the budget report is approved. Examples of such schedules are those relating to purchases of materials, operations of production departments, work of service departments, expense allowances for all factory departments, advertising program, and cash receipts and disbursements.

Appendix A contains the set of journal entries and supporting data on which the exhibits and schedules in Figure 5–1 are based. These serve to show how all the budget operations are assembled in the budget report. Moreover, for the reader who wishes to verify the figures in the report, they serve as a reference source.

ILLUSTRATIVE COMPANY

BUDGET REPORT

FOR THE THREE MONTHS ENDING MARCH 31, 19__

PREPARED DECEMBER 1, 19__
OR
(REVISED _____ 19___)

FIG. 5-1. Illustrative Company Budget Report
First Quarter, 19—

THE BUDGET IN FINAL FORM 89

 **ILLUSTRATIVE COMPANY**

New York, N.Y.

Date: December 1, 19__
From: Budget Director
To: President
Subject: Budget for First Quarter, 19__.

This is to present to you, for approval, the summarized budget for the first quarter, 19__. The report comprises three sections. The first section restates the directives which governed the budget's preparation and the extent of the conformity therewith. The second section contains five exhibits as follows:

    I. Forecast Operating Statement
   II. Forecast Statement of Return on Capital Employed
  III Forecast Sources and Applications of Funds
  IV. Forecast Changes in Working Capital
   V. Forecast Balance Sheets

The third section contains the following schedules in support of the foregoing exhibits:

  1-a. Forecast Sales and Factory Cost of Sales
  1-b. Forecast Selling Expenses
  1-c. Forecast General and Administrative Expenses
  1-d. Forecast Other Income and Deductions

FIG. 5-1 (*Continued*)

SECTION I

DIRECTIVES AND CONFORMITY THEREWITH

THE SALES PLAN FOR THE FORTHCOMING QUARTER IS TO BE DIRECTED PRIMARILY TOWARD AN IMPROVEMENT OF PROFITABILITY BY A CHANGE IN SALES MIX, WITH A SHIFT IN EMPHASIS FROM PRODUCT C TO PRODUCT A. DESIRED RATE OF RETURN ON CAPITAL EMPLOYED IS 30 PER CENT (ON AN ANNUAL BASIS).

It has been verified that the low rate of return earned on capital employed during the quarter just ended, approximately 17 per cent, is primarily the result of a low net operating profit realized on Product C and a poor turnover ratio of Product A. Consideration has been given the possibility of improving the net operating profit margin of Product C or of increasing sales volume sufficiently to compensate for this low margin. It has been agreed that measures to improve the net operating profit margin are not feasible during the forthcoming quarter. Moreover, it is not deemed advisable to attempt to increase the sales volume of this product. Consequently, this budget is directed at a change in the sales mix, with a gradual shift from Product C to Product A which will also improve the turnover ratio of Product A. Sales of Product A, in units, are planned as follows: 2,000 in January, 3,000 in February, and 7,000 in March, for a total of 12,000 units as compared with 5,250 for the quarter just ended. Product B sales are scheduled at 2,000 per month, the same as during the quarter just ended. Product C sales are planned as follows: 8,000 in January, 6,000 in February, and 4,000 in March, with a total of 18,000 for the new quarter as compared with 24,000 for the old quarter. Total planned sales for the forthcoming quarter amount to $2,130,000 as compared with $1,800,000 for the quarter just ended.

The foregoing sales, when related to the budgeted costs for the quarter, will yield the following returns on capital employed: 16.72 per cent in January, 19.64 per cent in February, 43.88 per cent in March, and 26.28 per cent for the quarter as a whole. It is believed that the new pattern of sales will provide, in ensuing budget periods, a rate of return close to the 30 per cent rate established as an objective. It should also be pointed out that, with reference to Product B, while no change is anticipated in the sales of this product during the first quarter, its position also is expected to improve during the second quarter.

FIG. 5-1 (*Continued*)

IN PLANNING SALES EXPENSES FOR THE QUARTER, PRIOR EXPERIENCE IS TO SERVE AS THE GUIDE, BUT THE SALES MANAGER AND CONTROLLER ARE TO DEVELOP METHODS OF ACHIEVING BETTER CONTROL OF THESE EXPENSES AND BETTER STATISTICAL DATA TO BE USED IN THE STUDY OF THE EFFECTIVENESS OF SALES EFFORT.

With the information presently available, it is not possible to evaluate adequately the effectiveness of the various selling costs. Consequently, in the preparation of this budget the same allowances have been made as experienced in the preceding quarter. Advertising has been budgeted at 5 per cent of planned sales, salesmen's commissions at 3 per cent, and salesmen's expenses at 5 per cent, and the other expenses the same as budgeted for the previous quarter. Steps are being taken, however, to ensure closer adherence to these allowances, and sales accounting procedures are now being instituted to provide better data for evaluation, in the future, of both the plan of sales compensation and the amount and direction of sales effort.

PLANNED CASH BALANCES IN THE FUTURE MUST BE LARGE ENOUGH TO PERMIT THE TAKING OF ALL DISCOUNTS, EVEN THOUGH OUTSIDE FINANCING IS ENTAILED. DISCOUNT TERMS ARE TO BE RESTATED IN PURCHASE ORDERS, AND INVOICE AND PAYMENT PROCEDURES ARE TO BE IMPROVED SO AS TO ENSURE THE TAKING OF ALL DISCOUNTS.

Steps have been taken to ensure better procedures and to achieve better control of the routines. Terms of purchase orders have been revised to relate the discount of 2 per cent in ten days to specified payment dates. Planned realization of discounts during the quarter is in the amount of approximately $9,800, as compared with only about $1,100 in the quarter just ended. The improvement would be still greater but for the time lag inherent in the change of procedure. As is pointed out below, this new policy of taking all discounts, in conjunction with other phases of the budget, will require temporary external financing in March.

INVENTORY STANDARDS ARE TO BE DETERMINED AND USED IN THE BUDGET, WITH DUE ALLOWANCE FOR A REASONABLY UNIFORM LEVEL OF PRODUCTION.

Analysis of the inventory requirements has resulted in the following conclusions:
1. To minimize month-end inventories of work in process
2. To stop the practice of stocking part B1
3. To stock part A1 in the amount of one-half month's production requirements for Product A in the following department

Fig. 5–1 (*Continued*)

4. To maintain finished product in inventory in the amount of one month's shipments
5. To maintain one month's supply of raw materials in inventory

The foregoing decisions have been recognized in the preparation of this budget. However, with reference to the first three decisions, their realizations are to be effected gradually over the quarter in the interest of achieving level production in the factory. Moreover, with respect to the desired inventories of finished product, it is recognized that some latitude must be allowed, again in the interest of level production. For the purpose of satisfying this directive and the following one, which are difficult of reconcilement, the planned inventories of Products A and B will exceed the desired amount during several of the months of the quarter, while that of Product C will be less. With reference to the excess inventories, it is believed that the costs related thereto are not excessive, as a means of improving the flow of production. The deficiency in the inventory in Product C presents a risk in connection with relations with customers, but the sales department believes acceptance of this risk is not hazardous. It is expected that, in ensuing quarters, as the new sales pattern develops, the problem of maintaining standard inventories and also level production will be less difficult.

With reference to the inventory of raw materials, it has been planned on the basis of closely timed purchases. It is understood, however, that market conditions may make it desirable to deviate from this schedule. If such deviations should appear desirable during the quarter, in the interest of economies of purchase, they shall be made only after consultation with the treasurer, since no development in this field may be allowed to interfere with developing a firm policy relating to purchase discounts.

PRODUCTION SCHEDULES IN EACH OF THE PRODUCTION DEPARTMENTS ARE TO BE ESTABLISHED ON A REASONABLY UNIFORM LEVEL THROUGHOUT THE QUARTER.

The budget provides for uniform monthly deliveries of finished stock to inventory. As pointed out above, this schedule visualizes deviations from the finished stock inventory standards and a gradual achievement of the standard inventories of work in process and finished parts during the quarter.

APPROXIMATELY $100,000 IS TO BE MADE AVAILABLE FOR CAPITAL IMPROVEMENTS OF WHICH AT LEAST THREE-FOURTHS MUST MEET THE TEST

FIG. 5-1 (*Continued*)

OF A 30 PER CENT RATE OF RETURN ON THE CAPITAL EMPLOYED, THE BALANCE BEING TENTATIVELY ASSIGNED "NONEARNING" PROJECTS. IN SELECTING PROJECTS IN THE FIRST CATEGORY, RATE OF RETURN ON CAPITAL EMPLOYED IS TO BE USED AS THE PRINCIPAL TEST.

Requests for capital improvements aggregating $325,000 have been analyzed, and the following have been selected as best meeting the directive.

1. Purchase of stamping machines to be installed in Department 2 for the purpose of producing component parts which heretofore have been purchased $40,000
2. Purchase of conveyor equipment, connecting Department 3 and finished stock room, for the purpose of achieving economies in handling finished product 36,000
3. Various projects in improving safety conditions in the plant and providing additional recreational facilities for plant employees... 24,000
$100,000

The foregoing improvements are scheduled for completion and payment in March.

* * * * *

In concluding this report, attention is called to the matters of dividends and external financing. Other than the discharge of the dividend liability outstanding at the beginning of the quarter, no provision has been made in this budget with respect to dividends. With regard to external financing, provision is made for borrowing $200,000 on March 1 on a 3 per cent demand note. The proposed financing is only temporary in nature and is occasioned primarily by changes in the nature of the working capital and not in its amount. The net increase in working capital for the quarter is approximately $18,000, which, together with the planned capital improvements, is to be financed by the planned net income of the period and depreciation provisions.

Request is hereby made for approval of the budget, as summarized in Sections II and III.

Respectfully submitted,

Charles F. Kunstmann
Budget Director

Fig. 5-1 *(Continued)*

SECTION II

EXHIBITS

Fig. 5-1 (*Continued*)

THE BUDGET IN FINAL FORM

EXHIBIT I

FORECAST OPERATING STATEMENT
BY MONTHS AND FOR THE QUARTER
FIRST QUARTER, 19___

	Previous Quarter Actual	January	February	March	Quarter
Sales (Schedule I-a)	$1,800,000	$620,000	$630,000	$880,000	$2,130,000
Factory cost of sales (Schedule I-a)	1,323,600	461,800	457,100	607,000	1,525,900
Gross margin	$ 476,400	$158,200	$172,900	$273,000	$ 604,100
Selling expenses (Schedule I-b)	268,000	90,600	91,900	124,400	306,900
General and administrative expenses (Schedule I-c)	60,000	20,000	25,000	25,000	70,000
Total expenses	$ 328,000	$110,600	$116,900	$149,400	$ 376,900
Net operating profit	148,400	47,600	56,000	123,600	227,200
Excess of other deductions over other income (Schedule I-d)	56,200	21,340	15,730	25,230	62,300
Income before income taxes	92,200	26,260	40,270	98,370	164,900
Income taxes	46,100	13,130	20,135	49,185	82,450
Net income	$ 46,100	$ 13,130	$ 20,135	$ 49,185	$ 82,450

FIG. 5–1 (*Continued*)

EXHIBIT II

FORECAST STATEMENT OF RETURN ON CAPITAL EMPLOYED
BY MONTHS AND FOR THE QUARTER
FIRST QUARTER, 19___

	Previous Quarter Actual	January	February	March	Quarter
Sales:					
Product A	$ 420,000	$ 160,000	$ 240,000	$ 560,000	$ 960,000
Product B	540,000	180,000	180,000	180,000	540,000
Product C	840,000	280,000	210,000	140,000	630,000
Total	$1,800,000	$ 620,000	$ 630,000	$ 880,000	$2,130,000
Capital Employed:					
Product A	$1,848,000	$1,855,500	$1,901,960	$2,010,130	$1,943,000
Product B	720,000	720,000	720,000	720,000	720,000
Product C	840,000	840,000	800,000	700,000	795,000
Total	$3,408,000	$3,415,500	$3,421,960	$3,430,130	$3,458,000
Net Operating Profit:					
Product A	$ 78,300	$ 28,200	$ 38,600	$96,800	$ 163,600
Product B	45,300	14,000	16,200	22,500	52,700
Product C	24,800	5,400	1,200	4,300	10,900
Total	$ 148,400	$ 47,600	$ 56,000	$ 123,600	$ 227,200
Percentage Turnover (ratio of sales to capital employed):					
Product A	90.90%	103.48%	151.42%	334.31%	197.63%
Product B	300.00%	300.00%	300.00%	300.00%	300.00%
Product C	400.00%	400.00%	315.00%	240.00%	316.98%
Average	211.26%	217.83%	220.93%	307.86%	246.39%
Operating Profit Percentage (to sales):					
Product A	18.64%	17.63%	16.08%	17.29%	17.04%
Product B	8.39%	7.78%	9.00%	12.50%	9.76%
Product C	2.95%	1.93%	.57%	3.07%	1.73%
Average	8.24%	7.68%	8.89%	14.05%	10.67%
Return on Investment (ratio of net operating profit to capital employed):					
Product A	16.95%	18.24%	24.35%	57.79%	33.68%
Product B	25.17%	23.34%	27.00%	37.50%	29.28%
Product C	11.80%	7.72%	1.80%	7.37%	5.48%
Average	17.42%	16.72%	19.64%	43.24%	26.28%

FIG. 5-1 (*Continued*)

THE BUDGET IN FINAL FORM

EXHIBIT III

FORECAST SOURCES AND APPLICATIONS OF FUNDS
BY MONTHS AND FOR THE QUARTER
FIRST QUARTER, 19___

	January	February	March	Quarter
Forecasted funds required for:				
Increase in working capital	$25,130	$32,135	$149,185	$206,450
Capital improvements	-	-	100,000	100,000
Current mortgage installment	-	-	12,000	12,000
Total funds required	$25,130	$32,135	$261,185	$318,450
Less, Funds to be provided by operations, as follows:				
Net income	13,130	20,135	49,185	82,450
Depreciation	12,000	12,000	12,000	36,000
	$25,130	$32,135	$ 61,185	$118,450
Funds to be obtained by bank borrowing	-	-	$200,000	$200,000

FIG. 5-1 (*Continued*)

EXHIBIT IV

FORECAST CHANGES IN WORKING CAPITAL
BY MONTHS AND FOR THE QUARTER
FIRST QUARTER, 19___

	January	February	March	Quarter
Changes in current assets, increase or (decrease):				
Cash	($ 4,640)	($ 56,430)	($ 47,180)	($108,250)
Accounts receivable (net)	(139,400)	(61,600)	95,800	(105,200)
Inventories:				
Direct materials	52,500	-	46,000	98,500
Finished parts	1,400	1,400	1,400	4,200
Work in process	(27,200)	(27,200)	(27,200)	(81,600)
Finished product	117,800	129,500	(23,900)	223,400
Prepaid expenses and deferred charges:				
Insurance	(2,000)	22,000	(2,000)	18,000
Excess of standard cost in finished product inventory over current standard	3,500	(3,500)	-	-
Deferred advertising	4,500	4,000	(8,500)	-
Net change in current assets	$ 6,460	$ 8,170	$ 34,420	$ 49,050
Changes in current liabilities, increase or (decrease):				
Accounts payable	(28,500)	(52,500)	46,000	(35,000)
Dividends payable	(15,000)	-	-	(15,000)
Accrued sales commissions	3,600	300	7,500	11,400
Accrued federal income tax	13,130	20,135	(170,815)	(137,550)
Accrued real estate taxes	7,100	7,100	7,100	21,300
Accrued interest on mortgage	1,000	1,000	(5,050)	(3,050)
Accrued interest on demand note	-	-	500	500
Net change in current liabilities	($ 18,670)	($ 23,965)	($114,765)	($157,400)
Net increase in working capital	$ 25,130	$ 32,135	$149,185	$206,450

FIG. 5-1 (*Continued*)

FORECAST BALANCE SHEETS BY MONTHS
FIRST QUARTER, 19___

EXHIBIT V

ASSETS:	December 31	January 31	February 28	March 31
Current assets:				
Cash on hand and in banks	$ 250,000	$ 245,360	$ 188,930	$ 141,750
Accounts receivable	500,000	373,000	324,000	437,400
Allowance for doubtful accounts	(10,000)	(22,400)	(35,000)	(52,600)
Inventories at standard cost:				
Direct materials	166,500	219,000	219,000	265,000
Finished parts	99,000	100,400	101,800	103,200
Work in process	81,600	54,400	27,200	-
Finished product	426,400	544,200	673,700	649,800
Prepaid expenses and deferred charges:				
Insurance	2,000	-	22,000	20,000
Excess of standard cost in finished product inventory over current standard	-	3,500	-	-
Deferred advertising	-	4,500	8,500	-
Total current assets	$1,515,500	$1,521,960	$1,530,130	$1,564,550
Fixed assets:				
Machinery and equipment	1,000,000	1,000,000	1,000,000	1,100,000
Depreciation taken to date	(200,000)	(210,000)	(220,000)	(230,000)
Buildings	800,000	800,000	800,000	800,000
Depreciation taken to date	(100,000)	(102,000)	(104,000)	(106,000)
Land	100,000	100,000	100,000	100,000
Total fixed assets	$1,600,000	$1,588,000	$1,576,000	$1,664,000
Total assets	$3,115,500	$3,109,960	$3,106,130	$3,228,550
LIABILITIES:				
Current liabilities:				
Accounts payable	$ 300,000	$ 271,500	$ 219,000	$ 265,000
Dividends payable	15,000	-	-	-
Accrued sales commissions	15,000	18,600	18,900	26,400
Federal income tax accrued	220,000	233,130	253,265	82,450
Real estate taxes accrued	14,200	21,300	28,400	35,500
Accrued interest on mortgage	4,000	5,000	6,000	950
Mortgage payable, current installment	12,000	12,000	12,000	12,000
Accrued interest on demand note	-	-	-	500
Note payable	-	-	-	200,000
Total current liabilities	$ 580,200	$ 561,530	$ 537,565	$ 622,800
Long-term debt, mortgage payable	$ 228,000	$ 228,000	$ 228,000	$ 216,000
Total liabilities	$ 808,200	$ 789,530	$ 765,565	$ 838,800
CAPITAL:				
Capital stock, 20,000 shares, common, par $100	$2,000,000	$2,000,000	$2,000,000	$2,000,000
Retained earnings	307,300	320,430	340,565	389,750
Total capital	$2,307,300	$2,320,430	$2,340,565	$2,389,750
Total liabilities and capital	$3,115,500	$3,109,960	$3,106,130	$3,228,550

FIG. 5-1 (*Continued*)

SECTION III

SCHEDULES

Fig. 5-1 (*Continued*)

THE BUDGET IN FINAL FORM

	FORECAST SALES AND FACTORY COST OF SALES BY MONTHS AND FOR THE QUARTER FIRST QUARTER, 19__				SCHEDULE I-a
	Previous Quarter Actual	January	February	March	Quarter
Sales volume in units:					
Product A	5,250	2,000	3,000	7,000	12,000
Product B	6,000	2,000	2,000	2,000	6,000
Product C	24,000	8,000	6,000	4,000	18,000
Sales, cost of sales, and gross margin:					
Product A:					
Sales	$ 420,000	$160,000	$240,000	$560,000	$ 960,000
Standard cost of sales	273,000	105,600	158,400	369,600	633,600
Standard gross margin	$ 147,000	$ 54,400	$ 81,600	$190,400	$ 326,400
Product B:					
Sales	540,000	180,000	180,000	180,000	540,000
Standard cost of sales	408,000	129,000	129,000	129,000	387,000
Standard gross margin	$ 132,000	$ 51,000	$ 51,000	$ 51,000	$ 153,000
Product C:					
Sales	840,000	280,000	210,000	140,000	630,000
Standard cost of sales	681,600	231,200	173,400	115,600	520,200
Standard gross margin	$ 158,400	$ 48,800	$ 36,600	$ 24,400	$ 109,800
Total sales	1,800,000	620,000	630,000	880,000	2,130,000
Total standard cost of sales	1,362,600	465,800	460,800	614,200	1,540,800
Total standard gross margin	437,400	154,200	169,200	265,800	589,200
Adjustments:					
Change of standards realized in sale of opening inventory:					
1,000 of Product A	-	800	-	-	800
3,000 of Product B	-	(7,000)	(3,500)	-	(10,500)
6,000 of Product C	-	3,000	-	-	3,000
Overabsorption of factory burden	39,000	7,200	7,200	7,200	21,600
Gross margin, actual	$ 476,400	$158,200	$172,900	$273,000	$ 604,100

Fig. 5–1 (*Continued*)

SCHEDULE I-b

FORECAST SELLING EXPENSES
BY MONTHS AND FOR THE QUARTER
FIRST QUARTER, 19____

	Previous Quarter Actual	January	February	March	Quarter
Advertising to be purchased	$ 90,000	$35,500	$35,500	$ 35,500	$106,500
Advertising to be deferred	-	4,500	4,000	(8,500)	-
Advertising expense	90,000	31,000	31,500	44,000	106,500
Salesmen's commissions	54,000	18,600	18,900	26,400	63,900
Salesmen's expenses	93,000	31,000	31,500	44,000	106,500
Fixed expenses:					
Sales administration	10,000	3,000	3,000	3,000	9,000
Sales salaries	15,000	5,000	5,000	5,000	15,000
Depreciation	2,400	800	800	800	2,400
Real estate taxes	3,000	1,000	1,000	1,000	3,000
Insurance	600	200	200	200	600
Total	$268,000	$90,600	$91,900	$124,400	$306,900

FIG. 5-1 (*Continued*)

THE BUDGET IN FINAL FORM 103

SCHEDULE I-c

FORECAST GENERAL AND ADMINISTRATIVE EXPENSES
BY MONTHS AND FOR THE QUARTER
FIRST QUARTER, 19___

	Previous Quarter Actual	January	February	March	Quarter
Administrative salaries	$18,000	$ 6,000	$ 6,000	$ 6,000	$18,000
Other salaries	29,000	9,000	9,000	9,000	27,000
Travel expense	2,800	800	800	800	2,400
Office supplies	700	300	300	300	900
Telephone and telegraph	1,700	600	600	600	1,800
Legal	2,100	500	500	500	1,500
Auditing	1,000	-	5,000	5,000	10,000
Dues	-	500	200	-	700
Contributions	500	1,000	200	-	1,200
Depreciation	600	200	200	200	600
Real estate taxes	300	100	100	100	300
Insurance	300	100	100	100	300
Miscellaneous	3,000	900	2,000	2,400	5,300
Total	$60,000	$20,000	$25,000	$25,000	$70,000

FIG. 5-1 (*Continued*)

SCHEDULE I-d

FORECAST OTHER INCOME AND DEDUCTIONS
BY MONTHS AND FOR THE QUARTER
FIRST QUARTER, 19___

	Previous Quarter Actual	January	February	March	Quarter
Other income: Purchase discounts	$ 1,120	-	$ 5,430	$ 4,380	$ 9,810
Other deductions: Sales discounts	18,120	$ 7,940	7,560	10,560	26,060
Interest on notes	200	-	-	500	500
Interest on mortgage	3,000	1,000	1,000	950	2,950
Bad debts	36,000	12,400	12,600	17,600	42,600
Total	$57,320	$21,340	$21,160	$29,610	$72,110
Excess of other deductions over other income	$56,200	$21,340	$15,730	$25,230	$62,300

FIG. 5-1 (*Concluded*)

Part II
BUDGETING FOR CONTROL

CHAPTER 6

ANALYSIS AND REPORTING OF VARIATIONS FROM BUDGET

	Page		Page
Purpose of chapter	107	General and administrative expenses	121
Significance of budget variations as a measure of efficiency	108	Other income and deductions	122
Significance of budget variations as a measure of validity of plan	109	**2. Analyzing and Interpreting Results**	
The essence of good planning	111	Analysis of operating data	123
Steps in budgetary control	111	Change in sales mix	123
		Analysis of variations in cost of sales	124
		Analysis of variations in selling expenses	126
1. Reporting Results		Analysis of variations in general and administrative expenses	126
Nature of budget reports	112	Analysis of variations in other income and deductions	127
Form of reports	114		
Exhibits—Illustrative Company Budget Report for January		Review of variation in net income and rate of return	128
Operating statement and return on capital employed	115	Analysis of variations from financial plan	128
Balance sheet	116	**3. Taking Action**	
Sources and applications of funds	117		
Changes in working capital	118	Action as a method of control	129
Schedules—Illustrative Company Budget Report for January		Promoting budget consciousness	129
		Improvement of individual performance	130
Sales and cost of sales	119	Budget revisions	130
Selling expenses	120	Who takes action?	130

Purpose of Chapter. Budgets serve the three purposes of planning, coordination, and control. The preceding chapters present an over-all view of the planning and coordination phases of budget preparation; the present chapter is devoted to an over-all discussion of the control aspects of budgeting. In this connection, the term "control" warrants careful definition. In the broad sense, the term "budgetary control" has two meanings. These refer to control at the planning stage and control at the executory stage of operations.

In the planning stage, control implies the fullest utilization of available information in weighing alternative courses of action and policy, and in shaping the plans so as to achieve the best possible accomplishment of the company's objectives for the budget period. In the executory stage, the period of actual operations, control is concerned with keeping the operations in conformity with the plan. It is this phase of budgetary control which is discussed in this chapter. The chapter deals with the nature of budget variations, and their analysis, as a basis for managerial action. The discussion is illustrated by examples based on the data and experience of Illustrative Company and thus is keyed in with the previous chapters.

Significance of Budget Variations as a Measure of Efficiency. On the assumption that the underlying plan of operations is valid under the circumstances prevailing and that the budget accurately reflects the plan, deviations from the budget measure the organization's efficiency in living up to the plan. Consequently, it is necessary to examine the types of variations which may occur and their significance. The variations may fall into three principal categories. The first concerns the realization of income; the second relates to the production of goods and services; and the third deals with the incurrence of costs. Each is discussed in turn.

With reference to the first category, the realization of income, the measure of performance is the comparison of actual with budgeted sales. There may be other forms of income, such as interest, for example, but the principal analysis obviously is concerned with the company's reason for existence—the sale of goods or services. It should readily be apparent that sales performance under the budget is an extremely important subject for analysis. This analysis should be prompt and should be in sufficient detail to permit management to take whatever action may be feasible or necessary. The mere comparison of total sales with the budget is not enough. Moreover, it should be recognized that sales in excess of the budget may conceivably cause concern as well as sales below the budget, although, admittedly, the concern may be of a different sort—with customer relations in the future rather than immediate profit in the present.

The second category of control concerns the physical operations rather than the monetary aspects of the budget. Comparisons in this area deal with the flow of production, the availability and utilization of equipment, the availability and utilization of manpower, and the like. It concerns the occurences and transactions which underlie the financial transactions. These comparisons are based not on the financial sections of the budget but on the nonmonetary sections relating to production. The comparison of actual quantities of product produced with the budgeted quantities is an example of the type of budget performance measure involved in this area. Production at less than planned levels may result from numerous causes, and it must be promptly explained and action taken to remove the causes.

The third category of control relates to costs. Analyses of cost variations are important, not only for their own sake, but also because they may be indications of deviations in the underlying transactions. It is in

ANALYSIS AND REPORTING OF VARIATIONS

this connection that the second and third control categories are related. Cost control, to the extent that cost variations are a function of action rather than price, is achieved by attention to both physical happenings and monetary transactions. Moreover, in the case of cost control, the problem frequently is complicated by the fact that in the area of indirect expenses comparisons must be made with the expense allowances at the actual operations rather than the budgeted operations.

In all of the above categories, comparisons of budget and actual data are the principal measurement available to management in determining the efficiency of operations under the budgetary plan. Since the achievement of attainable goals under the plan is management's principal function in the executory stage of operations, the need for such measure is paramount.

Significance of Budget Variations as a Measure of Validity of Plan. The preceding section discusses the significance of budget deviations on the assumption that the budget properly reflects the plan of operations and that the plan itself is valid in the prevailing circumstances. Actually, this may not always be the case. The plan itself may be unrealistic and impossible of accomplishment, or faulty integration of its various parts in the budget may preclude the smooth working out of a plan which is fundamentally sound. Moreover, a budget which was valid at its inception may prove invalid as the period progresses, because of changes in conditions which were either not foreseen or not foreseeable at the time the budget was prepared.

The preceding chapters have shown the importance of the sales forecast in budget preparation. The sales plan is the cornerstone of the entire budget. It not only indicates the amount of revenue to be expected, but it governs all the operations of the enterprise. Material requirements, labor requirements, amount of production, all are keyed into estimated sales.

At the same time, however, the sales plan, since it is based upon a forecast of market conditions, is the most difficult plan to formulate in most companies. Because so many of the factors governing sales are outside the realm of the company's direct control, the validity of a sales plan at the time of its adoption is the big question mark in budget preparation. Nevertheless, every effort must be made to distinguish between deviations from budgeted sales which are due to variations in the efficiency of sales effort and those which are due to the unrealistic nature of the plan itself. The former require managerial action within the framework of the budget; the latter may require a change in the budget, including the assumptions upon which the budget is based.

The sales forecast may be unsound from its inception. This is a matter of market analysis and economic forecasting. The amount of purchasing power available to the public, the consumer's scale of preferences for various products and brands of products, the state of competition, price schedules—all these are factors which should have been taken into account but any one of which may have been forecasted incorrectly. On the other hand, these factors may have been correctly gauged initially, but time has a way of changing things. New products, new competitors, and new forms of competition are constantly arising, so that a sales plan that was sound for the conditions prevailing at the time of its adoption may rather quickly become maladjusted to the present conditions. Moreover, developments outside the immediate area of market economics may have a strong influence on market conditions. In the area of political action, the outbreak of war, or the sudden cessation of war, or acceleration of the national defense effort, fluctuations in the money market, changes in foreign aid policies, and similar matters may have a tremendous impact on the market for the company's products. And these latter factors obviously may be impossible to forecast with any degree of assurance.

Whatever the reasons for the invalidity of the plan, it is of the greatest importance that they be recognized when they occur. Changing sales call for other changes all along the line—changed production schedules, materials purchase schedules, financial operations, and so on. Steps to measure and evaluate the effects of changes in the market for the budgeted products must be taken promptly in order to determine the extent to which budget revisions are in order.

The sales forecast may be accurate, but the production plan may be faulty. The factors of labor supply, materials availability, and others, relating to the production of goods and services, are also subject to changing conditions and must be forecasted as accurately as possible. Again, improper evaluations may have been made at the time of the preparation of the budget, or conditions may change quickly during the budget period. A sudden wave of labor unrest in the company, for example, leading to production interruptions, can wreck a plan just as readily as changes in the conditions affecting the booking of sales orders.

The area of costs is also a sensitive one. Forecasts of productive efficiency and prices of materials and supplies may prove incorrect. True, in the case of some costs the element of risk can be greatly reduced. A wage contract may eliminate the risk of change in labor costs for the budget period. Similarly, forward purchase commitments at firm prices may eliminate the price risk associated with the purchase of materials. Nevertheless, for many companies, changing costs are a hazard in planning, and, again, cost deviations from the budget must be classified

ANALYSIS AND REPORTING OF VARIATIONS

as due to variations in efficiency or in basic conditions. The latter may require a change of plans, namely a revision of the budget.

The Essence of Good Planning. The foregoing sections draw a sharp distinction between budget deviations arising from variations in the efficiency of the organization and those arising from the fact that the budget itself is unrealistic. Prompt measurement and evaluation of the former should lead to managerial action to bring the organization into line with the budget. On the other hand, efforts in that direction may be very unwise if the real cause of the deviations lies in the budget itself. Management's problem, therefore, is first to determine whether the budget is a good one. If it is determined that it is not realistic, management has a second problem, that of determining whether the budget-making processes are faulty or whether the unforeseen changes have occurred since the budget was adopted.

Faulty budget procedures must be detected, for, to be useful, the budget must be reliable. Consistently large errors in sales forecasts may be due to inadequate or improper forecasting methods. Similarly, poor cost records can lead to erroneous cost estimates. The question then arises as to what constitutes good planning, admitting that the most carefully laid plans may be upset by factors which in the nature of things cannot be accurately forecasted. It is believed that good planning has essentially two requirements. First, it calls for the availability of all the forecast data generally associated with the market in question and reasonably available to the specific company. Second, it calls for a sound use of that data. Obviously, a small or medium-sized company cannot afford the elaborate research organization frequently associated with the large concern. But this is no justification for completely disregarding the requirements of scientific method and using haphazard methods. First, there is little excuse for a company's not knowing at least its present costs. And every company has available its own sales experience to serve as a starting point in forecasting sales. The problem is to use judiciously the data already in its possession.

Steps in Budgetary Control. There are essentially three steps in the executory stage of budgetary control, that is, in the control of operations against a budget already adopted. These steps are:

1. Reporting the results
2. Analyzing and interpreting the results
3. Taking action, if action is indicated

The first two steps are directly related to the budgetary control procedure. The third rests squarely with management. The point is that all the reports in the world will not achieve control if they are not acted upon. The reports and analyses serve only to indicate the need for action and the possible courses of action. The action must be taken if causes of budget deviations are to be removed. The remainder of this chapter is devoted to a detailed discussion of each of these steps.

1. REPORTING RESULTS

Nature of Budget Reports. Budget reports are essentially action reports. They are designed to disclose the extent to which the budget is being realized (or not realized) and thus to serve as the basis for managerial steps in achieving fuller realization of the planned objectives. In designing such reports there are three principal considerations:

1. Content
2. Destination
3. Timing

Little need be said here concerning the third consideration, except to point to the obvious conclusion that action reports must be *timely*. This not only means that they must be issued promptly in order to permit remedial measures to be taken; it also implies that they must be issued with appropriate frequency.

The first and second considerations are somewhat interdependent. The contents of a report will be governed in part by whether it is intended for higher or lower levels of management. The former, generally, are interested only in aggregates whereas the lower levels are concerned with details. The subject matter, of course, also has a bearing on the data to be included, and the problem in this regard is to select only meaningful information and to present it concisely and understandably. These principles are summarized in the following statement:

A Report Should Have a Purpose—and Should Achieve It

To this point we have looked at types of reports and noted very briefly the contents of some of them and the purposes for which they are intended. What, now, are some of the yardsticks for measuring the effectiveness and desirability of reports? This and following paragraphs will consider the more important standards of usefulness. In the first place, every report should have a definite purpose. It is sometimes said that each report should have a single purpose. If, however, the accountant can combine two or more reports into one without sacrificing clarity and other attributes of a good report, so that the single report serves more than one purpose, he should be encouraged to do so.

Every report should contain the information required to serve the purpose for which it is intended. The readiness with which managerial action can be taken, based upon the information in a report, depends largely on the clarity

ANALYSIS AND REPORTING OF VARIATIONS

and accuracy with which the data are presented and the skill with which significant points are emphasized. It is most desirable, from this point of view, to arrive at a clear understanding with management on the kind of information it wants. An appropriate chart of accounts and procedures should then be established to develop and report this information, for it is the accountant's responsibility to see that a report tells the whole story. For example, the statement that inventory on a given date had a value of $5,000,000 becomes much more meaningful if management is informed of the number of months' supply this represents and the number of months' supply needed for production and sales commitments.

PRESENTING CHARTS AND SCHEDULES EFFECTIVELY

The clearest reports are sometimes the briefest. Brevity without loss of completeness is the goal for which we should strive. Accounting jargon should be avoided, because many executives are not familiar with accounting technicalities and terms. The effectiveness of charts and graphs should be utilized. This type of presentation can sometimes clearly demonstrate relationships that it would take pages to describe. No one likes to read several pages of description and pore over columns of figures to get information which would be apparent from a moment's look at a chart. A number of larger companies have adopted presentation by charts as a standard part of their reporting methods. The use of large wall charts, presented to groups, affords an opportunity for direct oral presentation by persons who prepared the charts. This technique is frequently much more effective than merely presenting written material for review.

The chart technique lends itself admirably to presenting in comparative form such ratios as net income to sales, cost of sales to sales, return on investment, expenses to sale, total investment to working capital, etc. It is useful also for showing trends in shipments, inventory levels, unfilled orders, manufacturing variances, property expenditures, etc. Break-even charts may be used to good advantage because they show the relationship of costs to sales, particularly in that they show the sales volume which must be maintained to break even. These charts are not usually prepared monthly. They should be prepared as often as there are significant changes in the relationship of costs to sales. The alert accountant will find many ways in which graphical presentation can be used to highlight and dramatize important data.

Full use should be made of the "exception" principle for executive review, under which normal or routine situations are given relatively less prominence, and unusual or exceptional items are stressed and explanatory comment is given concerning them. If there are no significant "exception" items in a report, this should be stated, so that the executive does not need to study this out for himself in what may be very limited available time.

To the extent that printed or typed schedules are used, they should be prepared with a view to highlighting essentials for quick and easy recognition. The listing of expenses in alphabetical sequence because they happen to be in the general ledger that way or the detailed restating of every item in a miscellaneous expense account, instead of a summary of expenses by more important classifications, should be avoided.[1]

---

[1] Milton B. Basson, "A Review of Internal Reports—and Reporting," *N.A.A. Bulletin*, Section 1, Sept., 1954, pp. 7-9.

Form of Reports. The form that budget performance reports should take depends partly on the nature of the individuals for whom they are prepared and partly on the level of management for which they are intended. Top levels of management need an over-all performance report, whereas lower levels are concerned with detailed reports of only their own operations. Thus, in the case of Illustrative Company, the president would be expected to receive all the exhibits and schedules paralleling those contained in the budget. Similarly, lower levels would receive reports based on their basic budget documents. With reference to the reporting of figure facts, the original budget documents should set the pattern for budget performance reports.

The basic purpose of the reports is comparison of the actual results with the planned results. Consequently, the basic form is as follows:

	Current Month			Year to Date		
Item	Actual	Budget	Over (Under)	Actual	Budget	Over (Under)

This form may be varied depending on circumstances and needs. Additional columns, for example, may be provided for reporting of percentages, either percentages of each item to the total or percentages of change. In the case of a flexible budget schedule, for example, a schedule of manufacturing burden, additional provision may have to be made for reporting performance in relation not only to the planned operations but also to the actual operations. Variations will be discussed further in succeeding chapters and for the purpose of this chapter it is considered sufficient to point out that comparison is the basic function of the reports.

Whether or not the reports should contain graphic material as well as figure data, and whether or not the exhibits and schedules should be supplemented by explanations and comments, depends largely on the individuals for whom the reports are intended. Where the recipients are trained in the use of figure facts, explanations are not as necessary as in the case of those who have less comprehension. In any case, however, the reader should be enabled to grasp the full significance of the data presented to him.

Following (Figure 6–1) are the exhibits and schedules which would be presented to the president of Illustrative Company covering the month of January. The comparison is only for the month, since, that being the first month of the budget period, there is no need for year-to-date comparisons. It will be noted that the exhibits and schedules parallel those contained in the budget report presented to him for approval in the preceding chapter.

ANALYSIS AND REPORTING OF VARIATIONS

EXHIBIT I

ILLUSTRATIVE COMPANY
OPERATING STATEMENT AND RETURN ON CAPITAL EMPLOYED
JANUARY, 19___

	January			
	Actual	Budget	Over (Under)	Per Cent of Change
Sales (Schedule I-a)	$589,400	$620,000	($30,600)	(4.94)
Factory cost of sales (Schedule I-a)	443,080	461,800	(18,720)	(4.05)
Gross margins	$146,320	$158,200	($11,880)	(7.51)
Selling expenses (Schedule I-b)	$ 89,582	$ 90,600	($ 1,018)	(1.12)
General administrative expenses (Schedule I-c)	20,360	20,000	360	1.80
Total expenses	$109,942	$110,600	($ 658)	(0.60)
Net operating profit	$ 36,378	$ 47,600	($11,222)	(23.58)
Excess of other deductions over other income (Schedule I-d)	20,388	21,340	(952)	(4.46)
Income before income taxes	15,990	26,260	(10,270)	(39.11)
Income taxes	7,995	13,130	(5,135)	(39.11)
Net income	$ 7,995	$ 13,130	($ 5,135)	(39.11)
Rate of return on capital employed	12.78%	16.72%	(3.94%)	

FIG. 6-1. Illustrative Company Budget Report
January, 19—

EXHIBIT II

ILLUSTRATIVE COMPANY
BALANCE SHEET
JANUARY 31, 19___

	Actual	Budget	Over (Under)
ASSETS:			
Current assets:			
Cash on hand and in banks	$ 229,340	$ 245,360	($16,020)
Accounts receivable	358,300	373,000	(14,700)
Allowance for doubtful accounts	(21,788)	(22,400)	612
Inventories at standard cost:			
Direct materials	238,600	219,000	19,600
Finished parts	100,400	100,400	
Work in process	54,400	54,400	
Finished product	559,870	544,200	15,670
Prepaid expenses and deferred charges:			
Insurance			
Excess of standard cost in finished product inventory over current standard	3,150	3,500	(350)
Deferred advertising	4,500	4,500	
Total current assets	$1,526,772	$1,521,960	$ 4,812
Fixed assets:			
Machinery and equipment	$1,000,000	$1,000,000	
Depreciation taken to date	(210,000)	(210,000)	
Buildings	800,000	800,000	
Depreciation taken to date	(102,000)	(102,000)	
Land	100,000	100,000	
Total fixed assets	$1,588,000	$1,588,000	
Total assets	$3,114,772	$3,109,960	$ 4,812
LIABILITIES:			
Current liabilities:			
Accounts payable	$ 287,500	$ 271,500	$16,000
Dividends payable			
Accrued sales commissions	17,682	18,600	(918)
Federal income tax accrued	227,995	233,130	(5,135)
Real estate taxes accrued	21,300	21,300	
Accrued interest on mortgage	5,000	5,000	
Mortgage payable, current installment	12,000	12,000	
Accrued interest on demand note			
Note payable			
Total current liabilities	$ 571,477	$ 561,530	$ 9,947
Long-term debt, mortgage payable	$ 228,000	$ 228,000	
Total liabilities	$ 799,477	$ 789,530	$ 9,947
CAPITAL:			
Capital stock, 20,000 shares, common, par $100	$2,000,000	$2,000,000	
Retained earnings	315,295	320,430	($ 5,135)
Total capital	$2,315,295	$2,320,430	($ 5,135)
Total liabilities and capital	$3,114,772	$3,109,960	$ 4,812

FIG. 6-1 (*Continued*)

ANALYSIS AND REPORTING OF VARIATIONS

EXHIBIT III

ILLUSTRATIVE COMPANY
SOURCES AND APPLICATIONS OF FUNDS
JANUARY, 19___

	January		
	Actual	Budget	Over (Under)
Funds applied to: Increase in working capital	$19,995	$25,130	($5,135)
Capital improvements			
Total funds applied	$19,995	$25,130	($5,135)
Above funds provided by operations as follows: Net income	$ 7,995	$13,130	($5,135)
Depreciation	12,000	12,000	
Total funds provided	$19,995	$25,130	($5,135)

FIG. 6-1 (*Continued*)

EXHIBIT IV

ILLUSTRATIVE COMPANY
CHANGES IN WORKING CAPITAL
JANUARY, 19___

	January		
	Actual	Budget	Over (Under)
Current Assets:			
Cash	$ 229,340	$ 245,360	($16,020)
Accounts receivable (net)	336,512	350,600	(14,088)
Inventories:			
Direct materials	238,600	219,000	19,600
Finished parts	100,400	100,400	
Work in process	54,400	54,400	
Finished product	559,870	544,200	15,670
Prepaid expenses and deferred charges:			
Insurance			
Excess of standard cost in finished product inventory over current standard	3,150	3,500	(350)
Deferred advertising	4,500	4,500	
Total current assets	$1,526,772	$1,521,960	$ 4,812
Current liabilities:			
Accounts payable	$ 287,500	$ 271,500	$16,000
Dividends payable			
Accrued sales commissions	17,682	18,600	(918)
Accrued Federal income tax	227,995	233,130	(5,135)
Accrued real estate taxes	21,300	21,300	
Accrued interest on mortgage	5,000	5,000	
Mortgage payable, current installment	12,000	12,000	
Accrued interest on demand note			
Demand note payable			
Total current liabilities	$ 571,477	$ 561,530	$ 9,947
Net working capital, Jan. 31, 19___	$ 955,295	$ 960,430	($ 5,135)
Net working capital, Jan. 1, 19___	935,300	935,300	
Net change in working capital, increase or (decrease)	$ 19,995	$ 25,130	($ 5,135)

FIG. 6-1 (*Continued*)

ANALYSIS AND REPORTING OF VARIATIONS

SCHEDULE I-a

ILLUSTRATIVE COMPANY
SALES AND COST OF SALES
JANUARY, 19___

	January			
	Actual	Budget	Over (Under)	Per Cent of Change
Sales volume in units:				
Product A	1,800	2,000	(200)	(10.00)
Product B	2,100	2,000	100	5.00
Product C	7,600	8,000	(400)	(5.00)
Sales, cost of sales, and gross margin:				
Product A:				
Sales	$144,000	$160,000	($16,000)	(10.00)
Standard cost of sales	95,040	105,600	(10,560)	(10.00)
Standard gross margin	$ 48,960	$ 54,400	($ 5,440)	(10.00)
Product B:				
Sales	$187,000	$180,000	$ 7,000	3.89
Standard cost of sales	135,450	129,000	6,450	5.00
Standard gross margin	$ 51,550	$ 51,000	$ 550	1.08
Product C:				
Sales	$258,400	$280,000	($21,600)	(7.71)
Standard cost of sales	219,640	231,200	(11,560)	(5.00)
Standard gross margin	$ 38,760	$ 48,800	($10,040)	(20.57)
Total sales	$589,400	$620,000	($30,600)	(4.94)
Total standard cost of sales	$450,130	$465,800	($15,670)	(3.36)
Adjustments:				
Change of standards realized in sale of opening inventory:				
1,000 of Product A	800	800		
2,100 of Product B	(7,350)	(7,000)	(350)	(5.00)
6,000 of Product C	3,000	3,000		
Overabsorption of factory burden	7,000	7,200	(200)	(2.78)
Purchase variance - direct materials (Material A1)	4,000		4,000	$4,000
Material usage variance, direct materials (Material B-2)	(400)		(400)	($400)
Cost of sales, actual	$443,080	$461,800	($18,720)	(4.05)
Gross margin, actual	$146,320	$158,200	($11,880)	(7.51)
Gross margin, standard	$139,270	$154,200	($14,930)	(9.68)

Fig. 6-1 (*Continued*)

SCHEDULE I-b

ILLUSTRATIVE COMPANY
SELLING EXPENSES
JANUARY, 19___

	January			
	Actual	Budget	Over (Under)	Per Cent of Change
Advertising to be purchased	$35,500	$35,500		
Advertising to be deferred	4,500	4,500		
Advertising expense	31,000	31,000		
Salesmen's commissions	17,682	18,600	($ 918)	(4.94)
Salesmen's expenses	30,800	31,000	(200)	(0.65)
Fixed expenses: Sales administration	3,100	3,000	100	3.33
Sales salaries	5,000	5,000		
Depreciation	800	800		
Real estate taxes	1,000	1,000		
Insurance	200	200		
Total	$89,582	$90,600	($1,018)	(1.12)

FIG. 6-1 (*Continued*)

ANALYSIS AND REPORTING OF VARIATIONS 121

SCHEDULE I-c

ILLUSTRATIVE COMPANY
GENERAL AND ADMINISTRATIVE EXPENSES
JANUARY, 19____

	January			
	Actual	Budget	Over (Under)	Per Cent of Change
Administrative salaries	$ 6,000	$ 6,000		
Other salaries	9,000	9,000		
Travel expense	950	800	$150	18.75
Office supplies	275	300	(25)	(8.33)
Telephone and telegraph	635	600	35	5.83
Legal	500	500		
Auditing				
Dues	500	500		
Contributions	1,000	1,000		
Depreciation	200	200		
Real estate taxes	100	100		
Insurance	100	100		
Miscellaneous	1,100	900	200	22.22
Total	$20,360	$20,000	$360	1.80

FIG. 6-1 (*Continued*)

SCHEDULE I-d

ILLUSTRATIVE COMPANY
OTHER INCOME AND DEDUCTIONS
JANUARY, 19___

	January			
	Actual	Budget	Over (Under)	Per Cent of Change
Other income: Purchase discounts	-	-	-	-
Other deductions: Sales discounts	$ 7,600	$ 7,940	($340)	(4.28)
Interest on notes				
Interest on mortgage	1,000	1,000		
Bad debts	11,788	12,400	(612)	(4.93)
Total	$20,388	$21,340	($952)	(4.46)
Excess of other deductions over other income	$20,388	$21,340	($952)	(4.46)

FIG. 6-1 (*Concluded*)

2. ANALYZING AND INTERPRETING RESULTS

Analysis of Operating Data. In line with the practice established in submitting the budget for approval, subsequent performance reports would include explanations and comments by the budget officer. In the interest of full explanation, however, this phase of the budget report is omitted and detailed discussion substituted.

Referring first to the operating statement, Exhibit I (p. 115), it will be noted that significant variations have occurred. While sales are down by less than 5 per cent, the net income is down by almost 40 per cent. Obviously, a close analysis of the data is called for. Two lines of inquiry are indicated. The first is an analysis to determine whether the total sales variation of 4.94 per cent (which is not unduly large) tells the entire story concerning sales performance. The second is to determine to what extent the difference in the sales performance ratio and the net profit ratio was due to the behavior of the costs and, if so, whether there is an inherent weakness in the cost structure, or merely poor operating performance.

Change in Sales Mix. The fact that Exhibit I reports a drop in total sales of 4.94 per cent but a drop in gross margin of 7.51 per cent indicates that the change in total sales does not disclose the full significance of variations in sales performance. Reference then must be made to Schedule I–a (p. 119).

That schedule shows both sales and cost of sales data. However, since standard costs are used, and since the "actual cost" adjustments are analyzed later, attention at this point is centered on sales alone. The reader should immediately note the unexpected discrepancy between the percentage change in unit sales of B and C and the percentage change in dollar sales of the two products. If unit sales increase or decrease by 5 per cent, it would be expected that the dollar sales would change proportionately. Actually, however, B sales, which were 5 per cent over the budget in units, were over the budgeted dollar amount by only 3.89 per cent. Similarly, a 5 per cent decrease in unit sales of C caused a 7.71 per cent decrease in dollar sales. It is apparent that scheduled prices are not being maintained. Since the scheduled price of B is $90, the actual sales of that product should have been $189,000, not $187,000. Similarly, the sales of C should have amounted to $266,000, not $258,400. Consequently, $9,600 of the $14,930 deficiency in standard gross margin was due to unscheduled price reductions. This is a direct responsibility of sales management and should require explanation.

If the January sales had been made at scheduled prices, the comparison of budgeted sales and standard gross margins and actual sales and standard gross margins would appear as shown in Figure 6–2. The budget data indicate that while Product A would produce the smallest percentage of total sales, it would produce the largest percentage of total profit. This results from the fact that the standard profit margins for the three products are: A, 34 per cent; B, 28.33 per cent; and C, 17.43 per cent. The importance of these differences to the sales mix is further signified by the fact that the actual sales and profit data show that the increase in the sales of B could not compensate, profit-wise, for the decreases in A and C. Moreover, it must be remembered that scheduled prices were not maintained in sales of B and C.

The foregoing analyses tell the story of sales performance as it is disclosed in the data presented. The need for further investigation is indicated as to why special prices were accepted, and why and where volume fell below expectations. These studies should be made by the sales department.

Analysis of Variations in Cost of Sales. Exhibit I (p. 115) indicates that the factory cost of sales was less than the amount budgeted by 4.05 per cent. While a reduction in costs, of itself, is favorable, it is apparent that the reduction did not match the reduction in sales. This requires explanation since, with the use of standard costs, a budgetary deficiency in sales might normally be accompanied by a corresponding budgetary reduction in costs. Schedule I–a (p. 119) tells the story.

Comparison of the standard costs of sales with the units of each product sold indicates, as would be expected, a matching of those quantities. Consequently, the discrepancy between costs and dollar sales, to the extent not accounted for by sales price variations, is explained by the adjustments to the standard gross margin. The variations from the scheduled adjustments are:

Change of standards realized in sale of opening inventory	$ (350)
Overabsorption of factory burden	(200)
Purchase variance—direct materials	4,000
Usage variance—direct materials	(400)
Total variations	$3,050

The first variation is a normal result of the variations in quantities of product sold. Consequently, no further analysis is needed for control purposes.

With reference to the second item, overabsorption of factory burden, it should be recognized that the production schedule for January was adhered to in spite of variations in sales. Since that schedule entailed overabsorption of burden, the budgetary deficiency can be explained only by excessive incurrence of this class of costs in the plant. Further analysis of this variance is discussed in Chapter 8.

Product	Budget					Actual				
	Sales	Per Cent	Gross Margin	Per Cent		Sales (at Scheduled Prices)	Per Cent	Gross Margin	Per Cent	
A	$160,000	25.8	$ 54,400	35.3		$144,000	24.0	$ 48,960	32.9	
B	180,000	29.0	51,000	33.1		189,000	31.6	53,550	36.0	
C	280,000	45.2	48,800	31.6		266,000	44.4	46,360	31.1	
	$620,000	100.0	$154,200	100.0		$599,000	100.0	$148,870	100.0	

FIG. 6-2. Analysis of Sale Mix: Sales at Scheduled Prices

The third variation, purchase variance—direct materials, is the largest of the group. No provision was made for this in the budget, and the variance results from the fact that the month's purchases of material A1, including the 9,000 units scheduled to be purchased plus 1,000 additional units purchased because of a favorable procurement situation, were made at a unit price of 40 cents below standard. Since 7,000 units of this material are unused at the end of January (the 6,000 scheduled inventory shown on p. 76 and the 1,000 additional units bought), only 30 per cent (7,000 units inventory from 10,000 purchased) of the variance applies to January consumptions of material. According to the company's accounting procedure, however, purchase variances are taken into income in the month when incurred. The significance of this variance to the present analysis, however, is the fact that it is a credit or profit variance and that, but for it, the total cost of sales would be further out of line with the sales than the comparison in Exhibit I indicates.

The fourth item, material usage variance, reflects excessive consumption of direct materials for the actual (scheduled) production. This is the responsibility of factory management. No direct labor variations are indicated in the reports.

Analysis of Variations in Selling Expenses. Selling expenses were 1.12 per cent less than the amount budgeted, as indicated in Exhibit I. Further analysis is based on the data reported in Schedule I–b (p. 120). This schedule indicates that there were three variations, one in connection with a fixed expense and two with variable expenses.

Of the variable expenses, the item of salesmen's commissions was below the budget in the same proportion as sales, 4.94 per cent. This is to be expected since the commissions are proportioned directly to sales. Salesmen's expenses, however, dropped only 0.65 per cent as compared with the 4.94 per cent decrease in sales. Since this expense is deemed to be fully variable with sales, the discrepancy needs to be explained by sales management. While the absolute amount of the variation is small, a repetition of such variation in succeeding months (in the same direction) would indicate either some looseness of control or a conceptual error in budgeting on the assumption that this expense is wholly variable with sales.

Analysis of Variations in General and Administrative Expenses. These expenses are budgeted on a fixed basis. Consequently the analysis of variations is not related to the level of operations, although if the over-all picture changed materially, steps could be taken to revise the scheduled costs.

ANALYSIS AND REPORTING OF VARIATIONS

The total variation amounted to only $360, or 1.80 per cent of budget, as shown in Exhibit I. Actually, however, four of the detail expenses varied from the budget, ranging from a minus variation of 8.33 per cent to a plus variation of 22.22 per cent, as reported in Schedule I-c (p. 121). Again, while the amounts involved are not large, the number and proportion of the variations suggest the need for closer control of these expenses.

Analysis of Variations in Other Income and Deductions. Exhibit I indicates that the excess of other deductions over other income was $952 under that scheduled for the month, a budget variation of 4.46 per cent. Schedule I-d (p. 122) indicates that this was due to a minus variation of 4.28 per cent in sales discounts and a 4.93 per cent minus variation in bad debts. Since the latter was scheduled on an accrual basis at a fixed percentage of sales, the per cent of variation coincides with that of sales and no further explanation is required.

The variation in sales discounts, 4.28 per cent, must be analyzed carefully since it reflects not only a decline in sales but also some change in expected receipts from sales consummated. The latter factor is important since it furnishes one clue to the promptness with which customers are paying invoices.

Since the scheduled discounts were related to both December and January accounts, the analysis involves reference to the original data shown in Chapter 5, as well as a breakdown of the cash receipt in January. The forecast balance sheets in Exhibit V of Figure 5–1 (p. 99) indicate that the accounts receivable on hand at December 31 amounted to $500,000. The explanation of the second of the journal entries presented in the Appendix (p. 373) shows that 5 per cent of these were expected to be paid in January, less the 2 per cent discount, and that 70 per cent were to be paid at the gross amount. Analysis of the January cash receipts shows the following data:

	Accounts Receivable December 31	Sales on Account January	Total
	$500,000	$589,400	$1,089,400
Paid in January..............	368,800	362,300	731,100
Discounts taken..............	300	7,300	7,600
Cash received...............	$368,500	$355,000	$ 723,500

Since the receipts from December 31 accounts were expected to be $375,000 (75 per cent of $500,000) and the discounts taken, $500 (.02 × .05 × $500,000), it is apparent that the estimates relative to these accounts were not entirely correct, although the proportionate error in total receipts is much less than in discount payments. In the case of the January billings, however, since 60 per cent were expected to be paid that month, all less the discount, it is evident that both the total and the discounted payments are in excess of the amount expected, based on the actual sales of the month (.60 × $589,400 = $353,640; discount should be $7,073).

Review of Variation in Net Income and Rate of Return. The foregoing variations add up to a decrease in net income of 39.11 per cent from that budgeted and a reduction in the rate of return on captial employed from 16.72 to 12.78 per cent. The very large percentage reduction in net income, larger than any of the detail percentage variations, results from the fact that the scheduled net income in January was low in comparison with the total operations. In that month the scheduled profit margin was so low that it was disproportionately affected by even minor percentage variations in revenue and costs. In such a tight operating situation close control must be exercised. While the forecasts presented in the preceding chapter indicate that an improvement is expected in the succeeding months of the budget period, the fact still remains that there is a strong leverage factor in the relation of revenue and costs to net profit. In the nature of things, this is typical of all business operations. The fact that many costs are fixed, regardless of volume, and that a small percentage of increase in any of a number of costs may produce a disproportionately large decrease in net profit emphasized the importance of careful planning and control.

Analysis of Variations from Financial Plan. The effect of variations in operations on the financial plan is shown in Exhibits II, III, and IV (pp. 116–18). Reference to Exhibit II indicates that there were no budget variations in either the fixed asset or long-term debt accounts. Consequently, the analysis of financial variations can be made solely from Exhibit IV, Changes in Working Capital. Of the budget variations shown in that exhibit, three—excess of standard cost in finished product inventory over current standard, accrued sales commissions, and accrued federal income tax—result automatically from the deviations in sales and net income. They are variable and, of themselves, noncontrollable.

Similarly, the behavior of accounts receivable, once acquired, is not subject to direct control. In the present case the variation in the receivable is due in part to the deviation in sales and in part to variations from the expected time pattern of payments. The significant changes, from the standpoint of controllability, are those which occurred in the inventories. The unscheduled increases in inventory of direct materials and

ANALYSIS AND REPORTING OF VARIATIONS

inventory of finished product were controllable. They were *permitted* to occur for valid reasons, but could have been prevented if necessary. The former increase was allowed in order to obtain the benefit of a favorable purchase price. The latter resulted from the fact that production schedules were not revised to accord with decreased sales. Perhaps the schedule could not economically be changed on such short notice, but the illustration shows the effect on current financial position of a lack of balance between production and shipments. The fact that it may not pay to revise production schedules on short notice does not negate the idea of controllability; rather, it sharpens it, in that management can and must weigh the advantages and disadvantages of maintaining an even flow of production in the face of an immediate decline in sales.

3. TAKING ACTION

Action as a Method of Control. Figures of themselves do not provide control. Control must be exercised at the source, where the sales are made and the costs incurred. The budget reports just discussed measure the financial effect of operational deviations and indicate the deviations, but they do not control them. Moreover, sales once made and costs actually incurred cannot be controlled. Knowledge of deviations which have already occurred is useful only for its value in preventing future deviations. But this requires that the knowledge be utilized in a positive manner.

While the control of various operating factors is discussed in detail in succeeding chapters, it is relevant at this point to discuss in general terms the lines of action which are available. Essentially only three types of action are available. The first concerns the awareness on the part of operating personnel of the importance of the budget, the second relates to the improvement of individual performance, and the third to budget revisions.

Promoting Budget Consciousness. The circumstances surrounding the acceptance of orders by Illustrative Company at less than scheduled prices and the incurrence of certain presumed fixed costs in excess of the amounts budgeted are not disclosed. These variations, however, should not have been permitted to occur, it is presumed, without express approval from top management. The awareness throughout all levels of management that the budget is for their guidance and control is a prerequisite of control. Knowledge that unauthorized variations will have to be explained and justified tends to promote adherence to the budget as a control device. This suggests, therefore, that the first line of action in securing better control is to devise and then adhere to a system of inquiry and review. Accountability, as among various levels of managements, should be an accepted principle.

It is important to note, however, that the system of accountability should be developed in the spirit of teamwork. Acceptance of the budget as an important managerial tool leads to its most effective use. The idea of the budget must be "sold" to all levels of management.

Improvement of Individual Performance. People are the heart of an organization. Human effort presents the largest area for managerial control; and training, supervision, and leadership are management's problems. Promoting the worker's effectiveness through training, whether he be in the factory, offices, or sales force; maintaining the company's disciplinary standards; and inspiring the worker to do his best—these constitute management's job under the budget.

The nature of the action to be taken in this category of individual performance is more difficult to define than in the category of promoting budget consciousness. Training, discipline, and inspiration involve intangible factors which cannot be accurately and precisely charted. These are the challenge of management, and the problems concern the relation not only of management, as a whole, to nonmanagerial employees but also of top management to lower management levels.

Budget Revisions. The final line of action is to change the budget for future months. The principal problem in this connection is to determine when and if a change is warranted. For example, does the sales deficiency of Illustrative Company in January result from factors which can be corrected in February and March, or does it portend continued deficiencies? And if the latter is the case, does their size warrant budget revisions?

Who Takes Action? All levels of management are involved in budgetary control action. This fact, however, necessitates a management *system* whereby action is properly initiated and directed. Just as the form and nature of budget performance reports are governed by the nature of the budget itself, so the nature of and the authority and level of managerial action are defined in the budget documents. Operations are controlled at the source. Consequently, in the first instance corrective action under a budget should always be taken by the immediate supervisor to whom a particular segment of the budget relates. Top management's control function, therefore, consists of (1) observing, measuring, and training the lower levels in action-taking, and (2) appraising the over-all results to determine when budget revisions are necessary.

CHAPTER 7

FLEXIBLE BUDGET ALLOWANCES FOR COST CONTROL

	Page
Purpose of chapter	131
Requirements in determining flexible cost allowances	132

1. Determination of Appropriate Measures of Activity

Validity of measure	132
Ease of application	134
Understandability of measure	135

2. Determination of Range of Activity Levels To Be Covered

Need for determination of activity range	135
Changing behavior of some costs	136
Factors influencing range of analysis	137

3. Determination of Costs for Each Activity Level

Danger of preconceived ideas of cost behavior	139
Costs a function of quantity and price	139
Determination of known fully variable costs	140
Determination of known fixed costs	141
Variability studies of other cost items	141
Engineering studies of variability	141
Statistical analyses of prior experience	142
Plotting the record	143
Determining the trend line	147
High-low method of trend determination	151

4. Promulgation of Cost Allowances

Form of schedules	153
Approval of allowances	153

Purpose of Chapter. In the previous chapters it has been observed that in order properly to coordinate all the activities of Illustrative Company it was necessary to lay plans based on a given volume of sales and level of activity. The budget there presented was fixed but subject to revision if and when deemed necessary. A material deviation of sales from the forecast, requiring a significant change in production schedules with corresponding changes in material requirements and other costs, would necessitate an over-all budget revision in order to achieve coordination at a different level of activity. For this purpose new cost allowances, other than standard unit labor and material costs, would have to be determined. This suggests the utility of predetermined allowances for various levels of activity.

But even though deviations in activity are not large enough to cause budget revisions, they may be substantial enough to require a series of cost allowances for the purposes of cost control. The analysis in the preceding chapter of the budget deviation in salesmen's expenses is a case in point. There it was noted that, although those expenses were less than the amount budgeted, the decrease was not proportional to the decline in sales. Whether the two items should have a fixed relationship at all levels of activity is not now the question. The mere fact that there is some relationship between them requires that the fixed budget be supplemented by other data, as a means both of determining how much cost should be incurred under conditions differing from those underlying the fixed or forecast budget, and of measuring the efficacy of cost control after the fact. These additional data take the form of flexible cost allowances for a range of activities. It is the purpose of this chapter to describe how such allowances are determined.

Requirements in Determining Flexible Cost Allowances. There are four steps in the preparation of flexible cost allowances for the guidance of operating personnel. These are:

1. Determination of appropriate measures of activity
2. Determination of range of activity levels to be covered
3. Determination of allowable costs for each activity level
4. Promulgation of cost allowances

Each step is discussed in turn.

1. DETERMINATION OF APPROPRIATE MEASURES OF ACTIVITY

Since each cost item, other than the fixed costs, is to be related in amount to the corresponding activity, it is necessary to determine what that activity is. For reasons noted below, this is not always a simple task. Actually, three requirements of a measure should be satisfied. The first requirement is that the activity measure be valid in the sense that there is a logical and practical relationship between the selected activity and costs. Second, the measure should be easy to apply, and third, it should be understandable.

Validity of Measure. The importance of the validity of a measure of activity for cost control purposes can be understood only in light of the use to which the measure is put. Essentially, the purpose of the measure is to serve as a benchmark for the determination of allowable expenses. Granting that expenses may be expected to vary with changes in level of activity, how may the level of activity best be measured?

The selection of an appropriate measure is not always a simple matter. Frequently a measure which at first appears useful proves to be invalid. Experience may indicate little correlation between expense behavior and the selected measure of activity, and the resultant analysis may indicate a lack of logical relationship. A better measure must then be sought. An example of the problem of selecting the appropriate measure is found in budgeting salesmen's travel expenses. Should the allow-

FLEXIBLE BUDGET ALLOWANCES FOR COST CONTROL 133

ance be based on total sales, as was the case in the preparation of Illustrative Company's budget? Or should it be based on the total number of units of product sold, or other factors? Conceivably, a change in the sales mix would render total sales invalid as a measure by reference to which travel expense allowances are determined. This could be true whether sales are measured in dollars or units. Moreover, the ratio of travel expenses to sales might reasonably be expected to differ from one territory to another.

Numerous other examples of the problem are available. Many are found in connection with production costs. In the case of stockroom labor, for example, should the allowance be based on activity as measured by units of product turned out, by direct labor cost, or some other factor? In this example, as well as the preceding one, it frequently is difficult to find a valid measure, and often the appropriate measure must be sought by the trial and error method. Since the measure is used not only in the preparation of a budget but also in evaluating performance, it must be determined fairly.

While we are concerned here with a measure of the capacity to be attained, we must not overlook the fact that the capacity itself may not always be accurately known. Following is a suggested program for establishing the capacity of the plant:

1. *Establish the working shift schedule*—The normal work week shift schedule for department and for total plant to be used for the capacity determination should be definitely settled upon. If overtime in certain departments is so frequent as to be the usual thing, the shift schedule should include the overtime hours.

2. *Tabulate all productive equipment*—The capital equipment records should first be obtained and a tabulation made of all equipment in the productive departments.

3. *Delete all service equipment from the tabluation*—An engineer from the tooling or manufacturing organization should then be consulted to determine which equipment items are directly productive and which are used for service functions. For example, in the milling department, a large milling machine would probably be used exclusively on production work. However, a small hand miller may be used for special repair or jig work not done by service departments. Tool bit grinders are typical equipment items which are found in most productive departments but over which work is rarely, if ever, scheduled.

4. *Check the equipment list for accuracy*—A complete physical check of each machine location by department, machine description, and tooling should be made to insure the accuracy and timeliness of the plant equipment records.

5. *Set up an inter-changeable machine test classification system*—Some variety of machine tool classification system should be devised with the methods or tooling engineer, so that inter-changeable production machines of similar size and capacity may be grouped together for measurement of a

single unit. Although the development of such a code system seems involved, it can be very simply done by using standard machine codings of the National Machine Tool Builders Association.

6. *Determine proper allowances for down-time and set-up*—Realizing that, by definition, the practical capacity of a machine is not just the full shift time that the machine is available but rather the shift time, less allowances for set-up, down-time, maintenance, etc., it becomes necessary to develop factors for these machine delays. This can be accomplished by securing a list of all standard parts worked on and operations performed in the various producing departments.

Consultation with foremen or methods personnel will provide estimates of the down-time and set-up requirements for each part and operation. If the timekeeping procedure is so constituted that the operator must punch on and off at the beginning and end of each machine run, it is possible to secure an accurate down-time estimate by analysis of the amount of down-time in comparison to machine running time.

7. *Allow for the increase in production resulting from incentives*—If an incentive system is in effect, it is necessary to take into account the fact that, although the time standards may indicate a standard machine time required for production, the operator may be able, as a result of incentive, to produce more than standard in the allotted time. It is, therefore, necessary to take this factor into account in determining productive capacity. This is accomplished by determining for at least a one-year period the average incentive response in each department working on incentive, and developing an average departmental per cent factor indicating the amount by which production has exceeded standard.

8. *Tabulate all these factors into the finished determination.*[1]

Ease of Application. Because of the need for prompt budgetary adjustments to changes in activity, and for prompt reporting of actual costs in relation to actual activity, activity measures should be easy to apply. In other words, the determination of allowed expenses and costs for a given condition of operations should be made readily. This requires that the measure or measures be precise and that the data be readily available.

Commonly, expense items are grouped under one measure. Where this is feasible, the allowances for a number of items of expense are determined by reference to one measure of activity. The convenience of this method is an advantage. It must be used with caution, however, since a sense of fairness must underlie cost control and cost evaluation procedures. This is particularly true when the grouped items involve different supervisory responsibilities. In grouping items, care must be exercised that the items have the same logical relationship to the measure of activity. Obviously, since production and sales do not necessarily coincide, separate measures must be used for these two activities.

[1] Thomas R. Torian, "Measuring Activity and Capacity for the Budget," *N.A.A. Bulletin*, Section 1, Oct., 1951, pp. 163–65.

FLEXIBLE BUDGET ALLOWANCES FOR COST CONTROL 135

There follow a few examples which illustrate how expense items may be grouped and allowances determined by reference to one measure of activity.

Expense	Measure of Activity
Labor expense Social security taxes Pensions Fringe benefits Compensation insurance First aid and safety	Total labor dollars
Automobile expense Gasoline Oil Tires Some repairs	Mileage
Material handling In-plant trucking Storekeeping Crane operation	Tons or pounds of product
Sales office expense Supervisory salaries Clerical salaries Stationery Postage Telephone, etc.	Number of salesmen

Understandability of Measure. If expense allowances for a given activity are reported in exact monetary or physical amounts, understandability of terms does not present a problem. On the other hand, if predetermined expense and cost allowance schedules are presented to supervisory personnel, based on certain levels of capacity, care must be exercised to ensure that the capacity measures have meaning for the supervisors. A stated percentage of capacity, for example, may mean different things, depending on the meaning of "capacity." By "capacity," do we mean normal capacity, maximum capacity, one-shift capacity, two-shift capacity? In general, the measure should be couched in terms which are closely related to the work of the particular department. The author has found from his experience that the adoption of a "universal" measure of 1 shift equals 100 per cent activity represents a solution to the problem of providing an understandable measure of activity.

2. DETERMINATION OF RANGE OF ACTIVITY LEVELS TO BE COVERED

Need for Determination of Activity Range. Bearing in mind that predetermined allowances are useful both in revising the budget and in applying cost control procedures under varying conditions of operation, the allowances should be readily available for all conditions likely to be encountered. If all costs were either wholly fixed or fully variable with operating level, this would present no problem. Or if a particular cost is partly fixed and the remainder fully variable, no problem is presented. Thus, for example, if a particular manufacturing expense never falls below $1,000 per month, but always increases beyond that amount at the rate of 10 per cent of direct labor cost, the allowed expense for any amount of direct labor could be determined very simply by reference to the formula:

$$\text{Allowed expense} = \$1,000 + 10\% \text{ D.L.}$$

Some items of cost and expense do behave in this manner and, for them, there is no need to delimit the range of activity to be covered in establishing expense allowances. In the case of many other items, however, this is not true.

Changing Behavior of Some Costs. Certain costs may fall into the foregoing pattern only within a narrow range of activity levels, but change radically beyond this range. It has been pointed out in an earlier chapter that so-called fixed costs frequently are not unalterable; that commonly they are fixed only by the decision of management. It is understandable, therefore, that management may determine a certain cost to be fixed for a period of time, having in mind a certain level of operations during that period, but reserving the right to change its determination if operations should depart radically from those planned. Actually, very few so-called fixed costs remain unchanged throughout the entire scale of operating levels, from zero to maximum capacity. However, in most cases it is not necessary or practical to budget the fixed costs for all levels, since wide variations are not expected to occur in short periods of time. Or, if they do occur, they will be of such short duration as not to demand a drastic revision of the fixed costs.

There is another class of costs, however, which presents a more difficult problem. These are the so-called stepped costs—costs which are fixed at one amount for a limited range of activities and at another amount for a different limited range. Clerical and supervisory personnel often fall into this category. It is with this class of costs, in particular, that the delimitation of the activity range promotes the ease of cost budgeting. If the forecast range of operations coincides with the range in which an expense of this type remains unchanged, it becomes in effect a fixed expense. On the other hand, however, if the forecast range is wider, the "stepped" nature of these expenses must be recognized and calculated.

FLEXIBLE BUDGET ALLOWANCES FOR COST CONTROL 137

Factors Influencing Range of Analysis. Where costs and expenses do not fall into the categories of wholly fixed or fully variable, but include items which vary either on a curved basis or a stepped basis with volume, it is generally considered necessary to schedule the allowances for specific volumes or activity levels. They commonly take the form illustrated in Figure 7–1, where the activity levels are set at intervals of 10 per cent of capacity, ranging from 60 per cent to 130 per cent of normal activity. But suppose that operations are scheduled at 82 per cent for a particular month, or that it is the activity that actually is achieved. How can the allowances for this unscheduled activity readily be determined? Obviously no problem is encountered in connection with general foremen, depreciation, or property taxes, for they are fixed for the entire scheduled range of activity. Similarly, there is no problem in connection with supplies or cartons and containers. These expenses are fully variable and directly proportional to activity. All the other items, however, are semi-variable.

If the semi-variable items are not "stepped" in nature but consist of a fixed portion and a fully variable portion, they can be broken down and treated as two separate items of expense, one fixed and one fully variable with activity. Another method is available, however, the method of interpolation. This method, which has the advantage of applicability to "stepped" expenses as well as to the type just described, is illustrated as follows:

Fuel cost at 90 per cent............................	$470
Fuel cost at 80 per cent............................	430
Increase in cost for 10 per cent increase in activity......	$ 40
Increase in cost for one per cent increase in activity ($40 ÷ 10)	$ 4
Allowance for 82 per cent: $430 + (2 × $4)	$438

The assumption implicit in this calculation is that, regardless of the behavior throughout the entire range of activity, this expense is fully variable with changes in activity between 80 per cent and 90 per cent. The method is based on the theory that the closer two points lie on a curved line, the more closely the segment of the line between them approximates a straight line. Therefore, granting that it may be impractical to schedule allowances for every per cent of normal activity, the smaller the interval between the schedules, the more accurate is the method of interpolation. Expediency therefore requires a balancing of the need for accuracy and the cost of establishing additional schedules of allowances.

The method of interpolation must be used with judgment, however. Reference to the item "Foremen" in the figure, for example, indicates

THE CONSOLIDATED CORPORATION
AIRCRAFT DIVISION
MANUFACTURING EXPENSE BUDGET

Department Subassembly
Department Head _____ Ship _____
Year 1955
Normal Activity 85,000
Base Standard Labor Hours

Account	60%	70%	80%	90%	100% (N.A.)	110%	120%	130%
Salaries								
General Foremen	$ 700	$ 700	$ 700	$ 700	$ 700	$ 700	$ 700	$ 700
Foremen	1,100	1,500	1,900	2,200	2,200	2,200	2,600	2,600
Clerks, etc.	700	700	950	950	950	950	950	1,200
Subtotal	$ 2,500	$ 2,900	$ 3,550	$ 3,850	$ 3,850	$ 3,850	$ 4,250	$ 4,500
Hourly Labor—Indirect	1,500	1,750	2,000	2,250	2,500	2,500	2,750	3,000
Fuel	350	400	430	470	510	530	570	620
Power	2,620	3,020	3,430	3,870	4,300	4,740	5,140	5,320
Water	210	220	230	240	250	260	270	280
Maintenance and Repairs	1,630	1,875	2,050	2,250	2,500	2,790	3,070	3,660
Supplies	270	315	360	405	450	495	540	585
Mule Expense	140	180	190	200	210	230	260	270
Traveling	70	70	100	100	100	100	120	120
Telephone and Telegraph	70	80	90	100	100	100	110	120
Cartons and Containers	150	175	200	225	250	275	300	325
Recreation and Welfare	30	40	50	50	50	60	60	60
Miscellaneous	120	130	150	160	175	190	200	210
Subtotal	$ 9,660	$11,155	$12,830	$14,170	$15,245	$16,120	$17,640	$19,070
Depreciation—Building	900	900	900	900	900	900	900	900
Depreciation—Machinery and Equipment	1,800	1,800	1,800	1,800	1,800	1,800	1,800	1,800
Property Taxes	1,200	1,200	1,200	1,200	1,200	1,200	1,200	1,200
Insurance	350	350	400	400	400	400	400	450
Total	$13,910	$15,405	$17,130	$18,470	$19,545	$20,420	$21,940	$23,420

SOURCE: Heckert and Willson, *Business Budgeting and Control* (2d ed.; New York: The Ronald Press Co., 1955), p. 63.

FIG. 7-1. Manufacturing Expense Budget

that while it is a "stepped" expense, it probably should not be interpolated. Between 80 per cent and 90 per cent activity, the cost increases $300. Since foremen are not divisible, it must be assumed that the increase took place either exactly at 90 per cent, or at one point between 80 and 90. On the other hand, interpolation of the total budget as between 80 and 90 per cent would be more nearly correct since differences of the type just described would tend to cancel one another.

Concerning the advisability of extending the scheduled allowances beyond the activity range illustrated (60 per cent to 130 per cent), it is not necessary to do so if foreseeable operations do not require it. And, in addition, it might be a waste of time, since operations either below or above those provided for might well call for a complete revision in the cost picture and nullify the work done in incorporating such schedules in the cost control budget.

3. DETERMINATION OF COSTS FOR EACH ACTIVITY LEVEL

Danger of Preconceived Ideas of Cost Behavior. In establishing schedules of cost allowances for various levels of operation for the several activities of the company—production, distribution, administration, and so on—the analyst should endeavor to free his mind of preconceived ideas concerning the variability characteristics of various items of cost. Expenses do not always behave in the expected manner. Cost-volume relationships at times are obscure, and only a searching analysis will disclose the correct relation. Shipping costs, billing costs, order-getting expenses, and factory supervision are some examples of costs concerning which only a careful analysis of cost and performance data can lead to proper allowances. It is assumed, of course, that the purpose in establishing allowances is to provide a good basis for real control of costs and not merely to reflect past experience. Thus, each item of cost must be studied to determine whether it is fixed, variable, or semi-variable in nature.

Costs a Function of Quantity and Price. All costs represent the consumption of labor, goods, or services at a price. For control purposes at some management levels, quantities alone may suffice. Thus, tons of coal burned in the power plant, hours of labor used on an assembly line, or square feet of sheet metal used in relation to quantities of finished production may be useful measures of efficiency. But for purposes of understandability at all levels of management and of budget preparation, it generally is necessary that these items be costed in monetary terms. Furthermore, it must be recognized that the monetary costs are not always proportional to the physical quantities consumed. Labor hours alone, for example, will not disclose all the additional costs arising from overtime work, nor the excess labor costs resulting from the use, in an emergency, of high-rate labor on a low-rate job.

Cost variances can be due either to quantity or price, and the two should be separated for a complete assignment of responsibility. Furthermore, since with many cost items price may fluctuate more than quantities used, it is obvious that cost allowance schedules must reflect both quantities and unit prices.

Determination of Known Fully Variable Costs. In preparing a flexible cost allowance schedule for a particular department or activity, one normally begins with the known items and by a process of elimination works toward those items which must be carefully investigated. Actually, the number of cost items readily known to be fully variable in many companies is rather small, although they may represent a sizable proportion of the total costs.

In the case of the budget of Illustrative Company, there was no question concerning the variability of sales commissions, for example, for the sales compensation plan provides for a flat rate of commission on all sales. Likewise, since standard costs are used, there is no concern with the cost allowances for consumption of either *direct* material or labor. In the case of the direct material it is understood that purchase price variances are accounted for at time of purchase, so that the production cost schedule is based on standard quantities at standard prices. The standard quantities, once determined, should represent fully variable costs. Direct labor standard quantities, at standard rates, should also represent fully variable production costs. In this connection, however, it must be recognized that the costs of the labor personnel involved are not necessarily in the same category. For example, if it be assumed that ten operators are needed on an assembly line and that the standard direct labor cost per unit of output is based on a specified speed of the line, the *standard* direct labor cost per unit will remain the same regardless of the speed of the line, but the *actual* direct labor cost will change as the line is speeded up or slowed down, unless the operators are paid solely on a piece-rate basis. In this case, standard costs are a costing device but not a budget-making device.

In the case of Illustrative Company, certain other items were budgeted on a variable basis, but the relationship with volume was not necessarily preconceived. Bad debts and salesmen's travel expenses were budgeted as variable items but both the nature of the relationship and the proportion had to be established by analysis, and the analysis would have to be a continuing one. Normally, certain other expenses, particularly in

FLEXIBLE BUDGET ALLOWANCES FOR COST CONTROL 141

connection with factory burden, would also tend to be fully variable, but it should be emphasized that in most companies very few costs can be *assumed* to be in this category. In most cases the relationships can be determined only by a study of the facts.

Determination of Known Fixed Costs. Costs in this category include those which are established by contractual arrangement and those which are determined by management with the expectation that they will not be changed during the budget period. Insurance, taxes, advertising, depreciation, and professional retainers are the more common costs for which commitments are normally made in advance and which cannot readily be changed.

The great bulk of administrative costs however, whether incurred in production, distribution, or general administration, are fixed only by management decisions. It is these costs which are subject to change if volume and profit undergo radical change. But these costs would be changed only by top management decision and are considered as unalterable by lower levels of management. For purposes of short-period budgets they present little or no problem of definition.

Variability Studies of Other Cost Items. Having determined those items which are obviously fixed or variable, the budget officer's job is then to analyze the variability characteristics of the remainder of the cost items. This is the difficult assignment since they may account for fully half of the budget items. These items may prove, on analysis, to be fully variable, semi-variable, or fixed, but analysis is required to establish the fact. Such analyses in general may be of two main types: the so-called engineering type of analysis, and studies of the company's past experience, the latter being based on a variety of mathematical and statistical methods.

Engineering Studies of Variability. The engineering type of study is one in which an attempt is made to determine what the costs should be rather than what they are likely to be on the basis of prior experience. The methods which are used in establishing direct material consumption and direct labor usage standards are applied to other cost items.

As applied to the labor force, a manning table is established in which every category of human endeavor in the company is covered for various levels of activity. The number of mechanics, janitors, stock clerks, billing clerks, and so forth, for each operating level is ascertained, not by reference to the past but by a careful study of actual requirements. This type of study presupposes a knowledge of each job and the availability of output standards in each job classification. Once these data are determined, their conversion to monetary costs requires only the application of the various rates provided in the salary and wage classification schedule.

Determination of material consumption standards, both direct and indirect, follows the same method. The analysis is based initially on quantities, not costs, of the various materials needed. Pricing these materials, however, may present a more difficult problem than in the case of labor, since prices of materials frequently are more volatile than labor rates.

Engineering determinations of both labor and material requirements vary in difficulty among industries. The method is most readily used in a process type of industry, where all operations are continuous and repetitive. It is much more difficult to apply in a custom-order or job type of company.

In either type, however, some expenses are not readily analyzed in such a precise manner. Sales effort, in particular, is not subject to the same precision of measurement as other effort. Advertising, notably, is an expenditure which cannot be engineered in the same sense as packing cost, although it can be studied statistically and experimentally. Managerial supervision also is not subject to precise measurement, except in a highly mechanized or routinized type of industry.

In the author's opinion, the engineering type of study represents the most scientific approach to the problem of determining cost allowances. However, in view of its difficulties in some situations, the mathematical and statistical analyses of prior experience next described are widely used. While such analyses are an indirect method of arriving at the desired information, they are a less expensive method of investigation which under some conditions produces reasonably satisfactory results. They also are useful as a checking device supplementing engineering studies.

Statistical Analyses of Prior Experience. Assuming that engineering studies are too costly or too time-consuming for immediate use, the alternative is to analyze the records of prior experience to determine how costs behave under various conditions of operation. There are three prerequisites of this method. First, the company must have had experience with various volumes of operation in all departments to provide a useful pattern of cost experience. Under the influence of certain economic and political pressures, companies may find their cost estimates to be unreliable simply because they are called on to operate at volumes far in excess of or far below that normally experienced. It goes without saying that a new company cannot use statistical methods— it must use the engineering type of analysis.

FLEXIBLE BUDGET ALLOWANCES FOR COST CONTROL

Second, the experience must be recorded in such a manner as to be useful. An adequate chart of accounts is extremely important. Too few accounts, with a resultant combination of numerous costs in one account, makes analysis impossible.

Third, the cost data must be comparable. Even though the company has had a varied experience, properly recorded, the data may not be satisfactory for the purpose at hand because of changes either in methods of operation or prices of labor, materials, and services. Particularly in recent years, changes of this type have been so frequent that an experience record of more than a year or two may be useless unless adjusted for the changes. Such adjustments may be so costly and time-consuming as to approach the engineering type of study in difficulty.

Assuming that the foregoing three requirements are met, it must be emphasized that the statistical analyses can only provide a pattern of costs based on prior experience. This can be very useful in financial budgeting, but its limitation for cost control must be recognized. This limitation lies in the fact that prior experience may not be a valid guide to what the costs *should* be under efficient conditions of operation or under entirely different operating conditions in the future. The succeeding discussion must be read with this limitation in mind.

Plotting the Record. Assuming the presence of an adequate and comparable record of the incurrence of a particular expense for a number of comparable time periods (weeks or months) of operations at various capacities, plotting the data on grid paper is the easiest way to determine the type of relationship existing between the expense and the level of activity. As an example, let us consider the relation of salesmen's travel expense to sales in one department of Illustrative Company. One problem that arises immediately is that of selecting the time period. In this case a month is used since it is the shortest period for which expense data are recorded in the accounts. Following are the expenses and sales for the twenty most recent months (that number is used since it is believed to afford a broad experience with little if any distortion due to changes in either the prices of the products or the level of travel costs of the company).

Month	Sales	Salesmen's Travel Expense
1	$70,000	$2,800
2	75,000	2,000
3	69,000	2,100
4	71,000	1,800
5	62,000	1,500
6	63,000	1,400
7	66,000	2,000

BUDGETING FOR CONTROL

Month	Sales	Salesmen's Travel Expense
8	50,000	1,900
9	54,000	2,000
10	30,000	2,200
11	31,000	2,400
12	64,000	3,000
13	40,000	2,000
14	50,000	1,700
15	58,000	1,900
16	62,000	1,700
17	60,000	2,200
18	48,000	2,100
19	81,000	2,300
20	74,000	1,600

For ease in plotting and in reviewing the data, the foregoing series of data are rearranged in a series in which the monthly data appear, not in chronological order, but in the order of the sales magnitudes. This is as follows:

Month	Sales	Salesmen's Travel Expense
10	$30,000	$2,200
11	31,000	2,400
13	40,000	2,000
18	48,000	2,100
8	50,000	1,900
14	50,000	1,700
9	54,000	2,000
15	58,000	1,900
17	60,000	2,200
5	62,000	1,500
16	62,000	1,700
6	63,000	1,400
12	64,000	3,000
7	66,000	2,000
3	69,000	2,100
1	70,000	2,800
4	71,000	1,800
20	74,000	1,600
2	75,000	2,000
19	81,000	2,300

This arrangement of the data makes it easier to determine by inspection whether there is a relationship between the things compared. It appears that the relationship is not close, but a final determination can best be made by plotting the data. This is done in Figure 7-2.

The pattern of plotted points in that scatter diagram confirms the impression gained from inspection of the foregoing data, that the relationship between sales in the particular territory and salesmen's travel costs is not clear cut and, consequently, not particularly useful as a basis for establishing cost allowances for cost control purposes. If, however,

FLEXIBLE BUDGET ALLOWANCES FOR COST CONTROL 145

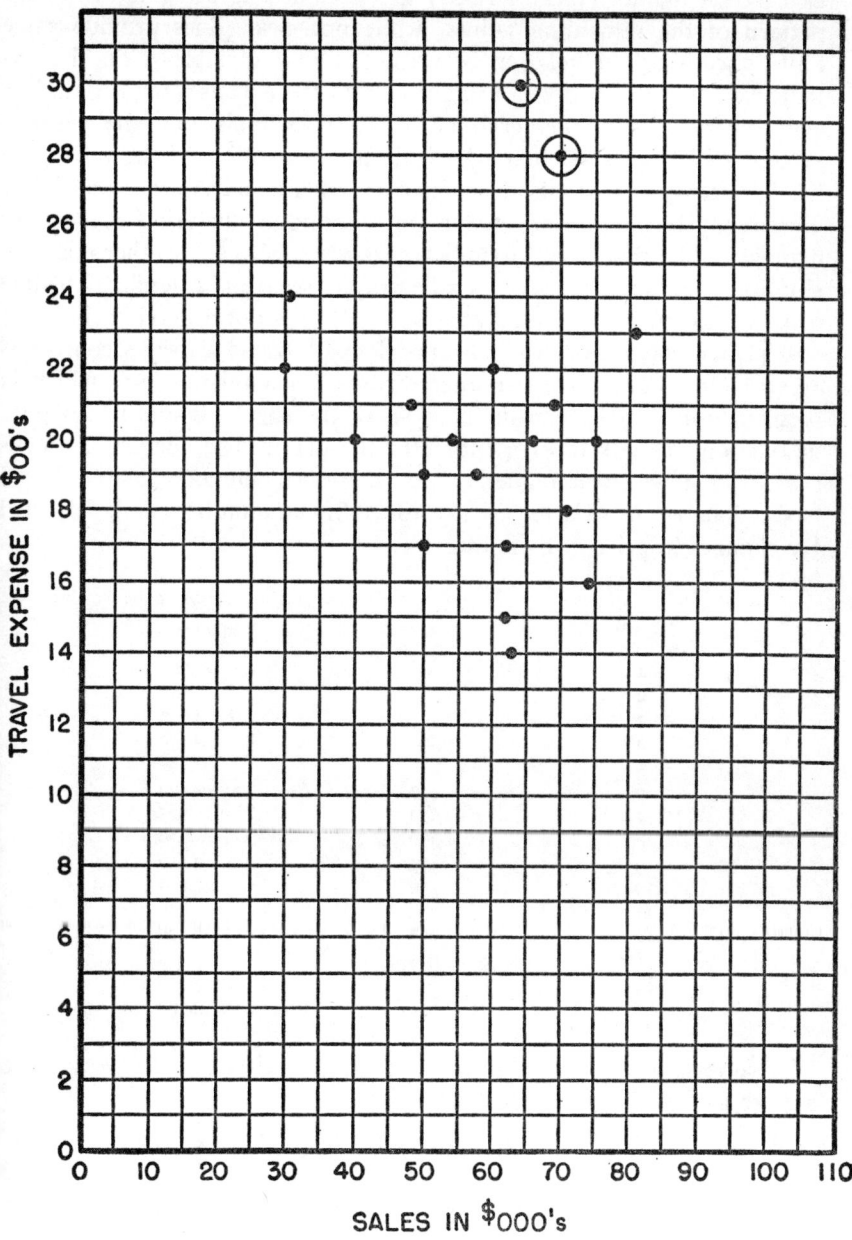

FIG. 7-2. Relationship of Sales and Salesmen's Travel Cost
A Sales Territory—Illustrative Company

two plotted points (those circled) are excluded as being freakish, the pattern of the remaining points, while not clear, does provide some hint concerning the relation between the two variables. To the extent that there is a pattern, it indicates that the expenses tend to decline as sales increase in the territory. Does this imply that the greatest volume of business is obtained within a short radius of the territorial headquarters and that salesmen are sent farther afield as volume shrinks? There may be significant answers in this line of analysis for the sales manager. The chart seems to indicate, however, that some other relationship must be found to serve as a basis for preparing a flexible schedule of travel expense allowances, that sales alone is not a good basis.

Further investigation of the problem of travel expense control is deferred to Chapter 10. Another example of a relationship, which is more definite, is found in the analysis of the cost of operating supplies in relation to the total work force in the plant. The analysis assumes that the supplies are accounted for on an as-used and not an as-purchased basis. The company's experience for a fifteen-month period, adjusted for changes in price, is as follows:

Month	Work Force	Cost of Supplies Used
1	600	$3,000
2	575	3,100
3	550	2,900
4	400	2,250
5	420	2,100
6	420	2,200
7	372	1,925
8	450	2,300
9	475	2,350
10	550	2,800
11	575	2,850
12	600	3,100
13	625	3,150
14	640	3,150
15	650	3,500

The same data, rearranged in the order of magnitude of the work force appear as follows:

Month	Work Force	Cost of Supplies Used
7	372	$1,925
4	400	2,250
5	420	2,100
6	420	2,200
8	450	2,300
9	475	2,350
3	550	2,900

FLEXIBLE BUDGET ALLOWANCES FOR COST CONTROL

Month	Work Force	Cost of Supplies Used
10	550	2,800
2	575	3,100
11	575	2,850
1	600	3,000
12	600	3,100
13	625	3,150
14	640	3,150
15	650	3,500

These data are plotted in Figure 7-3.

The data plotted on that scatter diagram show a close relationship, particularly if the circled point is eliminated as not being typical. It would appear that the expense has both a fixed and a variable element and that the latter tends to be fully variable with the size of the work force. If this is the case, a straight trend line may be developed to serve as the basis for setting reasonable allowances for any size of work force.

Determining the Trend Line. A trend line or relationship line may be determined either by drawing a straight line which visually constitutes a best fit for the points on the scatter diagram or by a mathematical computation. The latter method, while more accurate, may require a substantial amount of work, and hence some practitioners feel that the degree of error inherent in the visual method is not such as to bar its use in many circumstances. Nevertheless, the mathematical approach has the advantage of objectivity and theoretical accuracy and hence is illustrated in the following paragraphs. It must be emphasized, however, that the method is usable only if the relationship between the two variables is linear. It is not usable if the relationship is either curved or stepped. The calculation is made by means of the so-called "least-squares" method, a standard technique of statistics described in any standard work on that subject.

Attention is called to the basic formula for a straight line, namely: $y = a + bx$. In the example illustrated (y) equals the cost of supplies used; (x) equals the work force; (a) equals the fixed cost; (b) equals the variable cost per man.

The problem is to determine that value of "a" and that value of "b" which make the best fit for the various values of x and y represented by the company's experience. If the line is drawn by visual inspection, the values for "a" and "b" are read from the completed chart. If the values for "a" and "b" are to be computed mathematically, the equations for the calculation are commonly stated as follows:

(1) $\Sigma(y) = na + b\Sigma(x)$
(2) $\Sigma(xy) = a\Sigma(x) + b\Sigma(x^2)$

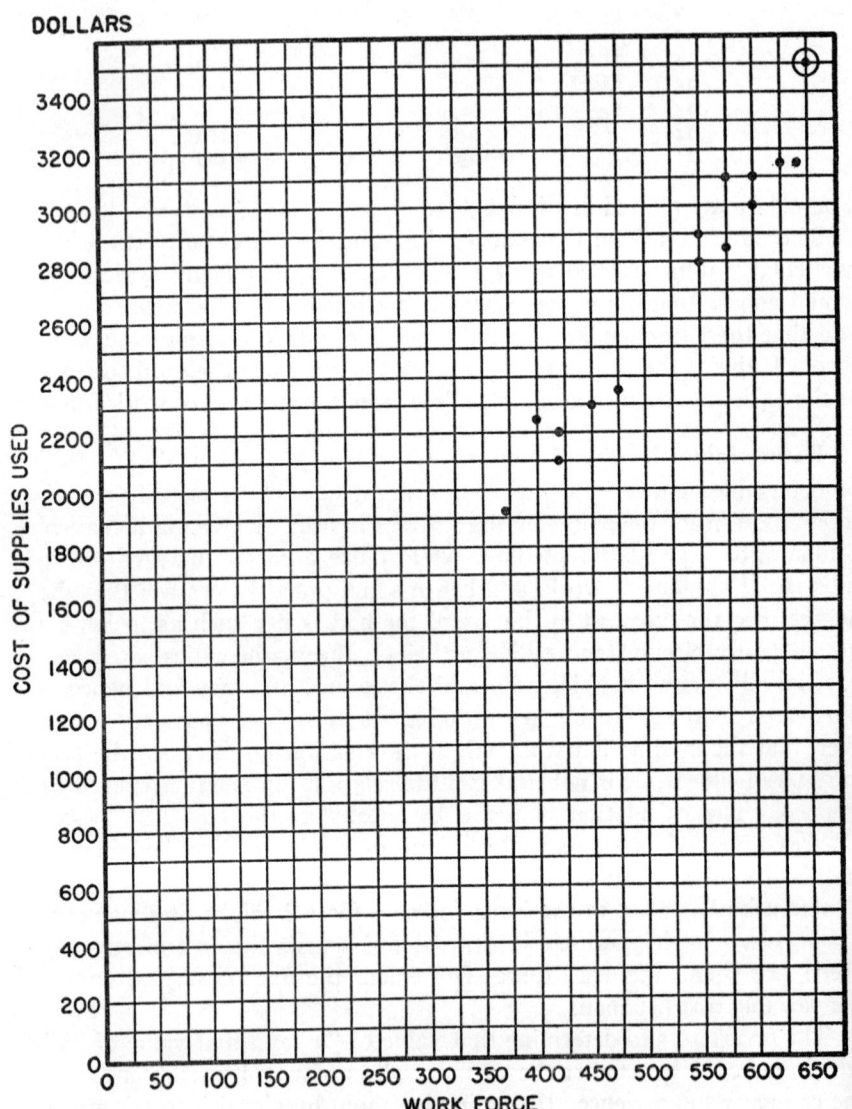

Fig. 7-3. Relationship of Work Force and Cost of Operating Supplies
Illustrative Company

FLEXIBLE BUDGET ALLOWANCES FOR COST CONTROL

where

(y) = the amount of monthly expense
$\Sigma(y)$ = the sum of the values of y
(x) = the monthly activity (work force)
$\Sigma(x)$ = the sum of the values of x
$\Sigma(xy)$ = the sum of the products of the paired x's and y's
$\Sigma(x^2)$ = the sum of the squares of the values of x
n = the number of points (months) plotted.

The computations are as follows (omitting the circled point):

x (Work Force)	y (Expense)	xy	x^2
372	$ 1,925	$ 716,100	138,384
400	2,250	900,000	160,000
420	2,100	882,000	176,400
420	2,200	924,000	176,400
450	2,300	1,035,000	202,500
475	2,350	1,116,250	225,625
550	2,900	1,595,000	302,500
550	2,800	1,540,000	302,500
575	3,100	1,782,500	330,625
575	2,850	1,638,750	330,625
600	3,000	1,800,000	360,000
600	3,100	1,860,000	360,000
625	3,150	1,968,750	390,625
640	3,150	2,016,000	409,600
7,252	$37,175	$19,774,350	3,865,784

Substituting these figures in the above equations, we get

(1) $37,175 = 14a + 7,252b$
(2) $19,774,350 = 7,252a + 3,865,784b$

Clearing out the a's by multiplying the first line by -518 $\left(\text{since } 518 = \frac{7,252}{14}\right)$, we get

$19,774,350 = 7,252a + 3,865,784b$
$- 19,256,650 = 7,252a - 3,756,536b$
$\overline{517,700 = 109,248b}$

Therefore 'b' (the variable cost per man) = $4.739.

Substituting this value in either of the original equations, we get a value for 'a' (the fixed cost) of $200.55. The formula for the cost of supplies used, therefore, is $200.55 + $4.739 per man. The trend line can therefore be drawn on the scatter diagram by starting at $200.55 on the left-hand margin and sloping it diagonally upwards at the rate of $4.739 per man. The effect is shown in Figure 7–4. Again it must be emphasized that the formula is representative only of past experience

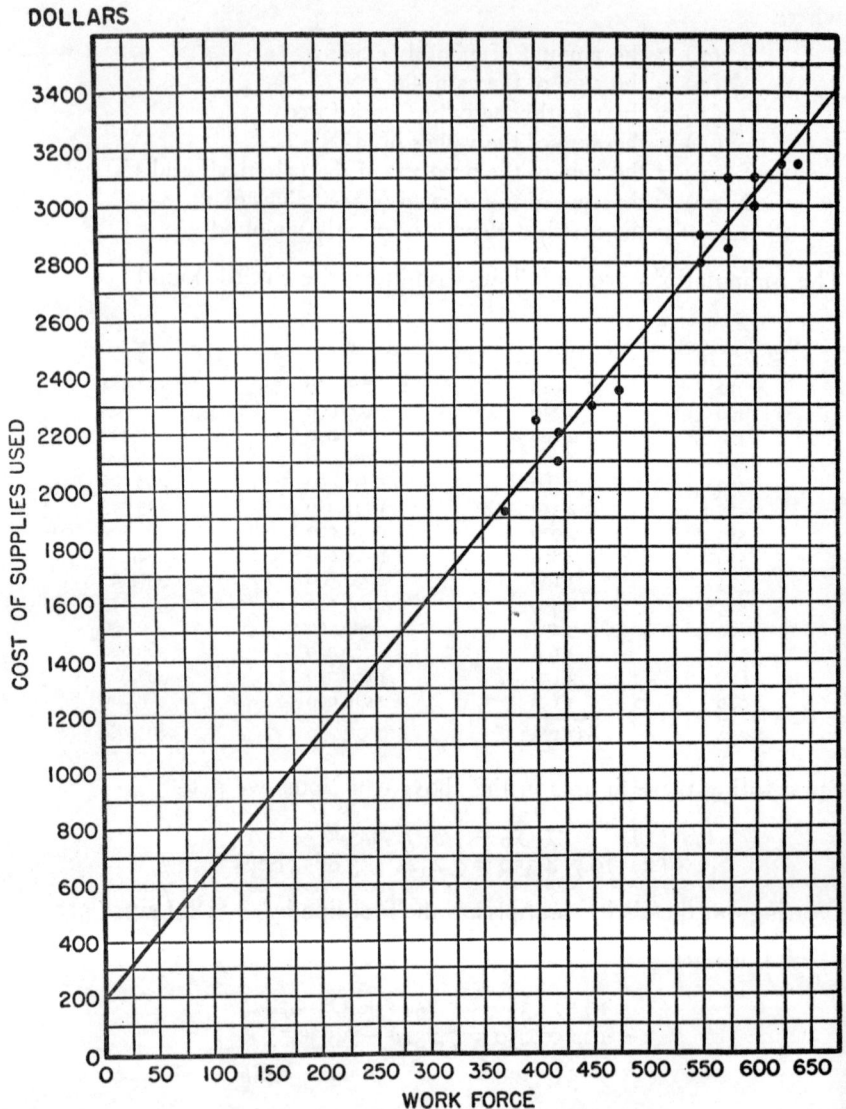

Fig. 7-4. Data from Fig. 7-3, with Addition of Trend Line

(except for the elimination of one point) and, consequently, is useful only insofar as past experience is valid as a guide for cost control purposes. With reference to Figure 7-4, it is pointed out that when the fixed cost (a) and variable rate (b) are computed, it is not necessary to construct the chart in order to determine cost allowances; these may be derived from the basic formula $y = a + bx$. However, the construction

FLEXIBLE BUDGET ALLOWANCES FOR COST CONTROL 151

of the chart is recommended, first, to aid in visualizing the cost relationship and, second, to observe whether or not there is in fact a linear relationship between the two variables. It is only in that circumstance that the foregoing calculation is valid.

It will not apply if the relationship is stepped or curved as shown in Figures 7–5 and 7–6. In the former case, a series of horizontal trend lines is indicated, rising in step form; in the latter a curved line is indicated. This also can be determined by a mathematical formula, but its use goes beyond the sphere of this work.

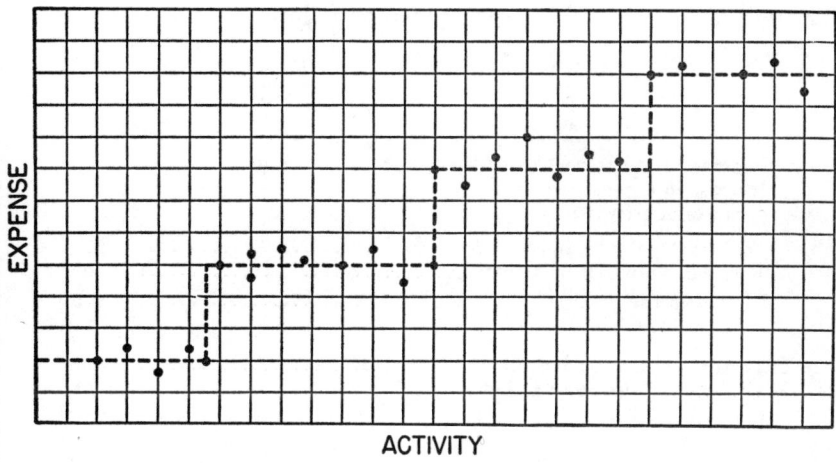

FIG. 7–5. Example of a Stepped Relationship

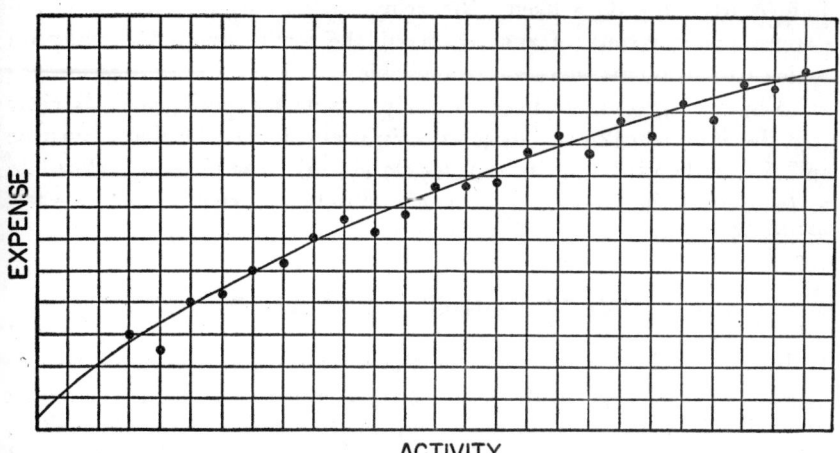

FIG. 7–6. Example of a Curved Relationship

152 BUDGETING FOR CONTROL

High-Low Method of Trend Determination. If past experience must be relied on in establishing cost allowances, and that experience covers only a few levels of activity, resort occasionally may be had to the so-called "high-low" method. Thus, for example, if only the following data are available:

Activity	Expense
80	$200
60	160

the indicated fixed expense would be $40, and the variable expense $2 per unit of activity. This is computed as follows:

Activity	Expense
80	$200
60	160
Increase........ 20	$ 40

Increase in expense per unit of activity, $2

Total expense at 80 activity	$200
Variable expense at 80 activity	160
Fixed expense	$ 40

or

Total expense at 60 activity	$160
Variable expense at 60 activity	120
Fixed expense	$ 40

This method, however, seems too dangerous to be used extensively. It assumes a linear relationship and a validity of data which cannot be judged from the data itself. Referring back to Figure 7-4, it is apparent that a variety of answers would be forthcoming depending on which pair of points were alone available.

Whatever method is used in analyzing past experience, it is clear that the experience must be recorded in useful form. Accounts must be sufficiently detailed and the expense classifications sufficiently refined so as to prevent the combination in one account of expenses whose variability characteristics are dissimilar.

4. PROMULGATION OF COST ALLOWANCES

Form of Schedules. Since flexible cost allowance schedules are designed for on-the-spot control of costs for activities which may or may not coincide with those provided for in the fixed or forecast budget, their formal establishment raises questions concerning both form and method of approval.

FLEXIBLE BUDGET ALLOWANCES FOR COST CONTROL

As to their form, it has already been indicated that the control data issued to operating supervisors may be in the form of columnar schedules, as illustrated in Figure 7–1, or cost formulae, or charts, or a combination of these. The form should be related to the level of comprehension of the supervisors to whom they are addressed. But an equally important question is that concerning approval.

Approval of Allowances. It goes without saying that the allowances must have the approval of top management, as an integral part of the company's budget. It is also apparent that if the allowances which are determined by any of the methods previously discussed do not permit the company's achievement of its profit goals, steps must be taken to improve them. In any case, however, it should be recognized that to be fully effective, the allowances should meet the approval of those directly concerned with them, as well as of top management.

The most careful investigation by engineers, statisticians, or cost accountants may fail to disclose conditions which only the operating man knows. Consequently, not to invite his cooperation in setting allowances is dangerous both in its effect on the workability of the budget and on the spirit of teamwork within the organization. For this reason, those who are to be controlled should have a voice in the preparation of the data.

CHAPTER 8

ANALYSIS AND REPORTING OF COST VARIANCES

	Page		Page
Purpose of chapter	154	2. Comparison of Actual and Allowed Expenses	
		Collecting the data	157
1. Departmentalization of Activity and Responsibility		What rate of activity?	157
		The problem of unabsorbed burden	159
Coordination of authority and responsibility	155	3. Useful Reports	
Departmentalization of activity	155	Report requirements summarized	161
Controllable vs. noncontrollable costs	156	Restricting contents of reports	164
		Examples of reports	164

Purpose of Chapter. If all operations of a company were exactly identical with those projected in the master forecast budget, it would suffice as a basis of evaluation of actual results. It rarely happens, however, that the plan works out exactly. Therefore, for the purposes of cost control, it is necessary that cost allowances be available for a variety of operating conditions in order that cost incurrence may be directed and evaluated in terms, not of the work planned, but of the work accomplished. The preceding chapter discusses the establishment and promulgation of flexible allowances; the present chapter is concerned with their use in evaluating cost performance after the fact.

Where cost standards for direct material and direct labor are available, they facilitate the control of those items of cost. It is the indirect costs which present the major problem of reporting, and they are the principal subject of this chapter.

The basic requirements in analyzing and reporting performance in cost incurrence control are:

1. Departmentalization of activity and responsibility
2. Valid comparisons
3. Useful reports

Each of these is significant and poses problems. The chapter is devoted to a discussion of them.

ANALYSIS AND REPORTING OF COST VARIANCES

1. DEPARTMENTALIZATION OF ACTIVITY AND RESPONSIBILITY

Coordination of Authority and Responsibility. It is axiomatic that costs are controlled at the source, that is, at the point of incurrence. Consequently, those who have authority to hire employees, authorize overtime, and approve purchase orders should also have the responsibility for the costs incurred. The spirit of teamwork cannot be developed if a supervisor is held responsible for costs which he himself did not authorize. By the same token, there can be no control if those who incur the costs are free of accountability for them. These considerations lead to the requirement of departmentalization of activities.

The traditional classification of operating expenses on the statement of income as to production, sales effort, general administration, and so on, is in part a recognition of the need for placing responsibility for various classes of costs. But this classification is primarily functional and, therefore, not adequate for cost control purposes. The breakdown of costs must be much finer and sharper for control purposes.

Departmentalization of Activity. The proper coordination of authority and responsibility, as it relates to cost control, requires a clear-cut definition and differentiation of activity centers in the organization. This may or may not coincide with the classifications made for cost accounting purposes. Thus, for example, a production department in the factory may be broken down into cost centers for product costing purposes, but considered as an entire department for cost control purposes. The decision in this respect should be based on the location of the authority and responsibility for cost incurrence within the department.

One of the problems arising in the fixing of responsibility relates to the cost of services incurred by one department for the use of another department. Power, maintenance, and space are typical examples. In the case of power (self-produced), for example, the consumption may be controllable in the department where used, but the cost per unit of power produced is controlled only in the power department. It is obvious that a foreman of a producing department would consider a report on his cost control performance as unfair if he were charged different costs for the same quantities of power consumed in two different time periods. This difficulty can be overcome by charging him for power at a standard rate per unit of power consumed and thus evaluating his performance only in relation to consumption. In the power department the comparison of actual costs with standard costs of power delivered to all other departments serves as a measure of the efficiency of power production.

A similar problem arises in the case of maintenance, when this work is done by a maintenance department. Again the work is done *for* the producing department, but *by* another department. Where should the costs be controlled? While similar to the power question, maintenance presents a more difficult problem because, while power consumption is directly related to level of operations, maintenance is in part discretionary. More or less, maintenance may be done without full regard for operations. It may be accelerated or deferred.

Thus, there arises a certain amount of unavoidable duplication in connection with the maintenance budget. Maintenance and repairs are properly placed in the budget of the particular department for the benefit of which the repair expenditure is incurred, but the maintenance department must also prepare a budget from which information will be derived as to the number of employees and repair materials needed and the probable cost.

The latter budget is in the nature of a summary of the maintenance requirements of all of the operating departments. Such duplication is unavoidable because both budgets are required for maintenance control, as part of the process of summarizing maintenance requirements for the payroll and personnel estimates and for the financial budget.

It becomes the function of the operating department supervisor to order maintenance and be responsible for maintenance cost. It is the function of the maintenance department supervisor to inspect facilities, to recommend maintenance projects, and to supervise their execution.

Space costs, representing the prorated costs of the building and its services, are another example of a utility consumed in one department but with the cost thereof controlled elsewhere. Of the three examples cited, however, this one presents the least difficulty, since it commonly is considered a fixed charge and only infrequently can a foreman control his space cost through control of the amount of space used by him.

Controllable vs. Noncontrollable Costs. Aside from the problem of assigning responsibility as between users and producers of services and utilities, there is the added fact that in all departments there are some costs which are fixed, either by the nature of things or by the decision of a higher level of management. This suggests that such costs should not be charged to the supervisor of a department for cost control purposes.

Moreover, it must be recognized that even in the case of variable costs, they frequently are affected by factors over which the supervisor has no control. For example, while he can control quantities, he frequently has no control over prices paid for goods or services. While he may be responsible for overtime premium costs where the overtime work

ANALYSIS AND REPORTING OF COST VARIANCES 157

results from production delays, he should not be held to account for them if the overtime results from an unexpected expansion of the production schedule. These ideas merely emphasize the principle announced earlier, namely, that costs are controlled at the point of incurrence, and this varies with circumstances.

It follows that as all costs are incurred, authorized, or committed for at some level of authority, the reporting structure should be designed to provide for appropriate identification of responsibility for all costs. This principle is further discussed later in this chapter (pp. 161–66).

2. COMPARISON OF ACTUAL AND ALLOWED EXPENSES

Collecting the Data. Promptness in analyzing cost performance is highly important to effective control of costs. After-the-fact analyses are useful only as a guide in future operations. This requires, first, that the report periods be short and, second, that the data be collected and analyzed speedily.

The promptness with which data can be collected and analyzed depends largely on the accounting system and procedures. These should provide an adequate chart of accounts and permit prompt completion and balancing of the period's records. With respect to the former, it must be recognized, when building the chart of accounts, that the requirements of cost accounting are not necessarily the same as those of cost control. Product costing may require a different flow of costs through the books than responsibility costing. This is evident in the case of the indirect expenses discussed above. It follows therefore that a chart of accounts should be developed which accomplishes the dual ends, namely, accounting and budgetary control. Prompt reporting of variances in direct costs is relatively easy, particularly if standard costs are used. In this case the variances are directly reported in the accounts themselves. In the case of indirect expenses, however, the reporting covers only the actual expenses incurred, and variances must be computed by reference to the scheduled allowance for the actual activity.

Reference to the activity, however, also suggests that a prompt recording must be made, not only of the actual expenses, but also of the activity data. Since activity frequently is measured in nonmonetary terms such as labor hours, machine hours, invoices billed, and so on, depending on the department involved, it is apparent that some data will not be obtained from the books of account and must otherwise be provided for.

What Rate of Activity? The selection of the best measure of activity has been discussed in a previous chapter. The question posed now concerns the rate of activity, appropriately measured, which should be used in determining the cost allowance against which actual costs are to be measured. Obviously, it should not be the budgeted rate if activity did not coincide with the budget; it should be the activity actually experienced. But suppose that the activity was not standard for the work accomplished. Should the cost allowance for indirect expenses be based on the efforts expended or on the actual output? As an example, if direct labor hours measure activity of a department and if the output for the period calls for 1,000 hours of work, but 1,100 were actually used, should the allowance for burden incurrence be that for 1,000 hours of direct labor, or 1,100 hours? This question would not arise if output itself were used as the measure of activity; hence one significance of the selection of the measure.

Practice in this respect differs among companies, partly from a difference in viewpoint and partly from necessity. If a homogeneous product is manufactured, quite frequently the amount of product turned out is used as the measure and the burden allowances based thereon. Where the product is not homogeneous, however, direct labor hours or a similar measure must be used, and it is primarily in this case that the question arises as to whether the allowance should be related to actual effort or standard effort for the work accomplished. The decision depends on managerial philosophy concerning cost control, but a problem of morale is also involved.

If the burden allowance for the 1,000 hours referred to above is $1,500, and for 1,100 hours $1,600, and the actual burden was $1,580, should the supervisor be criticized for over-running the budget $80, or praised for saving $20? There is no question but that the total excess cost of the period's output included both the direct labor cost of the 100 excess hours and the additional burden in the amount of $80. On the other hand, the foreman may argue that he has already been criticized for the excess labor and that, granting the validity of that criticism, he believes that the burden allowance should be related to production time rather than output and, consequently, he deserves some praise for retrieving some of the loss in production time through able management of the burden. The question is of some importance, partly from a morale viewpoint, but principally because it focuses attention on the need for clear identification of causes and results and a wise selection of the activity measure.

Similar questions may arise in connection with other activities. For example, should salesmen's travel expense allowances be related to sales or to the effort expended in obtaining the sales? Again, from a top-management viewpoint, excessive expenses in relation to sales are to be guarded against; but from the viewpoint of the salesman and his

ANALYSIS AND REPORTING OF COST VARIANCES 159

immediate superior, the matter of expense control may require that the relation be one of effort and cost, not of results and cost.

The Problem of Unabsorbed Burden. While this is a book on budgeting and not cost accounting, the two subjects are related and it is deemed advisable to fit the subject of burden cost variations into the entire scheme of burden accounting. Reference to Schedule I-a of Figure 6-1 (p. 119) shows that the Illustrative Company had overabsorbed factory burden, reported as a deduction from cost of sales. What is the nature of this adjustment and how does it relate to burden cost variances?

In the following discussion a different set of facts from those prevailing in Illustrative Company is used. This is done to set forth more clearly all the factors which should be recognized in such an analysis, even though they may not all be present in Illustrative Company.

First, it must be recognized that the rate of variability of burden with production is not identical with the burden absorption rate for product costing. The two are related, but while the former is used to determine cost allowances for any activity, the latter is based on one activity. For example, let it be assumed that:

Fixed monthly burden equals $50,000
Variable burden equals $5 per direct labor hour
Normal output (for costing purposes) requires 10,000 direct labor hours per month
Actual output for a month equalled 6,000 hours of labor, but required 6,200 hours for its accomplishment
Actual burden expenses for the month equalled $84,000

The normal or standard burden cost of an hour of direct labor, to be used for cost accounting purposes, must be based on normal volume and is computed as follows:

Fixed monthly burden	$ 50,000
Variable monthly burden at normal volume, 10,000 hours @ $5	50,000
Total monthly burden at normal volume	$100,000
Divided by normal production load in direct labor hours..	10,000
Standard burden costing rate, per hour	$ 10

Since the month's output called for 6,000 hours of work, the burden absorbed, at the standard hourly rate of $10, must amount to $60,000; and since the actual burden amounted to $84,000, an underabsorption of $24,000 is indicated.

Analysis of the reasons for this underabsorption is important to a full understanding of cost control procedures and their relation to cost accounting. Actually, three basic causes are present:

BUDGETING FOR CONTROL

1. Failure to achieve normal volume
2. Use of excessive labor time for the actual output
3. Excessive burden cost incurrence for the work done

As to the first cause, the underabsorption (assuming the costs fall into only two categories—wholly fixed and fully variable) represents the unchanged portion of the fixed costs. Since output was only 60 per cent of normal, the burden charged to product cost included only $30,000 of fixed burden, leaving $20,000 unabsorbed. In the language of standard costs, this is commonly described as a volume or capacity variance. The responsibility for it rests on that person responsible for achieving a production volume of only 60 per cent of normal. If the output at that rate was scheduled for the month, the responsibility obviously does not rest with the production department; it must be assumed by those responsible for over-all control and planning of operations. On the other hand, responsibility might lie with the factory management if the subnormal volume represented a failure to achieve scheduled output.

As to the second cause, 200 excess hours were required for the work done. Assuming again that the burden falls into only the two categories named above, this would necessitate the incurrence of $1,000 of additional burden—200 hours @ $5 variable cost. This represents the allowed excess burden cost of the excess hours, and the responsibility for it coincides with that in connection with the excess hours.

As to the third cause, overspending, it is assumed in the three-way analysis of the underabsorption that the excess spending is measured from the allowance for the actual hours (6,200) rather than the standard hours for the output achieved (6,000). Consequently, since the allowance for 6,200 hours equals $81,000 ($50,000 fixed, plus $5 per hour, variable) and the actual incurrence was $84,000, an excess spending of $3,000 is indicated. This presumably is the responsibility of the factory.

The foregoing results may be summarized as follows:

Actual burden	$84,000
Burden absorbed	60,000
Unabsorbed	$24,000
Accounted for as follows:	
Due to subnormal volume	$20,000
Due to excess hours for work done	1,000
Due to excess spending	3,000
Total	$24,000

If, instead of computing burden variances on a three-way basis, they were based solely on the standard hours for the work done (as must be done if burden absorption is measured solely by product produced), the $24,000 underabsorption would be accounted for as follows:

ANALYSIS AND REPORTING OF COST VARIANCES

Due to sub-normal volume	$20,000
Due to excess spending	
$84,000 − [$50,000 + (6,000 × $5)]	4,000
Total	$24,000

If, as is frequently the case, not all burden can be classified as wholly fixed or fully variable, but semi-variable costs are present, the calculations would take the following form:

Burden Cost Allowance Schedule

	6,000 hours	6,200 hours	10,000 hours
Fixed burden	$50,000	$50,000	$ 50,000
Semi-variable burden	15,000	15,000	20,000
Variable burden	18,000	18,600	30,000
Total	$83,000	$83,600	$100,000
Normal volume, in hours			10,000
Burden absorption rate, per hour			$10

Variance due to capacity or volume (Burden allowed for output—$83,000 minus absorbed—$60,000)	$23,000
Variance due to excess hours—difference between allowances for 6,000 and 6,200 hours	600
Variance due to spending ($84,000 − $83,600)	400
Total	$24,000

or

Variance due to capacity or volume	$23,000
Variance due to spending ($84,000 − $83,000)	1,000
Total	$24,000

The point of the foregoing discussion is that the entire burden cost which is not charged to product on a standard basis represents a cost variance which must be explained and for which responsibility must be fixed. From the nature of things, the responsibility may be varied and may rest with different segments of management. A cost control program seems incomplete if all aspects are not fully comprehended and covered.

3. USEFUL REPORTS

Report Requirements Summarized. It can be taken for granted that reports, to be useful, must be regular and prompt. It is also assumed that they will be issued to, and used by, all ranks of management responsible for the incurrence and/or supervision of incurrence of costs. Moreover, it must be observed that cost control reports, to be fully useful, should be issued *before* as well as *after* the fact. They include not only the reports on what has been done, but also the schedules of

BUDGETING FOR CONTROL

FOREMAN'S COST REPORT
(WEEKLY LABOR)

Week Ending _11-22-55_   Department_____

ACCT. NO.	ACCOUNT	LINE NO.	DOLLARS THIS WEEK* Allowed	Actual	Variance
	DIRECT LABOR	1			
	Standard	2	1500		
	Substandard	3	150		
	Total Direct Labor	4	1650		
	BURDEN LABOR	5			
	Waiting Time	6			
315	Waiting for Stores	7	—		
320	Waiting for Setup or Tools	8	1		
330	Waiting for Machine Repairs	9	8		
340	Power and Plant Breakdowns	10	2		
342	Waiting for Inspection	11	2		
344	Waiting for Work Assignment	12	1		
345	Parts and Materials Not Delivered	13	1		
	Total Waiting Time	14	15		
	Employee Activities	15			
158	Voting Time Pay	16	—		
164	Jury Duty Pay	17	—		
165	Reporting and Call-in Pay	18	—		
166	Accident Reporting Time Pay	19	—		
167	Employee Welfare and Services	20	2		
168	Union Activities	21	10		
169	Minnreg Veteran's Activites	22	2		
	Total Employee Activities	23	14		
	Training	24			
174	Instructing New Help	25	24		
175	Training School and Orientation	26	—		
	Total Training	27	24		
	Overtime	28			
190	Premium Pay Direct Departments	29	75		
	Setup and Adjustment	30			
157	Setup for Direct Labor—Reg. Production	31	80		
159	Setup Adjustment—Regular Production	32	16		
160	Setup for Direct Labor—Gov. Production	33	40		
161	Setup Adjustment—Government Production	34	15		
162	Tool Trouble	35	65		
	Total Setup and Adjustment	36	216		

SOURCE: Allan L. Rudell, "Planned Profits for the Factory," *N.A.A. Bulletin*, Section 1, Mar., 1955, p. 942.

FIG. 8-1. Foreman's Weekly Labor Cost Report

ANALYSIS AND REPORTING OF COST VARIANCES

	Salvage Created By:	37		
080	Operating	38	80	
081	Inspection	39	—	
082	Methods	40	—	
083	Production Planning	41	—	
084	Engineering	42	—·	
085	Procurement	43	18	
086	Prior Operating Departments	44	20	
	Total Salvage	45	118	
	Department Administration	46		
115	Group Leaders and Setup Supervisors	47	125	
120	General Clerical	48	125	
118	Scheduling of Manufacturing Operations	49	—	
119	Scheduling of Assembly Operations	50	—	
	Total Department Administration	51	250	
	Premiums	52		
192	Bonus for Night Shift Work	53	90	
193	Wage Adjustments	54	—	
163	Lunch and Wash-up Time	55	90	
196	Suggestion Awards	56	—	
	Total Premiums	57	180	
127	Labor Not in Standard—Misc. Production Labor	58	—	
	Repairs and Maintenance Labor	59		
187	Oil and Clean Machines	60	45	
258, 303	Tools and Machine Repairs and Maintenance	61	—	
	Total Repairs & Maintenance Labor	62	45	
	Repair and Rebuilding	63		
358	Ordnance Returned Goods	64	—	
360	Regular Customer Repairs	65	—	
363, 364	Rebuilding on Production Dept. R and T No.	66	—	
	Total Repair and Rebuilding	67	—	
	Miscellaneous Labor	68		
173	Experimental Work	69	—	
199	General	70	—	
116, 170	Stockmen, Inventory Control	71	—	
	All Other	72	—	
	Total Miscellaneous Labor	73	—	
	Total All Labor	74	2587	
	All Inclusive Ratio (Total all Labor/Stand. Labor)	75	1.72	

*Complete form also has month-to-date columns

FIG. 8–1 (*Continued*)

allowances to be incurred based on scheduled operations for the period. The principal problems, therefore, in designing reports in this area are:
1. Restricting contents to the responsibility involved
2. Making the reports understandable

Restricting Contents of Reports. It is axiomatic that as consideration shifts from top management to lower management, reports shift from summarization to detail. Top management must confine its appraisal of results to major segments of the organization; the control of details must be delegated. In this delegation, however, it is necessary that responsibility be defined clearly. Consequently, there must be no gaps in which operations are not adequately controlled.

In line with the principle of delegation of responsibility and authority, cost control reports should be designed to fit the needs of those concerned. Since reports are costly to prepare, the design is important and only useful data should be included in them. It is in this connection that the previously mentioned questions concerning controllable costs, assessed charges, and interdepartmental charges become important.

There are two schools of thought in this area. It appears that some managements provide data to supervisors which relate to costs not under their control, on the theory that such disclosure gives them greater comprehension of the cost problems of the division as a whole and thus fosters a spirit of teamwork. Other managements appear to believe that any data beyond those immediately useful tend to distract the attention of the supervisor from the essential data relating to his own activities. The choice, perhaps, depends on management's philosophy and the nature and size of the supervisory force. It should be recognized, however, that costs of preparation also are, or ought to be, considered in arriving at the decision.

Examples of Reports. On the preceding and following pages are some examples of types of cost control reports in actual use. Figure 8–1 shows a foreman's weekly labor cost report. Provision is made for the allowed expense, the actual expense, and the variance by accounts.

Figure 8–2 gives a graphic presentation of direct labor performance. Actual labor cost is plotted against standard labor, and the gains and losses are shown.

Figure 8–3 provides for the computation of performance indexes for various costs. In connection with the first index shown, it should be noted that the computations are based on the percentage of capacity attained.

It will be noted that in the aforementioned exhibits the emphasis is placed on the variances, and that every effort is made to highlight the record of performance in the control of costs.

ANALYSIS AND REPORTING OF COST VARIANCES

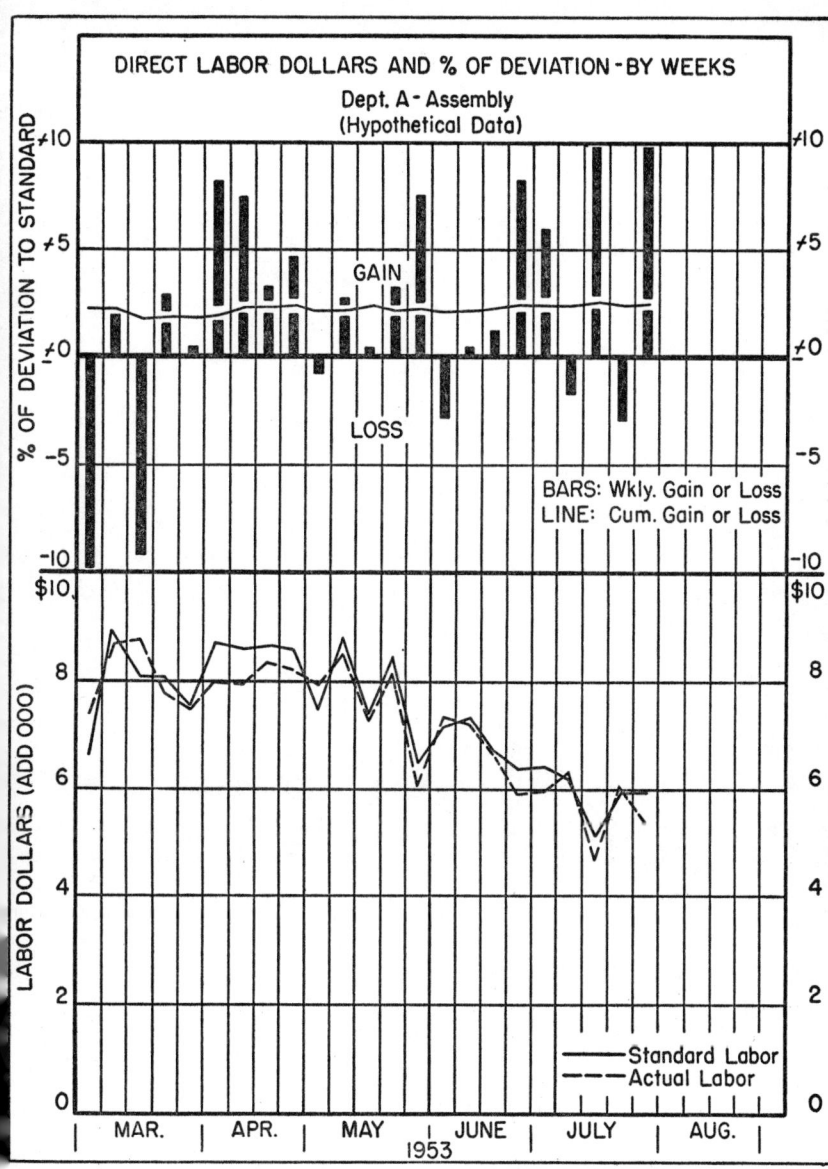

SOURCE: Robert E. Stockmeyer, "Helping the Foreman Control Costs," *N.A.A. Bulletin*, Section 1, Feb., 1954, p. 764.

FIG. 8–2. Direct Labor Dollars and Per Cent of Deviation

*PERFORMANCE INDEXES COMPARING RESULTS AT STANDARD AND ACTUAL

1. Index of Man Hour Usage: (Wages, Benefits, Salaries)
   Actual wages @ % = $
   Standard wages @ % = $
   Gain/Loss   = $
   Performance Index   %
   Performance Index—12 month period

2. Index of Material Usage:
   Value of Material Supplies   = $
   Standard Material Cost of Good Units Produced = $
   Gain/Loss   = $
   Performance Index   %
   Performance Index—12 month period

3. Index of Controllable Expenses: (12000, 13000, 13700)
   Actual Controllable Expenses   = $
   Budgeted Controllable Expenses   = $
   Gain/Loss   = $
   Performance Index   %   %
   Performance Index—12 month period

4. Index of Facility Utilization: (Building & Equipment)
   Actual cost of taxes, dep'n, insurance   = $
   Standard cost of taxes, dep'n, insurance = $
   Gain/Loss   = $
   Performance Index   %   %
   Performance Index—12 month period

5. Index of Overhead Utilization (15500 & 16000)
   Actual cost   = $
   Standard cost   = $
   Gain/Loss   = $
   Performance Index   %   %
   Performance Index—12 month period

* In practice there are also indexes representing categories 1–3, 4 & 5, and 1–5.

SOURCE: Oliver R. Altum, "Production Costing in a Pharmaceutical Company," *N.A.A. Bulletin*, Section 1, Jan., 1955, p. 705.

Part III

BUDGETING AND CONTROLLING TECHNIQUES

CHAPTER 9

SALES

	Page		Page
Purpose of chapter	169	The sales budget	184

Budgeting Sales

	Page
Determination of sales policy	169
Selection of products to be sold	170
Selection of sales method	171
Determination of price	172
Determination of quantities	175
Methods of forecasting sales	175
Jury of executive opinion method	176
Sales force composite method	178
Statistical analyses	179
Combination of methods	179

Controlling Sales

	Page
Interrelation of budgeting and control	184
Sales control standards	185
Determination of standard sales mix	185
Determination of standard order size	187
Standard territorial distribution	188
Sales standards reviewed	189
Comparison of actual and standard	189
Interpretation and action	190
Accounting requirements for controlling sales	191

Purpose of Chapter. Chapter 4 emphasized the position of the sales plan as the cornerstone of the company's entire operating budget. All the operations for the period are keyed to planned sales. It follows, therefore, that the determination of the sales policy and the amounts of products to be sold must be accomplished as the first step in planning for the forthcoming period or periods. And, after the budget is completed and operations are started, there is the continuing duty to analyze sales performance against the budget in order either to attempt to bring performance in line with the plan or to determine when and how the plan itself must be changed. This chapter, therefore, is concerned with both planning and controlling sales performance.

At the outset it must be recognized that sales cannot be planned independently of sales effort. Sales do not just happen. They are the result of sales effort of one type or another. Consequently, the best sales plan, profit-wise, is that one which achieves the best balance between results (income) and efforts (selling costs). In practice, therefore, the planning and control of sales and sales costs must go hand in hand. For convenience, however, it is desirable to separate the two factors of income and cost. The present chapter is confined to sales results and the following chapter to sales efforts.

BUDGETING SALES

Determination of Sales Policy. The determination of sales policy must be related to and made part of the company's entire profit-planning operation. Considerations in profit-planning have already been discussed in Chapter 2. The profit objective, the measurement of this objective, the facts of the fundamental volume-cost-price-profit relationships, and the tools for planning are all assumed to be known to management before attention is paid the specific problem of sales-planning. Granting this to be the case, the sales plan must take into consideration a number of specific sales problems, including the following:

1. Basis of competition—price, or nonprice (e.g., service, delivery, etc.)
2. Product mix in relation to profit margins—promotion of numerous items at varying margins to utilize capacity, as opposed to concentration on high-margin items
3. Method of distribution—direct selling, retail outlets, etc.
4. Geographical distribution of sales
5. Customer mix—concentration on a few large buyers as opposed to a wide market; or concentration vs. diversification of customers in particular industries or geographical areas
6. Development of new products
7. Company's desired share of market

Basically, these questions can be resolved into four main issues:

1. The products to be sold
2. By what methods
3. In what amounts
4. At what prices

Each of these issues is discussed in turn.

Selection of Products To Be Sold. This question has both long-range and short-range significance. It is obviously long-range to the extent that it involves the development of new products and the rearrangement of facilities and resources involved in major changes in product mix. In the short run, however, that is, for the immediate budget period of a year or less, the decision relates primarily to relatively minor shifts in emphasis on the various products for which capacity and resources already exist.

Ideally, every product should earn the same rate of return since, if given a choice, management would concentrate only on the most profitable items. In the short run, however, it frequently happens that there will be considerable variation in the profitableness of the several products. This arises from a number of causes. At any given time some products will be in the process of market development. Either they have not yet reached the planned annual volume, or production difficulties may not yet be smoothed out, or special introductory prices may be in effect as a means of developing the market. Whatever the cause, a substandard profit rate on these products during the forthcoming budget period may be warranted for the sake of profit-maximization in the long run.

In other cases, products may have to be repriced or budgeted in lower volume than originally achieved. In either case, the profit rate drops; but so long as some profit is realizable, management has no immediate alternative to continuing the product in the line for the very practical reason that, even though more profitable substitute products are potentially available, the change-over takes time.

Still other products may be handled on a short-run basis simply because they make *some* contribution to total profit through their utilization of capacity which otherwise management may not be able to use in the immediate future. In extreme cases, such products may even lose money on a total cost basis but be retained because they produce gross income in excess of their out-of-pocket costs.

With the foregoing types of situations in mind, it is readily understood that the short- and long-range considerations in planning may be quite different. Long-range planning is directed toward achieving the desired profitability of all product items, but the immediate budget frequently is aimed at achieving the highest total profit realizable from the products now available. The presence of fixed costs and the rigidity of plant and organizational arrangements thus confront management with two factors which, together, make total volume very important. This need for volume, therefore, commonly results in planning a sales mix which entails a wide range of product profitability.

It is also readily understood that the foregoing factors tend to place short-run planning in conflict with long-run planning. Because of their immediate effect on total volume and total profit, items may be kept in the line which should be dropped to make way for new items which will be more profitable in the future. Profit maximization in the long run may involve present sacrifices of profit. This conflict must be resolved In addition, the necessity for continuous product research and development cannot be overemphasized. The history of industry in this country has been one of product innovations in a constant drive to keep abreast of and forge ahead of competition.

Selection of Sales Method. The question of sales method refers both to the type of sales organization and the channels of distribution. The first question refers to internal matters of responsibility, sales compensation, and promotion of the most effective promotional and sales effort. The second relates primarily to external matters.

In this latter area the manufacturer is faced with a basic problem of how to get those things done in the field which are fundamental requirements to assure sales in sufficient volume, not only currently but over an extended period. A number of alternatives are available, such as sales branches, owned retail outlets, or use of brokers, wholesalers, jobbers, or manufacturers' agents.

The interrelated questions to which answers are required may be summarized as follows:

1. How far should the manufacturer spread his own business structure?
2. What is the most effective method of distribution at both the wholesale and retail level?
3. How broad and deep should distribution coverage be?
4. How much control over legally independent enterprises is desirable or necessary?

Various factors govern the choice, including:

Conditions surrounding the manufacturer (primarily financial)
Nature and extent of the market
Nature of the product or the product line
Availability and competence of distributive outlets

It should be observed, however, that the problem of method, as well as of product selection, is long-range in nature. It is a problem which merits constant study. Changes of methods, however, are not readily made. Consequently, short-range planning usually treats the methods as fixed for the period.

Determination of Price. Price setting obviously should be directed toward profit maximization in the long run. The basic problem, of course, is how much control the manufacturer has over price. Is price set by the market, or does the manufacturer have considerable latitude in price policy determination?

Some of the factors which govern the degree of independence in pricing are:

Special features of the product, of significance to consumers
Competition of directly competing products with little or no differentiation
Competition of substitute products which, though not directly competing, do give the consumer a choice of values
Elasticity of demand
The possible effect of price on the encouragement of new competition

Thus while the range of independence is wide depending on the extent that one manufacturer's product differs from that of others, it is extremely important to judge correctly and recognize the degree of latitude in price policy decisions.

Although cost-plus pricing seems to be the basis of the price structure in a majority of cases, the circumstances related above have lead businessmen to develop a variety of methods and compromises, such as flexible market pricing, pricing by intuition, following the price structure of the principal producer, and other methods which presumably have one characteristic in common. They attempt to lead to establishment of price targets that would yield satisfactory profits when operating at capacity.

The great variety of pricing methods which appear to be used are largely a reflection of managements' lack of knowledge, or lack of confidence in their knowledge, of the basic facts of either the demand or the supply of the product. While the cost-plus pricing method is the most common, it does not necessarily mean that it is the best available method because:

1. It ignores demand. It fails to take account of the buyer's needs and willingness to pay, which govern the sales volume obtainable at each of a series of prices. What people will pay for a product bears no necessary relationship to what it costs any particular manufacturer to make that product.
2. It fails to adequately reflect competition. Buyers' alternatives in the form of competitive and substitute products, the effect of a price upon rivals' reactions and the effect upon the birth of potential competition are all omitted from a simple cost-plus formula. In general, a pricing formula operates to cut off potential profit at the top of the line and cut off potential sales at the bottom of the line, i.e., products which are intensively competitive. Thus in a sense it is a two-edged sword for restricting profits.
3. It overplays the precision of historical costs. In multiple-product firms, the cost of individual products cannot usually be determined exactly, because of the arbitrary nature of allocation of common costs. Equally defensible bases of apportionment yield significantly different product costs. Hence, the figures on full costs used in the formula are generally less exact, even as history, than they appear to be.
4. It is based upon a concept of cost that is frequently not relevant for the pricing decision. It is usually not current costs and certainly not past costs that are needed but forecasts of future costs. For many decisions, moreover, incremental costs rather than full costs are appropriate. Finally, economic costs rather than accounting costs are germane for pricing. As a consequence of inflation, accounting costs may seriously misrepresent true economic costs.[1]

To the extent that the foregoing remarks correctly characterize the shortcomings of accounting data, the accounting profession has a real job on its hands—that of making costs more useful in spite of the obvious difficulties. Actually many companies in recent years have made great strides in improving cost accounting procedures and in developing the concept of different costs for different purposes. Even in these cases,

[1] Joel Dean, "Pricing Policies and Cost Analysis," *National Association of Accountants Conference Proceedings—1949*, pp. 35-36.

however, managements recognize that pricing is a job that requires great flexibility and adaptation to market situations.

We begin our commercial planning a year in advance. The sales and merchandise divisions compile a proposed commercial plan for the coming year, which lists models and quantities, with proposed list prices and proposed discount patterns. For each of these models, we must have an estimated standard cost. From this information, we prepare a tabulation of the standard gross margin by model and the total standard gross margin expressed in dollars and percentage. To be sure of our prospects, we carry this out to a forecast profit and loss statement on which we forecast the variances and expenses and the net profit for the year, but, in many management meetings, the subject never gets beyond the indicated standard gross margin percentage.

If this figure is unsatisfactory, which it usually is for Plan 1, we put together Plan 2. This may consist of changes in proposed prices, quantities and discounts, or it might consist of a change in specifications for certain proposed models, or a different line-up of models. If the revised plan involves no physical change in the merchandise, it is simply a computation job. If, on the other hand, management recommendations indicate physical changes or additions, or deletions from the merchandise line, additional work by the cost group with the engineering department is involved. Usually, the plan finally accepted by management as our program for the coming year is some such number as 67G or 92K, indicating that not only approximately 100 basic plans have preceded it, but that there have been many variations of some of the basic plans!

Do not be misled into believing that list prices are determined solely on the basis of cost and standard gross margin. In our highly competitive business, suggested list prices are primarily established by competition. Obviously, if the basic price level in the industry for a television table model is $199, we could not arbitrarily elect to create a sales program around an RCA Victor table model television line beginning at $259. Although competition is the major factor in establishing price ranges, our standard cost system does provide the necessary tool in further developing and refining our sales program to fit into the price requirements as established by competitive pricing.

Furthermore, it should be pointed out that, in planning a complete sales program, including all models from the lowest price to the more expensive, it is not possible to price every individual model in its logical price sequence based solely on the expected standard gross margin of the individual model. It becomes necessary, sometimes, to knowingly price a model with specific features which will yield somewhat less gross margin than should be forthcoming. In many instances, this is very good business. The total profit for the department may, in such circumstances, even be increased. If, for instance, in the opinion of our commercial people, the total quantity of sales for the year can be substantially increased, thus giving us additional manufacturing volume and (more importantly) additional sales revenue, this type of program pricing can result in substantially increased profit per dollars. It is also possible, under certain circumstances, by including in the line some models which are planned to earn less than the normal standard gross margin, to make sure of the sale of a greater quantity of higher priced models which earn a somewhat better standard gross margin than normal.

This method of forecasting has proven so accurate over a period of years that our management has complete confidence in the standard cost system. As a matter of fact, the accuracy is taken for granted. Experience has shown that, when a forecast sales program carries to the end of the year without major quantity or price changes, the profits earned and the original forecast profit are so close that it is hard to believe.[2]

Determination of Quantities. While the preceding discussion and quotations indicate that price and quantity are closely related, there still remains the question of how much is to be sold *at a price*. The importance of volume has already been recognized. The question of the quantity of sales at a price in the forthcoming period, therefore, takes one of two, or both, forms: how much can be sold, and how much must be sold? The latter question is a matter of budgetary policy and assumes that certain goals exist and have been clearly defined. The former question relates to the state of the market for the company's products at a price and is the most difficult and, at the same time, the most important problem in budgeting.

Methods of Forecasting Sales. How much can be sold at a price is management's important question. In reviewing the various forecasting methods below, it must be recognized that the difficulty of forecasting will vary from company to company and from time to time depending on circumstances. Many companies making and selling nationally advertised products base their sales forecasts on the concept of anticipating their "share of the market." In the first instance, they refer to certain economic indexes or studies which forecast national sales of the line of product. Such forecasts may be broad and related to indexes such as new housing construction, freight car loadings, and the like. In the second step, statistics are developed showing past relationships of the company's share of the market to the national sale of the product. Third, for the immediate future period to be budgeted, estimates are obtained from executives, from the sales force, and from advertising and market research people, as to the company's anticipated share of the market in the coming year.

During and immediately following a protracted period of acute shortages of goods, many companies find that the ability to sell is governed entirely by the ability to produce—plant capacity sets the sales budget. This type of situation, however, cannot be looked upon as normal.

Companies which sell to only a few customers frequently can obtain accurate information concerning those customers' needs for the period, and in such cases forecasting poses no problem. Companies which sell a staple product generally can predict sales volume more easily than those selling style merchandise. Frequently, too, sales of low unit price goods involve less error of prediction than those of high unit price goods.

[2] G. K. Bryant, "Standard Costs in Control and Planning," *N.A.A. Bulletin*, Section 1, May, 1954, pp. 1112–13.

Companies whose sales are controlled by economic conditions have a somewhat different prediction problem from those whose products have a close relationship to climatic conditions. Whatever the degree of difficulty, however, the forecast must be made by whatever means possible, and as accurately as possible.

It must also be recognized that the forecast, to be useful, cannot be made simply in terms of total sales for the budget period. As illustrated in Chapter 4, the sales budget must be stated in quantities as well as dollars, by product items, and by months (or even weeks or days).

Four principal methods of forecasting are commonly recognized:

1. Jury of executive opinion
2. Sales force composite
3. Statistical analyses
4. Combination

Jury of Executive Opinion Method. The first method represents a more or less formal polling of the top executives of the company concerning their ideas as to sales possibilities during the forthcoming period. Where the company does not provide either for the accumulation or the study of relevant forecast data, this method may represent no more than group guessing. The guesses, however, may be quite intelligent if the executives polled have a keen sensitivity to market factors and are in close touch with market operations. In many small companies this method frequently is the only one available. Even in those companies, however, where more elaborate forecasting procedures are used, executives still may be polled for their opinion of the validity of the scientifically determined findings, recognizing that even the most elaborate forecasting methods are not foolproof. Statistical analyses, in particular, assume a continuation of a certain pattern of underlying factors, but this pattern can easily be upset by noneconomic developments such as the outbreak or cessation of war, new legislation, or changes in people's outlook. For example, the quick emergence of a public concern with the relation of cigarette smoking and cancer is a factor which statistical analyses cannot predict. Where a forecast must be based on assumptions in the political, religious, or psychological fields, for example, the normal statistical procedures must be adjusted to one or a series of assumptions, and it is in the selection of these assumptions that the opinion of the executives may be useful. The advantages and disadvantages of the jury of executive opinion method of forecasting have been described as follows:

Advantages—
1. Can be made easily and quickly.
2. May not require the preparation of elaborate statistics.

SALES

3. Brings a variety of specialized viewpoints together for a pooling of experience and judgment.
4. May be the only feasible means of forecasting, in the absence of adequate data.

Disadvantages—
1. Is inferior to facts as a basis of forecasting, since it is based on opinion.
2. Requires costly executive time.
3. Is not necessarily more accurate because opinion is averaged.
4. Disperses responsibility for accurate forecasting.
5. Presents difficulty in making breakdowns by products, time intervals or markets for operating purposes.[3]

Following is an example of how one company uses the method:

The sales forecasting procedure starts with the sales manager. Drawing on his own experience, knowledge of impending sales, and of plant capacity for various products, as well as upon the suggestions and opinions of his branch managers, the sales manager prepares an annual estimate of sales for the coming year. This estimate is broken down to show the product content (types and sizes of machines to be sold), which is of prime importance for planning production.

The sales manager's preliminary forecast is then given to the controller, who has the responsibility of translating it into a forecast profit and loss statement. To do this it is necessary, on the basis of the individual judgment of various executives and on an accurate determination of past results, for him to make a series of assumptions as to costs, labor and manufacturing efficiency, plant capacity, and numerous other factors which may influence the total profit outlook. This phase of the preparation of the forecast is under the active direction of the controller. The company has a costing system which provides the forecaster with up-to-date standard costs (for various types of products) to be used in making cost conversions.

The controller usually discusses the progress of his forecast with the company's principal executives. His forecast therefore represents, to some extent, a blending of their opinions and judgment.

When he has completed his job, the preliminary sales forecast and the forecast profit and loss statement are submitted to the operating committee of the company. This committee is composed of the president, general manager, and the vice-presidents in charge of sales, production, and engineering, and the controller and other top executives. The committee meets in an all-day session to discuss point by point the assumptions which were used in making the forecasts and to approve or correct them. In the event that the basic assumptions are altered, the preliminary forecast must be adjusted and the effect of these changes has to be worked back into the cost and profit statements.

As noted, the sales manager is responsible for making the original estimates of sales, and the controller is responsible for converting these sales into a profit and loss statement. But management, through the medium of the operating committee, assumes responsibility for the assumptions used in setting the final forecast and for seeing that it is achieved.[4]

[3] National Industrial Conference Board, *Forecasting in Industry*, Studies in Business Policy, No. 77, 1957, p. 7.
[4] *Ibid.*, p. 8.

Sales Force Composite Method. Under this method of forecasting sales, the future sales outlook is determined, more or less formally, by polling the sales force. This may be done by the top sales executive or by the salesmen's immediate superiors in the field. Under the more formal method, the salesmen are instructed to report in writing their appraisal of the market, on special forms. Frequently they are supplied with a historical record of their sales to be used as a starting point in the appraisal.

The advantages and disadvantages of the method have been listed as follows:

Advantages—
1. Uses specialized knowledge of men closest to the market.
2. Places responsibility for the forecast in the hands of those who must produce the results.
3. Gives sales force greater confidence in quotas developed from forecasts.
4. Tends to give results greater stability because of the magnitude of the sample.
5. Lends itself to the easy development of product, territory, customer, or salesmen breakdowns.

Disadvantages—
1. Salesmen are poor estimators, being either more optimistic or more pessimistic than conditions warrant.
2. If estimates are used as a basis for setting quotas, salesmen are inclined to understate the demand in order to make the goal easier to achieve.
3. Salesmen are often unaware of broad economic patterns which are shaping future sales and are thus incapable of forecasting trends for extended periods.
4. Sales forecasting is a subsidiary function of the sales force, for which sufficient time may not be made available.
5. Requires an extensive expenditure of time by executives and sales force.
6. Elaborate schemes are sometimes necessary to keep estimates realistic and free from bias.[5]

In spite of the foregoing disadvantages, the *Forecasting in Industry* study previously cited indicates that the method is popular and apparently quite effective in a number of companies where over a period of time the margin of forecast error was only 5 per cent. Apparently, too, a number of devices can be used to lessen the force of the disadvantages, such as:

1. Putting past performance records in hands of salesmen for their guidance in making estimates.
2. Having the regional manager discuss the forecasts with each salesman.
3. Adjusting local advertising and promotional support to the sales forecast (useful only when salesmen receive a commission on sales).
4. Cross checking estimates within the sales department where the department is organized along two or more lines, such as territorial and product divisions.[6]

[5] *Ibid.*, p. 12.
[6] *Ibid.*, p. 13.

Statistical Analyses. A discussion of statistical procedures and of types of data useful in forecasting goes beyond the objectives of this book; this is a special field of knowledge with a large body of literature. It should be recognized, however, that statistical studies can be made of the trend of the company's own sales alone, or in relation to certain selected external factors, and that they may be applied in analyzing general business trends as a background for the company's own forecast. Studies of the latter type, in particular, require specialized training and generally are made only by larger companies which can afford the necessary staff and facilities.

One rather simple statistical procedure, however, which is apparently quite successful in many companies, merits some attention in this work. The method involves essentially only two steps. The first is to analyze past records to determine whether monthly sales of each product, in relation to annual sales, follow a definite pattern. In some companies a more significant relationship may exist between orders received and annual sales. If such a pattern exists and can be determined, then the second step is to divide the actual sales of the month in which the forecast is being made by the percentage of total annual sales represented in the pattern by that month.

For example, if analysis shows that the month of December normally accounts for, say, 10 per cent of the year's sales of a product, and if this December's actual sales of the product amount to 1,000 units, then it may be assumed that sales for the next twelve months will amount to 10,000 units distributed throughout the year in accordance with the monthly pattern. For this method to be useful, a pattern by months must exist. Moreover, the estimate is valid only so long as the conditions prevalent in December continue to hold true. On the other hand, since the estimate is based on actual performance immediately preceding the beginning of the new budget period, it does have the advantage of the greatest possible currency of forecasting data.

The method is particularly useful when used in conjunction with short budget periods, and in this connection it should be noted that many companies today budget for a period of less than a year. Where the method is used in connection with quarterly budgets, it has considerable merit so long as the basic pattern holds true. Moreover, the computation, monthly, of an indicated annual sales volume furnishes a good basis for comparison with budgeted sales as a means of determining when the original forecast must be revised and plans reset.

Combination of Methods. No method of sales forecasting is foolproof. Therefore, whenever possible, a combination of methods should be used. In practice, probably few companies use one method exclusively. And it would seem that even where the sales force composite and statistical methods are used, there still is room for the jury of executive opinion method. In one company, where all three methods are used, the annual sales forecast is a synthesis of:

1. Territory salesman's forecast for his territory.
2. Division manager's forecast for his division.
3. Region manager's forecast for his region.
4. Sales management's forecast for the company.
5. Budget director's forecast for the company based on two statistical methods:
    a) Recent experience, adjusted on five-year data to an annual basis.
    b) Long-term trend method.
6. Executive or top management's economic forecast.[7]

The way in which the foregoing synthesis is developed into a budget is described as follows:

Building the Sales Staff Composite Forecast

In the fall of the year the Budget director prepares a one-year summary of sales, by grade and container, of all significant items sold in each territory or division. The year used includes the last quarter of the preceding calendar year and the first three quarters of the current year. The term, significant items, means those which are important in the sales of a particular territory or division. There are two good reasons for limiting the number of items the salesman is asked to forecast. It can readily be seen that, if a salesman is requested to forecast sales of an item not yet generally sold in his territory, he may make some wild guess to impress the home office. Also, if he has to estimate territory sales for the entire range of products sold in it, he will throw up his hands and ask, "What do they want me to do? Sell or spend my time doing paper work?"

To determine the items on which the salesman should make a forecast, we have followed a "rule-of-thumb." If an item represents less than two per cent of total volume, it is not considered a "significant" item. An exception to this is that we ask every salesman to forecast his sales of all items which we alone sell or which we specialize in. They are items which the company, either for advertising or other reasons, want to sell as widely as possible. Generally, it turns out that we ask each salesman to forecast sales for approximately twenty to twenty-five items out of the more than two hundred which comprise our line. For our forecasting procedure we always work on the theory that, although the region manager has a broad understanding of his region and knows the larger accounts, the territory salesman is closer to all customers than anyone above him. He knows the local conditions and is able to talk to the buyers who are familiar with the community.

The one-year summary of significant items which the budget director prepares for each salesman is in terms of tonnage sold and the salesman supplies his forecast of tonnage, as in the table below. From this table, two other features will be noted. The first is that a five-year classified tonnage summary is appended for the salesman's guidance. The second is that a section for "addi-

[7] C. E. Manteuffel, "A Case Study in Systematic Forecasting," *N.A.A. Bulletin*, Section 1, Mar., 1954, p. 820.

tional items" is included. Each man is familiar with our entire line, and he may feel that he will develop sales of items which have not been significant in his territory in the past year. The form supplied each salesman is, in its general features, as follows:

1954 FORECAST OF SALES
TERRITORY/DIVISION XXX
John Smith

	TONS SOLD YEAR 10/1/52–9/30/53	YOUR ESTIMATE YEAR 1954
Rock—100 lb. Multi-wall Bags............	100	(150)
50 lb. Multi-wall Bags............	150	(200)
Rock Gran—100 lb. Cotton Bags............	200	(175)
Total Rock Sales	700	(800)
Total Evaporated Sales	300	(400)
Total Significant Items	1,000	(1,200)
Miscellaneous Items	100	(100)
Total Tons Sold	1,000	(1,300)
Additional Items	–	(1,500)

Past Five-Year Summary

	ROCK	EVAP.	FLAKE	TOTAL
1949.........................	–	–	–	–
1950.........................	–	–	–	–
1951.........................	–	–	–	–
1952.........................	650	250	75	975
1953.........................	750	350	100	1,200

(Note: Figures in parentheses are those inserted by the salesman.)

Each division manager, using similar data furnished him for his division, prepares an independent estimate of expected sales for his division for the coming calendar year. This is one time we ask our Territory Salesman, Division Managers, and Regional Managers to act independently of each other. In forecasting, we do not want an individual to be influenced by another's thinking.

The underlying information is furnished to the field about November 1, and all estimates are returned directly to the Budget Director by November 15. The Budget Director reconciles or (for lack of a better word) blends each Division Manager's forecast with the total of his Territory Salesmen's forecasts. An example will serve best as an explanation, with attention directed to the "total" and "composite" columns:

	DIV. MGR. FORECAST	TERR. 1 FORECAST	TERR. 2 FORECAST	TOTAL TERRITORY FORECAST	COMPOSITE
Rock A—100 lb. MW....	500	150	300	450	475
50 lb. MW....	–	200	–	200	200
Rock Gran—100 lb. Cotton	200	175	250	425	313
Totals	3,000	1,300	1,500	2,800	2,900

It will be noted in the example Rock A, 50 lb. MW was not a significant item to the division manager or Territory 2. In this case, the salesman's forecast for territory 1 was used as the composite figure for the division. In the case, of Rock A, 100 lb. MV, the division manager forecast 500 tons, whereas the sum of his territory salesman's forecast was only 450 tons. Either the Division Manager was overoptimistic or the territory men were overpessimistic. It will be noted that, for the composite, we took a straight arithmetic average of the two figures. This usually proves fairly accurate. Experience has also shown us that some men are of the over-cautious type, while others will soar to heights all too readily. Knowing the salesmen helps the Budget Director to evaluate the forecasts. Later, partly as a procedure to obtain better forecasts, we advise each man of the final forecast for his territory or division and notify him monthly of results against forecast. A man who is constantly behind forecast will tend to lower his sights on his next forecast, while the man who is constantly ahead will tend to do the opposite.

Contributions to the forecasting process do not stop with divisional sales management. To top sales management, consisting of Vice President-in-charge-of-sales, the sales office supervisor, and their assistants, the Budget Director furnished a five-year summary for each division, showing total tons sold of the three principal types of salt. In return, he receives a forecast for each division, again by November 15. It is to be noted that top sales management deals only in salt-type totals, not individual items, and breaks down its figures for the divisions only.

The budget director takes the forecast of a division as made by the sales management group and averages this total with the composite resulting from the forecasts of the respective Division Manager and his territory salesmen. Assuming that the sales management group expects 3,200 tons from the division, for which figures have already been shown, the procedure would be to average this expectation with the 2,900 composite, arrived at before, resulting in a sales department forecast of 3,050 tons. This figure will be used by sales management as a yardstick, as it is strictly developed by the sales department, although according to budget procedure this forecast may or may not be made by top management.

Averaging-in the Budget Director's Statistical Forecasts

The Budget Director prepares two statistical forecasts of sales by tons, for each division. The first forecast is made by using the third quarter of the current year, seasonally adjusted on a five-year history. For this purpose, records are kept of each divisions' sales, by months, of total tons of each grade of salt. A typical sale of a grade for a year might reflect the following:

MONTH	TONS	PERCENTAGE
January	10	5.0
February	15	7.5
March	5	2.5
April	10	5.0
May	10	5.0
June	15	7.5
July	25	12.5
August	35	17.5
September	40	20.0
October	15	7.5
November	10	5.0
December	10	5.0
Total	200	100.0

It can be seen that the third quarter sales of this particular grade in this particular division amounted to 100 tons out of the total year's sales of 200 tons, or 50 per cent. This would be a highly seasonal sales characteristic. It could just as readily be in any other three-month period, depending on the particular grade and geographic location. Let us assume that the five-year record results in the same seasonal indication and that during the current third quarter this division sold 150 tons. If this is 50 per cent of annual sales, it results in 300 tons, which we put down as our expectancy for the following year's sales of this grade. This is done for each grade in each division and the total for each division is the forecast for the following year.

The second forecast prepared by the Budget Director is the straight-line trend corrected for season variation, using the previous six years as a base. This is also called the method of least squares, or root-mean-square line of best fit. It is prepared for each grade in each division, using the same basic information which was described in connection with the foregoing method.

The Budget Director then prepares his final statistical forecast by projecting the mean of the two statistical forecasts. Generally, the two forecasts will be relatively close. This final statistical forecast is then averaged, in total tons for each division, with the final composite of the sales department. Assume that the statistical mean total for the division referred to before, is 3,100 tons. The final sales department composite was 3,050 tons. Averaging gives a final forecast of 3,075 tons.

The Budget Director then revises the various division forecasts and, in turn, their respective territory figures to reconcile them with the final forecast.

Over-all Economic Adjustment to Forecast by Top Management

It is the responsibility of top management, consisting of the officers of the company, to prepare, either individually or collectively, a general forecast of business conditions, giving an interpretation of its net effect on company sales during the coming year. Consideration is also given to the introduction of a new product, change of company policy, adjustment of prices, or a major advertising program to be undertaken in the following year. This group determines to what extent the particular findings will affect company sales, e.g., business will be off 5 per cent, remain steady, or possibly increase 10 per cent. The Budget Director is advised of top management's decision and he may be instructed to adjust the combined forecast accordingly.

From Tons to Dollars

The Budget Director takes the final forecast of tons of product to be sold by each division and assigns them to each month of the year, based on each respective division's seasonal-to-total sales ratio for the previous three years, regardless of the various grades. The individual seasonal characteristics of the various grades are taken care of in the part they play in determining the monthly seasonal variation in total sales.

The next step is to determine the sales value of these monthly sales. When principal price changes from the current year are known, the forecast for each month's tonnage sales for each division is extended at the average price per ton received for the respective months during the current year. A summary is then prepared reflecting total tons to be sold during the various months of the coming year, and the resulting sales dollars.[8]

[8] *Ibid.*, pp. 820–25.

The Sales Budget. The actual sales budget schedule, similar in form to that illustrated in Chapter 5, is prepared from the forecast. The forecast sets the upper limit on the sales volume that is expected to be obtainable, but there still remain the tasks of (1) relating this volume to the desired utilization of production capacity, and (2) preparing the sales schedules both by products and by time periods, quarters, months, or weeks, depending on circumstances, and in both dollars and units.

With reference to the first task, it is conceivable that the company either cannot or decides not to accept all the business potentially available. Selectivity may be important in achieving the best sales mixture in the interest of profit maximization. It is in this connection that the determination of the budgeted sales requires the cooperation of various segments of management, production, accounting, and sales.

Concerning the second task, it is obvious from previous discussion that a true budgeting plan requires close scheduling of all operations, beginning with sales. Attention is called to this fact, however, that in many businesses there is a sharp distinction between consummated sales and orders taken. Where this is the case, different types of schedules are required; "sales" in the form of orders taken must be distinguished from shipments. The latter control the immediate production plans, while the former represent backlog.

CONTROLLING SALES

Interrelation of Budgeting and Control. The phrase "control of sales" actually has two meanings. The first relates to the decisions reached in the planning stage concerning the where, when, why, how, etc. of sales. This is where the alternatives are considered and the most profitable course of action is adopted. The second meaning relates to the comparison of actual results with the budget and to the analyses which are made to determine:

a) What steps must be taken to make the budget more effective
b) Whether to change the budget

The two meanings obviously are interrelated, first, because the decisions arrived at in the planning phase of control in effect establish the standards to be used in the performance phase, and second, because the information gained through the ceaseless study of sales performance aids in improved planning control in the preparation of new budgets.

The essence of control at the performance stage is the comparison of actual with planned results and the interpretation of the variations to indicate the type of corrective measures that should be taken. The budget is the standard and it is because of this that the establishment of the budget and control of operations under the budget are so closely related. Consequently, discussion of sales control must begin with the analysis of the standards to be established.

Sales Control Standards. The planned sales of Products A, B, and C shown in the budget of Illustrative Company in Chapter 5 constitute the standard total sales of the several products by months and for the budget period. These are based, however, on a number of detailed standards each of which should be carefully established by consideration of the various possible alternatives.

The ultimate objective of the sales plan is to produce the maximum profit consistent with any other goals management may establish. This objective requires consideration of both sales results and costs of sales effort since the two are interdependent. A matching of results and costs is needed in order to determine the best balance. Since, for convenience, the discussion of sales cost control is deferred until the next chapter, it will be assumed for the purpose of this chapter that the proper determinations in this regard have been made. Given the information concerning the volume-cost relationships for various products, the principal considerations in drafting the standard sales objectives refer to sales mix, size of order, and territorial distribution of sales. It should be remembered that, as has previously been pointed out, questions of price, change of products, and change of methods of distribution do not permit managements much freedom of action in the short run, although they are important in the long run.

Determination of Standard Sales Mix. The standard sales mix is that which is determined for the budget being prepared and represents that combination of product sales which will provide the most satisfactory profit under prevailing conditions. If all products and all product lines could be made to earn the same rates of return, the problem of the sales mix as it relates to total profit would be nonexistent. At any given time, however, such a condition seldom prevails. Differences will exist as between commercial business and government business, or between established products and new products, or between sales to one type of outlet and those to another type; and frequently unavoidable differences may exist temporarily within any one of the categories. Since it may be necessary, in the short run, to take some business in all categories, the problem becomes one of selecting the best combination under the circumstances, establishing the sales plan and standards on this basis, and then controlling performance so as to meet the standards.

This can be illustrated by reference to a table of assumed profit rates, based for convenience on sales.

Established products

A	20 per cent
B	18 per cent
C	25 per cent

New product

D	15 per cent
Government work	10 per cent

Let it also be assumed that the total desired profit for the period is $100,000. To earn this profit entirely through the sale of only one of each of the products would require sales as follows:

Product A only	$ 500,000
Product B only	555,555
Product C only	400,000
Product D only	666,666
Government work only	1,000,000

For reasons of policy as well as market and production limitation, it may be necessary to sell all products. Therefore, the problem is one of striking the best balance possible under the circumstances. Sales ability is one circumstance, but so is production ability. For example, if it be assumed that the several products require productive capacity in proportion to sales volume, and if it be further assumed that the practical capacity limits total sales to $600,000, it is obvious that $100,000 of profit simply cannot be earned solely through government business. If the management wished to take all the government business possible, in combination with only the most profitable of the other products (Product C), the maximum amount that could be taken, to earn a total of $100,000 with total sales of $600,000, would be $333,333, determined as follows:

Let government business equal x.

$$.10x + .25(600,000 - x) = 100,000$$
$$.10x + 150,000 - .25x = 100,000$$
$$.15x = 50,000$$
$$x = 333,333$$

Proof

Government sales	$333,333 @ 10% =	$ 33,333
C sales	266,667 @ 25% =	66,667
Total	$600,000	$100,000

Similarly, it would be impossible for the company to devote all its capacity to promotion of the new product (Product D) since $600,000 of sales at 15 per cent would not yield $100,000 of profit. If the company wished to sell as much of D as possible, again in combination with Product C, the maximum amount of D that it could afford to sell would be $500,000, determined as follows:

$$.15D + .25(600{,}000 - D) = 100{,}000$$
$$.15D + 150{,}000 - .25D = 100{,}000$$
$$.10 = 50{,}000$$
$$D = 500{,}000$$

Sales of D	$500,000 @ 15% =	$ 75,000
Sales of C	100,000 @ 25% =	25,000
Total	$600,000	$100,000

When all products are to be sold, the computations become more involved, but the foregoing examples portray the type of determination that should underlie the selection of the sales plan and the resultant sales performance standards.

Determination of Standard Order Size. Planning the total sales of each product item is not enough. Whether these sales are obtained in large or small orders is also important. While this chapter does not discuss the costs of selling as such, the fact remains that the form in which sales are made can be just as important as the total amount. We were concerned above with selective selling as it relates to products; here we are concerned with selectivity as it relates to customers.

A careful analysis of customers and the cost of selling them and servicing their orders will disclose many surprising situations in which such cost may actually exceed the total margin obtained from product sales. Sometimes the orders are too small to be processed and filled at a profit. Special handling or shipping requirements may eat up the profit on the transaction. The cost of serving and selling an account may be all out of proportion to its profit potentialities. The skilled cost analyst will not be content to accept these conditions on the explanation that they are necessary in order to have complete coverage of the market. He will rightfully question whether there is any such thing as complete coverage under any condition and will be the first to demonstrate that handling a volume of unprofitable business is too high a price to pay for a nebulous object.

In studying the relative profitability of customers, it is necessary to determine the break-even point, at which distribution costs and gross margins are equal. This will lead to the establishment of the minimum order which the company can accept profitably. The results of a customer profitability cost analysis may indicate that a great share of the total profit of the company results from a relatively small percentage of total orders and that a small, but nevertheless important, percentage of orders results in a loss. Such an analysis is shown in [Fig. 9–1]. With this knowledge, salesmen should concentrate efforts on bringing all orders up to the minimum.[9]

Granting that various sizes of orders may have to be accepted in achieving the desired total sales, a standard average size should be determined and used as a basis for measuring performance under the budget.

[9] Lawrence L. Ellis, "What Cost Reduction Means in Distribution," *N.A.A. Bulletin,* Section 1, Sept., 1950, pp. 43–44.

188 BUDGETING AND CONTROLLING TECHNIQUES

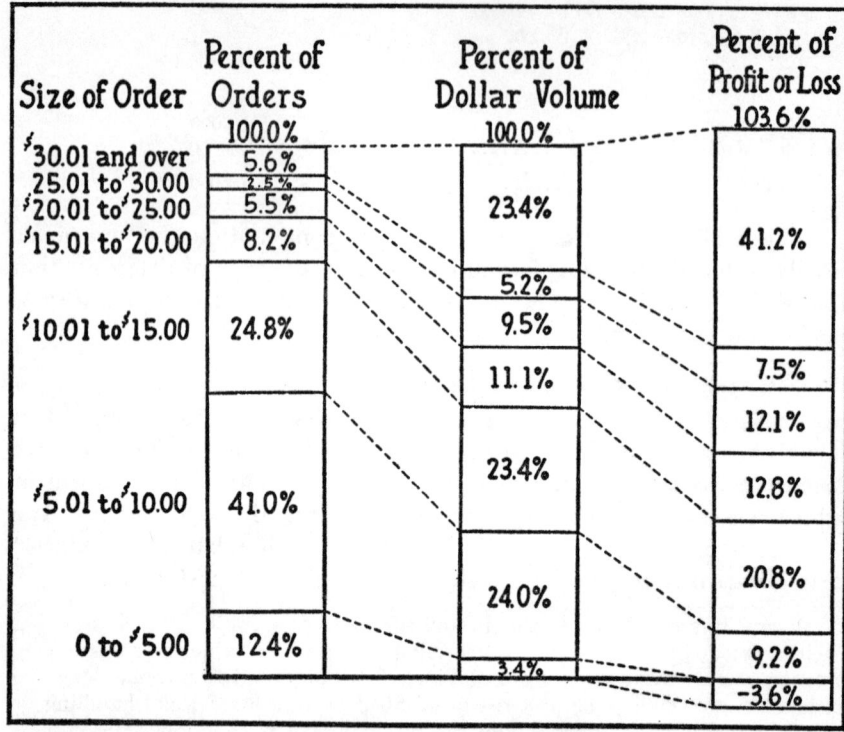

Source: Lawrence L. Ellis, "What Cost Reduction Means in Distribution," *N.A.A. Bulletin,* Section 1, Sept., 1950, p. 44.

Fig. 9-1. Analysis of Profit by Size of Orders

Standard Territorial Distribution. Another factor in the determination of planned total sales volume is the territorial origin of the sales. Given a number of established sales territories, it is essential that each territory contribute its share of total sales. The same is true of individual salesmen, but it can be assumed here, for reasons of convenience, that control of salesmen's efforts is achieved through control of the territories. Aside from the cost control aspects of a proper territorial distribution of sales, the importance of breaking total planned sales down to territorial budgets lies in its usefulness in analyzing sales performance under the budget.

If total sales are planned in the amount of $100,000 for a period, and the sales actually amount to only $85,000, correct explanation of the difference must begin with detailed observations, first at the territorial level, and then at the salesmen's level. Variations simply cannot be explained in terms of total sales alone.

How much volume and what proportion of total volume should be produced by a particular territory is a function of two factors. The first is the sales potential, and this is determined by the sales forecast. The second is the comparative cost of selling and delivering in a particular territory. Some territories cannot be as profitable as others. Thus the territorial mix is almost as significant as the product mix, and it is necessary to direct the sales effort, and hence to apportion the sales, in the most profitable manner. Achieving the best balance of profit contributions from the several territories requires a selective determination of territorial quotas. In this process, of course, signs may be developed which point toward a rearrangement of territories.

Sales Standards Reviewed. Whether in relation to total sales, product item sales, average size of order, or territorial sales, the budget, as finally determined, sets the standards of performance. It is by comparison of actual results with these standards that sales performance control is started. The sales schedule appearing in the operating budget, therefore, is supported by numerous detail schedules. Each sets the performance standard for some detailed operation. Sales are budgeted both in dollars and units for:

> Entire company by product items
> Territories by product items
> Districts by product items
> Salesmen by product items

All schedules also are broken down to time periods. Other items also may be scheduled, particularly the profit contribution of each of the foregoing divisions.

Comparison of Actual and Standard. With the foregoing standards established and constituting, in the aggregate, the budgeted sales, the first step in controlling sales under the budget is that of comparing actual sales with the planned sales and reporting the comparisons in a useful form. This step is then followed by interpretation and managerial action.

The method of reporting performance is easily arrived at if the standards themselves are properly defined and detailed. The principal decision concerns whether to report in monetary terms and/or unit terms, or in percentages of achievement, or both. The facts to be reported, however, should not be in question. Following are examples of performance reports.

The first example shown in Figure 9–2 reports graphically on performance of various subdivisions. The second example (Figure 9–3) shows variation of subdivisional reporting.

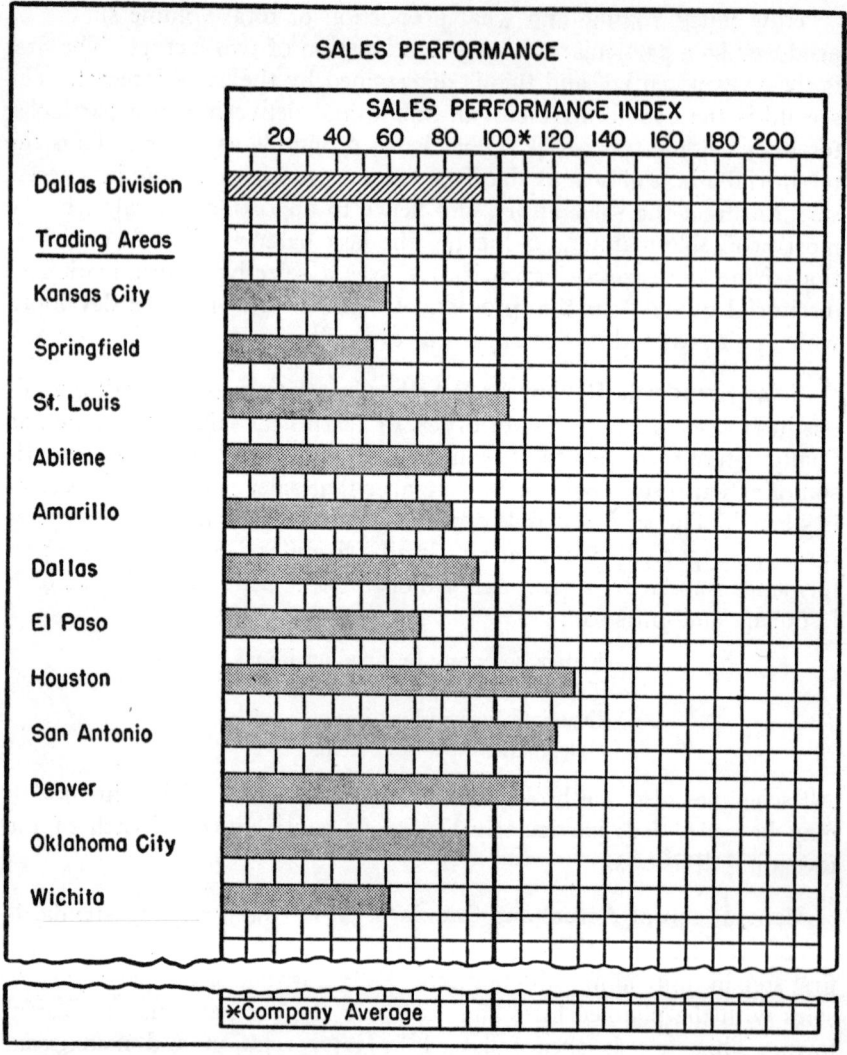

Source: J. S. Ebright, "The Accountant's Part in Market Development," *N.A.A. Bulletin*, Section 1, June, 1952, p. 1232.

FIG. 9–2. Sales Performance Index

The basic scheme in reporting is that of comparison—showing variations from the budget. Most commonly the data are shown for the current month (or shorter period) and the budget period to date on a cumulative basis.

Interpretation and Action. The use of the budget as a tool of control stops when significant comparisons have been made of results and plans.

COMPARATIVE NET SALES TO DATE BY DISTRICTS AND TERRITORIES									
District and Territory	Total Net Sales	% Inc. or dec. last year	Quota	% Performance against quota	Total selling expense	Expense percentage to sales	Dollar sales by product group			
							A	B	C	etc.
Los Angeles	$	%	$	%	$	%	$	$	$	$
Salesman Jones Smith Brown, etc.										
Portland										
Salesman Doe Roe etc.										

SOURCE: "Cost Control for Marketing Operations—Order Getting," Research Series, No. 26, N.A.A. Bulletin, June, 1954, p. 1374.

FIG. 9-3. Comparative Net Sales to Date by Districts and Territories

If the forecasts and planning determinations are valid, failure to achieve planned results generally rests with personnel. Budget comparisons indicate and localize the areas of poor performance, but the corrective steps now become the responsibility of sales management. Operational weaknesses are corrected by managerial action, not figures. It is the responsibility of the budget analyst, however, to indicate to the sales management the areas of poor performance.

There is always the possibility, however, that the budget standards themselves are faulty and incapable of achievement. Consequently, the budget analyst must always be alert to the possible need for a revision of the sales plan.

Accounting Requirements for Controlling Sales. As is indicated above, the control of sales involves control both at the planning stage and the executory stage of operations. At the planning stage, there are essentially two problems—determining what can be done, and determining what should be done. These are in essence the problems of forecasting and differential analysis.

With respect to the problem of forecasting sales, accounting requirements are related only to the company's own experience, but this experience should be adequately reflected in the accounts. The essential

ACCOUNT CODING PLAN

Product Code			Customer Code		
Product Line	Product Item	Order Size	Customer Class	Territory	Salesman
0	0	0	0	0	0

Product Code	ACCOUNT CODE		Customer Code	ACCOUNT CODE	
	Product Code	Customer Code		Product Code	Customer Code
Line I	100	000	Customer Class A	000	100
Product A	110	000	Territory X	000	110
Order Size 1	111	000	Salesman 1	000	111
Order Size 2	112	000	Salesman 2	000	112
Order Size 3	113	000	Salesman 3	000	113
Product B	120	000	Territory Y	000	120
Order Size 1	121	000	Salesman 4	000	124
Order Size 2	122	000	Salesman 5	000	125
Order Size 3	123	000	Salesman 6	000	126
Product C	130	000	Territory Z	000	130
Order Size 1	131	000	Salesman 7	000	137
Order Size 2	132	000	Salesman 8	000	138
Order Size 3	133	000	Salesman 9	000	139
			Customer Class B	000	200
Line II	200	000	Territory X	000	210
Product D	240	000	Salesman 1	000	211
Order Size 1	241	000	Salesman 2	000	212
Order Size 2	242	000	Salesman 3	000	213
Order Size 3	243	000	Territory Y	000	220
Product E	250	000	Salesman 4	000	224
Order Size 1	251	000	Salesman 5	000	225
Order Size 2	252	000	Salesman 6	000	226
Order Size 3	253	000	Territory Z	000	230
Product F	260	000	Salesman 7	000	237
Order Size 1	261	000	Salesman 8	000	238
Order Size 2	262	000	Salesman 9	000	239
Order Size 3	263	000	Customer Class C	000	300
			Territory X	000	310
			Salesman 1	000	311
			Salesman 2	000	312
			Salesman 3	000	313
			Territory Y	000	320
			Salesman 4	000	324
			Salesman 5	000	325
			Salesman 6	000	326
			Territory Z	000	330
			Salesman 7	000	337
			Salesman 8	000	338
			Salesman 9	000	339

FIG. 9–4. Sales Chart of Accounts

data for this purpose comprise a historical record of information in detail concerning:

Total sales—in dollars

By products and product lines
By territories
By salesmen
By classes of customers

Product item of line sales—in dollars and units

By territories
By salesmen
By classes of customers
By order sizes

It is only through the use of such data that the company's sales trends can be determined and correlations with external data computed and tested.

Given the sales possibilities for the various products, there remains the planning problem of determining the most profitable course of action. The profit contribution of products, territories, classes of orders, and so on are the essential data for this purpose. But these involve, in turn, cost data as to both product costs and costs of sales effort.

The types of data required for performance control are governed by those used at the planning stage. The only accounting problem peculiar to this stage is that of timeliness in assembling, classifying, and reporting the data.

The chart of accounts, obviously, is the key to the basic data needed in the control of sales. Considering only the sales and excluding the cost phase of sales control, it is apparent that the sales accounts must provide for numerous classifications of data. Figure 9-4 is one example of a sales chart of accounts.

While the following account classification pertaining to sales may be fairly representative of those commonly used, it is not established as a model. Accounts, to be useful in budgetary control of sales, must be organized to satisfy the requirements in each case.

CHAPTER 10

MARKETING AND DISTRIBUTION COSTS

	Page		Page
Purpose of chapter	194	**Controlling Marketing and Distribution Costs**	
Budgeting Marketing and Distribution Costs		Control procedures affected by nature of costs	207
Relation to sales budgeting	196	Controlling fixed marketing and distribution costs	209
Nature of the costs	197	Controlling the variable costs of order-filling	209
Budgeting the fixed costs	198	Controlling variable warehousing costs	210
Budgeting the variable costs resulting from sales	198	Controlling variable transportation costs	210
Budgeting variable sales compensation costs	199	Controlling variable clerical costs	214
Budgeting variable warehousing costs	200	Controlling advertising and sales promotion costs	214
Budgeting variable transportation costs	201	Controlling selling costs	217
Budgeting variable clerical costs	202	Controlling marketing administration costs	218
The managed costs of obtaining sales	202	Controlling direction of sales efforts	218
Budgeting advertising and sales promotion costs	203		
Budgeting selling costs	206		
Budgeting marketing administration costs	207		

Purpose of Chapter. In this chapter we are dealing with the costs associated with the flow of goods to customers. These costs frequently are referred to only as marketing costs. When the two terms "marketing" and "distribution" are used, the latter term generally refers only to the physical handling of the goods, the former term applying to all the other marketing activities. The particular terminology is unimportant so long as it is understood that the present chapter deals with those costs which are incurred in getting and filling orders. That these costs are many and varied is illustrated by the following functional classification of marketing and distribution expenses provided for in the uniform accounting manual of a manufacturing industry:

1. Investment in finished goods:
    Taxes on stock
    Insurance on stock

2. Storage of finished goods:
    Rental expenses, or
    Maintenance and repairs to buildings
    Taxes on buildings
    Insurance on buildings
    Heat, light and power
    Outside storage space

MARKETING AND DISTRIBUTION COSTS

3. Inventory control, finished goods:
    Salaries—stock-record clerks
    Salaries—merchandise distribution (allocation of stock to district and branch warehouses and preparation of orders on factory)
    Overhead—space, equipment, supplies, and supervision charges

4. Order assembly (physical handing):
    Salaries—warehouse labor
    Overhead—space, equipment, supplies, and supervision charges

5. Packing and shipping:
    Material
    Labor
    Overhead—space, equipment, supplies, and supervision charges

6. Transportation (on merchandise shipped from factory or branch to customer and from branch to branch, and on returned goods):
    Freight
    Truck
    Express
    Parcel post
    Transportation on consigned merchandise, factory to branch

7. Sales solicitation:
    Salaries—salesmen
    Commissions—salesmen
    Commissions—agents
    Commissions—brokers
    Traveling expenses—salesmen
    Entertainment—salesmen
    Overhead:
        Salaries—sales executives
        Salaries—merchandise department managers
        Salaries—district branch managers
        Sales employment and personnel
        Sales training
        Sales research
        Sales engineering service
        Adjustment
        Sales records
        Space and equipment charges

8. Advertising:
    Advertising space:
        Newspapers
        Magazines
        Posters
        Outdoor signs
        Electric signs
        Advertising agency services
        Art work—outside
        Radio

Displays
Motion pictures
Electros
Overhead:
Salaries—advertising managers and assistants
Advertising expenses
Space and equipment charges

9. Order entry:
Salaries—clerical
Overhead—space, equipment, supplies, and supervision charges

10. Billing:
Salaries—clerical
Overhead—space, equipment, supplies, and supervision charges

11. Credit extension:
Salaries—clerical
Overhead—space, equipment, supplies, and supervision charges

12. Accounts receivable.
Salaries—clerical
Overhead—space, equipment, supplies, and supervision charges [1]

The foregoing classification obviously would not apply uniformly to all companies. Nevertheless it serves to show the comprehensiveness of the costs under consideration and to hint at the budgetary problems involved. The purpose of this chapter is to discuss (1) the problems and practices in budgeting these costs, and (2) methods of control.

BUDGETING MARKETING AND DISTRIBUTION COSTS

Relation to Sales Budgeting. It was pointed out in the previous chapter that sales and sales costs are interdependent. The formulation of the most profitable sales plan cannot be independent of consideration of the related costs of order-getting and order-filling. In the prebudget planning of what to sell, where, in what quantities, and at what price, the interrelation between sales income and sales costs must be carefully analyzed. For the purpose of this section of the present chapter, however, it is assumed that those analyses have been made. At this point, consequently, we are concerned only with building the budget schedules of marketing and distribution costs to fit in the framework of sales decisions already made.

[1] Charles H. Sevin, "Distribution and Administrative Cost Analysis," pp. 870–72 in *Industrial Accountant's Handbook,* Wyman P. Fiske and John A. Beckett (eds.). Copyright, 1954, by Prentice-Hall, Inc., Englewood Cliffs, N.J. The functions and the primary expense accounts are based, in part, on those suggested by the *Uniform Accounting Manual for the Rubber Manufacturing Industry,* published by The Rubber Manufacturers Association, Inc.

Nature of the Costs. Because of the variety of activities and costs in the marketing and distribution of products, the presentation of budgetary methods related thereto can encompass a great deal of detail and repetition. The outline presented above shows twelve areas of activity. It would be possible to take each one in turn and illustrate the budgetary procedure related thereto. To some extent this is done in the succeeding pages of this section, but it seems more important, first, to view the costs as a whole and attempt to formulate a pattern of behavior. An understanding of the nature of the costs will serve to show the objectives to be achieved, and the extent to which the budgeted costs result from decisions already made.

Whether the marketing and distribution costs be classified as above, or simply as order-getting and order-filling costs, or as

1. Direct selling expense
2. Advertising and sales promotional expense
3. Transportation expense
4. Warehousing and storage
5. General distribution expense

in the classification presented by Heckert and Willson,[2] they all fall into three basic categories for budget purposes. These categories are:

1. Fixed or capacity costs
2. Variable or volume costs resulting from sales
3. Managed costs of obtaining sales [3]

In this classification the fixed or capacity costs of marketing and distribution are those costs which tend to remain the same throughout *several* budget periods. Other than for price changes, they will not be changed except through revision of the sales organization or sales methods. These costs include "the relatively permanent administrative staffs related to selling, advertising, warehousing and handling, credits and collections, and any other distribution activities, as well as the costs of the permanent facilities used by those departments."

The variable costs resulting from sales comprise principally the non-fixed costs associated with order assembly, packing and shipping, transportation, sales solicitation, order entry, billing, and accounts receivable. These costs result from sales and are true volume costs. It should be noted in this connection that the author conceives that sales commissions, for example, are a cost resulting from sales, rather than a cost of obtaining sales, since commissions are not earned unless sales are effected. It should also be noted that many of the variable costs in this category are not necessarily wholly variable with sales volume, but are

---

[2] *Business Budgeting and Control* (New York: The Ronald Press Co., 1955), p. 231.
[3] Cf. Sterling K. Atkinson, *N.A.A., 1947, Conference Proceedings*, pp. 88–95.

semi-variable in nature. Moreover, their variability will differ depending on whether sales volume is measured in physical or monetary terms. For example, while sales commissions frequently are related to money values, packing costs more commonly are a function of physical quantities.

The so-called "managed" costs of obtaining sales are peculiar to marketing activities. Many of them are in the nature of appropriated costs, determined in fixed amounts for the budget period. They differ from fixed costs in that their amounts are newly determined for each budget period in relation to the sales objectives of the period. The advertising appropriation is a common example of this type of expense.

Other managed costs are variable in that they can be increased or decreased at the will of management. But the variability is not necessarily based on sales, or to the extent it is so based, the variability ratio may be an inverse one. As sales fall, effort in the form of travel and customer calls may be intensified.

While the foregoing classification of marketing and distribution costs is not a hard and fast one (any classification of costs according to variability must be relative), it is a convenient device for studying the budgetary problems in the area. Its usefulness lies in the fact that, regardless of the number of activities encompassed by the sales organization, or the number of territories and other classifications, all activities can be analyzed in the same manner. All costs must of necessity fall into one of only three classes.

Budgeting the Fixed Costs. Budgeting fixed marketing and distribution costs is no different from budgeting fixed manufacturing or fixed administrative costs. The principal problem is that of determining what costs are expected to remain unchanged (except, perhaps for price changes) over a certain range of operations—and the extent of the range. Once that is determined, and assuming that current operations are expected to fall within the specified range, the data are assembled in the budget schedules merely by reference to preceding budgets, after giving consideration to any plans for revision of the sales organization or sales methods. Referring to the preceding outline by Sevin, this procedure automatically disposes of a portion of the costs in each of the twelve groups of distribution expenses.

Budgeting the Variable Costs Resulting from Sales. These costs, as indicated above, are principally the nonfixed costs associated with order assembly, packing and shipping, transportation, sales solicitation, order entry, billing, and accounts receivable. Actually, they are the nonfixed costs of sales compensation, warehousing, transportation, and clerical work.

In general, these costs can be budgeted on the basis either of percentages of sales or unit standards.[4] The first basis, however, has its limitations in part because of the semi-variable nature of some expenditure items, and in part because factors other than sales may govern the variability. Unit standards usually are preferable and are established by methods applicable to standard cost procedures generally.

Steps taken to establish standards for order-filling costs are:

1. Broad functions are broken down into work centers in which operations are reasonably homogeneous. Elements in the function which require thinking and judgment (e.g. supervision of others' work) are separated from elements which are repetitive and mechanical in nature, for operations of the latter type can be standardized while operations of the former type cannot. An individual work center should be under a single responsibility although the same person may supervise more than one work center.
2. The independent variables influencing cost in each work center are determined by analysis of the work done. To the extent possible, these variables are reduced in number by standardizing operations and conditions under which the work is done.
3. A unit is selected for measuring production in each work center. This unit should (1) fairly reflect the principal activity in the center and (2) be one for which production records can be kept without undue clerical expense.
4. Physical standards are set, based upon past experience modified by judgment or upon industrial engineering studies. These standards provide the basis for budgeting the number of man-hours and employees, quantity of supplies, and any other items needed to handle the anticipated work load. Physical standards also are used to make unit comparisons with actual performance and to aid in analysis of cost variances by source and cause.
5. Manpower budgets and other physical budgets are translated into budgeted costs. These budgets provide financial goals and dollar measures of the significance of variances from budgets.[5]

It is understood, of course, that the unit standards are translated into budget schedules by reference to the expected volume of sales activity.

Budgeting Variable Sales Compensation Costs. Variable sales compensation costs arise only if the plan of compensation of salesmen provides for commissions or bonuses which depend in some degree on sales actually effected. Where this is the case, the amounts can readily be scheduled by reference to the scheduled sales. In the case of Illustrative Company, the compensation was budgeted merely by applying the uniform commission percentage to the scheduled sales of each month.

[4] "Cost Control for Marketing Operations—Order Filling," Research Series, No. 27, *N.A.A. Bulletin*, Section 2, Aug., 1954, pp. 1649–51.
[5] *Ibid.*, p. 1651.

It should be noted that frequently different rates apply to different products and if a bonus arrangement is in effect, the bonus will not be a wholly variable cost.

Budgeting Variable Warehousing Costs. Storage costs of finished product can arise in connection with either public warehouses or company-owned warehouses. In the former case the costs tend to be solely of the variable type. The cost depends, however, on the amount and duration of the storage and handling. Since these are controlled in part by sales effected and in part by the general operating plan, the cost is in part a cost resulting from sales and in part a managed cost of obtaining sales.

In the case of company-owned warehouses there is a combination of fixed and variable costs and also of variable costs resulting from sales and managed costs of obtaining sales. The nature of the costs involved is indicated by the following subaccounts used in connection with one of a number of warehouses operated by one firm:

13. Salaries and wages
20. Automotive operating costs
24. Storage and shipping supplies
32. Telephone and telegraph
33. Electricity
34. Heating
37. Pallet materials
64. Rental on real estate
77. Maintenance and repair of equipment
78. Maintenance and repair of building
81. Depreciation on equipment
84. Fire and general insurance
93. Real and personal property taxes [6]

Typical warehousing operations include:

Receiving, regular
Receiving, carload
Bin stockkeeping
Bin order-filling
Light bulk stockkeeping
Heavy bulk stockkeeping
Assembly—B/L—ship
Inventory taking [7]

The nonfixed costs, consisting primarily of the labor costs of the foregoing operations, can best be incorporated in the budget on the basis of flexible cost schedules. These in turn should be based on unit stand-

[6] "Cost Control for Marketing Operations—Order Filling," Research Series, No. 27, *N.A.A. Bulletin*, Section 2, Aug., 1954, p. 1655.
[7] *Ibid.*, Exhibit 2, p. 1656.

ards developed for each operation. Since the total activity of a warehouse will depend on the amount of sales, the foregoing variable costs will be budgeted in relation to the scheduled sales. It should be recognized that where a number of warehouses are operated in different geographical locations, the activity in a particular warehouse will be governed, not by total sales, but by sales in that area.

Budgeting Variable Transportation Costs. The importance of these costs to budgeting depends in part on whether they are absorbed by the company or charged to the customer. Even in the latter case, however, the company's share may be sizable, depending on the nature of its operations. The variety of transportation charges on finished product is illustrated by the following list of accounts used by one company:

40. Transportation Charges on Finished Goods
    1. Between production plant warehouses
    2. Between production plant warehouses and temporary warehouses
    3. From production plant to distribution and transit warehouses
    4. Between warehouses
    6. To customers from production plant—by railroad
    7. To customers from production plant—by truck
    8. To customers from outside warehouses—by railroad
    9. To customers from outside warehouses—by truck
    10. Transportation on export sales
    11. Special charges for protection (against freezing, etc.)
    12. Fire and general insurance on goods in transit [8]

It is obvious from the foregoing list of charges that a number of variable factors must be considered in budgeting transportation costs. Location of customers and method of shipment are factors which tend to stress the relation between sales and costs. On the other hand, intracompany shipments conceivably may be based on other factors than sales, or to the extent sales are a controlling factor, the costs may have an inverse relation to sales. Where standard shipments to known points are common, standard costs can be determined for use in the budget schedules. Where, however, special situations are the rule, requiring in each case special routing and analysis by the traffic department, the budget figures may have to be based on past experience, giving effect to sales volume and other known variables.

Where the company maintains its own transportation facilities, standards to be used in budget schedules can be more readily determined. Typical costs include:

Fixed charges
Mileage charges
Drivers and helpers

[8] *Ibid.*, p. 1661.

Insurance
License fees
Travel expense
Tolls
Cargo handling
Miscellaneous [9]

Budgeting Variable Clerical Costs. Clerical effort is involved in all the marketing and distribution activities. Much of it is a fixed cost and presents no short-term budget problem, although for long-term budgeting the problems of work simplification are extremely important. The variable clerical costs which are primarily associated with order-filling should be budgeted on the basis of flexible cost schedules related to the specific activity. For this purpose, unit standards are desirable.

The Managed Costs of Obtaining Sales. As pointed out previously, these costs are the nonfixed costs which are planned for the purpose of obtaining sales. From period to period they do not necessarily bear a fixed relation to sales but represent heavier or lighter doses of sales effort depending in part on the state of the market, and in part on management's selection of an over-all operating plan designed to obtain that combination of costs and results which will maximize profits in the long run. Some of these costs may be determined in fixed amounts for a budget period, based on the budgeted sales, but with no expectation that they will vary with sales during the period. Generally, however, management will feel free to make budget revisions where deemed necessary to achieve budgeted sales—to the extent that changes can be made on short notice. For example, a management may decide to increase the advertising appropriation to bolster sagging sales, but its freedom to do so may be limited by the time requirements of obtaining space and mapping the campaign.

The difference between the budgeting of order-getting costs and that of other costs is brought out in an explanation appearing in one company's budget manual:

> Sales force, advertising media, and deals are all tools for getting and maintaining business. They are controllable in the sense that the management can change them at will; however, they do not fall into the usual classes of fixed, semi-variable, or directly variable expenses. Certainly they are not fixed. If they were to be classified as variable, they would be variable only in relation to sales. To budget the amount of selling expenses as a predetermined percentage of sales would be to prestate the amount of sales, whereas they depend in a large part upon the selling efforts to be put forth. . . . To budget sales . . . without relation to selling efforts, advertising and promotional deals and then to budget selling expenses as a predetermined percentage of the budgeted sales

[9] *Ibid.*, p. 1664.

MARKETING AND DISTRIBUTION COSTS 203

is to oversimplify the whole matter of determining the selling effort and expenses and resulting sales volume.[10]

The principal types of order-getting costs are those associated with advertising and sales promotion, selling, and marketing administration, although the latter is also partly associated with order-filling costs. Each of these is discussed in turn.

Budgeting Advertising and Sales Promotion Costs. The principal problems in this connection are (1) how much to spend, and (2) where and how to spend it. Much has been written on the first question but, unfortunately, the question is one of the most difficult for management to answer scientifically.

One author lists the following factors as determinants of how much to spend:

1. *How large is the market?* How many customers should be reached? Is it a newly developed market or a market nearly saturated?
2. *What are the characteristics of the potential customers?* Are they widely scattered geographically or concentrated? In what economic groups—age groups—which sex—what economic levels?
3. *How well established is the product?* Will reminder advertising alone stimulate sales, or does the selling involve acceptance of new ideas as well as a new brand?
4. *What is the product's competition*—with respect to price—with respect to promotion expenditures?
5. *How responsive is the product to advertising?* Here, historical records of past advertising expenditures on a percentage basis of dollar sales or on a unit basis are most helpful. To what type of advertising has it been most responsive?
6. *What advertising is suitable and what is available* and what are its costs?
7. *How much promotion* will the gross margin and anticipated volume afford?
8. *How much money* is needed to do a minimum advertising job and how much to do an optimum job?
9. *How rapidly* is it wise to try to reach the ultimate sales potential in the light of the answers to questions (7) and (8)?[11]

The N.A.A. research study (Research Series, No. 26) lists the following guides:

1. Past experience expressed in ratios of advertising and sales promotion expenditures to sales.
2. Amount of advertising and promotion being carried on by competitors.

[10] "Cost Control for Marketing Operations—Order Getting," Research Series, No. 26, *N.A.A. Bulletin,* June, 1954, p. 1353.
[11] Charles G. Mortimer, Jr., "How Much Should You Spend on Advertising?" pp. 112–14 in *Advertising Handbook,* Roger Barton (ed.). Copyright, 1950, by Prentice-Hall, Inc., Englewood Cliffs, N.J.

3. Specific objectives such as introduction of a new product or a given increase in consumer recognition for a brand name.
4. Tests to determine results that can be expected from increments in expenditure on given types of advertising and sales promotion.
5. What the company can afford to spend for increased sales volume after considering cash needs for other purposes.
6. What the company should spend to gain efficient utilization of manufacturing and warehousing facilities through continuous movement of inventories.[12]

The cornerstone of the analysis is the effectiveness of advertising and sales promotion expenditures. The matching of efforts against results should be the basic consideration in budgeting these costs. Unfortunately, such matching is extremely difficult except in broad, general terms. Ideally, it would seem that the total budgeted expenditure should be built from the bottom up, determining the requirements for each product, each locality, and each medium and thus arriving at the total. In practice, however, it frequently is necessary to work down from the top since it is easier to establish a measure of over-all effectiveness of expenditures than it is of detail effectiveness. A practical short-term approach to the problem, but one which also illustrates the basic weakness in this area, is to start with last year's expenditures and attempt to measure the effect of increased dosages.

Before advertising expenditures or commitments are made, it is desirable for management to determine how much money is to be made available for the year or other fiscal period. The amount to be budgeted or appropriated may be arrived at by several different methods. One possibility is the use of a predetermined rate per sales unit, applied to the volume estimates made by the sales department, or a percentage applied to the estimated dollars of sales. Another is the computation of the appropriation from last year's expenditures, plus or minus whatever amount management or the advertising agency believes is necessary to accomplish the desired sales goal—all based on analyses of prior performance.

A more scientific method involves estimating the increased volume which might be obtained from various additional amounts of advertising, using past experience or test markets as a basis, and then determining the point at which income on the additional volume equals all out-of-pocket costs including the additional advertising expense. . . . Assuming ample plant capacity, it is profitable to spend advertising money up to the point at which advertising expense plus other out-of-pocket expense equals the gross profit over material cost on the additional volume obtained. Spending more than this amount produces a loss on the additional volume. Sometimes, even this is desirable in order to broaden the distribution base of a product. In any case, many estimates and intangibles enter into the calculations of the advertising budget and the final appropriation is likely to be predicated on a combination of these and other factors.

[12] *N.A.A. Bulletin*, June, 1954, p. 1357.

After the total budget is determined, the amount is divided between the portion to be spent by the company and the portion allocated to the agency or agencies, and detail budgets of their respective amounts are prepared by both parties.[13]

The preparation of the detail budgets involves the allocation of expenditures to various media and localities by time periods. The following list illustrates the variety of expenditures to be scheduled:

Consumer advertising
  Radio
    Time, talent, and mechanical
  Television
    Time, talent, and mechanical
  Magazines and newspapers
    Space
    Mechanical
  Trade papers
    Space
    Mechanical
  Educational
    Space
    Mechanical
    Visual
    Printed matter
    Exhibits
    Other
    Postage
  Office services
    Labor
    Overhead
Sales promotion
  Material and outside contracts
    Store display material
    Direct mailing
    Price sheets
    Mats and electros
    Miscellaneous sales promotion
    Exhibits
  Postage and shipping
  Labor from production division
  Office services
    Labor
    Overhead
  Money-back guarantees
  Cooperative advertising
  Miscellaneous
  Advertising experience adjustment based on sales
  Administrative expense [14]

[13] Glen M. Harold, "Advertising Expense Accounting and Control," *N.A.A. Bulletin*, Section 1, Aug., 1953, p. 1591.
[14] From Exhibit 3, Research Series, No. 26, *supra*, p. 1362.

It again should be pointed out that these expenses are "managed"; they do not follow sales and actually may have no fixed relation to sales during the budget period. Management spends more or less in this area based on its view of the immediate requirements. Budget revisions in this are frequent, and many companies apparently review this phase of the budget more frequently than other phases.

Budgeting Selling Costs. Selling costs are the costs of personal solicitation and promotion of business. They are the costs of maintaining and operating a field sales organization. Aside from the costs associated with field office space, they consist primarily of compensation and salesmen's expenses. Typical costs are shown in the following classifications applicable to sales offices and field salesmen:

Applicable to district sales office:
1. Clerical salaries
2. Hotel and meals
3. Transportation
4. Donations and dues
5. Telephone and telegraph
6. Postage and stationery
7. Entertainment
8. Rent
9. Miscellaneous general

Applicable to salesmen:
1. Salary
2. Hotel and meals
3. Transportation, other than automobile
4. Automobile
    a. Storage
    b. Repairs
    c. Tires
    d. Gasoline and oil
    e. Depreciation
    f. Insurance
    g. Miscellaneous auto
5. Donations and dues
6. Telephone and telegraph
7. Postage and stationery
8. Entertainment
9. Miscellaneous general [15]

Unlike advertising expenses, selling expenses are much more susceptible of budgeting from the bottom up since a closer relationship can be established between effort and results. Field selling costs are primarily a function of the number and the location of the customer calls

[15] Sebert Schneider, "Sales Territory Cost Control," *N.A.A. Bulletin*, Section 1, June, 1952, pp. 1225, 1226.

MARKETING AND DISTRIBUTION COSTS

to be made, and since the customers are known, the pattern of sales effort in relation to results is more definite than in the case of advertising. The basic procedure in budgeting these costs, therefore, is contained in the following steps:

1. Establish the territorial sales quotas needed to achieve the total budgeted sales.
2. Determine the man-days of sales effort needed in each territory.
3. Compute the cost of these man-days, giving effect to the territorial differences occasioned by
    a) Differences in costs of hotels, meals, etc.
    b) Differences in travel time—in concentration of customers and distances to be covered.

Past experience concerning the number of calls required to achieve a given sales objective and daily salesmen's costs should provide the basis for realistic expense schedules on a territorial basis.

Budgeting Marketing Administration Costs. These are the costs of formulating and administering marketing plans. In general, they are either of the fixed type of expense or the "managed" type, but in either case they tend to be determined in fixed amounts for the budget period. An example of how one company prepares this section of its budget is shown in Figure 10–1.

CONTROLLING MARKETING AND DISTRIBUTION COSTS

Control Procedures Affected by Nature of Costs. If all the plans incorporated in the company's operating budget were certain to be realized, control of all expenditures would involve merely a matching of actual expenditures and budgeted expenditures. Since in the nature of things there are bound to be deviations from plan in one or more of the company's activities, control must take these deviations into account as a means of ensuring that what is accomplished is accomplished in the most efficient manner. This implies that the first problem is to determine what has been accomplished, and it is in this area that marketing and distribution costs differ most from production activities.

In the case of the factory, all costs are related to one principal activity—the production of finished product, and the control objective is clear-cut. While the costs may be fixed, semi-variable, or wholly variable, the pattern is adjusted to output. In the case of marketing and distribution costs, however, the fact of the separation in nature of order-filling and order-getting costs poses a more complex problem in defining

MARKETING ADMINISTRATION OPERATING EXPENSE BUDGET

..........Section (Department)
..........Budget Period

Expenses	Source	Total Six Months	January July	February August	March Sept.	April Oct.	May Nov.	June Dec.
Salaries	Form BWP 1001	Department Head will budget overtime anticipated during the period: calculate at 150% of current rates.						
Overtime	Dept. Head							
Total								
Social Security Taxes	Sum of above % of Total Salaries	Budget Dept. will supply % to be applied to salary budget.						
Supplies—Office	Dept. Head	This expense will be budgeted at the average monthly rate for the latest 12 months adjusted for: (1) elimination of nonrecurring expenses in this 12 months average, (2) known unusual expenditures to be made during the budget period.						
Toll Calls & Telegrams	Dept. Head	Same as above.						
Travel and Entertainment	Form BWP 1005	Form BWP 1005 will be used to detail by employee the major trips and/or entertainment anticipated plus an amount to cover small trips and use of company auto pool.						
Associations & Publications	Form BWP 1005	Form BWP 1005 will be used to detail each association and publication expenditure anticipated during the budget period. A small allowance may be added to cover cost of ordinary publications, such as books.						
Professional Services (including Market Surveys)	Form BWP 1005	Budgeted, by Marketing Vice President only, form BWP 1005 will be used to detail each service to be purchased during the budget period setting forth type of service to be rendered and products to which applicable.						
Sales Training Expense	Form BWP 1005	Form BWP 1005 will be used to detail (1) each of the meetings to be held giving number of men to attend and breakdown of the costs, (2) sales training aids to be purchased, (3) sample cases to be purchased, etc. This expense budgeted only by the Field Sales Manager.						
Miscellaneous Expense	Form BWP 1005	Budget only anticipated extraordinary expenses which are not classifiable in the above expense accounts. Detail on Form BWP 1005.						
Building Occupancy—Admin. Bldg.	Budget Dept.	Budgeted, by Marketing Vice President only, at amounts supplied by the Budget Department as determined by Office Manager.						
TOTAL EXPENSE	Sum of above							

Source: "Cost Control for Marketing Operations—Order Getting," Research Series, No. 26, *N.A.A. Bulletin*, June, 1954, p. 1379.

objectives and control methods. Consequently, in the balance of this chapter control of marketing and distribution costs is approached on the basis of the threefold classification presented earlier in the chapter, namely:

Fixed costs (of both order-filling and order-getting)
Variable costs of order-filling (arising from sales)
Managed costs of order-getting

It is pointed out that, in the case of marketing and distribution costs, great consideration must frequently be given to the individuality of certain types of costs, which may have greater bearing on their budgetary treatment than a planned pattern of variability. Factors to be considered range from experience, trends, and competition to market conditions, trade practices (as in advertising), or traditional personnel practices (as in salesmen's compensation). Nevertheless the author feels that virtually all such costs lend themselves to the classification and treatment now discussed.

Controlling Fixed Marketing and Distribution Costs. The costs in this category have already been defined. And just as there is no difference between the budgeting of these fixed costs and that of any other fixed costs, so also there is no difference in the control procedures. These consist solely of comparing the actual with the scheduled costs and reporting and explaining the differences, if any.

From the viewpoint of the broader aspect of cost control which is involved in the planning of operations, revisions of fixed marketing and distribution costs may be more numerous than those of other activities, because of the semiexperimental nature of many marketing operations and their readier adaptability to changing conditions.

Controlling the Variable Costs of Order Filling. These costs were previously classified as variable sales compensation, warehousing, transportation, and clerical costs. It is in connection with these that flexible cost schedules are fully applicable, although the flexibility is not necessarily based on sales dollars.

To the extent that variable sales compensation takes the form of straight commissions, no problem of control should be presented. While the commissions earned may differ from the budgeted commissions in the operating budget (as in the case of Illustrative Company), the difference should automatically be accounted for by corresponding deviations in sales. The standard of performance is established in the compensation plan in the form of rates of commission. Except for faulty accounting or clerical errors, there should be no variations from the standard cost for the sales effected.

However, with respect to the other variable costs of order-filling, the control standards are less precise and merit fuller discussion.

Controlling Variable Warehousing Costs. Space utilization and handling costs are the principal subjects of control. The former is of less importance for short-run control purposes because of the fact that space charges commonly take the form of time commitments—for a number of budget periods if the property is owned, and for either a fraction of or an entire budget period if it is rented. For short-run control purposes, the handling costs are the more controllable.

These costs can best be controlled through the use of standards. Since warehouses may vary in the nature of the items handled, and also in the nature of the available handling equipment, separate standards may have to be established for each. Standard costs may be related to either units of product or units of weight, such as tons, hundredweights, and so on. Once these standards are established, comparison of the actual costs for the period and the weight of materials handled should readily disclose variations in efficiency. Again, it is to be remembered that efficiency is measured on a basis of work actually done rather than budgeted work.

Variations in handling standards and in utilization costs among several warehouses are not unimportant, but they must be considered at the time the budget is prepared rather than during the budget period.

Controlling Variable Transportation Costs. Transportation costs are governed in part by the quantities transported and the distances, in part by the selection of routes and conveyances, and in part by the costs inherent in a particular route or conveyance. Control of these costs, therefore, is more complex than that of warehousing costs. An illustration follows of how one company analyzes transportation expense, showing the form of report used and typical interpretations.

Cost of transportation is effectively controllable through the information provided by sound reporting procedures. Here is one of the major items of marketing expense, the cost of transporting finished goods from manufacturing to sales locations and to customers. The Transportation Expense Statistical Report [Fig. 10-2] is an operating report which is produced from accounting records. Finished goods transportation is accounted for in four major categories:

1. Plant to warehouse
2. Plant to customer
3. Intra-sales
4. Warehouse to customer

The transportation accounting plan is primarily for the operating manager to use in the control of expense. However, transportation expense, as a service cost, is charged to sales divisions and product groups and the accounting is done for this purpose also. On the control side, the transportation expense statistical report enables a district operating manager and the transportation staff at headquarters to get a bird's-eye view of what is going on without the work necessary to review hundreds and even thousands of freight bills. They are

MARKETING AND DISTRIBUTION COSTS

able to make comparisons of actual transportation costs with the standard cost of movements of every product to each sales district.

The hypothetical figures . . . may be used for typical questions which would be directed to the district operating manager so that he may take the appropriate control steps. The figures raise these questions in a simple and natural manner.

1. Shipments of only 16,000 pounds of malt from the plant, with sales of 76,000 pounds, indicates overstocking the previous month. Also, the rate from plant to warehouse is too high when compared with the statistical standard. Why were not these shipments combined with other products or with the plant to customer shipments to reduce the rate?

2. Shipment of 74,000 pounds of dough improvers from warehouse to warehouse seems unnecessary. Was the cost of $504 justified? Why were these shipments not made from the plant?

3. Why was a small shipment of tea balls made from the plant at the high cost of $4.87 per hundredweight? This rate is considerably above the standard. If the shipment was necessary, why was it not combined with other products from the same plant to get a lower rate?

4. The report shows 823,000 pounds of shortening shipped from plant to warehouse and 713,000 pounds from warehouse to customer. With this volume, why were not more shipments made direct from plant to customer?

5. Shipments of instant coffee from plant to warehouse should have been combined with other products in order to obtain a lower rate. The actual hundredweight cost of $4.54 compares with a standard of $2.35 when included in a combination load.

6. The high hundredweight costs of $.71 and $.67 for warehouse to customer shipments compare unfavorably with the standard rate. With the large volume lower costs are expected. With proper use of route layouts, contract carriers, etc., the average warehouse to customer cost would be $.55 and $.51 per hundredweight, respectively.[16]

Where the company maintains its own transportation equipment, standards can be determined for the various costs involved. For example, the time element in making home deliveries of milk on a suburban community milk route may be standardized as follows:

Typical Results of Home Delivery Time Study for Suburban Community Milk Route

	MINUTES
"Per Day" Jobs	
Check in, get orders, books, etc.	1.50 per day
Get vehicle, gas and oil, return vehicle to garage after delivery	8.18 " "
Arrange truck during delivery	6.50 " "
Settle accounts at plant	36.00 " "
Personal time and unavoidable delay	50.50 " "
Total "Per Day" time	102.68 per day
"Per Customer" Times	
Deliver	.94 per customer delivery
Collect	1.10 " " "
Record delivery and/or collection	.18 per customer collection

[16] E. W. Kelley, "Distribution Cost Control—and Beyond," *N.A.A. Bulletin*, Section 1, Apr., 1951, p. 916.

TRANSPORTATION EXPENSE STATISTICAL REPORT

DISTRICT A District
MONTH - YEAR August 19

LINE	PRODUCT GROUPS	PLANT TO WAREHOUSE			PLANT TO CUSTOMER			INTRA SALES		WAREHOUSE TO CUSTOMER		TOTAL	TRANSP. COST OF MONTHS SALES		
		GROSS WEIGHT	AMOUNT	COST CWT.	GROSS WEIGHT	AMOUNT	COST CWT.	GROSS WEIGHT	AMOUNT	GROSS WEIGHT	AMOUNT		GROSS WEIGHT	AMOUNT	COST CWT.
COLUMN NO.		(1)	(2)	(3)	(4)	(5)	(6)	(7)	(8)	(9)	(10)	(11)	(12)	(13)	(14)
CALCULATION				(2÷1)			(5÷4)					(2+5+8+10)		[(12-4)×3]+[5+8+10]	(13÷12)
1															
2	MALT	3,410	65.02	1.90	12,442	190.12	1.52	21,392	142.07	51,802	370.20	767.41	76,086	1,911.63	2.51
3	LEAVENERS	49,794	660.53	1.32				25,338	156.38	15,343	109.65	926.56	59,590	1,052.62	1.77
4	DOUGH IMPROVERS	188,325	2,471.61	1.31				73,727	503.88	119,799	856.14	3,831.63	144,891	3,258.09	2.25
5	FROZEN EGGS	250,176	936.46	.37				149,048	848.19	1,536	10.98	1,795.63	252,832	1,794.65	.71
6	FROZEN FRUIT	25,110	251.19	1.00				24,773	165.77	960	6.86	423.82	26,048	433.11	.67
7	COFFEE - INSTITUTIONAL	192,334	1,496.07	.77				302	1.34	4,472	31.96	1,529.37	202,639	1,593.62	.79
8	" - FROZEN EXTRACT	2,925	96.95	3.31	750	16.20	2.16	185	1.28			114.43	3,936	122.94	3.12
9	TEA BALLS AND BAGS	300	14.62	4.87				1,523	8.99	63	.45	24.06	3,773	193.19	5.12
10	GELATIN - INSTITUTIONAL	9,860	233.68	2.37				4,970	34.50	1,106	7.91	276.09	9,202	260.50	2.83
11	PUDDING - INSTITUTIONAL	8,925	197.19	2.20				1,604	10.46	226	1.90	209.55	4,209	104.96	2.50
12	BAKER'S MARGARINE	218,430	305.80	.14				6,201	22.05	29,521	210.97	538.82	51,832	305.58	.59
13	SHORTENING	823,337	3,968.76	.48	60,896	470.90	.77	39,593	254.97	713,112	5,095.90	9,790.53	824,570	9,487.40	1.15
14															

38	COFFEE - GROCERS	428,980	514.75	.12	68,141	438.17	.64			644,860	4,296.05	5,248.97	712,001	5,506.85	.77
39	" - INSTANT	8,400	382.10	4.54						7,531	50.17	432.27	7,522	391.67	5.20
40	TEA - PACKAGES	800	23.32	2.91						3,081	20.53	43.85	3,070	109.87	3.58
41	" - BALLS GROCER	10,000	285.92	2.85				1,146	8.24	3,492	23.26	317.42	3,473	130.48	3.76
42	" - INSTANT			2.62											
43	GELATIN - SMALL			1.90						30,783	205.08	205.08	30,716	788.68	2.57
44	PUDDING - SMALL	46,125	887.84	1.90				15,938	114.62	35,014	233.26	1,235.72	34,966	1,012.23	2.89
45	BAKING POWDER			1.32											
46	MARGARINE - 1 LB.	425,572	7,369.63	1.73	272,623	2,142.40	.78			378,093	2,518.85	12,030.88	643,977	11,085.67	1.72
47	BUTTER - 1 LB.			1.85											
48	DRESSING AND SPREADS	37,223	30.36	.08	213,930	1,296.88	.60			67,253	448.04	1,775.28	249,313	1,773.23	.71
49	CHEESE	143,064	2,219.08	1.55						155,708	1,037.33	3,256.41	153,115	3,410.61	2.23
50	TOMATO JUICES	164,212	2,069.07	1.26	40,096	585.40	1.46			140,124	933.51	3,587.98	180,220	3,284.47	1.82
51	CEREALS	72,036	1,087.74	1.51	20,142	328.31	1.63			81,744	544.58	1,960.63	101,886	2,107.22	2.07

N B

68	SUB TOTAL - DIVISION B	1,336,412	14,869.81	xx	614,932	4,791.16	xx	17,084	122.86	1,547,683	10,310.66	30,094.49	2,120,259	29,600.98	xx
69															
70	COST PER CWT.	xxx	xxx	1.11	xxx	xxx	.78	xxx	.7191	xxx	.6662	xxx	xxx	xxx	1.40
71	ERROR ADJUSTMENT	20,119	291.73		(20,119)	(291.73)									
72															
73	GRAND TOTAL	3,129,457	25,859.42	xx	668,901	5,176.65	xx	365,776	2,272.74	2,485,633	17,013.58	50,322.39	3,779,867	50,119.27	xx
74	COST PER CWT.	xxx	xxx		xxx	xxx		xxx		xxx		xxx	xxx	xxx	

SOURCE: E. W. Kelley, "Distribution Cost Control—and Beyond," *N.A.A. Bulletin*, Section I, Apr., 1951, p. 914

FIG. 10–2. Transportation Expense Statistical Report

214   BUDGETING AND CONTROLLING TECHNIQUES

"Per Case" Times [MINUTES]
Load cases to truck.............................. .12 per case
Unload empties .... .06 per case

"Per Mile" Times
Drive to route and return......................   3.60 per mile
Drive on route *............................... 12.60 "   "

*Dependent on number of stops per mile.[17]

The foregoing time standards, when costed at standard wage rates, provide labor cost standards. These, together with the standard costs of other transportation expenses, not only provide the basic data for budget preparation, but also serve to control costs during the budget period. Budget variations can quickly be analyzed as to those which result from volume changes and those which result from operating inefficiency. The former may be uncontrollable in the short run, but the latter always should lead to corrective action.

Controlling Variable Clerical Costs. Since the control of the variable clerical costs of marketing and distribution presents no problems not encountered in the control of clerical costs generally, full treatment of this topic is deferred to Chapter 15. Suffice it here to point out that, again, standards are the best basis of control.

Controlling Advertising and Sales Promotion Costs. Advertising frequently makes up the bulk of the expenditures in this category. Control of these costs has two aspects: (1) keeping the expenditures in line with the budget and (2) measuring the effectiveness of the expenditures.

Companies generally do a good job in controlling the expenditures against the budget, and frequently it is a very important job because of the large expenditures involved and the variety of the expenditures as to type and place and time. Figure 10–3 illustrates an advertising budget performance report.

The accounting for and auditing of advertising expenditures can present an imposing task, particularly where a number of advertising agencies are retained to handle the advertising. This, together with the budgetary control of the advertising expenditures, is a major task, as described below:

> One of the most important functions of the advertising accounting department is the control of advertising expense to determine that actual or proposed expenditures are within the budgeted amounts or that over-runs are called to the attention of the advertising manager, so that he can request additional appropriations or approval to exceed the budget. It has been described earlier how detailed schedules are prepared by both the agencies and the company to support the amount of budgeted money allocated to each spending unit and how

[17] W. D. Holdsworth, "Bringing Delivery Route Costs Under Standards," *N.A.A. Bulletin*, Section 1, Oct., 1952, p. 258.

MARKETING AND DISTRIBUTION COSTS

Month of ....   Product Division No. ....

ADVERTISING BUDGET PERFORMANCE REPORT

CLASS OF EXPENSE	BUDGET		EXPENDED		UNEXPENDED	BUDGET BALANCES		
	CURRENT MONTH	YEAR TO DATE	CURRENT MONTH	YEAR TO DATE		COMMITMENTS		NOT COMMITTED
						REVOCABLE	IRREVOCABLE	
SPACE								
Magazine—Space								
" —Production								
Trade Publications—Space								
" —Production								
Customers Publications								
Consumer Direct—Space								
" —Production								
" —Sales								
TOTAL SPACE								
PRINTING								
Catalog								
Price Lists								
Printed Matter								
Special Customer Cat. Pgs.								
" Printed Matter								
Imprinting								
Postage on Mailings								
TOTAL PRINTING								
MISCELLANEOUS								
Customer Electros								
Postage and Express								
Exhibit Expense								
Display Material								
Mdse. Given Away								
Type Salvage								
Training Material								
Sales Development								
TOTAL MISCELLANEOUS								
Reserve								
TOTAL EXPENSES								
Coop. Advertising								
TOTAL ADV. EXP.								

SOURCE: "Cost Control for Marketing Operations—Order Getting," Research Series, No. 26, *N.A.A. Bulletin*, Section 3, June, 1954, p. 1360.

FIG. 10-3. Advertising Budget Performance Report

BUDGETING AND CONTROLLING TECHNIQUES

these budget schedules are, in turn, based on schedules and estimates on which complete particulars are presented.

With this detailed planning behind the total appropriation, it would seem that very little additional control would be necessary during the year. However, this assumption does not hold true because:

1. The best laid plans change on account of competitive conditions, special merchandising problems, etc.
2. Publishers and broadcasters raise or lower their rates.
3. Credits arise from failure to broadcast or from preemptions of stations or networks.
4. Talent and production costs vary from estimates, depending upon script requirements, etc.
5. Art and mechanical costs deviate from estimates because of variations in subject material, color requirements and ad size.
6. Redemptions on coupon or mail-in offers may vary substantially from estimates.
7. Administrative expense invariably fluctuates from the original budget.

Some safety margin for these contingencies should always be included in the original plans but, in addition, careful follow-up and control is necessary to avoid ending the year with overexpenditures. This control is exercised principally through two sources. First, the schedules and estimates are brought up to date as often as is possible and practicable. Secondly, postings of payments to the commitment records are scrutinized monthly to detect items not included in the estimates or exceeding amounts provided in the budget. All such additional expenses, if of substantial amount, are posted to a schedule of budgeted expenditures maintained for each product. These schedules then show the current position in relation to the budget and are used to keep management informed.[18]

In controlling the effectiveness, as opposed to the amount, of advertising expenditures, however, progress is not nearly so satisfactory. The N.A.A. field study, previously referred to, indicates that little has been accomplished in this direction.

Some of the principal reasons for this situation are brought out in the following comments made by company representatives during field interviews.

"We watch sales before and after but we can't be sure what effect the advertising has because so many other factors influence sales."

"The inquiries which are generated by our ads and promotions are the principal measures of effectiveness, but it is very difficult to correlate inquiries with actual sales."

"Most of our advertising is directed toward maintaining the company's market position and developing the long-range demand for the products. It does not produce immediate sales which can be traced to individual advertising expenditures."

The most widely used ultimate measure of advertising and sales promotion effectiveness is net sales attained. However, this measure does not tell whether or not the same sales volume could have been attained by more effective use of a smaller expenditure. Some of the companies interviewed use thumb-rule

[18] G. M. Harold, "Advertising Expense Accounting and Control," *N.A.A. Bulletin*, Section 1, Aug., 1953, pp. 1597–98.

measures such as cost per sales dollar or per unit sold. One company compares rates of change in advertising expenditures and sales by plotting the two series of figures on a semilog chart for each product. Figures for an extended period are charted to allow for lag between advertising and sales. The above and other similar measures are admittedly rough and they are known to have a low degree of reliability.

Under favorable conditions, somewhat more significant measures can be obtained for specific projects. Where the project is designed to sell a specific item within a limited time, it is easier to trace actual sales to a given advertisement or promotion. . . .

For the most part, measurement of advertising effectiveness is viewed as a market research function rather than as an accounting function in the companies interviewed. The accounting department supplies various data such as sales analyses to serve as the basis for statistical studies made by market research personnel. Data from other sources, including outside advertising research agencies, are utilized in addition to accounting figures. While comparative effectiveness of alternative types of advertising copy can sometimes be measured, evidence available seems to indicate that a real measure of the over-all effectiveness of advertising remains to be developed.[19]

Controlling Selling Costs. As in the case of advertising cost control, the control of selling costs has both a quantitative and a qualitative aspect. Unlike advertising, however, the quantitative aspect of selling cost control involves more than just money; it relates directly and primarily to human effort and action. The distances covered and the number of calls made by salesmen measure the activity which, in turn, controls expenditures.

The overhead costs of selling and salesmen's salaries are controlled against the budget. Generally, these costs are either fixed or of the appropriation type. The field selling expenses, however, must be controlled in terms of:

1. Salesmen's efforts
2. Salesmen's expenses
3. Results

The efforts are measured by the distances covered and the calls made. The expenses are those of travel, hotels and meals, and miscellaneous. The results are the orders obtained. With reference to salesmen's efforts, control is achieved through territorial standards and salesmen's reports. While the discussion of Illustrative Company's budgets in the introductory chapters assumed selling expenses to have a fixed relation to sales, a careful coordination of budgeted sales and budgeted selling expenses normally results from the analysis of territorial coverage of customers upon which the former is based. In effect, therefore, the establishment of the sales targets sets the standards of sales efforts for each territory or district.

[19] Research Series, No. 26, *supra*, pp. 1365–66.

BUDGETING AND CONTROLLING TECHNIQUES

Once the standards are established, they provide the basis for evaluation of reported efforts. Sales call reports not only measure salesmen's efforts but, when posted to quota cards, serve as basic information for control of *direction* of effort. These call reports should provide for basic data as follows:

1. Sales call—order received
2. Sales call—no order
3. Service call (any call where immediate sale is not the prime reason)
4. Sales call—buyer out [20]

Control of salesmen's expenses is related to the individual salesmen. It is primarily a matter of analyzing each salesman's reported expenses against his reported efforts. Practice in this regard varies among companies. Some call for detailed expense reports; some use an "advance" system with or without detailed documents supporting reimbursements. In any case, however, control can be exercised only through some form of expense standards related to the conditions prevailing in a specific territory. The major problem in controlling salesmen's expenses, aside from that of internal auditing, is related to the control of the direction of sales effort, discussed at the conclusion of this chapter.

The control of sales results has been discussed in the preceding chapter. It is mentioned here since the results must be viewed, together with efforts and costs, to measure the over-all effectiveness of the sales organization.

Controlling Marketing Administration Costs. These costs, for the most part, are either fixed in nature or "appropriated." The control procedure is based simply on a comparison of actual expenses with the budgeted expenses.

Controlling Direction of Sales Efforts. In the case of production activities, the relation between costs and results (goods produced) is normally so well determined that control can readily be exercised. A shift in production schedules from one product to another automatically calls merely for a substitution of one set of cost standards for another. In the case of sales activities, however, because of the peculiar nature of order-getting costs, there must be a constant analysis of sales efforts and sales results to achieve the best profit results. It is partly in this connection that the present chapter is so closely related to the preceding chapter.

In order to bring sales up to the budget, how much additional effort is justified, and where should the effort be expended? It is questions

[20] Cf. Sebert Schneider, "Sales Territory Cost Control," *N.A.A. Bulletin*, Section 1, June, 1952, p. 1224.

of this type that create the need for distribution costs accounting. While this subject is too large to be treated in this volume, it should be emphasized that decisions concerning the location, type, and amount of sales effort to be expended at any time must be made in light of data concerning the contribution of the expenditure to net profit. It is in this sense that the material of this chapter and the preceding chapter are interdependent. Sales require sales efforts, and the two must constantly be matched. Presumably this matching, as to products, territories, order size, and so on, has been the basis of the budget plan. But during the budget period, the matching of actual results is not only a means of comparison with the plan, but also the basis for local changes in amount and direction of effort where necessary to achieve the over-all plan.

Territorial profit contribution reports, product profit contribution reports, salesman profit contribution reports, and others provide the data needed for an intelligent control of sales and sales activities. The principal role of distribution cost accounting is to facilitate the preparation of such reports through the necessary classifications of marketing and distribution expenses.

CHAPTER 11

INVENTORIES

	Page		Page
Purpose of chapter	220	Financial limits on inventories	228
Budgeting Inventories		**Controlling Inventories**	
Nature of inventories	221	The amount of inventory	229
Interrelation of quantitative inventories	221	Inventory standards and the budget	231
The reason for inventories	222	The problem of deviations from the budget	231
Measuring the requirements—prevention of delays	224	The use of standard inventory ratios	232
Measuring the requirements—economy of acquisition	226	Control reports	234
		Importance of records	234

Purpose of Chapter. Depending on their size (and in many companies the size is significant) the importance of inventories arises from two facts. First, they represent an investment of company funds and, second, they involve substantial carrying charges. That in many companies inventories represent a substantial investment, aggregating very often from 20 to 30 per cent of the total investment, is common knowledge. On the other hand, insufficient recognition is given to the carrying costs, which, depending on the industry, may amount annually from 5 or 6 to 20 or 30 per cent of the inventory investment. These costs, which are periodic charges against income, represent an addition to the cost of doing business and a corresponding pressure on profits.

The foregoing facts, as well as the fact that inventories do not just occur but are consciously planned to meet the company's requirements, indicate that inventories must be carefully budgeted and controlled along with the other aspects of operation. Moreover, the problems encountered in the budgetary control of inventories are perhaps more difficult and complex than in many of the other expenditures. The determination of inventory objectives involves consideration of a number of factors, some of which are not easy to measure. With these facts in mind, the devotion of a separate chapter to the topic can well be understood. Accordingly, it is the purpose of the chapter, first, to discuss the problems associated with the budgeting of inventories and, second, those related to their control during the budget period.

The location of this chapter in the book, following the chapters on sales and marketing and distribution costs and preceding the chapters

INVENTORIES

on material usage, factory labor, and so on, is the result of a deliberate choice. It is designed to emphasize that fact that inventories represent, not a result of operation, but a planned factor in operations. Production schedules are governed by both current sales and planned inventory requirements. Just as sales and selling costs are interrelated in determining the best sales plan, so are sales and inventories linked in determining the most suitable production plan. Consequently, it appears logical to treat the problems of sales *and* inventories before taking up the costs of production and administration.

BUDGETING INVENTORIES

Nature of Inventories. Inventories, as reported on financial statements, represent an investment of funds and are reported in monetary terms. Basically, however, they represent an investment in things: units of various kinds of finished product, units of production in process of manufacture, units of various kinds of finished parts, and units of various kinds of direct and raw materials (supplies are not considered in this chapter). The balance sheet data merely reflect the cost (or some other financial measure) of these quantities. If unit costs and prices never changed, the distinction between monetary and quantitative values would not be important (apart from the question of inventory mix) but things being as they are, the distinction must be recognized and inventory budgeting must begin with physical quantities.

Interrelation of Quantitative Inventories. At this point, the reader is reminded to review the budget procedures of Illustrative Company described in Chapter 4. The steps, as they relate to inventories, may be outlined as follows:

Finished Products
1. Estimate current and future shipments in units
2. Determine inventory requirement in relation to *future* shipments
3. Determine required number of product completions, by the following formula:

$$\text{Month's shipments} + \text{Desired inventory, end of month} - \text{Inventory, first of month}$$

4. Modify the foregoing to the extent necessary to achieve greater stability of production if that is desirable

Work in Process and Finished Parts (assuming level production)
1. Compute required completions for each department, based on foregoing determination

2. Determine required end-of-month inventories
3. Adjust for opening inventories, to determine production, by the formula:

$$\text{Required completions} + \text{E.O.M. inventories of work in process} - \text{Opening inventories of work in process}$$

Direct Materials
1. Measure materials needed in foregoing production
2. Determine required end-of-month inventories of materials
3. Adjust for opening inventories, to determine required purchases, as follows:

$$\text{Current requirements} + \text{E.O.M. inventories} - \text{Opening inventories}$$

From the foregoing outline it is obvious that the determinations of the several quantitative inventories are closely interlocked and that the order of determination is from finished product back to direct materials. It is recognized that as a matter of practice, many companies budget inventories in a much less formal manner. Frequently the determinations are only financial in nature, based on historical ratios of inventory investment to sales, or some other data. The basic weaknesses of this method are (1) that the ratios are based on past experience which may not be a good guide and (2) that the determinations are in totals only, thus furnishing no clue as to the proper detailed composition of the inventories. The method does not promote precise analysis and may account for the numerous cases where inventories get "out of control." More precisely, it may be said that they are inadvertently planned "out of control." It would appear that an investment in inventories should receive the same careful attention as is given any other investment of funds.

Why are inventories required? As pointed out above, they should not just happen as a result of overproduction or overpurchases. They are planned and are needed. Following is a brief discussion of the needs which give rise to the several inventories.

The Reason for Inventories. The basic reasons for inventory accumulation are as follows:

1. Prevention of delays
2. Stabilization of production
3. Economy of acquisition
4. Anticipation of price increases and/or shortages

All of the reasons apply to each of the several inventories, but under varied circumstances. The first reason concerns respectively delays in

a) Shipments to customers of *finished product*
b) Completion of finished product from *work in process*
c) Sequential manufacturing operations involving *direct material*

The first delay is of obvious significance and is directly related to the company's principal reason for existence—sales at a profit. Orders are usually contingent on ability to make timely delivery. In very few industries can products be completely processed on a moment's notice; hence the need for stock on hand from which to make deliveries.

Delays arising in connection with work in process generally relate to finished parts and components of product. In addition to the fact that most work in process inventories result simply from the time-consuming nature of production, a stock of parts and of started work must be available to permit an even flow of operations throughout the various departments of the factory. The fact of time-consuming sequential operations alone explains the inventory requirement.

The need for materials in production and the recognition of the time factor involved in their procurement are sufficient to explain the need for materials inventories.

The second reason for inventories, stabilization of production, may be inherent in the nature of the industry—some operations simply cannot be quickly adjusted to short-term changes in product demand. But quite commonly stabilization of production results from either cost considerations or the management's concern for the work force. Whether because of seasonal cycles in the industry or short-run economic variations in the market, the maintenance of a stable work force may require the accumulation of inventories as a means of leveling out production.

By economy of acquisition is meant economy of both the manufacture of product and the purchasing of materials. Long production runs are less costly, measured on the basis of a unit of product, than short runs. Set-up and re-training time are expensive. And, in the case of materials, quantity discounts may be significant.

The final reason for inventories, anticipation of price increases and/or shortages, is more a matter of company policy than of operating management, particularly as it relates to price increases. Inventory build-ups to engender inventory profits are speculative in nature and should be recognized as such. However, speculation is inherent in inventory management in view of the speculative characteristics of the forecasts upon which decisions must be predicated. Moreover, management cannot disregard the necessity for procuring its raw materials at favorable market prices. The solutions to problems of this complexity are being sought aggressively by many companies through the application of "Operations Research" techniques. Essentially this approach is directed toward minimizing total costs rather than inventory costs only.

BUDGETING AND CONTROLLING TECHNIQUES

Measuring the Requirements—Prevention of Delays. In discussing the problems of measuring inventory requirements, reference is made to only two of the four reasons for having inventories—prevention of delays and economy of acquisition. The other two reasons relate to high company policy rather than normal operations.

The prevention of delays, as it relates to finished product inventory, is aimed at the protection of customer goodwill and the promotion of sales. The measurement problem, therefore, is one of determining the size of the inventory necessary to ensure that orders can be filled promptly. Essentially, this involves the estimated timing of orders, the availability of productive facilities and the length of the production cycle. If the latter averages two weeks, if sales are spaced evenly throughout the month and if facilities are always available for the particular products sold, then it is evident that when the inventory gets down to a two-weeks' supply, production for replenishment must begin. Note this is not the same as saying that the minimum inventory must equal two-weeks' supply, but that the two-weeks' supply signals a new run of production. During the two weeks of the production cycle the inventory would decline on a straight-line basis to zero, but the moment it reaches zero the stock is replenished from the production run.

Generally, however, the distribution of the sales in time does not follow a precise straight-line pattern, although frequently some pattern is discernible. Consequently, it is necessary to build a safety factor in the inventory. It is this factor which calls for careful analysis and judgment. It should also be pointed out that the safety factor, or reserve inventory, need not necessarily be large enough to provide 100 per cent protection. Full protection may cost more (in inventory costs) than it is worth.

Moreover, the calculation of the reserve factor may be complicated by the fact that production facilities may not always be immediately available when needed. Consequently, when planning the inventory requirements, consideration must be given the probable distribution in time of future sales, the length of the manufacturing cycle, and the availability of facilities—to say nothing of the most economic production run, which is discussed in the next section.

It is to be assumed that the management of Illustrative Company took the foregoing factors into consideration when (see Chapter 4) it was decided that one month's sales should be inventoried. This refers, of course, to future sales, not current. The fact that the management of that company finally agreed to a modification of this policy in the interest of stabilizing production does not change the principle. In gearing inventory to the succeeding month's sales it must be recognized, of course, that the future sales and their timing must be estimated. This really is the crux of the problem. The manufacturing cycle is known, but the flow of sales of the product under consideration and of the other products which also utilize the common facilities must be estimated. Again we are impressed with the importance of the sales forecast as the keystone of the entire budget-making process. Observe, too, that the determinations must be made for individual products; hence, quantitative measurements are necessary. A financial measurement of a total inventory of finished product is meaningless for the purpose under consideration.

In a going concern there is always work in process because of the time factor of production. Aside from this simple fact, however, the presence of a number of departments devoted to sequential operations and the fact that these operations generally have different time cycles require that certain inventories of unfinished work, including finished parts, be stocked in order to ensure an even flow of the work needed to achieve the budgeted production. (Note that the idea of an even flow of sequential operations is not the same as stabilized production, which, in this book, is considered to relate to the ironing out of economic swings.) This is a matter of production scheduling, and its object is to synchronize as much as possible the flow of work into the final assembly of the product. While the inventory of work in process is measured in terms of manufacturing operations, its size ultimately is controlled, in part, by the inventory requirements of finished product, since this is a factor in the scheduling of the current month's production of each product.

The measurement of the quantities of direct materials to be stocked involves the matching of production schedules with the procurement cycles and is subject to the same analysis as finished product. Whether a two-weeks' or four-weeks' supply is the signal for reorder is a matter of the time needed to process the purchase order and get delivery of the materials modified by the safety factor and the economics of purchasing.

Similar problems in inventory management occur in commercial, wholesale, or general distribution activities not involving manufacturing. Order and shipping time from sources of supply must be given proper consideration in determining the minimum quantities to be maintained. Order and shipping time includes the time required by the company to determine that it needs something, to prepare the paper work such as a purchase requisition and purchase order, to obtain bids where necessary, to mail purchase orders and receive confirmations; vendor's time to process the company's incoming purchase order, to prepare shipping papers and documents, to select the stock, arrange for transportation; the actual trucking, rail, or air freight time; and finally, the company's own receiving time necessary to unload the merchandise and place it on the warehouse stock shelves, available for shipment.

Measuring the Requirements—Economy of Acquisition. The inventory requirements to prevent delays, however, may not be the only consideration. They tend to establish the floor below which inventories must not be permitted to drop but do not necessarily establish the ceilings. Economy of acquisition in the form of production of finished products and component parts and procurement of direct materials may dictate that larger inventories be accumulated than necessary solely for prevention of delays.

The maintenance of minimum inventories to satisfy the foregoing requirements for a number of products whose manufacture utilizes common facilities after appropriate change-over setups have been made, may lead to such frequent change-overs as not to yield economical unit costs. The stocking of larger quantities may be indicated. The problem is that of finding the most economical production run, giving effect to the various cost factors.

The importance of the calculation of the most economical production run arises from (1) the fact that change-overs incur costs of making the actual change-over of facilities, of retraining workers, and of clerical routines associated with starting a new run, and (2) the fact that inventories create costs in the form of storage charges and costs of invested funds. Fewer setups reduce the setup and starting load cost per piece of a given product, but they also increase the inventory maintenance cost per piece. Consequently, the most economical run is that in which the total inventory and setup cost per piece is the lowest, as shown in Figure 11–1.

Various mathematical formulae have been developed for the calculation of the most economical run. The Norton formula is one of the most widely used and is stated as follows: [1]

$$Q = \sqrt{\frac{S}{K}} \qquad (1)$$

where
$$K = \frac{(B+I)C + 2A\left(1 - \dfrac{U}{P}\right)}{2NU} \qquad (2)$$
and

Q = The lot size
S = Total preparation cost per lot (dollars), including cost of preparing manufacturing orders, cost of setting up machines, and any other similar costs which are independent of the number of pieces in the lot

[1] W. Van Alan Clark, Jr., and William E. Ritchie, "Economic Lot-Size and Inventory Control," *N.A.A. Bulletin*, Section 1, Feb., 1953, p. 775.

INVENTORIES

$P =$ Pieces made per day
$U =$ Pieces used per day
$N =$ Days worked per year
$C =$ Material, direct labor, and overhead per piece (dollars)
$A =$ Cost of storing one piece for one year (dollars)
$B =$ Taxes, insurance, etc., per cent per year on inventory
$I =$ Desired return on capital, per cent per year

In formulae of this type certain assumptions have to be made, and as with all formulae, the validity of the results depends on the soundness of the assumptions. The four principal assumptions are:

1. It is usually assumed that storage costs are truly variable both as to space and to time. This means that the firm should have no idle floor space or funds and that the incremental cost of more spare floor space or more working capital is fairly constant over a wide range.

2. Another common assumption is that manufacturing techniques remain the same, no matter what the lot size, throughout the range of lot sizes studied.

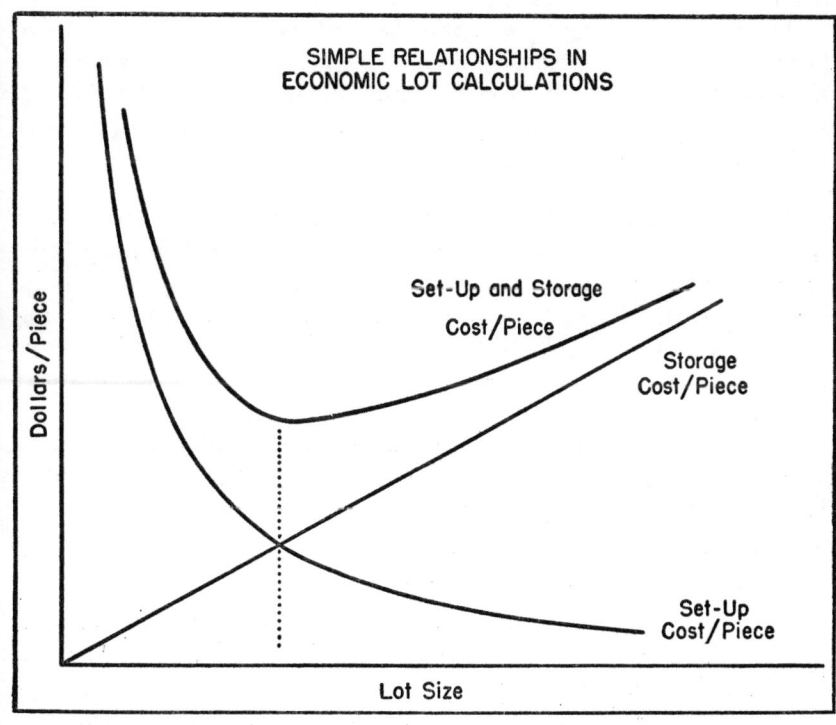

SOURCE: W. Van Alan Clark, Jr., and William E. Ritchie, "Economic Lot-Size and Inventory Control," *N.A.A. Bulletin,* Section 1, Feb., 1953, p. 774.

FIG. 11–1. Simple Relationships in Economic Lot Calculations

3. In much the same way, it is assumed that costs are not reduced in larger lots because of an increase in operator skill.
4. Further simplification is also introduced in that withdrawals from inventory are commonly assumed to be on a straight-line basis.[2]

Obviously, these assumptions may not always apply. Aside from the assumptions which have to be evaluated, the use of formulae of the above type requires careful cost determinations. Set-up costs, storage costs, and so on, must be known, and this frequently is no easy task. Moreover, where many products are manufactured, it may not be practical to apply the formula separately to each one, particularly where the cost factors are subject to changes over a period of time. Consequently, determinations of this type may have to be (1) somewhat generalized, (2) made for families of products rather than individual products, and (3) constantly reviewed. The full study of this subject is outside the scope of this work; the foregoing is designed to call attention to it and show how it relates to budgeting.

Similar analyses are useful in the case of direct materials. Granting that minimum inventories are necessary to ensure the proper flow of production, should larger inventories be maintained in order to achieve the most economical purchasing and storing? Here again, it is a matter of balancing storage and inventory costs against costs of purchasing. And again, the purchases should be arranged so as to achieve the lowest total cost per unit of material.

Financial Limits on Inventories. In the preceding two sections we have been concerned with (1) the number of units of inventory to be planned for in the interest of protection against delays and (2) the number of units of inventory to be planned for as a means of achieving economy of acquisition. In both sections we were concerned with inventory quantities. But now attention must be given the financial aspect of inventories.

Inventories represent invested funds, and consequently two questions arise in the evaluation of inventory policies designed to provide protection and economical acquisition:

1. Can the inventories be financed?
2. Will the investment yield an adequate return?

In companies which are not adequately capitalized, the first question may be very serious and may make it difficult to achieve desirable inventory goals. The effect of inventories on cash position was illustrated in the budget of Illustrative Company. There, short-term financing had to be arranged for, but in that illustration, the problem was temporary

[2] *Ibid.*

INVENTORIES

because of a shift in inventory policies. As a practical matter, however, inventories represent a permanent requirement and their size may be limited by the company's resources. Inventory objectives, therefore, must be viewed in the light of the capital available.

But, granting the available financial resources, will the investment designed to achieve the objectives of protection and economy of acquisition, yield the desired rate of return? Obviously, the higher the investment in inventories, other things being the same, the lower will be the rate of return on total investment from a given volume of business. But the factors of protection, economy, and rate of return are interrelated as follows:

1. Protection (of customer goodwill) relates to price and volume of sales.
2. Economy of acquisition relates to profit margin.
3. Inventory size relates to turnover and investment yield.

The question, therefore, is: Will the additional protection and additional economy adequately compensate for the additional investment?

The relation of the savings, from more economical acquisition, to additional investment, can be measured precisely, depending on the validity of the factors used in the production and purchasing formulae. Admittedly, however, the relation between prompt shipments and sales is less easily defined and may vary with the state of the market.

One very important conclusion may be drawn from this analysis. Granting that, practically, some minimum inventory requirement is associated with every product, if the investment in that inventory does not yield the desired return, then the adoption into the line of the product itself was ill-conceived. So long as the product is in the line, however, planned inventories should be determined on the basis of the analyses called for in this chapter.

One question should be raised here concerning inventory turnover ratios. Should they be standard, or should they vary with changes in sales? If the formula presented above, relating to the inventory safety factor, is correct, then the safety factor should vary with the square root of the sales. Thus, if sales were quadrupled, the safety factor should only be doubled. Obviously a higher turnover would be expected with increased sales.

CONTROLLING INVENTORIES

The Amount of Inventory. In considering how much inventory will be on hand during a given period of time, it must be recognized that the preceding analysis deals with the *maximum* required inventories at

BUDGETING AND CONTROLLING TECHNIQUES

particular points in time, but not with *average* inventories over a time period. The determination of the economic lot and of the safety factor is designed to provide one target figure for the *beginning* of a depletion period (probable sales for that period plus the safety factor), and another target for the end of the period (only the safety factor). Thus, assuming:

1. Sales as follows (in units):

    January 5,000
    February 4,000
    March 6,000
    April 8,000

2. No beginning inventory
3. Safety factor (end-of-month inventory) equal to one-half of next month's sales
4. A short production cycle

the inventory position for the first three months would be determined as follows, assuming further that production was continuous throughout the period:

	January	February	March
Sales	5,000	4,000	6,000
Required ending inventory	2,000	3,000	4,000
Total required	7,000	7,000	10,000
Less: Beginning inventory	–	2,000	3,000
Required production	7,000	5,000	7,000
Average inventory:			
Beginning	–	2,000	3,000
Ending	2,000	3,000	4,000
	2,000	5,000	7,000
Divide by 2	1,000	2,500	3,500

But now let it be assumed that the most economical production under the circumstances is achieved by producing 19,000 units in the first month. The inventory analysis would then be as follows:

	January	February	March
Production	19,000	–	–
Beginning inventory	–	14,000	10,000
Total	19,000	14,000	10,000
Less: Sales	5,000	4,000	6,000
Ending inventory	14,000	10,000	4,000
Average inventory:			
Beginning	–	14,000	10,000
Ending	14,000	10,000	4,000
	14,000	24,000	14,000
Divide by 2	7,000	12,000	7,000

The foregoing analyses show the effect of the economy factor on inventories, but they also show that both for each month and for the three-month period the inventory varies.

Inventory Standards and the Budget. As in all the previous discussions of budgeting control, the question of standards is the starting point. In the case of inventories, the purpose of control is to keep inventories "in line." In line with what? If all aspects of the master budget are attainable, it and it alone (including its various underlying determinations and schedules) should serve as the standard by which to evaluate the inventory position during the budget period.

Since the budget contains both financial and quantitative determinations, the question arises as to which data should be used for control purposes. Unquestionably, quantitative data should be used. Financial data suffer from three defects for this purpose. First, the inventory costing method—Fifo, Lifo, average, and so on—injects an accounting factor into the comparisons, which may be misleading for control purposes. Second, because of production inefficiencies, the financial inventory may contain excessive costs which are a function of the control of production efficiency rather than of inventory control. (This reason would not apply if standard costs are used in costing inventories.) Third, financial data frequently appear as aggregates and thus may conceal detail deviations. Referring to the last reason, it should be recognized that financial measures do have a usefulness, which is discussed later. The method of control, therefore, involves the comparison of actual quantities on hand at a given time with the standard quantities.

The Problem of Deviations from the Budget. As with other aspects of operation, budget deviations may be due to inefficiencies or to the fact that the budget itself does not reflect actual operating conditions. Causes of deviation are now discussed with respect to each type of inventory, starting with finished stock.

The finished stock inventory budget is planned by reference to estimated future sales and production schedules. Inventory variations, therefore, may be due to two principal causes:

1. Deviations in sales
2. Deviations in product completions

The first reason commonly is the more important. If sales run behind the budget, production schedules should be curtailed accordingly. But these schedules frequently cannot be altered overnight. Depending on the length of the manufacturing cycle and the complexity of the pattern of operations, it may require days or weeks to revise a schedule and put it into effect. In the meantime, finished product is piling up in the warehouses and the inventory gets out of line. Similarly, an unexpected jump in sales may require production facilities which cannot immediately be made available.

The second reason relates to the flow of production. Production difficulties may result in an inventory's being below the requirement. Or, the reverse may be true: the factory may beat its efficiency goals and turn out the required production in a shorter time than planned. Temporarily, inventory will be higher than planned.

In the case of the work in process inventory, the same factors are present since it is a result of production. The amount of work in process at any given time is naturally directly related to current production. To the extent that this inventory includes component parts which are produced and stocked pending the start of succeeding operations, the time factor is especially important. The earlier the operation in the budget period, the less it can be adjusted to later changes in the budget. Excess parts may be frozen in inventory.

The time factor is also of real significance in the case of direct materials. Depending on the availability of materials on short notice (where sales jump ahead of the budget) and on the economics of purchasing whereby large quantities are ordered early in the budget period (significant when sales decline), the materials inventory during a period of changing sales may be harder to control than the others. Orders for materials not yet delivered may be subject to cancellation or revision in anticipation of a reduction in production schedules, but materials already on hand represent an inventory increase which will not be in line with curtailed operations.

Thus, the coordinated nature of operations is again emphasized. The several inventories are interrelated since the various aspects of operation are tied one to the other. But the problem of coordinating changes in plans is made difficult because of the time factor. This, plus the fact that sales usually cannot be forecast in detail with complete accuracy, means that inventories seldom will be exactly balanced with sales. All of this points to the importance of sales performance as the key to inventory control. The detailed budget schedules set the standards of inventory accumulation; the problem is one of determining when and how much the schedules should be revised to correspond to changes in the sales picture.

The Use of Standard Inventory Ratios. Much has been written concerning the use of various ratios in the control of inventories. These may take the form of turnover ratios or balance sheet ratios. The former are designed to show the relation between the inventory and the related activity. The following turnover ratios are typical:

$$\frac{\text{Cost of sales}}{\text{Finished stock inventory}}$$

$$\frac{\text{Material usage}}{\text{Materials inventory}}$$

$$\frac{\text{Total production cost}}{\text{Work in process inventory}}$$

The balance sheet ratios show the proportion of total assets invested in inventories.

Both types of ratios are useful in measuring over-all effectiveness of operations, provided standard ratios have been determined. They suffer from several weaknesses, however, for the purposes of control under a budget. First, they reflect past experience and do not recognize the fact that present inventories are designed for *future* business. Thus, an unusually large inventory accumulated to take care of an expected large increase in future sales, would have a distorting effect on this period's turnover data. Second, they do not measure the efficiency of inventory operations per se under the plan, but are primarily useful in determining the need to revise the budget plans. A declining turnover of finished stock, for example, or an unusually high inventory balance sheet ratio for finished stock does not necessarily imply failure to adhere to inventory operating policy, but rather that the policy needs revision. Thus, for example, inventories of finished products may be exactly in line with the protection policy decided on, based on the actual sales, but it may be that the policy itself is too costly. Perhaps the company must assume greater risk of running out of stock, at least for certain products.

The implication of the last point above is that the real use of the ratios is in the planning and control that precedes the building of the budget rather than in control under the budget. It is granted, of course, that the ratios have some historical usefulness in indicating the need for a major overhaul of control procedures. But it is contended here that control under the budget is a matter of quantitative analysis and review of inventories in detail.

To the extent, however, that standard ratios are used, the determinations of the standards are important. They may be either external standards or internal standards, but it would seem that, at least in the short run, the standards would have to be based on the company's own situation and experience. Moreover, the standard ratios, particularly the turnover ratios, should be flexible; that is, they should vary with sales. If the reserve factor varies with some constant times the square root of sales, the turnover must increase as sales rise. This idea has been recognized by some writers who indicate that a useful device in budgeting inventories is to segregate them according to fixed and variable amounts, only the latter portion increasing with sales.[3]

Control Reports. It hardly needs mentioning that inventories merit the closest attention at all times. A constant review of stock must be maintained and deviations from planned accumulation promptly reported. Both failure to conform to the budget and the need for budget changes should be observed as soon as possible. Figures 11–2 and 11–3 are illustrative, the former presenting a report of surplus items and the latter an inventory analysis report.

SURPLUS ITEMS REPORT
September 1953

Raw Materials:

Material #35	$30,000
Due to tight market, we built up stocks. This represents three months' excess over normal requirements.	
Material #88	25,500
Inactive stock due to specification change requiring immediate change in material. Will try to dispose of this stock.	
Material #103	20,500
Accumulation of new program material. When program is actively producing, this will be considered active inventory.	
TOTAL—Raw Materials Surplus Stock	$76,000

Finished Goods:

Stock #22	$25,000
Seasonal increase in production in order to level department operating hours and provide for Fall Peak demand.	
TOTAL—Finished Goods Surplus Stock	$25,000

SOURCE: Charles H. Gleason, "Inventory Control Through Budgeted Turnover," *N.A.A. Bulletin*, Section 1, Dec., 1953, p. 538.

FIG. 11–2. Surplus Items Report

Importance of Records. Good records are important in all phases of budget work, but their importance in the case of inventories should be emphasized. Physical control of inventories is difficult. The great volume of transactions; the large number of items involved; the numerous movements, both in and out of the company and within the company; and the variety of personnel engaged in their handling require elaborate recording procedures and supervision. The importance of this is gener-

[3] Cf. P. M. Chiuminatto, "How Will Capital Requirements Vary With Sales Volume?" *N.A.A. Bulletin*, Section 1, June, 1950, pp. 1215–22.

ally recognized in connection with income determination, but it is equally important for budget control purposes. And while the auditor can always resort to an end-of-year physical inventory as a final check on the records, this would be too late to serve the purposes of budgetary control.

DIVISION SUMMARY—INVENTORY ANALYSIS REPORT
September 1953

Raw Materials

Product Plant	Total Inventory	Surplus Items	Net Inventory	Months' Stock Actual	Months' Stock Budget	Allowable Stock	Inventory Excess
A	$ 580,000	$ 76,000	$ 504,000	2.70	2.50	$ 466,000	$38,000
B	670,500	55,500	615,000	3.45	3.40	606,000	9,000
C	178,700	—	178,700	2.20	2.55	207,000	(28,300)
D	619,000	20,000	599,000	2.35	2.30	585,000	14,000
Total	$2,048,200	$151,500	$1,896,700			$1,864,000	$32,700
August	$2,062,600	$158,000	$1,904,600			$1,843,000	$61,600
July	2,048,100	165,000	1,883,100			1,795,400	87,700
June	2,020,200	140,000	1,880,200			1,850,500	29,700

Finished & In-Process

A	$ 570,000	$ 25,000	$ 545,000	1.06	1.00	$ 517,000	$28,000
B	577,000	—	577,000	1.62	1.50	535,000	42,000
C	380,000	—	380,000	3.05	3.00	373,000	7,000
D	1,090,000	75,000	1,015,000	2.60	2.75	1,075,000	(60,000)
Total	$2,617,000	$100,000	$2,517,000			$2,500,000	$17,000
August	$2,640,500	$110,000	$2,530,500			$2,495,000	$35,500
July	2,563,000	118,000	2,445,000			2,420,000	25,000
June	2,544,000	109,000	2,435,000			2,390,000	45,000

Note: 1. Total inventory figures are before any deductions for balance-sheet reserves.
2. Excess inventory represents amount the net inventory is over the budget stocks for going rate of sales and production.

SOURCE: Charles H. Gleason, "Inventory Control Through Budgeted Turnover," *N.A.A. Bulletin*, Section 1, Dec., 1953, p. 540.

FIG. 11-3. Division Summary—Inventory Analysis Report

CHAPTER 12

DIRECT MATERIAL COST

	Page		Page
Definition of direct material	236	How the standard purchase price is established	240
Direct materials contrasted with direct labor	236	The budgetary treatment of variances	243
Purpose of chapter	237	**Controlling Direct Material Costs**	
Budgeting Direct Material Costs		Control function of the standards	243
The elements of direct material cost	237	Controlling the price variances	244
How standard quantities are determined	238	Controlling the usage variances	245

Definition of Direct Material. Direct materials are those which enter directly into a product. This would seem to be a very simple and precise definition. In practice, however, the classification of materials as direct or indirect, for costing purposes, is governed by the ease of measurement. It should be remembered that the significance of the direct material classification lies in the purpose to identify material costs with specific products or lots of production. For major items of direct material, this can readily be accomplished by the normal cost accounting routines. Some materials, however, which do become part of the product may do so in such small quantities that the measurements may be too expensive relative to the values added. In such case, it may be decided that those materials will be treated as factory overhead rather than direct materials and apportioned over all production instead of being identified with particular products. This decision may in turn be affected by the nature of the cost system in use. In a process cost system, particularly one in which only one product is processed in a department, the problem of identification is simple, but in a job order cost system it may be much more difficult. Thus, the nature of the system, the nature and value of the materials used, and the management's viewpoint concerning the relative usefulness of extreme accuracy of product costing all affect the classification adopted for materials.

Direct Materials Contrasted with Direct Labor. In many respects direct materials and direct labor are similar, and it might appear desirable and convenient to include both in this chapter. There are certain differences, however, which for budgetary control purposes call for separate treatments. These differences result from the fact that whereas the purchase and usage of labor coincide, the purchase and usage of

DIRECT MATERIAL COST

materials do not. The time factor is significant. Moreover, the purchase price of material frequently is harder to forecast than that of labor. In addition, the separation of purchases and usage, as in the case of materials, poses a different problem of control. For the purposes of this book, therefore, the differences may be listed as:

1. Difference in time
2. Difference in accuracy of forecasts
3. Difference in location of responsibility

Because of these differences, direct materials and direct labor are treated separately in this book.

Purpose of Chapter. Because of the distinction between the purchase of direct materials and their use, and the fact that the purchases may be for inventory as well as for current consumption, the purchase budget generally differs from the cost budget. Since, however, the budgeting of inventories has already been covered and since all the purchases, whether for immediate consumption or for inventory, are determined ultimately by consumption requirements, the treatment in this chapter of the budgeting and control of direct materials centers around the standard requirements for production. It is the principal purpose of this chapter, therefore, to discuss the relation of these standards to both the budgeting and budgetary control of direct materials transactions.

BUDGETING DIRECT MATERIAL COSTS

The Elements of Direct Material Cost. The actual cost of direct material used in an accounting period includes:

1. Standard requirements for the period's production, at the standard price
2. Variations in purchasing price
3. Variations in usage

In this listing it is assumed that the company uses standard costs. Where this is not the case, some target figures must be used, whether for budgeting, profit determination, or pricing; and since standard costs are desirable, the discussion in this chapter is based on their use.

The recognition of the foregoing elements in the budgeting of direct material costs is discussed below under the following headings:

1. How standard quantities are determined
2. How the standard purchase price is established
3. The budgetary treatment of variances

How Standard Quantities Are Determined. Reference to Chapter 4 and its description of Illustrative Company's budget procedures shows how the material quantity standards serve as basic data in preparing the budget schedules for direct materials. Given this data and assuming no variances, the quantity schedules can quickly be drawn up on the basis of scheduled production (and inventory accumulation).

Quantity standards can be determined in three ways, as now described.

1. Engineering studies to determine the best kind of material for the purpose and the proper quantity to use. This requires a consideration of the production methods to be used, quality of the product to be made, expected yield, and similar factors.
2. Analysis of past experience in usage of materials for the same or similar products. In setting standards by this method past performance is averaged or the standards are based on jobs or periods which are selected as typical. The use of unadjusted past experience may include in the standards an undetermined amount of past waste and excess usage. Known excess usage may be eliminated in setting the standards or the standards may be tightened by an arbitrary percentage reduction in the quantity of material allowed, but the method does not focus attention on finding the best combination of quantity, methods and product quality as does the engineering study method. However, the use of past experience may be less costly and quite satisfactory in setting standards for minor items of cost or perhaps for obtaining temporary standards.
3. Test runs under controlled conditions. This method avoids some of the principal shortcomings of the preceding method in that conditions can be standardized and extraneous causes of variation eliminated. Most companies use a combination of the above methods in setting their material quantity standards, although approximately two-thirds of the companies interviewed reported that they rely principally on engineering studies.[1]

An important question for budgetary purposes concerns the tightness of the standards. For cost control purposes it may be desirable to set the standards tightly. For purposes of financial budgeting, however, the data must be realistic—in the form of either reasonably attainable standards, or tight standards but with a provision for variances. It is important, therefore, that the standards be established with full recognition and knowledge of the managerial philosophy involved.

Where the second and third of the three foregoing methods are used, allowances automatically are made for normal inefficiencies. Under the first method, however, they must be separately provided for.

When material quantity standards are set by engineering study, the calculation of standard quantities from drawings and product specifications yields

[1] "Standards to Aid Control of Manufacturing Costs," Research Series, No. 12, N.A.A. Bulletin, Section 3, Mar., 1948, pp. 903-4.

theoretical or ideal quantity standards to which allowances must be added to get the attainable standards needed for control. While the allowances that are made depend partly upon the nature of the production processes, nearly all of the companies interviewed increase the quantities of material included in the standards to cover a certain amount of wastage and loss that is considered impossible or impracticable of elimination.[2]

Methods of setting material quantity standards and the problems encountered are indicated, for certain industries, in the following descriptions:

A Chemical Company

In the fine chemical industry, there are many conditions to be considered in establishing both the bill of material and the labor standard. In other industries, the standard material requirements may be accurately predetermined by the engineering staff. In the chemical industry the problem is not so easily solved. Admittedly, the portions can be determined through chemical equation, but other factors enter in which may play a major role. Among these are purity of crude, extent of process control, degree of mechanical perfection, and the human factor. The bill of materials then becomes the normal or average yield of the various lots of crudes used. Included in this average must also be normal losses. This is the factor which is most nearly a matter of judgement. By way of illustration, a 100 per cent yield is theoretically possible. However, the chemist is able to obtain only an 80 per cent yield under controlled conditions in the laboratory. The standard is set at 70 per cent, reflecting normal plant losses.[3]

A Wire Cloth Manufacturer

Wire Cost Standards.—Weight per hundred square feet of each mesh is first determined. Assuming that this calculation has been made on 18 × 14 mesh and that the average weight per hundred square feet turns out to be 12.8 pounds, the standard material unit cost will be the product of this figure times the per pound cost of steel wire.

Finishing Material Standards.—When it comes to finishing, there is added material cost. Again, steel mesh will supply the example. Standard practice dictates that a fixed percentage of zinc be deposited on the cloth. For the purpose of illustration, it may be assumed that this ratio is to be 5½ per cent and that the mesh is again 18 × 14. In this instance, 5½ per cent of 12.8 pounds (which is the weight per hundred square feet of 18 × 14 mesh) will give the number of pounds of zinc to be deposited on one hundred square feet of cloth. This figure, multiplied by the cost per hundred pounds of zinc anodes, gives the material cost per one hundred square feet of wire.[4]

A Steel Company

For each product rolled, a standard cost sheet is developed. . . . At this stage primary concern is with the standard for each cost element. . . . It may be assumed that the material standard for Product A, which is rolled from

---

[2] *Ibid.*, pp. 904–5.
[3] Kenneth Schweller, "Material Control in a Chemical Company," *N.A.A. Bulletin*, Section 1, Nov., 1950, p. 304.
[4] W. S. Hildebrand, "Standard Costs in Wire Cloth Manufacture," *N.A.A. Bulletin*, Section 1, July, 1951, pp. 1331, 1332.

Number 1 ingots, is wanted. By means of scientific measurement, tempered by past experience, it is found that the yield factor for Product A is 82.97%. This ratio . . . indicates that for every ton of raw material (ingots) charged, .8297 tons of finished Product A result under good and achievable operating conditons. . . .[5]

The standard raw material required for one ton of finished product, therefore, is 1.205 tons.

A Clothing Manufacturer

The material quantity standards for the major materials of the garment are determined by the use of templets or patterns designed for the average size chosen. These templets are arranged to give the best usage of the material, and the standard yardage is determined from these areas plus an allowance for end pieces and lappings. . . . Standard quantities for the miscellaneous items of material such as buttons, zippers, tags, purchased pockets, etc. are obtained by inspection of the garment. . . .[6]

The above descriptions serve to illustrate the fact that quantity standards for direct material are based primarily on physical measurements established by reference to laboratory tests, past experience, or judgment, and with or without allowances for losses depending on the circumstances. In general, these standards are the easiest to establish.

How the Standard Purchase Price Is Established. In the case of quantitative usage of material, control rests solely with the user, and, as noted above, standards can be established quite accurately and with confidence. The price to be paid for these materials, however, poses a more difficult problem, for not all the price factors can be controlled by the purchaser. The difficulty, of course, varies, depending on the nature of the market and the stability of the demand and supply factors.

In a market where changing prices are the rule, it is common practice to set the standard material prices on a basis of what the company will have to pay for them. The determination of this in turn involves two steps:

1. Estimating price trends for the budget period
2. Selecting the best suppliers on the basis of the available knowledge concerning their operations

The relative importance of these two steps depends on the nature of the materials to be purchased. If the material is in the nature of basic raw material, the first step is the more important since the price of such material tends to be affected by nationwide or worldwide conditions

---

[5] A. J. Penz, "Standard Costs in a Small Steel Company," *N.A.A. Bulletin*, Section I, July, 1951, pp. 1350–51.
[6] How Standard Costs Are Being Used Currently, *Special N.A.A. Publication of Complete N.A.A. Standard Cost Research Series*, p. 82.

DIRECT MATERIAL COST

and to be uniform among suppliers. In the case of manufactured materials, however, the second step assumes greater importance.

The farther the material is removed from the basic raw materials category, that is, the greater the conversion factor, the more the supplier's own methods and production costs become a factor in the price. Consequently, selective purchasing of fabricated materials and parts should be based on the greatest possible knowledge, on the part of the buyer, concerning the economics of that fabrication. Thus a company which itself makes some of this material and buys the rest is in a good position to know what price it should expect to pay outside suppliers.

In setting standard material prices, the purpose must be kept in mind, and it is in this respect that materials pose a different problem than other cost items. For the purposes of budgeting cash expenditures, the standard is significant with respect to purchases only, and not usage, because of the factor of inventories. On the other hand, for the purpose of budgeting actual cost of sales, the accounting will vary depending on how beginning inventories of materials are costed into production. In any event, for the pricing of finished product, it would seem that current material price standards are most practical.

The difficulties and alternative procedures for setting the material price standards are described as follows:

How do you establish a standard cost on a purchased component? It was suggested that the solution was simple enough. Just get the buyers in the purchasing department to obtain three quotations on each item. The lowest quotation would be the standard. That decision almost cost us the ball game! In the first place, the lowest quoting vendor often did not get the business because of a variety of reasons: poor quality history, poor performance, inability to deliver on time, lack of capacity, history of repeated price increases and many other reasons. Also, because our standard cost system was part and parcel of the cost estimating system, we were requesting these quotations on all parts considered for future business. After several months, our purchasing department had such a backlog of requests for quotations they could not get their current buying job done. We were so far behind on standard costs and estimates, because of lack of quotations, that the commercial plans of the sales department were delayed and already people were being criticized for not meeting standard cost.

Then came a second decision equally "brilliant." It was decided that purchased material standard cost be determined at the average of three quotations on each part. This change in policy accomplished two things. Obviously, the dollar level of the standards increased, since we were using average cost rather than the lowest cost. Furthermore, our work load increased considerably, since we had to average three quotations instead of discarding two of them. Other than that, we had all the same troubles and inefficiencies we suffered before. . . . Therefore, [now] we engineer our own standards. . . .

First of all, we break down purchased material standards into two categories: standards for items we either process or buy, and standards for those we only buy. The parts we do not process are made up of shelf items, such as lock washers, screws, nuts, etc. These, for the most part, are stock items sold on a very competitive market and usually can be purchased at the same price from a number of sources and suppliers. The standard cost on these items is established at the current market price.

The items we do process, with the alternative of buying them, consist of such items as wood cabinets, plastic cabinets, plastic parts, stampings, screw machine parts, coils, transformers, speakers, controls and all such other special items. Since our standard costs remain in effect for one year, once each year we analyze the current market value of all basic materials. We determine the mill price on steel in all of its forms, and on copper, aluminum, bronze, zinc, etc. We determine the market price on wire, paper, plastic powder, plating materials, paint materials, wood, glue, foil, and all other basic raw materials. We had our personnel department through its wage and salary division, find out the average wage rates in certain geographical locations, the rates for occupations such as punch press operators, screw machine operators, assemblers, winders and hundreds of other occupational rates. We acquired through two sources, our purchasing and personnel departments, the average prevailing overhead liquidating rates in geographical areas by machine centers. From this basic data, we established standard labor and overhead rates to be used as the standard rate for the coming year.

With this preliminary work accomplished, we were ready to go to work in establishing our standard costs for items in the make or buy category. Every individual component or part is designed by engineers, drafted and blueprints made. A copy of the blueprint is received by our cost estimating department and the same day a standard cost is issued. Specialists in manufacturing methods, time study and processing are employed in this section. From the blueprint and their knowledge of manufacturing methods, they determine the weight or volume of materials needed per 1,000 pieces. This is priced out at the standard value of raw material and allowances are made for normal cutoff and scrap, based on efficient utilization of the material.

Next, we turn to the processing operations for the parts, in sequence, and synthetic time values are applied. These time values are extended by the standard wage rate data and a standard overhead allowance is applied. Allowances are made to convert select time to standard time. The synthetic time values used, or pre-rates as they are sometimes called, are identical to those used in our own manufacturing plants prior to the actual time study. Assembly operation allowances vary with restrictions of difficulty, just as allowances for tight tolerances vary on machining operations. Experience with many tens of thousands of estimates, later time studied, has proven the accuracy of these pre-rates.

The cost of material, labor and overhead at this point is totaled. It is known to us as the "efficiency standard." This is the cost we would expect our own plant to incur in the production of this item if they manufactured it. However, to this cost we must add an allowance for administrative costs and profit. This total cost becomes the purchased material standard. The engineering of these standards assumes modern methods and tools, the economical purchasing of material on the part of the vendor, and reasonable allowances for administrative cost and profit.[7]

[7] George K. Bryant, "How We Built Standard Costs Into Control and Planning," *N.A.A. Bulletin*, Section 1, May, 1954, pp. 1101-4.

The Budgetary Treatment of Variances. Having set the quantity and price standards for materials by reference to which variances will be measured, the question now arises as to whether provision for variances should be made in the forecast budget. As to the purchase or price variances, representing the difference between actual and standard prices on purchases, if the price standards are based on an appraisal of expected conditions, the budgeted variances should not be large and therefore need not be budgeted.

In the case of usage or quantity standards, however, representing the difference between standard and actual quantities used in a given amount of production, the question of the tightness or looseness of the standards is significant. For cost control purposes they obviously should be tight. On the other hand, if their determination is based on a desired rate of efficiency which will require several years to obtain, and if, accordingly, substantial variances are expected to occur in the immediate future, a realistic appraisal of current financial requirements would necessitate a provision in the budget for the variances. Psychologically, however, it seems desirable to avoid having two sets of standards, one for cost control and a different one for the forecast budget. The author believes that standards should be revised currently, based on an attainable degree of efficiency, and that consequently variances need not be budgeted. The cost control standards may then also be the basis of the forecast budget.

CONTROLLING DIRECT MATERIAL COSTS

Control Function of the Standards. While the forecast budget is based on the purchase of specified quantities of material at standard prices and the use of standard quantities required for specified production, the price and quantity unit standards permit a measurement of performance even though the forecast purchases and production are not achieved. A failure to make the quantities of material purchased conform with the budget is significant for the purposes of financial budgeting, but for the purposes of cost control the essential factor is the meeting of the price standard in the case of the purchases actually made. Similarly, a failure to produce scheduled quantities of products may have a serious effect on the over-all plans, but, again for cost control purposes, it is the amount of material used in the actual production which counts. Budget deviations in purchase and usage of materials, consequently, may be both qualitative and quantitative in character. That is to say the deviations may arise from material used or price paid at variance with standards (qualitative) or from production or purchases which differ in total from forecasted quantities (quantitative).

Accounting procedures for standard costs provide for measuring and recording the qualitative deviations but not the quantitative. The latter are a matter of budgetary analysis alone. Assuming no deviations, in prices paid, variations in the amount purchased are ultimately reflected in current financial position, that is, in cash and inventory. Such variations of themselves have no effect on the period's profit, but they do affect the operation of a closely integrated budgetary plan.

Again assuming no qualitative usage variances, a quantitative variation from the budget for material usage must result solely from variations in production. Again, such variations of themselves have no effect on profit (unless a shortage of product causes loss of sales), but they do throw the plan out of gear.

Controlling the Price Variances. Price variances measure the difference between the actual price and the standard price of the quantities purchased. It should be recognized that such variances, once incurred, are historical and measure the cost of failure to adhere to the standards. Much has been written to the effect that costs are controlled at the time and point of incurrence and not afterwards. Granting this, it follows that the presence of price standards should serve to prevent variances since, ideally, no purchases should be made in excess of standard. Practically, however, variations will occur. Unforeseen difficulties may absolutely require the immediate purchase of materials at an excessive price. Market conditions, too, may change and make the standards temporarily or permanently invalid. The reporting of variances incurred serves, not to control the purchases already made, but to point out the need for closer analysis of future transactions.

Where variances do occur, a question arises as to when they should be reported. In the normal accounting procedures for standard costs, price variances are recorded when the invoice is received and the liability recorded. The standard entry is:

> Dr. Stores
> Dr. Price Variance
> Cr. Accounts Payable

It has been suggested by one writer, however, that this is too late, and that the variance should be reported at the time the purchase order is issued.

> ... we firmly believe that control of material prices at the source (purchase order) is preferable to waiting for receipt of an invoice. There is also no need to sacrifice cost and statistical data. Purchase orders can be tabulated by commodities and compared with the material price standards set for control purposes as well as the standard costs used for inventory valuation purposes. Trends of control and material costs can then be forecast much sooner than by

DIRECT MATERIAL COST

waiting until invoices are received. Typical advantages resulting from this advance material price information would be:

1. Sales departments could be made aware of material price changes days and even weeks ahead of those competitors whose accounting departments follow the textbook approach to material price variance computation and control.
2. Design engineering could be advised of high cost raw materials and excessive cost design features such as non-standard threads, special tooling, and fine tolerances.
3. Production engineering could be advised of these material price trends so that they might institute prompt cost reduction programs.[8]

An important question relates to the placing of responsibility for material price variances. It would seem that primary responsibility should rest with the purchasing department. Admittedly, since prices are not subject to the same degree of control as usage, the purchasing department may not be at fault. Nevertheless, it should be forced to exert its fullest effort in the direction of selective purchasing.

Controlling the Usage Variances. Usage variances represent the differences between standard and actual quantities of material used in a given amount of production. They measure the efficiency of usage and are the primary responsibility of the production departments. In many companies, direct materials constitute the largest single item of cost; hence the importance of this phase of cost control. Moreover, because of the importance of usage variances and of the fact that the causes tend to be controllable, much more progress has been made in this field than in that of price variance control.

A common method of control involves the use of excess material requisitions. Standard quantities are issued for a production job or run. If excess materials are needed to complete the required production, they are issued only on the basis of a special requisition. This ensures both a reporting of the excess usage and an explanation of it. The reasons may include faulty material, defective equipment, poorly trained operators or "green" help, or poor supervision. The determination of the real cause and its correction are of great importance. It should be observed, however, that where many items of material are used, attention should be directed principally to those variances whose monetary values are really significant.

In some industries the nature of the material usage is such that control can most readily be achieved through the control, not of issues, but of scrap. In metal-working industries and foundries where scrap is normal to the processes, its control is an effective means of achieving material cost control. Figure 12–1 shows one form of scrap report.

[8] Nieson N. Shak, "Before the Fact Control of Material Prices," *N.A.A. Bulletin*, Section 1, Sept., 1955, p. 75.

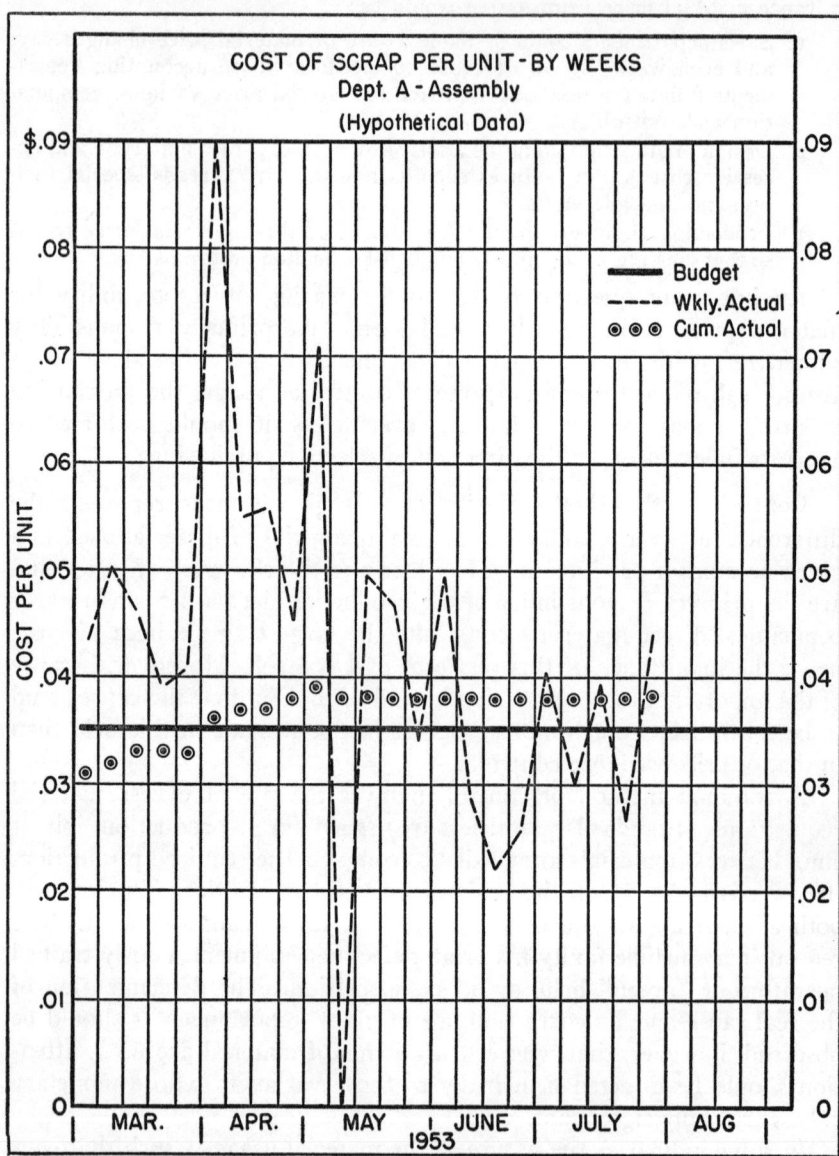

SOURCE: Robert E. Stockmeyer, "Helping the Foreman Control Costs," *N.A.A. Bulletin,* Section 1, Feb., 1954, p. 762.

FIG. 12-1. Cost of Scrap Per Unit—By Weeks

CHAPTER 13

DIRECT LABOR COST

	Page		Page
Definition of direct labor	247	Budgetary treatment of variances	252
Purpose of chapter	248		
Budgeting Direct Labor		**Controlling Direct Labor**	
Elements of direct labor cost	248	Control function of the standards	252
How labor time standards are determined	248	Controlling the price variances	253
How labor price standards are determined	250	Controlling the time variances	254

Definition of Direct Labor. Direct labor commonly is thought of as that labor which is applied directly to products. As in the case of direct material, however, the definition loses some of its apparent precision in practice, particularly when a distinction is made between the physical labor and its cost.

With respect to the physical aspects of direct labor, the term originally had clear meaning since it was used to designate that labor which actually worked on, and could be charged to, units of production. However, as production becomes more automatic and mechanized, physical contact between worker and product becomes less common and the term "direct labor" increasingly tends to imply a cost relationship rather than a physical relationship. Moreover, this cost relationship frequently is difficult to define. The separation in labor categories of machine operators and machine maintainers, for example, does not follow a precise pattern. And an operator who tends a group of machines working on different products or cost-units of production may present a difficult problem of cost classification by products or jobs. Classification of labor as direct, therefore, tends to become a matter of practicability and expediency.

When one turns to the financial aspects, as opposed to the physical aspects, of direct labor cost, the problem of classification poses even more questions. The writer refers to the costs of overtime premiums, vacation allowances, idle time, setup time, payroll taxes, and so on. Theoretically, if these costs are associated with the work of "direct" workers, they would be considered as direct costs. Difficulties in assigning these costs to products, however, may, and frequently do, necessitate their being classified as indirect costs.

Because of the foregoing difficulties in cost classification, this chapter must be read with the understanding that it is concerned with the principles of budgeting and controlling direct labor but that the definition of direct labor may vary from company to company. It is assumed, however, that direct labor is that labor for which a reasonably direct relationship *should* exist between quantity of physical effort and quantity of product, and that direct labor costs include only those related costs which can readily be assigned to units of product.

Purpose of Chapter. As was pointed out in the preceding chapter, direct material and direct labor are treated in two separate chapters, instead of being combined as prime production costs, because of differences both in precision of determination of standard quantities and in timing of purchase and usage. Because of the nature of the work, the establishment of labor time standards is less objective and more subjective than that of material quantity standards, and the problems of labor *cost* allocation are more difficult. In addition, whereas material is purchased and stored prior to usage, the purchase and usage of labor are simultaneous transactions. These differences are important in budgeting; hence the separate treatment of direct labor. Therefore, it is the purpose of this chapter to discuss the budgeting and budgetary control of direct labor only.

BUDGETING DIRECT LABOR

Elements of Direct Labor Cost. The total direct labor cost of an operating period will consist of:

1. Standard labor time requirements of the period's production, at the standard labor price
2. Variations in labor usage
3. Variations in labor price

This listing, as in the case of direct materials, assumes the use of standard costs, but even though they are not used formally, it must be assumed that some form of standard is used even if it is nothing more than an estimate based on past experience. The recognition of the foregoing cost elements in budgeting is treated under the following headings:

1. How labor time standards are determined
2. How labor price standards are determined
3. Budgetary treatment of variances

How Labor Time Standards Are Determined. The determination of labor time standards is a function of industrial engineering. For obvious reasons, it cannot be as precise as the determination of material quantity standards. The measurement of the normal effort of a normal

DIRECT LABOR COST   249

worker in the plant involves consideration of intangible and subjective factors which cannot be reduced to rigid formulae. Standard operation times should be set by one of three methods as described below:

Time and Motion Studies.—Time and motion studies furnish by far the most satisfactory direct labor time standards upon which to base standard labor costs. In fact it is the only method that can be depended upon to yield standards sufficiently reliable to permit other than a crude analysis of variations. Operation time standards set by averaging past performance or from estimates not based upon careful observation methods of time study work are always open to question when variations arise, since it is impossible to say to what extent the standard was wrong and to what extent there was a variance resulting from lack of efficient work.

Time study aims to analyze the manual and machine operations into distinguishable elemental motions and, by making careful measurements of the time required to perform these when working under given conditions, *time usage standards* are set for operations to be performed. These labor time standards contain not only the time set as standard for performance of the operation, but also allowances for rest, for necessary machine delays, for set-ups (if this is not to be considered a separate operation), and any other allowances regarded as essential.

Average of Past Performance.—A second method is to take an average of past operation times shown on time cards. When a job order cost system has been in operation, actual time for direct labor operations is available and can be used as the source of data. If extreme figures are first eliminated (because they probably represent unusual conditions or mistakes) and the remaining ones averaged, this average of past experience serves as an actual expected time standard.

If changes in production methods have been made, the setting of standards must await the accumulation of new experience. Another unsatisfactory situation occurs where there is excessive variability in the operation time as a result of conditions over which workers have no control; for example, nonuniformity in material, machine failures, or working conditions that prevent concentration on the job. Such a situation can generally be recognized by the existence of a very wide dispersion in the past operation times or by inspection of the factory. Working conditions must first be standardized before a standard cost system can operate with any degree of satisfaction, for responsibility cannot be fixed or causes of variations traced when the sources of variations are too numerous.

Advance Estimate.—Another method of determining operation time standard is to estimate it in advance. This method is particularly useful where an operation has not been performed before in exactly the same way, is not to be repeated, and represents an operation of considerable consequence. Thus construction of a building, ship, or a large special job of any other sort furnishes an occasion where this method of setting standards is useful. Quite often estimates are made first to establish a basis for bidding or quoting a price to the customer; after the order has been obtained, these same estimates may be utilized as standards to facilitate the control of actual operations in order to make sure that the profit anticipated is realized.

Such estimates obviously must be based upon a thorough study of the situation and an assembly of all relevant data available. This includes definite knowledge of what is to be done, comparison with past experience in similar operations, and inclusion of allowances for uncertainties. The magnitude of the latter item depends upon the type of standard; that is, whether it is to be actual expected, normal, or ideal, although where some estimates are to serve as a basis for pricing, only actual expected standard can be used for direct material and labor costs.

In some circumstances it is feasible to develop *empirical formulas,* schedules, tables, or curves from which standards can be set for operations not previously performed. This is essentially the case with a flexible standard, for the formula represents a change in allowed operation time as some dimension of the production process is varied. Development of such a formula proceeds by analysis of the process to determine what elements are concerned, and then studying the way the operation time varies as the other elements are varied. This variation is expressed in the schedule, curve, or formula from which any value within the range of experience can be derived. The method is a familiar one to time study workers who call it *synthetic time setting.* It consists of analyzing classes of operations into those which are common to all, and those which are variable.[1]

The labor time standards, once determined on a unit of production basis, are applied to the scheduled production for the period to determine the quantity of labor time required.

How Labor Price Standards Are Determined. The determination of labor price standards varies with the type of pay plan. If a straight day-rate or hour-rate plan is used, the problem is very much the same as that of setting a standard purchase price for material. The standard rate is that which the company expects it must pay, giving effect to local and industrial labor conditions. Commonly, today, the rates are included in the negotiated labor contract. If all the labor in a given department or operation is paid at the same rate, the price standards will be the same as the contract rates. If, however, this is not the case because of variations related to length of service, experience, and the like, then the standard must be calculated on the basis of some form of expected weighted average hourly or daily rate.

If the pay plan is related, either wholly or partially, to amount of output, as in the case of straight piece rates, or bonus plans, or a combination plan, the determination of the price standard is tied in with the determination of the quantity standard. If a straight piece rate is provided for in the labor contract, the negotiation of the rate involves, in effect, the negotiation of both price and quantity. This rate sets the standard labor cost per unit of output.

If, on the other hand, price and quantity are negotiated in connection with some form of premium or bonus plan, an additional step is needed in setting the standard labor price per piece because of the vari-

---

[1] Theodore Lang (ed.), *Cost Accountants' Handbook* (New York: The Ronald Press Co., 1944), pp. 291–93.

ability of the unit labor cost under different conditions of output. These plans, depending on their nature, provide for either increasing or decreasing unit labor costs as output per worker (or group of workers) increases. Furthermore, the increases or decreases may be curved or stepped in nature. The problem of setting a price standard therefore becomes one of setting a standard output per worker. Hence, price and quantity both are involved in setting the price standard. At least two different practices are followed with respect to this problem, as is reported below.

1. To assume that 100% level of output is a reasonable one that ought to be attained and to set the standard at the wage rate paid for this degree of efficiency. When examining the resulting variance figures, management must keep in mind that a debit balance in the *labor rate variation* account may be justified when it has resulted from a high level of output under a wage system that has been deliberately designed to yield an increasing *unit labor cost* with increases in worker output.

2. To assume that the standard labor rate should include the *average bonus* or *premium earned*. This method differs from the foregoing only in the level at which the standard is set. However, in setting the standard it becomes necessary to study past performance records to ascertain what bonus is most commonly earned.

The choice between the above levels is best made according to the underlying policy upon which the wage payment plan has been constructed. Where the 100% level gives the rate of production and compensation which the average worker is expected to earn, it is the preferable level at which to set the standard. On the other hand, if the wage payment curve is constructed in such a fashion that the average worker is able to earn a bonus consistently, then the labor price standard should be set at this level.[2]

The close relationship between the development of an incentive pay plan and the standard price is clearly described as follows:

If a reasonably scientific plan of wage incentive is in use, based on sound time studies and adequate job evaluation, the per cent of bonus to add to the rate standard will usually be calculated rather than developed from the average of past experience for the given job. For instance, the time standards used for setting up the labor cost standards will be the ones used as the basis for setting the wage incentive rates. By considering this allowed time, the evaluated hourly rate, the efficiency rating of the operators studied, and a standard bonus factor, the wage payment rate will be developed. In instances of this sort, the effective bonus allowance in the final wage rate will be the factor of increase to apply to the rate standard shown in the job evaluation plan in order to obtain the final rate standard to use for standard cost purposes, as applied to the labor time standards. This procedure places the entire operation on a predetermined standard basis, including allowed time, evaluated rate per hour, and standard bonus allowed in the incentive rates.[3]

[2] *Ibid.*, pp. 296–97.
[3] Clinton W. Bennett, "Building Standards," p. 284 in *Industrial Accountant's Handbook,* Wyman P. Fiske and John A. Beckett (eds.). Copyright, 1954, by Prentice-Hall, Inc., Englewood Cliffs, N.J.

252 BUDGETING AND CONTROLLING TECHNIQUES

Budgetary Treatment of Variances. As in the case of direct materials, making budgetary provision for labor variances would be necessary if the standards were set so as practically to be unattainable. This practice is not recommended, however, and consequently no such provision is deemed necessary.

One possible exception might be made in the case of overtime premium payments, depending on the accounting disposition of the premiums. For example, in budgeting operations for a productive department for a period, overtime work may be scheduled. The incurrence of overtime premium costs during this period would raise the effective hourly rate of pay for the workers concerned, and yet it would not normally be advisable to change the labor price standard. If it is the company's practice to treat the premium as an item of factory burden and not as direct labor cost, provision would be made for it in the budget schedule for burden and the question of direct labor price variance would not arise. If, however, the accounting practice is to treat the premium as a direct labor price variance, then it should be budgeted. Note, however, that this recommendation presupposes that overtime work is scheduled. No provision for the premium should be made, whether as direct labor price variance or as burden, if the premium results from a failure to conform to the production time schedule.

Another exception perhaps should be made in the case of a new product in the early stages of production. Here, while the labor standards are deemed attainable within the budget period, variances which are anticipated until necessary experience is acquired should be recognized in the budget.

CONTROLLING DIRECT LABOR

Control Function of the Standards. Again, as in the case of direct materials, the direct labor costs in the forecast budget, which is based on the labor standards for the budgeted production, serve as a control over direct labor costs only if actual production coincides with that which is budgeted. Where actual production differs from that scheduled, the underlying labor standards must be referred to for control purposes. If, for example, 1,000 units of production are scheduled and the standard direct labor cost per unit is five hours at $2.00 per hour, the budgeted direct labor cost would be $10,000.00. If the actual labor cost for the period was $9,200.00 for 4,550 hours, and only 900 units of production were completed, the labor variations for control purposes would be measured by reference to the actual work done rather than the scheduled work. Thus, using the facts assumed above, the variances would be as follows:

DIRECT LABOR COST

Actual cost	$9,200.00
Standard cost	9,000.00
Total variance	$ 200.00
Time variance, 50 hours @ $2.00	$100.00
Price variance $9,200.00 − $9,100.00	$100.00
Total variance	$200.00

The standards thus provide in effect for flexible budgeting, but with a uniform unit labor cost at all levels of activity. It will be observed that the only difference between the variance accounting for direct material and direct labor is in the timing of the price and quantity variances. In the case of materials they may fall in different time periods because of the separation of purchase and usage; but with respect to direct labor, the purchase and usage are simultaneous transactions.

Controlling the Price Variances. It cannot be overemphasized that control of costs takes place at the time they are incurred, not afterwards. The reporting of price variances, for example, measures a control failure; the report is useful only in directing attention to the causes in order to attempt to prevent their recurrence. However, this must not be interpreted as suggesting a rigid conformity to a budget under all circumstances. For example, while a labor budget price schedule directs that labor be employed at a standard hourly rate, a foreman would not be justified in shutting down a machine because the only available operator had to be paid a rate in excess of the standard for the operation. A labor price variance would be unavoidable under the circumstances, but if such variance recurred, a study of the underlying causes would be indicated.

Ordinarily, since labor rates are commonly contracted for, it would at first appear that labor price variances should not occur. They do, however, for various reasons as described below:

There are many circumstances which may cause a rate variance. For example, the hiring of a large number of apprentices or a general wage increase will cause a rate variance if standard rates are not adjusted. Also, when standard and actual labor is reported by cost center and standard rates are set for each center, any change in the makeup of the labor skills within that center may cause a variance. For instance a department may be set up to employ five machinists and ten machine operators. If, during an accounting period, this department should employ ten machinists and only five machine operators the actual rate paid will be greater than the standard. This problem is especially prevalent in manufacturing companies with a seasonal pattern in their manufacturing cycle. It is often necessary to reshuffle employees to retain those with longer seniority and greater skills thereby causing higher rates to be paid in certain cost centers than were originally contemplated when standards were set up.[4]

[4] George B. Cleveland, "Getting Down to Causes on the Labor Variance," *N.A.A. Bulletin,* Section 1, Sept., 1955, p. 83.

The foregoing suggests that the control of labor price does not rest solely with the foreman but reaches back to those who are responsible for volume, scheduling, and personnel.

Controlling the Time Variances. The control of direct labor time ordinarily is the most important aspect of the control of direct labor cost. As noted above, this is achieved primarily through the use of time standards. With reference to these standards, however, it should be pointed out that frequently current shop standards differ from the standards used in accounting and in preparing the labor cost budget. These differences result from the fact that in many companies it is not possible to keep the formal standards adjusted to the changes in method resulting from the continuous effort in improving efficiency and reducing labor costs. Nevertheless, the two standards should be in agreement as far as practicable.

While, for the purposes of over-all budgeting and budgetary control, labor time financial costs are the data used, for the purpose of detailed control at the departmental level, manpower measurements, rather than financial cost measurements, are the more useful. The foreman is dealing with people, not dollars, and his job is to train and lead them to achieve standard output. But to do this properly, his labor force must be adjusted to the work to be done. Hence, for the foreman a manpower budget may be much more useful than a dollar cost budget.

... the supervisor's labor budget is his plan for manpower requirements and utilization, based on the organization's production planning and scheduling. If the planning is sound and if the supervisor is able to follow the plan, his labor costs will be under control as far as he can control them. The requirements, then, for a sound labor budget are a production schedule which indicates the work expected from the department during the budget period, and some form of standards by means of which the production schedule can be translated into manpower requirements.

The foregoing statement, of course, presupposes the availability of adequate equipment and tools, that work from other departments will feed through on schedule, and that materials, parts, and components will be available as required. These presupposed conditions usually are not the responsibility of the production supervisor whose budget is being discussed and delays or other costs due to failures in such matters should be isolated, measured, and accounted for as variances controllable by others than the supervisor under discussion.[5]

The varied causes and sources of variations, as indicated in the foregoing statement, call for good reporting of labor performance. A variance in one department may be unavoidable because of failures elsewhere in the organization. Corrective action may have to be initiated at a

[5] Alwyn M. Hartogensis, "Manpower Budgeting for Control of Labor Costs," *N.A.A. Bulletin*, Section 1, Mar., 1955, pp. 948–49.

DIRECT LABOR COST

DEPARTMENTAL MANUFACTURING EFFICIENCY ON COMPLETED OPERATIONS

——— Plant

Dept. No. . . . .

Code	Reason for Variance		Month of			Year to Date		
			Actual Hours	Variance Hours	Cost	Actual Hours	Variance Hours	Cost
0	No reason variances less than 10 per cent.	C						
1	Estimated running time too high. Reported to Stds. Dep't.	N						
2	Estimated set-up time too high. Reported to Stds. Dep't.	N						
3	Men's effort and/or ability above average.	C						
5	New machine, standard has not been changed.	N						
6	Change in methods, standard has not been changed.	N						
7	New or improved tools, standard has not been changed.	N						
8	Used set-up from previous job.	C						
9	Time set for man operating one machine. Ran two.	C						
10	Time clock registers to 0.1 hour only.	N						
11	Work done under special supervision.	C						
	Total Gains							
0	No reason variances less than 10 per cent.	C						
51	Standard too low. Reported to Standards Department.	N						
52	First time job was made.	C						
53	Slow or obsolete machine used.	N						
54	Planning not correct. Was changed. Stds. Dep't. notified.	N						
55	Could not follow oper. as planned, delivery requirements.	N						
56	Operations in previous departments not performed as planned.	C						
57	Time set for man operating two machines. One available.	N						
58	Quantity too small.	N						

SOURCE: Research Series No. 22, The Analysis of Manufacturing Cost Variances, *N.A.A. Bulletin*, Section 2, Aug., 1952, pp. 1558–59.

FIG. 13–1. Departmental Manufacturing Efficiency on Completed Operations

BUDGETING AND CONTROLLING TECHNIQUES

Code	Reason for Variance	Month of			Year to Date		
		Actual Hours	Variance Hours	Cost	Actual Hours	Variance Hours	Cost
59	Extra set-up result of machine break down.	N					
60	Extra work.	N					
61	Two men had to be assigned to job due to nature of job.	N					
62	Learner, apprentice, or student.	N					
63	Man inexperienced. Undergoing instructions.	N					
64	Different operators used due to difficulty of job.	C					
65	Assisting inexperienced operator on another machine.	N					
66	Man's effort and/or ability below average.	C					
67	Oper. not performed correctly. Add'l time required.	C					
68	Parts spoiled. Had to make additional parts.	C					
69	Tools not available at time job was started.	N					
70	Trying out new tools.	N					
71	Tools not correct when job was started. Had to be corrected.	N					
72	Broke tool. Time lost redressing and sharpening.	C					
73	Oversized material used.	N					
74	Castings warped, but are within Foundry tolerances.	N					
75	Castings not to dimensions. Time lost waiting for instructions.	N					
76	Material too hard. Frequent sharpening of tools required.	N					
77	Improper supervision.	C					
79	Illegible Blue Prints.	N					
80	Blowholes and porous castings	N					
81	Sheet stock—Secondary material or scrap ends used.	N					
99	Full quantity or operations not complete.	N					
	Total Losses						
	Total						
	Efficiency % Controllable by Foreman	C					
	Efficiency % Noncontrollable	N					
	Efficiency % Overall						

Fig. 13-1 (*Continued*)

higher level of management than the departmental level because of the interlocking nature of interdepartmental activities.

Labor performance reports assume many forms, depending on circumstances. The time element in reporting obviously is of great importance and many companies require daily labor efficiency reports. Because of the many possible reasons for variations from standard time, the accurate reporting of them frequently is difficult but, nevertheless, important. Figure 13-1 provides for a comprehensive reporting of causes, classified according to their controllability at the departmental level.

CHAPTER 14

FACTORY EXPENSE

	Page		Page
Nature of factory expense	258	Indirect materials	265
Purpose of chapter	259	Time charges	265
Budgeting Factory Expense		**Controlling Factory Expenses**	
Indirect labor—producing departments	260		
Indirect labor—service departments	262	Departmentalization of factory expenses	266
Idle time	263	The point of control	266
Supplementary labor costs	264	Measurements	268

Nature of Factory Expense. The term "factory expense," which has various synonyms, such as "factory burden," "manufacturing overhead," "indirect factory costs," and so on, denotes the cost of all the factory materials and services not directly adding to or readily identifiable with the products which the factory manufactures. Those costs frequently are larger in the aggregate than either direct material or direct labor, and they constitute a very important budgetary item or group of items. Aside from its quantitative importance, factory expense poses difficult budget-making problems because of the varied nature of the component costs.

These costs differ from direct costs, first, with respect to their variability with volume of production. Whereas direct costs tend by definition to vary fully with volume, factory expense includes items which are fixed, other items which are fully variable, and still other items which are semi-variable. Problems of variability classification and behavior, therefore, are basic in the building of budget schedules for factory expense.

A second distinctive feature of factory expense is the varied nature of the items with reference to their primary account classifications. Whereas direct material and direct labor refer respectively only to material and labor, factory expense includes items of labor, material, time costs—such as depreciation and taxes, and purchased services. A typical list of cost items included in factory expense is as follows:

                Supervision
                Clerical
                Indirect labor

FACTORY EXPENSE

Idle time
Supplementary labor costs
Materials and supplies
Maintenance and repairs
Insurance
Taxes
Depreciation
Other factory expenses

The factory expense items also differ from direct costs as to the point of incurrence. Direct costs can readily be departmentalized for control purposes. Factory expenses, however, are incurred at many places in the factory, and quite commonly their benefit is so diffused and so far removed from the source that where to control them presents a serious problem.

Purpose of Chapter. In considering the purpose of this chapter, the reader must bear in mind that this is a treatise on budgeting and not on cost accounting. The latter is concerned primarily with the identification of costs with products and, as it applies to factory expense, presents as its principal problems the departmentalization of expenses and their eventual application to product costs through the use of overhead rates determined for producing departments only. While these refinements are useful in the budgeting of cost of sales, they are not of prime consideration in budgeting factory expenses, where the purpose is to schedule expenditures in proportion to manufacturing activity, but without regard to specific products.

The fact, however, that there are both producing and service departments in the factory does present a budgetary problem in the determination of the volume of activities (or range of volumes) for which the budget schedules are to be drafted. In the case of a producing department, the expense schedule is related solely to that department's activities. In the case of service departments, however, the activities ultimately are governed by the operating levels of all the departments served by them. This suggests, therefore, that in discussing the preparation of expense budget schedules, the treatment of the expense items should be from two viewpoints: that of producing departments and that of service departments.

With reference to the specific expenses to be discussed, it is observed that the foregoing list may be reduced to basic elements as follows:

Indirect labor—all labor, other than direct, and including supervision, clerical, and repair labor

Idle time—labor normally classified as direct, but reclassified where no work is done

Supplementary labor costs
Indirect materials—including repair materials
Time charges—insurance, taxes, and depreciation

It is pointed out that in this chapter devoted to factory expense the discussion includes a number of costs which are frequently treated as direct labor variances, for example, idle time and rework. Similarly, setup labor is sometimes treated as direct labor. These and similar items are discussed in Chapter 13, which is devoted to direct labor cost, but are again taken up in this chapter in view of the alternative treatment as factory expense.

The first purpose of the chapter, therefore, is to discuss the budgeting of the foregoing items as they apply to producing and service departments. The second purpose is to discuss their control, and it is in this connection that some reference to cost accounting is made. The reader is reminded that Chapters 7 and 8 discuss at some length the principles of cost behavior and variability determination, the use of flexible budgets, and expense control.

BUDGETING FACTORY EXPENSE

Indirect Labor—Producing Departments. The nature of indirect labor in a producing department will depend in part on the accounting classification, but the following activities are commonly classified as indirect:

Supervision (salaried)
Supervision (hourly)
Clerical
Cleaning
Inspection
Rework
Setup
Material handling
Machinery repairs

On occasion, some of the foregoing items may be restricted to service departments, but for the purpose of this section of the chapter they are considered to arise in producing departments.

As to budgeting direct labor costs, it was noted in the preceding chapter that the factors used are (1) scheduled production and (2) unit standard labor costs, the latter being determined by reference to unit time standards and wage rate standards. Full variability with volume is the basic assumption. In the case of indirect labor, however, **it is not that simple.** Most of this labor is not fully variable with volume.

FACTORY EXPENSE

In addition, for much of it, precise time standards cannot be set. Resort must be had, therefore, to a manpower budget based on a manning table. This table may be established on a flexible basis (and should be, for cost control purposes), and from it the necessary indirect manpower can be budgeted in relation to scheduled production. Costs are computed by applying the salary and wage rates to the manpower requirements. Figure 14-1 illustrates a flexible manpower schedule related to number of direct labor employees.

	Number of Direct Labor Employees						
	Below 75	76–90	91–105	106–120	121–135	136–150	151–165
Assistant foremen	4	5	5	6	6	7	8
Clerks	2	2	2	3	3	3	3
Setup men	2	2	3	3	3	4	4
Materials handlers	3	3	4	4	5	5	6
Sweepers	2	2	2	2	3	3	3

SOURCE: Alwyn M. Hartogensis, "Manpower Budgeting for Control of Labor Costs," *N.A.A. Bulletin*, Section 1, Mar., 1955, p. 953.

FIG. 14-1. Department Budget Allowances for Indirect Employees

The determination of the allowances is based on study and observation.

The actual allowances may be determined by past experience or by careful observation and analysis of the work performed. In some cases, standards can be developed by time study, but these standards, alone, will not be adequate for the purpose. For example, a standard time allowance might be developed for setup of various classes of work on various machine tools, but it is still necessary to forecast or estimate the number of setups for each class of work on each tool in order to arrive at the total manpower requirement. This involves so many variables, in most shops, that it will be far more simple, and also probably more accurate, to estimate the total requirements, based on past experience modified by an expected possibility of improvement on past experience. The actual observation and analysis should then be directed to the possible amount of improvement on current practice, rather than to the actual amount of work required.[1]

While standard times for indirect labor have not been developed to the same degree as for direct labor, it should not be concluded that they are not desirable. But to the extent they can be developed, they must result primarily from methods study rather than time study.

[1] Alwyn M. Hartogensis, "Manpower Budgeting for Control of Labor Costs," *N.A.A. Bulletin*, Section 1, Mar., 1955, p. 953.

Occasionally, in budgeting an item of indirect labor, the determination depends on the efficiency of direct labor. A case in point is rework labor. The budget-maker has a twofold responsibility. He must estimate both the amount of rework and its indirect labor requirement. The former is a function of the efficiency of direct labor in relation to the direct materials to be connected. In this case there is a close relationship between the direct production standards and the budgeted rework. Following is a description of how one rework budget is established.

The first step in budget preparation is the developing of a workmanship re-work percentage to the direct labor of each department. This takes into account the relative liability and is established in conjunction with the opinions of qualified production personnel, and historical, factual data from the accountants. As examples of different percentages, let us consider an automatic screw machine operation where one operator keeps several machines functioning, compared to hand lathe operations where there is one operator per machine. The multiple machine gives rise to more repairs per direct labor dollar than the hand lathes because of the process. Newer machines and better facilities produce finer, more accurate work with equal or less skill than some older facilities.[2]

Another troublesome problem in budgeting indirect labor concerns maintenance labor (here assumed to be part of the indirect labor of a producing department). Again, the problem is twofold, involving the determination, first, of the required amount of maintenance in relation to scheduled production and, second, the manpower necessary to its accomplishment. For short periods of time, maintenance needs may be unpredictable, but over long periods they generally are believed to have a very close relationship to volume of production. The key to successful budgeting of this cost is an experience record based on adequate maintenance reporting and accounting.

Indirect Labor—Service Departments. The factory service departments commonly include the following:

> Factory accounting
> Maintenance
> Machine shop
> Methods and time study
> Production control
> Building service
> Power plant
> Tool crib
> Storeroom
> Intraplant materials handling

---

[2] F. Gordon Foster, "Re-work Costs Yield to Budgetary Control," *N.A.A. Bulletin*, Section 1, Mar., 1953, pp. 916–17.

Much of the labor of these departments is fixed over a wide range of operating levels. To the extent, however, that it is variable, the first budget problem is that of determining the proper measure of activity to be used in the cost-volume relationship. The problem arises from the fact that in the case of many of the foregoing departments the service is rendered to many departments of varied nature. For example, if Producing Department A goes on a reduced schedule, the effect on the indirect labor requirements of that department is relatively easy of determination; but what of the effect on, say, the work of the Methods and Time Study Department, which serves the entire factory?

With respect to maintenance, while it is pointed out above that in the long run it has a close relationship with production, nevertheless, in short periods the relationship may be an inverse one because of the greater ease of some types of maintenance when a department is idle.

It is clear that manning tables for service department labor (all of which is classified here as indirect in spite of the fact that within a service department frequently some of the labor is classified as direct to that department) require for their preparation an intimate knowledge of the flow of services throughout the factory. With such information, the tables can be developed, on a flexible basis, in a manner similar to those of producing departments.

The problem of labor time standards is similar to that of indirect labor in producing departments. Some progress has been made in this direction; more can be done in many companies; but in general the setting of time standards is more difficult than for direct labor.

Idle Time. Idle time in this chapter refers to earned hours of direct labor employees which were not used in either production or indirect operations and thus are lost. The wages represented thereby are idle time costs which are classified as factory overhead. The common causes are:

>Setups
>Lack of material
>Lack of manpower
>Lack of scheduled work
>Lack of proper tools
>Machine breakdown

Where there is enforced idleness on the part of direct employees whose pay, nevertheless, runs on, the idle time cost represents a loss of the wages earned. To the extent the employees can be assigned other useful tasks, the loss is reduced. In many instances, however, this is not feasible on short notice. While idle employee time frequently is associated with idle machine time, this is not necessarily the case.

Whether or not idle time cost should be budgeted depends on the degree of certainty of its incurrence. If the nature of the company's operations, for example, involves frequent setups of equipment and specialized setup labor, idle time probably will be inevitable and should be budgeted. If, on the other hand, it results from causes which should be controllable, the decision to budget it should be consistent with the company's over-all view regarding the budgetary provision for all types of controllable variances.

Where idle time is to be budgeted, the necessary estimates require adequate experience records, and these, in turn, depend on accurate timekeeping and a properly classified set of labor accounts. Not only must idle time be accounted for as such, but the reasons also must be known and recorded. Only in this manner can the cost be classified according to degrees of controllability.

Supplementary Labor Costs. Supplementary labor costs, frequently referred to as "fringe benefits," include:

>Holiday pay
>Vacation pay
>Unemployment and old-age taxes
>Pension costs
>Overtime premium
>Shift differentials
>Paid lunch periods
>Washup time
>Union activities (time paid for by employer)

These costs may be incurred in connection with both direct and indirect labor. Quite commonly, however, they are treated as factory burden and are not classified in the accounts as to the labor classification to which they relate.

With the exception of overtime premium, all the foregoing items are capable of reasonably accurate estimation and should be budgeted. Overtime premium, too, may be budgeted if the scheduled operations call for overtime work. In the case of fringe costs associated with indirect labor, the same budgetary problem is presented as in the case of indirect labor itself, namely, the added difficulty of budgeting the work load of service departments. All labor costs should be geared to the ultimate production, but the service departments are two steps removed. Whereas the fringe benefits associated with the labor of a production department can be adjusted to its production schedule alone, those of the service departments must be related to total factory operations and frequently (for short periods) may be unrelated to the production schedules.

Indirect Materials. While terminology with respect to indirect materials is not standardized, the term "indirect materials" is here used to denote both indirect materials and supplies. Where a distinction is made between the two, the former usually denotes materials which are incorporated in the product but which are not accounted for as direct materials for reasons of convenience; the latter term refers to materials which are not incorporated in the product but are essential to production processes. Examples of indirect materials are glue, thread, paint, and minor items of hardware. Examples of supplies are lubricating oils, grease, cleaning rags, brushes, paint (not used on product), janitorial supplies, fuel, and repair parts. In the case of both the materials and supplies the accounting procedures are the same and require an adequate expense classification in the accounts.

For the purposes of budgeting, the principal distinction between indirect materials and factory supplies lies in the ease of estimation. The indirect materials which are in effect direct materials, but not accounted for as such, can be related with reasonable accuracy to some measure of production such as quantity of direct materials, direct labor time, or units of product. With such relationships established either as percentages or as unit costs, they can be budgeted with reasonable accuracy in relation to scheduled production.

Factory supplies, on the other hand, are consumed in various degrees of variability with production. Moreover, their consumption occurs in both production and service departments.

Only a careful analysis of past experience will provide necessary budget information. Frequently, the validity of the experience record is open to question because of loose accounting. This is particularly true where—for whatever reason—the supplies are accounted for on an as-purchased rather than an as-used basis. Needless to say, the larger items of supply expense must be properly accounted for.

Time Charges. These include such items as insurance, taxes, and depreciation—those items which normally require monthly entries to record periodic expense accruals and expirations. Whether incurred in connection with production departments or service departments, they present no serious budget-making problems for they are primarily fixed expenses. Their incurrence either follows from an earlier decision (as in the case of the decision to build the plant and acquire equipment) or from year to year policy decisions (the amount of protection to be carried, for example).

CONTROLLING FACTORY EXPENSES

The basic principles underlying the control of factory expenses have been described in Chapter 8. Additional discussion of them at this point is limited to (1) departmentalization, (2) the point of control, and (3) necessary measurements.

Departmentalization of Factory Expenses. With regard to the departmentalization of factory expenses there must be a clear distinction between the purposes of cost accounting and those of budgetary control. A review of cost accounting procedure as it applies to factory expenses will aid in posing the departmental problems of control and in clarifying the distinction between product costing and expense control.

It is recognized that the factory comprises both producing and service departments and that expenses include those which are incurred in and are directly chargeable to a department, and those which are incurred on a plant-wide basis and must be prorated to the various departments, both producing and service departments. It is further recognized that the expenses of the service departments must be redistributed to the producing departments for the purpose of allocating these expenses to product cost. The procedure can best be illustrated by a *pro forma* expense distribution sheet (see Figure 14-2), which is illustrative of the type which would be prepared as part of the budget-making procedure.

If the foregoing procedure, which may vary in detail from company to company, is followed in the established cost system, then it should also be followed in preparing budget forecasts. There is a growing trend in cost accounting to avoid elaborate and complicated redistribution of service department costs on an interim periodic basis. Since budgetary procedures must be consistent with the cost accounting methods regularly employed by the company, this will likewise affect the procedure in budget forecasting. The estimated distribution is also useful in budget-making to the extent that the financial statements in the forecast budget include the over- or underabsorption of expense.

The Point of Control. As is pointed out in Chapter 8, expenses are controlled at the point of incurrence and not at the point where they are ultimately charged. The problem then is one of determining responsibility for the incurrence. That this problem is not always a simple one is pointed out in Chapter 8, where reference is made to the duality of responsibility in the case of power costs and centralized maintenance. Both the production of a service and its use must be controlled. If too much power is used, but it is produced efficiently, the using department is responsible. On the other hand, in the case of efficient usage but inefficient production, the power producer is responsible. Measurements

FACTORY EXPENSE

Pro Forma Expense Distribution Sheet

	Service Departments			Producing Departments			
	General Factory	Power	Store Rooms	1	2	3	4
Directly incurred expenses:							
Supervision—general	x						
Supervision—departmental .	x	x	x	x	x	x	x
Clerical	x	x	x	x	x	x	x
Idle time				x	x	x	x
Supplementary labor costs .	x	x	x	x	x	x	x
Materials and supplies	x	x	x	x	x	x	x
Maintenance and repairs ...	x	x	x	x	x	x	x
Time charges—direct:							
Depreciation	x	x	x	x	x	x	x
Time charges—prorated:							
Taxes	x	x	x	x	x	x	x
Insurance	x	x	x	x	x	x	x
Total expenses	x	x	x	x	x	x	x
General factory redistributed		x	x	x	x	x	x
Power redistributed			x	x	x	x	x
Store rooms redistributed				x	x	x	x
Total expenses charged to producing departments				x	x	x	x
Expenses applied to product cost				x	x	x	x
Over or (under) applied				x	(x)	x	x

Fig. 14–2. *Pro Forma* Expense Distribution Sheet

of this type can be made through the use of standards, either of quantity or of cost.

But what of time charges, such as depreciation, taxes, and insurance? These charges in general result from earlier decisions at top management levels; they represent commitments incurred at the time of acquisition of facilities. In the short run, nothing can be done about them, and there is some disagreement as to whether any purpose is served by including them in cost control reports to department heads. For those who urge their inclusion, the principal argument would seem to be in connection with their long-run significance. If efficiency can be so improved as to make certain facilities unnecessary, a long-run reduction of investment costs is indicated. Consequently, the decision concerning inclusion of these items in departmental cost control reports rests on management's viewpoint concerning the relative importance of the short and long run. Poor performance needing intensive effort for its correction may lead management to conclude that the attention of foremen and supervisors should be concentrated on those items within their immediate control. Short-run objectives are paramount and no useful purpose is served by reporting noncontrollable costs. On the other hand, where long-run improvement is a more important present consideration, every effort should be made to inform foremen fully on all aspects of operation.

A similar problem arises in the case of the proration of that group of expenses included under the heading of general factory. These consist primarily of the services of general factory supervision, the general factory technical services (production control, timekeeping, method and time study, works accounting, and so forth), and space costs (costs associated with the ownership, protection, and maintenance of buildings). Some of these costs are the result of prior commitments, some are a result of company policy, and some are not susceptible to control standards. None of them are controllable at the level of the department to which they are charged. For the purposes of cost control, should they be reported to the assessed departments? Again, the answer is not fully agreed upon in management circles. The advocates of noninclusion believe that a foreman's attention should be concentrated on his own problems. The advocates of inclusion feel that a foreman can better perform his tasks if he has wide comprehension of company problems as well as of his own department's problems. This is a matter of managerial philosophy concerning which, perhaps, there is no final and conclusive answer.

One point on which there is fairly general agreement is that the most effective cost control under a budgetary system occurs where the foreman or supervisor has a voice in the determination of his expense budget schedules. It is common practice to secure beforehand his approval of the flexible expense schedules. This serves to ensure his confidence in the control system whereby his performance in the control of expenses is to be measured.

Measurements. Control of present costs takes place at the time of incurrence, not afterwards, and a historical record of performance is useful only for the improvement of control in the future. Cost control budgets, therefore, are essentially directives governing present actions. The significance of this is that under a flexible budget system, providing cost directives for various levels of operation, the foremen must be fore-

FACTORY EXPENSE

warned of changes in operating level in time to effect necessary changes in work force and other cost factors. The measurement of activity level, therefore, must be clear. This suggests that the language of operating directives must be appropriate to the nature of the work of the various departments. It further suggests that performance records must be similarly phrased. And in line with the earlier reference to manpower budgets, it follows that frequently the most effective reporting of actual cost incurrence takes the form of nonmonetary measures. A comparison of actual and budgeted hours of labor may have more meaning at the point of control than the comparison of actual and budgeted dollars of labor.

Quantitative measurements of this type are especially significant in the interpolation of allowed costs as between two operating levels covered in a flexible budget. The procedure of interpolation has been described in Chapter 8. It must be used with care since, while dollar amounts can be interpolated, quantities may not be susceptible of interpolation. A workman cannot be fractionalized! This suggests that in a case where the flexible budget schedules cover operating levels 80 per cent and 90 per cent, and actual output is at 87 per cent, the performance report may have to assume that the allowance is 90. This problem and its disposition become clearer when quantitative measurements are used.

A final matter of measurement is now referred to, which has a bearing on the preceding discussion relative to the inclusion, in departmental cost control reports and budgets, of the general factory expenses. Aside from managerial philosophy in the matter of reporting costs to a foreman who has no voice in their incurrence, there is the problem of current proration. This problem is also inherent in the procedures of cost accounting for product costing purposes. So many assumptions have to be made that confidence in the prorations frequently is undermined. For product costing purposes the problem has to be faced and solved in as satisfactory a manner as is possible under the circumstances. For the purposes of cost control, however, this is not true. This consideration should have some bearing on management's decision concerning the inclusion of these data in control reports.

CHAPTER 15

GENERAL AND ADMINISTRATIVE EXPENSES AND OTHER ITEMS

	Page		Page
Purpose of chapter	270	Other credits to income	278
Budgeting		Purchase discounts	278
		Interest earned and investment income	279
The nature of general and administrative expenses	271		
Salaries and wages	272	**Controlling the Items**	
Professional services	273	Fixed and appropriated general and administrative expenses	279
Supplies	274		
Equipment costs	274	Flexible general and administrative expenses	280
Space costs	275		
Telephone, telegraph, and postage	275	Departmentalization of general and administrative expenses	280
Travel costs	275		
Subscriptions, dues, and memberships	276	Control of sales discounts	281
Donations	276	Control of bad debts	281
Other charges to income	276	Control of interest expense	281
Sales discounts	276	Variations in income taxes	283
Bad debts	277	Control of purchase discounts	283
Interest expense	277	Control of interest earned and investment income	284
Income taxes	277		

Purpose of Chapter. The purpose of this chapter is to discuss the budgetary and control problems of those operating charges and credits not covered in detail in the preceding chapters. These include that group of expenses commonly referred to as "general and administrative," and other miscellaneous items of income and expense which are variously reported in internal operating statements. These include purchase discounts, investment income, sales discounts, bad debts, and interest expense. As pointed out in Chapter 2, accounting classifications used in statements for internal management purposes frequently are at variance with generally accepted accounting classifications used in published statements.

In the aggregate, the foregoing items constitute a significant segment of total operations, and for several reasons the problem of their control is somewhat different from that of the operating items previously discussed. First, many of the items are the result of decisions at top management level and, because of their nature, are not susceptible to precise evaluation. Second, some of them are the result of policy decisions, the pattern of which may vary from time to time. Third, some of the items (sales discounts and investment income, for example) are

GENERAL AND ADMINISTRATIVE EXPENSES

difficult to budget and control because of external factors. On the other hand, some of the items are subject to the same type of standards as are used in other routine operations of the company.

As in the preceding chapter, the method of treatment is by nature of the item rather than on a departmental basis. The first section of the chapter is devoted to the budgeting of the main categories of general and administrative expenses, followed by a brief discussion of the other items of income and expense. The second section discusses the budgetary control of the same items.

BUDGETING

The Nature of General and Administrative Expenses. The administrative organizations of companies vary both in form and in degree of centralization. In general, however, they embrace general executive departments, the controller's department, the treasury department, the purchasing department, the legal department, and the personnel and industrial relations department. Typical expenses are:

Salaries—officers and executives
Salaries—general office employees
Travel expense
Legal and auditing
Maintenance and operation of office building
Depreciation—furniture and fixtures
Stationery and office supplies
Telephone and telegraph
Postage
Rental and equipment
Subscriptions and dues and association activities
Donations

Some of these expenses are common to all departments of the company and, to that extent, the principles here set forth are similar to those previously discussed in the preparation of the budgets of the sales and production departments.

While, in practice, each department of the general office submits a budget schedule of all its costs, and their summation provides the budget for general and administrative expenses, the treatment in this chapter is based on the primary nature of the expense rather than the department. For convenience the expenses are discussed according to the following classification:

1. Salaries and wages
2. Professional services
3. Supplies

4. Equipment costs
5. Space costs
6. Telephone, telegraph, and postage
7. Travel costs
8. Subscriptions, dues, and memberships
9. Donations

Salaries and Wages. In this section we are concerned with the compensation paid all employees in the administrative division of the company. The employees include the president and other corporate officers, department heads, professional employees (lawyers, tax experts, accountants, industrial relations specialists, etc.), secretaries, clerks, machine operators, messengers, and so forth. In the case of the president and other corporate officers, compensation commonly is determined by the board of directors and represents a fixed charge for budget purposes. Below that rank, the compensation generally is determined by the operating management, but in all cases it should be on the basis of a formal salary and wage schedule based, in turn, on job classifications. Only in this manner can there be an orderly determination of starting salaries, periodic increments, and promotional increments. Given such a program, the budgeting of compensation is greatly simplified.

Much of the administrative payroll cost is fixed in nature, and that portion which is executive or professional in nature cannot be determined by reference to accurate time standards. The main problem in regard to these employees is that of determining how much executive and professional service can be used effectively. This obviously is a question which can be decided only by the highest authority. So long as the services are used, they should be compensated for in accordance with the compensation schedule.

On the other hand, a significant portion of the payroll costs relates to work of a standardized, routine nature. Billing, posting, filing, addressing, and card punching are examples of work for which accurate time standards can be set, and these operations should be scheduled by reference to flexible manpower budgets in the same manner as factory labor budgets are determined. The number of employees in each of these categories to be provided for in the budget depends on the volume of work to be done, and this is related to the over-all level of company activities. In this connection, the budgeting of routine, administrative employees presents the same problem as that encountered in factory service departments, namely, the relation of the general office work load to the volume of company business. It is one thing to determine unit time standards for each routine job in the office, but the quantity of help to be provided requires a forecast of the amount of office work to be done. Does this vary with sales, or with production, or with a combination of factors? It is obvious that the latter determinations are necessary to the application of sound budget procedures to this aspect of the general and administrative budget.

In setting time standards for routine, clerical operations, the same methods are used as in the setting of factory labor standards. Moreover, there must be the same urge to improve old procedures and devise new ones. The tremendous increase in paper work and the resulting increase in clerical staffs to a point where they tend to be in the ratio of one clerk to two factory employees has resulted in recent years in the serious study of office routines. The office methods staff is now important in almost every large company. Its functions are as follows:

1. Conduct research into the best clerical methods successfully employed within the corporation or in other businesses.
2. Prepare formal written procedures covering clerical operations in existence within the corporation.
3. Standardize clerical procedures throughout the company, so far as is compatible with varying local conditions.
4. Survey existing procedures and clerical methods for improved efficiency.
5. Design and install simple low-cost clerical procedures.
6. Set clerical performance standards.
7. Determine work loads and the number of employees required to perform each operation.
8. Investigate office equipment, machines, and other facilities, and make recommendations concerning specific applications to clerical procedures.
9. Survey and make recommendations concerning office space and efficient layouts.
10. Survey and make recommendations for effective and efficient filing systems.
11. Design forms and engineer their standardization.
12. Set up standards for control of printing and stationery purchases and costs.[1]

Once the standards are established, and the activity levels forecasted, the clerical budgets can readily be prepared by reference to the salary classification schedule.

Professional Services. Professional services purchased on the outside include legal, accounting, and others. Some are purchased on a retainer basis and some on a project basis. The former generally are on a continuing basis from year to year at the direction of top management or the board of directors. The charges are fixed and present no budget problem. The latter may be planned in advance and easily budgeted or may result from unforeseen events. In this latter case some provision should be made on an estimated basis from past experience modified by a look to the future.

[1] S. D. Flinn, "Continuous Methods Work Will Control Clerical Costs," *N.A.A. Bulletin,* Section 1, Sept., 1951, p. 29.

Supplies. Office supplies if material in amount present troublesome problems. One of the problems arises from the fact that commonly they are expensed as purchased rather than as used, and the accounting for their use frequently costs more than it is worth. On the assumption that the departmental requisitions from the supply storeroom are costed, departmental supply cost information is useful in budgeting only if there is a system of inventory control whereby it is ensured that the users do not accumulate substantial inventories. The necessity for this may appear obvious, but it must be recognized that there may be a penalty for close departmental control in the form of excessive requisitions and deliveries. This is a matter for study by the office methods staff.

Whether or not supplies expense should be budgeted in total for the general office, or departmentalized, depends on the adequacy of the data and on the nature of the operations. In any case, they are costly and their use should be carefully controlled. An important aspect of the cost side of the picture is the nature of the supplies. Efforts should be directed toward the reduction of this cost through improvement of procedures and through a critical review of the purposes to be served. Needless to say, a review of forms is closely related to the study of procedures generally.

As with office labor, determining the relation between the amount of supplies used and the forecast level of company operations is a prerequisite to accurate budget determinations. This is important not only for cost budgeting, but also to prevent overaccumulation of supply inventories. Overaccumulation is to be avoided particularly where obsolescence is a factor, as it is in the case of catalogs and periodically changed items, and in those companies where methods studies lead to frequent changes in the process of improving clerical procedures.

Finally, it should be observed that efficient purchasing is also a factor in supply budgeting to the extent that the forecasted purchases must be priced.

Equipment Costs. Equipment costs include depreciation, repairs, and rental of all forms of office equipment. As mechanization proceeds in the office, these costs assume more importance. Depreciation and rentals commonly are fixed charges during the budget period. Repairs, however, tend to vary with usage but frequently present no budget problem since commonly they are contracted for on an annual basis.

A growing budget problem relates to departmental charges in those companies developing centralized installations of very expensive electronic data processing equipment. The using departments are charged for the service by the use of rates which are designed to liquidate the entire periodic cost of the servicing department.

A major problem in such installations is to provide for the fullest use of the equipment through good scheduling. The avoidance of bottlenecks and the fullest possible utilization require that utilization studies and records be developed similar to those used so successfully in manufacturing.

Space Costs. These costs include all the costs associated with the occupancy of general office buildings. The extent to which they are designed to give prestige value is determined by company policy. Otherwise, except for the fixed charges of occupancy, they should be determined by standards of operating efficiency similar in nature to those established for factory buildings. The costs are scheduled by the building superintendent. Repairs, cleaning, heating, lighting, and the like, should be estimated on as scientific a basis as is possible in the circumstances.

A major problem associated with space is its effective utilization. Because of its cost and also of the relation of layout to the entire problem of office and clerical efficiency, it is apparent that space requirements, clerical procedures, and equipment are closely intertwined.

Generally, there is no need to allocate space costs to office departments for ordinary budget purposes. It is advisable, however, to consider space costs when studying proposed changes in procedure which would necessitate major changes in total space requirements.

Telephone, Telegraph, and Postage. These three items are grouped for convenience since they present similar budget problems. First, it is difficult to relate them to some over-all measure of activity, and, second, it frequently is considered not worth the trouble to attempt to departmentalize the costs.

In the case of telephone and telegraph facilities the cost usually consists of a fixed charge and a variable charge, depending on the extent of the usage. Ordinarily, it is not considered worth the clerical effort to charge the costs to individual departments. The principal budget-making problem is to relate the variable costs to the company's activity.

While postage costs are fully variable, they too are hard to forecast on a scientific basis because of the frequent lack of apparent relationships with activity. In both cases statistical analyses are the means of establishing a basis for cost estimation.

Travel Costs. Travel costs, as they relate to the general office, may not be subject to the same scrutiny by the budget officer as are the other costs of administration. But when consideration is given to travel costs throughout all divisions of the company, when incurred for administrative purposes, there is no satisfactory basis for judging the effectiveness of the expenditure. In short, good judgment and intentions must be relied on largely in budgeting these costs. They cannot be judged by ordinary standards. On the other hand, significant changes in *total* travel expenditures should be brought to light in the course of budget preparation.

Subscriptions, Dues, and Memberships. These, for the most part, are annual fixed charges. The principal concern with them is to review their usefulness. The literature, exchange of ideas and information, and other benefits obtained from association memberships frequently are of great value. It is suggested, however, that a clear case of advantage should be made for each of such expenditures.

Donations. Corporate donations generally are a matter of high corporate policy. In the aggregate they are becoming a very important source of funds for charitable and educational institutions. Whether budgeted at a flat amount or as a percentage of net income, the decision is one for top management or the board of directors to make. Where the amount is large, approval should come from the board since stockholders might question management's right to "give profits away." Unless the gifts are made to specified donees and at prearranged dates, a problem will arise in the allocation of the expenditures to the several months of the budget period. Consideration of this problem is useful, particularly in drafting the financial budget schedules.

Other Charges to Income. Sales discounts, bad debts, interest expense, and income taxes are variously classified in operating statements. However, since the classification in the operating statement has no bearing on the budget procedures, the foregoing items are all treated in this chapter.

Sales Discounts. Sales discounts are a function of (1) sales, (2) invoice terms granted by the company, and (3) financial condition of customers. Budgeting the discounts requires that the experience pattern of discounts in relation to sales be analyzed. The first step is to determine the average ratio of discounts to sales over a period of time. If the terms, for example, are 2/10, *n*/30, the average discount normally will be less than 2 per cent because of slow accounts and worthless accounts.

For complete accuracy in scheduling discounts on a monthly basis, consideration must be given the fact that discount periods may extend into the month following that in which the sale is made. Failure to take this into account where sales do not flow evenly in time would render the forecast useless for the purposes of monthly budgeting and control.

GENERAL AND ADMINISTRATIVE EXPENSES

Where, however, there is an even flow of sales by months, the errors would tend to cancel out and the simpler procedure would be satisfactory.

Aside from the significance of the discounts, the analysis of payment patterns is very important in budgeting cash receipts. Whether customers pay promptly or one or two months following the sale has a direct bearing on the nature and amount of the company's working capital requirements.

Bad Debts. Some companies account for bad debts on the "direct charge-off" basis. Under this method, the charge must wait for a final determination of worthlessness. The timing of the charge-off, therefore, is very uncertain, and month-to-month scheduling is difficult.

It is a more common practice, however, to accrue an allowance for doubtful accounts on the basis of past experience. Subsequent determinations of worthlessness result in the bad accounts being written off against amounts previously provided. Since the company's experience with bad accounts generally is reviewed carefully for income tax as well as budget purposes, data are available for a reasonable estimate on a monthly basis. Again, the analysis is also important in scheduling cash receipts.

Interest Expense. Whereas the scheduling of interest payments on fixed obligations and on current obligations incurred in the preceding budget period is a simple matter, the scheduling of payments on new, short-term loans is the last of a whole series of budget preparation steps. The reader is referred to the earlier illustration in connection with Illustrative Company. The amount of expense to be incurred, and its timing, depends on the outside financial aid expected to be required, and this can be determined only by reference to the cash schedules which are assembled from an analysis of all expected cash transactions. Moreover, since short-term bank rates are subject to quick change, the forecast must include not only the amount and time of borrowing, but also the bank rate expected to be in effect at that time. Obviously, the budget schedules must provide for expense accruals as well as cash payments.

Income Taxes. Scheduling income taxes involves a forecasting both of net income subject to tax and the rates of tax. The problem of tax forecasting, moreover, is complicated by the nature of the tax laws. Graduated rates, allowable and unallowable deductions, carry-backs and carry-forwards, special treatment of capital gains and losses—all these when considered beforehand and on an estimated basis make this phase of budgeting quite burdensome. Since the amounts involved are substantial in relation to profits, the forecast is most important both from the point of view of the operating statement and from that of the financial statement and cash position.

An interesting problem arises in month-to-month budgeting where, because of graduated rates and credits, the effective rate of tax on net income varies from month to month as the year progresses. This is not important to the cash budget, but it is important in forecasting monthly operating results. Generally, the difficulty is resolved by accruing the taxes on the basis of the estimated effective rate for the year as a whole.

Other Credits to Income. These include such items as purchase discounts, interest earned and investment income, and miscellaneous income (sale of scrap, sale of seconds, profit on sale of capital assets, etc.). These, like the other charges to income, are reported under various headings in the operating statement, but are discussed in this chapter for reasons of convenience.

Purchase Discounts. Purchase discounts, like sales discounts, are a function of three variables: (1) purchases, (2) terms of purchase, and (3) the company's financial status. With respect to the first factor, purchases include not only direct material but also indirect material and supplies. The scheduling of direct material purchases generally is well done since the need for these materials can be forecast with reasonable accuracy on the basis of scheduled production and inventory requirements. The scheduling of other purchases, however, frequently is more difficult, first, because of the wide variety of items involved and, second, because the frequent looseness of inventory control and the common practice of expensing rather than inventorying of these purchases render the experience record less useful as a basis of forecasting. Where this is the case, rough estimates must be made. It should be recognized, however, that these estimates are important in cash forecasting as well as for budgeting discounts. Hence, they do deserve careful study and should not be treated lightly.

In connection with the terms of purchase, it is to be recognized that these terms may be imposed by the vendor or by the buyer, depending on circumstances. In the latter case, the budget problem is simplified, but in the former it requires estimation on the basis of past experience.

Needless to say, the factor of financial position is important. The effective interest rate inherent in normal discount rates is such that ordinarily no company can afford not to take all offered discounts. However, companies with insufficient working capital and poor credit may have to forego the privilege of discounting invoices. In the case of these marginal companies, the scheduling of purchase discounts, like that of interest expense discussed above, must wait for the completion

GENERAL AND ADMINISTRATIVE EXPENSES

of the various steps leading to the forecast of monthly cash position. It should also be observed that the timing of the discounts on a monthly basis presents the same problems as does the timing of sales discounts.

Interest Earned and Investment Income. Interest on both short-term notes and long-term investments and dividends on long-term investments are the subject of this paragraph. The taking of interest-bearing notes is common in some industries, particularly those dealing in costly items of capital equipment. On the other hand, the practice of making temporary investments of excess cash or of making long-term investments either for sinking fund purposes or purposes of corporate policy is not peculiar to any one industry.

Where the income takes the form of interest, the forecast depends on the nature and purpose of the asset acquired. If notes are received from customers in the normal course of business, the forecast must be related to that of sales. If income is to be earned on short-term investments, the amount of cash to be invested, the duration, and the interest rate must be estimated. On the other hand, the income from long-term interest-bearing investments presents no problem. As to dividends, they obviously contain an element of uncertainty.

CONTROLLING THE ITEMS

In discussing the budgetary control of the foregoing items of expense and income, the general and administrative expenses can appropriately be separated from "other charges" and "other credits." The general and administrative expenses are primarily of two kinds for control purposes. Either they are fixed or appropriated expenses which are not expected to change during the budget period, or they are flexible and adjustable to changes in volume. The former are not susceptible of control through standard measurements, whereas the latter are (or should be) capable of such control. On the other hand, the "other charges" and "other credits" are neither fixed nor easily controlled, and to the extent that they are controllable the control is not one applied to routine operations, where worker efficiency is the key, but to the performance of executives in nonroutine positions.

Fixed and Appropriated General and Administrative Expenses. As described in another chapter, the distinction between fixed and appropriated expenses is one of timing. The former normally are fixed for several budget periods while the latter are fixed for the current period only, in an amount determined with only this period in mind. Officers' salaries, for example, are fixed expenses, whereas travel costs and donations are appropriated.

While the foregoing distinction is not always clear-cut, it is significant for control purposes. The fixed expenses, by their nature, normally do not present a control problem. The expenditures are automatic and in line with a predetermined pattern so that variations normally cannot arise. In the case of the appropriated items, however, the spending is neither automatic nor periodic. Consequently, the expenditures must be watched for conformity with the budget. Moreover, because of the lack of precise timing of these expenditures in the budget, there frequently may be month-to-month budget variations without any inference as to the annual conformity. This very fact, however, requires special efforts toward control. Over-run expenses early in the year may tend subsequently to restrict desirable expenditures. In such cases it must be remembered that the budget is a managerial tool only, and not an end in itself. On the other hand, subnormal expenditures early in the year may tend to encourage excessive spending later on. This, too, is to be guarded against. Because of this lack of precision in timing and because the normal control standards of performance do not exist, the appropriated general and administrative expenses should receive special attention.

Flexible General and Administrative Expenses. These constitute that large segment of expenses incurred in connection with routine, daily work for which standards can in large measure be established. They contain a mixture of fixed and variable expenses of the type for which flexible budgeting is appropriate.

Unit time standards are the key to control of many of these expenses, and control reports are of the type which measure actual time against standard time for work done. Figure 15–1 illustrates such a report as prepared for the work of billing and invoicing.

Departmentalization of General and Administrative Expenses. It is axiomatic that expenses must be controlled at the point of origin and this normally is in the department where the expense is incurred. In dealing with the factory, the department generally is of sufficient size to make the control unit significant. In the case of the general offices of all but very large companies, however, the several departments are of such small size as to militate against aggressive cost control efforts. In the first place, it may not be considered worth while to departmentalize such expenses as supplies and telephone and telegraph. Consequently, budget variations, reported in total only for the entire general office, become no one's responsibility. In the second place, where all expenses are departmentalized, the variations in each office may appear insignificant while being of real significance when aggregated.

Considerations of the type just mentioned tend to present serious obstacles to cost control in the general office. They, together with the

GENERAL AND ADMINISTRATIVE EXPENSES

fact that many of the persons involved in the expenditures are high in authority, perhaps help to explain why cost control in the office has, over the years, lagged far behind that of the factory.

Control of Sales Discounts. In analyzing the difference between actual and budgeted sales discounts, consideration must be given, first, to possible variations in sales and then to possible changes in the ratio of discounts to sales. Thus, there are two variables in the analysis. The following data illustrate this fact:

Budgeted sales	$500,000
Budgeted discounts	8,750
Actual sales	550,000
Actual discounts	8,800

In this case it is obvious that the effective rate of discount is less than that scheduled. The fact is important primarily as a symptom of a slowing down of payments.

One point is mentioned here for the sake of completeness, although it is principally a matter of internal control and auditing, and that is the possibility of discounts being improperly allowed. Increases in the effective rate of discount may result from careless work in the accounts receivable section, permitting discounts to be taken after the discount period has expired.

Control of Bad Debts. This item is controllable basically only at the time the sale is made. The analysis of budget variations, however, is difficult in the case of bad debts because of the uncertainty as to when a debt becomes worthless. Since the monthly accrual of the allowance for doubtful accounts commonly is based on a fixed percentage of sales, variations in the accrual result solely from variations in sales and have no significance in controlling the expense.

While it was stated that bad debts are controlled basically at the time the sale is made, one should not overlook the work of the collection department. Worthlessness may only be apparent, but not real, depending on the action taken to collect slow accounts.

Analysis of bad accounts should be sufficiently detailed to serve as a guide to better credit administration in the future. To the extent that an increase in such accounts reflects a change in economic conditions, the analysis again may be significant.

Control of Interest Expense. Budget variations in interest expense may be the natural result of changes in operating conditions or may reflect poor administration of funds. Reference to the budget illustration of Illustrative Company in the early part of the book shows how the interest charge is scheduled only after the cash schedules are pre-

CLERICAL COST CONTROL		
EFFICIENCY PERFORMANCE OF CONTROLLED POSITIONS		
Analysis of Performance	Department	Billing & Invoicing
	For Month of	

1. Earned standard hours............................		3151
2. Special assignments...............................		28
3. Total hours of work earned.......................		3179
4. Regular hours attended...........................		3420
5. Overtime hours...................................		24
6. Total scheduled hours attended...................		3444
7. Scheduled hours (over-under) hours of work earned		265
8. Performance percentage...........................		92%
9. Unattended hours paid (vacation, holiday, illness, etc.).......................................		40

Analysis of Dollar Cost Variance

Performance Variance

A. Scheduled hours attended.........................		3444
B. Salaries paid for scheduled hours attended (Exclusive of O.T. premium)......................		$4305.
C. Average hourly rate of pay........................		$ 1.25
D. Salaries paid for scheduled hours attended (including O.T. premium)........................		$4320.
E. Value of hours of work earned (C × 3)............		$3974.
F. Dollar cost (over-under) hours of work earned.....		$ 346.

Other Variance

Unattended hours paid

Vacation		
Holiday		
Illness		$ 50.
G. Total other variance..............................		$ 50.
H. Total salaries paid (G + D)......................		$4370.

Detail of Special Assignments

Total ....

SOURCE: F. Ray Friedley, "Clerical Cost Reduction and Control," *N.A.A. Bulletin*, Section 1, Oct., 1953, p. 182.

FIG. 15-1. Clerical Cost Control

pared and the necessary short-term financing determined. A change in almost any segment of the operations may necessitate a change in month-to-month financing. Consequently, a budget variation in this item may merely reflect related changes in the basic operations. On the other hand, however, it may also reflect poor financial management, either at the planning stage or in the execution of the plan.

As to the former, poor judgment may have been used in the determination of the cash requirements, in that insufficient allowance may have been made for the day-to-day variations from the budget. Even though the budget for the period as a whole proved to be essentially correct, interim variations could occur which would affect the timing of cash receipts and disbursements. An inadequate margin of safety provided in the plan could entail additional short-term financing and corresponding interest charges. In the execution of a sound budget plan, additional financial requirements and corresponding interest charges normally would arise only from a failure to provide financial implementation for budget changes, or from carelessness in reducing loans promptly.

Variations in Income Taxes. Budget variations in income tax accruals may occur for several reasons (assuming the original accruals were properly budgeted). First, a change in taxable income may affect the accrual disproportionately because of credits and graduated rates. Second, the law may be changed, requiring new determinations. Third, a review of prior years' returns by the taxing authorities may result in unanticipated determinations. Finally, and this is applicable primarily to state income taxes, the geographical origin of transactions may shift (without any change in total budgeted transactions) in such a manner as to affect the aggregate amount of state income taxes.

Because of the complicated nature of many tax computations, a month-to-month review of the accruals may not always be worth the effort. In the case of major developments, however, budget revisions are in order.

Control of Purchase Discounts. Because the customary discounts allowed for prompt payment of invoices are equivalent to a high rate of interest, steps must be taken to ensure the taking of all allowable discounts. Unfortunately, it is difficult to analyze a budget variance in this item. If the discounts are less than the budget calls for, is it because of fewer purchases, a change in the terms allowed by suppliers, or simply failure to make timely payments?

If purchases for one reason or another are not in accord with the budget as to amount, there naturally would be a corresponding change in discounts realized. If the terms allowed by suppliers differ on average from the budgeted effective discount rate on all purchases, the difference may be due to a change in terms by the company's regular suppliers, or it may reflect a shift in suppliers originating with the purchasing department. If the terms generally are undergoing change, the knowledge is important in preparing future budgets; if a shift of suppliers is the cause, perhaps the purchasing department is at fault.

If, however, discounts are lost either because of careless processing of invoices for payment, or poor management of cash, requiring late payment of invoices, the cause should be promptly removed. But how can it be determined whether discounts have been lost, and how much? Where the accounting for discounts takes place only at the time of payment, the determination is very difficult, except by means of a time-consuming audit of invoices paid. If the purchase and payment entries are as follows:

(1) Purchases 100
    Accounts Payable 100
(2) Accounts Payable 100
    Cash 98
    Discounts 2

only realized discounts are recorded. A different recording, however, would automatically disclose lost discounts, as follows:

(1) Purchases 98
    Accounts Payable 98
(2) Accounts Payable 98
    Discounts Lost 2
    Cash 100

These entries may have to be varied in practice to meet specific internal accounting requirements, but they do serve to measure failure to achieve expected results with a minimum of effort and time.

Control of Interest Earned and Investment Income. With respect to this item, little can be done except to ensure that excessive cash balances, as determined in relation to working and safety requirements, are invested promptly. In this connection it should be noted that caution must be observed. Overzealous regard for the last dollar of interest income may result in a too hasty investment of seeming excess cash, only to incur a loss subsequently in a too hasty, enforced reconversion to cash.

Because of the number of items of income and expense discussed above, little attention was given to the location of the control points. However, the principle of control at the source has already been fully discussed. To the extent that variations are related to the internal operations of the several divisions of the general office, each of those divisions is responsible. On the other hand, where the variations relate to results obtained, the cause may have to be sought in other departments or in external, noncontrollable factors.

CHAPTER 16

RESEARCH AND DEVELOPMENT COSTS

	Page		Page
Purpose of chapter	285	**Controlling Research and Development Costs**	
Types of research	286		
Budgeting Research and Development Costs		Control of over-all costs	297
		Control of project costs	297
Planning the total expenditure	287	Form and use of project reports	298
Selection of projects	289	Control of purchases	299
Form of project requests	291	Control of equipment costs	300
Nature of the costs	293	Control of supplies	300
Financial accounting for the costs	296	The role of top management	300

Purpose of Chapter. Research and product development are very important activities in the struggle to maintain and improve one's position in the market. In Chapter I it was pointed out that a company cannot stand still. The forces of competition and of capital accumulation require constant effort in the improvement of present products and of productive methods, and in the development of new products. This can be accomplished only through constant research.

The budgeting and controlling of expenditures in these activities are difficult because of the nonstandard character of the work. How much must be spent, where it should be spent, and the effectiveness of the expenditures are questions which are difficult to answer. While somewhat similar to the problems encountered in dealing with sales effort, their complete unpredictability both as to cost and as to results sets research expenditures apart from the other activities of the enterprise as a special budget and control problem.

The growth of scientific research departments in American industry has given rise to numerous relatively new problems of administrative control. A group of highly trained scientists engaged in research cannot be managed by techniques the same as those used, for example, in line-production operations. Scientific research necessarily is nonstandard and individualistic. The very circumstances, however, which render it difficult to exercise effective administrative control over scientific research activities also intensify the need for such control. The executives who are accountable for the proper utilization of the financial resources of a corporation have just as great a responsibility for the funds used in scientific research as for the funds which are invested in plant and equipment, or for those which are used in the purchase of materials, in manufacturing operations, and in sales activities.[1]

Because of both the nonstandard character of the work, and its importance, it merits a separate chapter. This chapter, consequently, is devoted to a discussion of the budgetary and control problems peculiar to research expenditures. The decision to locate this discussion in this chapter rather than an earlier one was based, first, on the need to establish clearly the common budgetary principles and practices before treating a problem which is somewhat exceptional in nature, and, second, on the accounting classification of the expenditures. Here we are dealing with expenditures which may or may not be capitalized or deferred, depending on their outcome and on the accounting policy of the firm.

Types of Research. Industrial research comprises three primary areas of activity:

> Basic research (general scientific studies)
> Product development
> Process development

Each of these may involve either short-range or long-range projects. Moreover, the work may be done by the research organization as an independent and separate budgetary entity, or it may be done in conjunction with, and for, other divisions of the company. The comprehensive nature of the work is illustrated in the following classification of experimental and research activities.

1. Pure research, i.e., direct research or experimentation on general problems having no particular connection with the various products currently being manufactured by the plant.
2. Projects directing experimental or developmental effort toward the creation of new processes or new product or group of products to be manufactured by the plant.
3. Projects directing experimental or developmental effort toward any improvement to a specific product already being manufactured by the plant or an improvement in an existing process.
4. All further work beyond the developmental stage necessary to get a new product, model, or item of equipment ready for normal production and sale.
5. Projects for the purpose of designing and constructing new types of equipment or improvements to existing equipment which shall be used in our manufacturing processes and which will effect a change in any existing process in the plant.[2]

[1] From Foreword by Melvin T. Copeland to Robert N. Anthony's *Management Controls in Industrial Research Organizations* (Boston: Division of Research, Graduate School of Business Administration, Harvard University, 1952).

[2] Adopted from Maurice J. Moss, "Developmental Costs Incurred in the Plant," *N.A.A. Bulletin,* Section 1, May, 1954, pp. 1115-16.

The wide range of activities is also shown by the following excerpt from an illustration of a budget of one company's research and development division.

1. Present products
    a) Projects in progress
        (1) Product X improvements
        (2) Product Y usage
        (3) Product Z quality
    b) New projects
        (1) Product X new process
        (2) Product Y quality control
        (3) Product Z new use
2. New product research
    a) Projects in progress
        (1) Product XX
        (2) Product YY
    b) New projects
        (1) Product P
        (2) Product Q
        (3) Product R
3. Pure research
    a) Projects in progress
        (1) Item S
        (2) Item T
    b) New projects
        (1) Item U
        (2) Item V
4. Sales Department service
    a) Projects in progress
        (1) Product X
        (2) Customer Z
    b) New projects
        (1) Product Y
        (2) Product Q [3]

BUDGETING RESEARCH AND DEVELOPMENT COSTS

Planning the Total Expenditure. Ideally, the total amount to be appropriated for research and development work should be determined by aggregating the estimated costs of the several projects which it is believed the company must undertake, modified by its ability to finance them. In practice, however, this normally is not feasible. In the first place, detailed project costs cannot always be estimated with any reasonable degree of accuracy. Second, the nature of scientific research is such that the research division must be given large discretion and flexibility

[3] Adolph G. Lurie, "Controlling Research Costs With a Budget," *N.A.A. Bulletin*, Section 1, Mar., 1953, pp. 898-99.

in the spending of its funds. Some projects may have to be abandoned because they prove to be impractical; others may suddenly and unexpectedly disclose great promise and warrant heavier spending than that scheduled; and conditions may arise which require the shifting of research personnel from one project to another. Consequently, the more common practice appears to be that of making lump-sum appropriations to the division, supported by a report describing a general plan showing a broad allocation of the funds in the various areas of research.

According to one study of practice in a number of companies, in 73.4 per cent of the cases all or most of the funds are appropriated on a lump-sum basis.[4] And even in those cases where the appropriation is by projects, no attempt is made to support the requests by detailed estimates of the various items of expense to be incurred on each project. This does not mean that top management is not informed of the nature of the work to be done, but that the work is described in broad terms as to its expected costs, objectives, and results.

Given the research manager's request for total funds, top corporate management must decide how much can be afforded. Practice in this regard varies considerably. One writer lists four commonly used bases, as follows:

    1. Competitive parity
    2. Per cent of sales
    3. "All you can afford"
    4. Rate of return [5]

He points out that none of these is the right answer in all situations.

Another writer suggests that the following considerations or combination of considerations may be basic:

1. The total amount of the budget may be based upon the sales for the past period or it may be a fixed percentage of the estimated sales for the ensuing period.
2. It may be desirable to budget a percentage of net profits before taxes.
3. Management may decide to base the budgeted expenditure upon the amount that had been spent previously, modified either upwards or downwards by changes in volume of sales, changes in profits, or similar considerations.
4. The research budget may be dependent upon the operating budget and the amount determined from the forecast of sales or upon budgeted profits before research and development.
5. A general review and study of economic conditions, future prospects, competition, etc., may influence the establishment of the budget.

[4] Anthony, *op. cit.*, p. 104.
[5] J. W. Gladson, "Financial Bases for Research Budget Planning," *N.A.A. Bulletin*, Section 1, May, 1955, pp. 1140–43.

6. The least scientific method of approaching this problem is to fix the amount by arbitrary determination.⁶

The problem is not unlike that of determining the advertising appropriation, where there is also a lack of precise performance standards to serve as a basis for rational budgeting. There would appear to be a close analogy, for example, between basic or "pure" research and institutional advertising. Even in this case, however, the research budget problem is peculiar in that the objectives cannot be clearly defined.

It must be concluded that there is no scientific method available for the determination of the amount of funds to be spent on research. Certainly, management must be clear as to its long-range objectives. These, alone, provide the starting point for consideration of research appropriations. While some specific research projects may be capable of reasonably precise evaluation of costs relative to the objectives, others represent pure speculation. The latter constitute a gamble which, in the nature of things, must be undertaken, but some balance must be maintained as between the less speculative and more speculative projects.

Several laboratory directors have pointed out the importance of preparing a program which is properly balanced as to risk. For some projects, while the probability of success is high and the estimated time required to complete the work is short, the returns may not be great. For others, the risk is very great and the completion date is remote, but the possible return may be correspondingly large. It is probable that in most research organizations any balance among types of projects classified by risk is a matter of accident, but in some well-managed laboratories the director makes a conscious effort to achieve a balance among projects which places the proper emphasis on both the immediate and the long-run benefits of research.⁷

Selection of Projects. On the assumption that the total appropriation has been arrived at, the next problem is that of allocating the research and development funds to the several projects under consideration. This is primarily a matter for divisional planning as opposed to over-all planning, although the two are related and overlap somewhat. Although, as indicated above, the total appropriation is not arrived at without some knowledge on the part of top management concerning the general nature of the major projects under consideration by the division, nevertheless, in the nature of things, the full allocation of funds has to be treated separately from the determination of the total allocation. This allocation has to be accomplished by the head of the research division, in consultation with other members of both his own staff and the management staff, and with the approvals requisite to adequate internal control of expenditures.

⁶ Lurie, *op. cit.*, p. 894.
⁷ Anthony, *op. cit.*, pp. 128–29.

Suggestions for projects may come from the research director himself, from researchers, from operating divisions of the company, and even from customers. Frequently, the funds represented by the proposals greatly exceed the amounts available and, as in the case of other activities of the company, a selection must be made. The selection is important and, in the long run, determines the effectiveness of the company's research and development activities. Between the urge to approve projects which appear to have a reasonable chance of succeeding and the fear of turning down projects which, while risky, may prove to be bonanzas, the responsibility of selection is great.

Numerous factors must be considered and some of them, by their nature, are both controlling and measurable.

In one oil company evaluation of the ideas for research is based on:

1. Emphasis placed on the items to the discovery or recovery of which the proposal is directed
2. Time required to perform the work
3. Availability and capability of personnel
4. Anticipated benefits
5. Likelihood of success
6. Prior research by others [8]

In a large chemical company the considerations are reported to be as follows:

Potential markets are one factor of prime importance. Is there a real need for the new product? At what price would it be attractive to customers now using competitive products? How elastic would the demand be, that is, how much of this product could be sold at various price levels? . . .

Technical feasibility is another consideration. Has a workable process been developed? Is commercial equipment available to carry out the various steps of the process or must new equipment be devised before the process can be scaled-up to commercial size? Can quality of product be controlled at an acceptable level? . . .

The economics of the project are also determining. The decision of research management to continue or drop a research project will depend heavily upon economics.[9]

A comprehensive list of items to be determined before a research project is begun, used by General Foods Corporation, appears below:

1. Describe idea or job as completely as possible.
2. What are the reasons for doing the work? What are the ultimate objectives?
3. What is the dollar value of these objectives?

[8] W. L. McKinnon, "Planned Control of Costs in the Research Division of an Oil Company," *N.A.A. Bulletin,* Section 1, June, 1950, pp. 1197–98.

[9] John C. Tallman, "How Cost Estimates Help Guide Chemical Research," *N.A.A. Bulletin,* Section 1, Aug., 1955, pp. 1655–56.

RESEARCH AND DEVELOPMENT COSTS

4. Is there any reason why the result might not be used? Does it conform with corporate policy for expansion? Does it conform with G. F. merchandising policy? Does it appeal to the merchandising group who will have to market it? Does it require excessive installation costs, space requirements, or promotion capital? Are there unobtainable materials or objections from the production viewpoint? Does it conflict with existing or interrelating processes? Are there any patent or other legal reasons?
5. Is this part of an existing project or a new project?
6. Who has the primary responsibility? Is everyone informed of this and in agreement?
7. What is the nature of the research required? Are specialists required? Is special laboratory equipment needed? Will pilot plant work be carried out? Will extensive analytical or similar work be required? Where will raw materials come from? Will material be required that is available only at the plant or somewhere in the field?
8. Where can the research be carried out most effectively? Is this closely related to other work being carried out anywhere in the corporation?
9. Have literature and patent surveys been made?
10. Has the corporate report system been examined for the same or similar work in the past? If the same idea was proposed before but not carried out, why?
11. Have all the sources of ideas required for preliminary evaluation been contacted? Research staff, including divisional laboratory, Central Laboratories' Library, and the New York Office? Production Department? Engineering Department? Sales and merchandising departments? Law Department? General management? Others where indicated by the nature of the job?
12. What will the research cost? Is it likely that additional research by other departments will be required?
13. What is the priority of the job? How rapidly should it be carried out? Should it be started now or deferred? Dependent on priority, when can it be expected to be completed? [10]

It is now apparent that the selection of research and development projects is not a matter to be treated lightly. It should also be observed that periodic selection also involves periodic review of what is being done. To the extent that the periodic allocation of funds involves continuing projects as well as new ones, there must be constant evaluation of work already started. Nevertheless, it is clear that the ultimate selection involves a large amount of judgment. In the nature of things it cannot rest solely on a comparison of financial and cost data.

Form of Project Requests. The degree of formality, or informality, of project proposals and the extent to which cost estimates are detailed depend on the nature of the work to be done. A higher degree of formality and completeness generally is associated with applied research

[10] Anthony, *op. cit.*, pp. 17-18.

and developmental work; a lower degree with pure research. Since the latter is concerned mainly with ideas, it obviously cannot be pinned down to the same degree as work involving a clear-cut objective.

Moreover, the number of proposals also tends to vary with the definition of a project. What is a project? The variety of definitions is indicated as follows:

> It may be a single experiment or test, or one stage—such as the applied research stage—of the development of a new product or process, or *all* the work related to the development of a new product or process, or all the work done in one department for a stated period of time, such as a month or a quarter. The amount of money involved in a single project may run from a few dollars up to several hundred thousand. A major program may be defined in a single project, with various aspects of this program being broken down as subprojects, or even sub-subprojects. In short, a "project" is as big or as small as management wants to make it.
>
> The definition of a project in a specific case is influenced by two considerations: (1) the amount of control which management at all levels wishes to exercise over the conduct of the technical program, and (2) the nature of the technical work itself. If management gives broad latitude to the individual research workers for the conduct of the technical program, there are likely to be few research proposals active at any one time, each one covering a fairly large fraction of the work being done in the laboratory. If, on the other hand, management desires to have a fairly close check over the work being carried on, there is likely to be a larger number of projects. In the latter case, two dangers exist: (1) that the program will be so fragmented that an individual project does not define a logical unit of work, and (2) that the system will become so cumbersome, because of frequent changes, excessive paperwork, and detailed record keeping, that it breaks down. Under such circumstances a large number of separately defined projects results in looser control, rather than in tighter control, over the work being done.[11]

While, obviously, budget data are necessary in over-all planning, the application of budgetary principles to individual projects frequently cannot be as complete as the budget executive would like it to be. The experimental nature of much of the work and the danger of lessening the effectiveness of highly trained technical researchers through requiring too much attention to record-keeping puts this type of work in a somewhat special category for the purposes of financial control. Consequently, the financial requirements of individual projects frequently are indicated only in a very rough manner, depending on the nature of the work—pure research or specific developments. Technical manpower and equipment requirements may be more important for this purpose than refined cost estimates. A major managerial problem in connection with research and development work is that of determining a proper balance between the requirements of good budgeting and the conditions conducive to the best intellectual effort on the part of research personnel.

[11] Anthony, *op. cit.*, p. 114.

RESEARCH AND DEVELOPMENT COSTS

Again, it must be recognized that project authorization requests will vary in form and detail, depending on the nature of the work to be done. In the case of pure or basic research, a description of the nature of the experimentation and an estimate of manpower and equipment requirements may be all that is provided. On the other hand, a project relating to the development of a new machine, for example, to be used in the plant, will be described fully, not only as to estimated costs, but also as to estimated savings to be obtained from the improvement. An example of this form of request is shown in Figure 16–1.

Even in the case of pure research, however, there must be some financial control. Top management must know what its financial commitments are. This is accomplished through its control of the over-all research and development costs. It is in the detailed allocation of funds that a large amount of discretion may be left to the head of the research and development division. It is the responsibility of this person to make proper allocations of allowed funds and to determine the data necessary for this purpose.

Nature of the Costs. The chart of accounts of a research and development division will vary, depending on the nature of the work done, and on the size of the division. And, although it does not differ basically from that of a factory division, in that it contains the equivalent of direct labor, materials, and overhead, there are differences in detail which warrant a brief review of the nature of the costs to be incurred. They include:

1. Payroll
    a) Productive
        (1) Professional technical
        (2) Nonprofessional technical
        (3) Clerical
    b) Administrative
        (1) Professional technical
        (2) Other
    c) Patent services
    d) Library and technical information service
    e) Service departments
2. Supplies and materials
    a) Productive
        (1) Expendable equipment
        (2) Operating supplies
    b) Service departments
3. Other directly incurred costs
    a) Books, dues, subscriptions, etc.
    b) Travel expenses

EXPERIMENTAL WORK ORDER REQUEST
(——— Department)

To: <u>Plant Manager</u>

E. W. O. 1253—Design and Construct a New Type Spooling Machine

1. Department making request	Roll Film Department
2. Date of request -	October 1, 195-
3. Reason for project -	To design and construct a new type roll film spooling machine which will overcome current maintenance problems and reduce substantially our manufacturing cost.
4. Expected results -	We expect to develop a spooling machine which will be flexible to the extent that it can handle all widths and operate on a three trick basis. By combining several operations and increasing speeds, it is hoped to reduce costs by about $50,000 per year.
5. Estimated time to complete -	Originally requested January 195- and to be completed by the end of 195-
6. Estimated cost of entire project -	$ 50,000
7. Estimated cost for year -	
(a) Cost of engineering and construction work.	$ 25,000
(b) All other costs.	$ 5,000
Total	$ 30,000
8. Estimated cost in first quarter -	$ 10,000
9. Any other information which might be of interest to management -	Maintenance costs and downtime have been an increasing problem during the last two years. With increased production requirements forecast for the future years it is imperative that this machine be developed to meet the forecast work load with the present space and work force.
10. Recommended cost distribution -	All roll films
11. Percentage of completion to which this appropriation will carry the project -	100%

SOURCE: Maurice J. Moss, "Developmental Costs Incurred in the Plant," *N.A.A. Bulletin,* Section 1, May, 1954, p. 1117.

FIG. 16–1. Experimental Work Order Request

c) Technical, engineering, and consulting fees
   d) Fringe payroll costs and taxes
4. Assessed charges
   a) Taxes, insurance, depreciation
   b) Light, heat, and power
   c) Space
   d) Miscellaneous

The foregoing are the costs which must be budgeted for the department as a whole. Because the salaries of relatively high-priced professional workers constitute a large proportion of the total cost, the preponderance of the costs tend to be fixed in nature. Flexible budgeting can be applied, however, to nonprofessional technical workers in those cases where a considerable amount of routine testing and other routine work is done.

To the extent that detailed budgeting is applied to individual projects, the problem of overhead allocation is important. The selection of the basis of allocation is difficult because of the presence of two kinds of "direct" labor, professional technical and nonprofessional technical. Moreover, because of the nonstandard nature of the work, the accounting for "other direct" project charges becomes important. Whereas power costs, for example, may be treated as a departmental overhead item in some laboratories, in others it may be treated as a direct project charge because of the heavy power costs associated with some projects.

Overhead accounting may be further complicated in those divisions containing several departments, such as chemical research, physical research, metallurgical research, etc. A project within a department may then be charged with a share of the department's overhead and a share of the division's overhead. In the research division of one oil company the following principles of distribution were formulated and approved:

1. The general principle of the project cost accounting procedure is that all direct project labor, including that of service departments, should be charged to the specific project receiving the benefit of such labor.
2. All other labor of a nature that benefits more than one specific project, including indirect overhead, should be equitably spread over all projects.
3. The cost of material, supplies and equipment may be charged direct to projects or pro-rated, according to the policy of the laboratory considering the problem. The type of material and equipment purchased for general research work is so interchangeable, however, that direct cost accounting could very easily prove more burdensome and costly than the benefits to be derived from such a procedure. Consequently, we have elected to pro-rate this type of cost.
4. Appropriation costs applicable to specific projects should be charged to projects receiving the benefit of such work. All other construction costs should be charged to overhead and pro-rated equitably over all projects.

5. The method of distributing overhead and other pro-rated charges must rest with the appropriate level of management responsible for the unit. The research and development department management has approved a procedure whereby laboratory overhead is distributed to project sections on a percentage of manpower in each section as against the total project manpower in the laboratory.

6. In turn, section overhead is pro-rated to projects on a percentage of project manhours worked.

7. Service groups such as machine shops, carpenter shops, pipe-fitters, insulators, painters, analytical groups, performing duties of a general nature, should charge their time to the groups who originated the work requisitions.

8. Service groups performing duties of a plant maintenance and repair nature should charge their time to general overhead.

9. Administration, office, cafeteria, industrial relations, library, safety and fire prevention groups should charge their time to general overhead, since their services are all-inclusive and applicable to all departments.[12]

It is because of these cost allocation problems, combined with the indeterminate nature of some projects, that individual research projects tend to be budgeted more loosely and informally than detailed activities of other divisions of the company. As indicated earlier, the allotment of professional manpower and technical equipment frequently is the important consideration in project budgeting.

Financial Accounting for the Costs. Since this is not a work on financial accounting principles, it is not intended to pass judgment on the propriety of capitalizing or charging off research and development costs. Since, however, accounting policy in this regard does have a bearing on the preparation of forecast operating statements and balance sheets, attention must be called to it. Pure or basic research expenditures commonly are treated as period costs because it is usually difficult to determine in advance the benefit, if any, that may result therefrom in future periods. In the case of applied research and development work, however, the question arises as to whether the costs should be charged to current income, or capitalized (assuming the project is successful) and subsequently amortized. In the latter case, the period of amortization is often difficult to determine. Moreover, in the case of those projects extending over a period of several years, and where the final outcome is not known at the time of the early expenditures, decision to capitalize the costs would necessitate, in effect, a tentative cost deferment pending the completion of the project.

[12] A. J. Gallantier, "Project Costing in a Research Laboratory," *N.A.A. Bulletin*, Section 1, Sept., 1955, p. 31.

CONTROLLING RESEARCH AND DEVELOPMENT COSTS

Control of Over-all Costs. The procedure for controlling research and development costs under the budget is affected by the manner in which the budget itself is prepared. The fact that research and development funds frequently are appropriated in lump sums supported by a broad statement of objectives, and that the project allocation of funds is made within the division, suggests that there are two levels of budgetary control in this division. First, there is the control of over-all expenditures, without regard to project differentiation.

In this aspect of control, the purposes are (1) to ensure that the total appropriation is not over-run, and (2) to ensure the application of control standards to those activities which are routine and repetitive in nature and for which standard costs can be determined.

A portion of the division's expenditures are incurred in the operation of service functions, such as storeroom, maintenance, janitorial, and clerical. Still other expenditures are related to routine technical operations which can be standardized regardless of the project in which they are used. Cost control as applied to these items implies the use of standards and the relating of costs to the amount of work accomplished. It is in connection with these costs that the principles of variable budgeting are applicable.

The major portion of research and development expenses, however, tend to be fixed or appropriated in nature. The budget provides for certain numbers of chemists, physicists, engineers, and other researchers, and their supporting staffs. Control of these costs also serves two purposes. The first is that of ensuring that the appropriation is not overspent. The second, and more important, purpose is to make sure that the staff and facilities are fully utilized in the most useful research. It is in this phase of control that the second level of control becomes important. This is the control of costs at the project level.

Control of Project Costs. The control of costs at the project level is also affected by the method used in establishing the budget. As noted above, a lump-sum appropriation is made to the division, and it is primarily the research director's duty to allocate funds to projects which may be subject to top management review and approval. But, again, these allocations tend to be of the lump-sum variety because of the difficulty of estimating accurately the detailed costs. The allotments tend to be made on the basis of estimated research time, and on the assumption that there is a fairly stable relationship of costs to time.

Since commonly there is no detailed budget for projects, obviously there can be no detailed comparison of amounts budgeted and spent.

But even if the project budget were detailed, it would be difficult to gauge the performance of expenditure control for any short period of time for the simple reason that with many projects (perhaps with all projects in pure research) the amount of work done cannot be measured accurately. Since the essence of cost control as applied to direct or productive costs is to relate costs to production, and since production in research cannot be reduced to standard measurements, cost control at the project level is extremely difficult.

This lack of cost standards is significant. It not only means that efficiency of detailed operations on the project cannot be measured; it also means that the qualitative evaluation of the total effort on the project must be largely subjective.

Some means of forming judgments about performance is used in all situations where people work together; but in many situations quantitative information is not used, or is used only incidentally, as a basis for these judgments. A research laboratory seems to be one of these situations. Apparently, it is not possible in a research organization to set standards of performance in quantitative terms. There seems to be no counterpart in the laboratory for cost per unit of product, quantity manufactured per day, percentage of rejects, monthly sales per salesman, or other quantitative measures which are useful to the production manager or the sales manager. It is not difficult to find out approximately what a research worker spent on a certain project or what he spent in a month, but there seems to be no way of ascertaining whether what he spent was the correct amount in view of what was accomplished.[13]

Form and Use of Project Reports. Since there are no cost standards for use in control of professional technical work, and since even the budgeted total costs of a project are likely to be only approximations, the principal purpose to be served in reporting project costs to date would appear to be that of a check on the estimated total cost. This, together with a periodic, subjective evaluation of the status and progress of the several projects, is the only basis for determining the validity of the over-all research plan for the period. Figure 16–2 illustrates progress and cost reports on a project.

Reference to Figure 16–2 makes clear the fact that there is no basis for evaluating the current period's expenditure. On the other hand, the new estimate of completion date (not changed) and of total cost (increased $1,000) is very important. Since the revised cost estimate exceeds the original appropriation (or allocation) of funds, the research director must decide whether to

1. Reduce the scope of the project
2. Abandon the project
3. Utilize savings from other projects

[13] Anthony, *op. cit.*, p. 67.

Appropriation Number	Description	Expenditures Current Period	Expenditures To Date	Appropriation
	PRODUCT DEVELOPMENT REPORT			
82-650	Development of a spectrophotometer	100	10,000	12,000

		Completion Date		Expenditures	
	PROJECT PROGRESS REPORT				
	Objectives and Progress to Date	Original Estimate	Present Estimate	Original Estimate	Present Estimate
82-650	To develop a low-cost instrument for the measurement of color. Engineering 75% completed. Drafting instructions issued.	12-1-53	12-1-53	12,000	13,000

SOURCE: Walter E. Arthur, "Developmental Costs Incurred in a Company Laboratory," *N.A.A. Bulletin,* Section 1, May, 1954, p. 1129.

FIG. 16–2. Examples of Reports on a Development Project

4. Shift funds from other projects
5. Request a supplemental appropriation of total funds

This forces a re-study of the entire program, and herein lies its value.

Again referring to Figure 16–2, it should be noted that the data reported therein relating to probable completion date and total cost are not the automatic products of the recording system. They are the results of estimates which, as the project progresses, should become more accurate. Moreover, since the estimates can hardly be prepared by an independent cost control division, the reports differ from cost control reports in the factory which are prepared by other than the persons over whom control is to be exercised. Nevertheless, the requirement that the estimates be reviewed periodically is the only control device available in many instances.

The periodic review of the status of all projects is important, not only for cost control purposes, but also for the more important purpose of directing research effort into the most productive channels. The position of the research director is unique in its responsibility. He must both select and administer projects. Consequently, budgetary control for him assumes a dual purpose, that of policy formation and that of policy administration.

Control of Purchases. Research and experimental equipment is expensive, and the demand for it on the part of professional research workers appears to be insatiable. Commonly, the requests cannot be valued by the ordinary economic analyses, since the research projects themselves frequently have no known immediate monetary value. How much should be budgeted for these items normally can be determined only by professional judgment, modified, of course, by the availability of funds for the purpose. Once such items are budgeted, the purchases present no control problem. Frequently, however, research workers request equipment during the course of their work and after the budget has been approved. Where the amounts involved are large, a question of proper authorization arises. Even though there may be funds available in the budget which can be diverted to this purpose, if the amount is substantial it is recommended that approval be required of someone outside the research division. The establishment of spending limits in different amounts for different levels of responsibility in the division is believed to be normal practice and is approved.

Control of Equipment Costs. One phase of cost control in the laboratory relates to the utilization of special equipment and apparatus. While some equipment is so highly specialized as to purpose as to have no general utility, other equipment may be adaptable to a number of research projects. The problem, particularly in the larger laboratories and in the multiple-laboratory divisions, is to maintain equipment records in such form that the availability and location of equipment is known at all times. Through such records, costly duplication of equipment items can be avoided. Purchase requests, when checked against such records, can be screened for duplication. Figure 16–3 illustrates such records, the first record being an alphabetic listing of equipment and the second record being a locational listing.

Control of Supplies. Another cost control problem that is somewhat peculiar to the research and development division is the efficient management of inventories of research supplies and materials. Where there are a number of professional research workers, each with his own laboratory or laboratory section, numerous inventories tend to accumulate. This may be due to the inconvenience of location of the central storeroom or poor storeroom service, or it may be due to the hoarding instinct. To the extent that the materials have common properties, the decentralized accumulations represent an excessive investment. The problem is not unlike that of the control of supplies in the general office (see Chapter 15), but it is, perhaps, more acute because of the lack of standardization in the use of research materials and supplies.

The Role of Top Management. In most company activities, control procedures which are independent of the controlled divisions lead to

ABC RESEARCH LABORATORY
NEW YORK, N.Y.

Equipment Classification

MANUFACTURER OR TYPE	DESCRIPTION	MODEL NUMBER	LOCATION	DIRECTOR
MICROSCOPES				
See Corp.	w/paired 10x20 widefield eye pieces	M-430	Chicago	I. M. Spatula
Look Company	31-28-54-12	14x3	New York	O. P. Tical
View Master	M1-4928 Recording	1953	Chicago	J. M. Glass
QUARTZ UNITS				
Through Corp.	30-44 mc in HPB Holder tolerance ± .005	AL-40	Chicago	J. M. Glass
XYZ Company	3 pin mounting range 1-1.5 mc	C-1000	Chicago	J. A. Edwards
Specie Analyzer	two pin banana type 1.75 to 12.5 mc	03471	New York	R. M. Wilson

Laboratory Location: Chicago — Equipment Location

CLASSIFICATION	MANUFACTURER OR TYPE	DESCRIPTION	MODEL NUMBER	TAG NUMBER
		J. M. GLASS		
Microscope	Viewmaster	M1-4928 Recording	1953	63-207
Quartz Units	Through Corp.	30-44 mc in HPB Holder Tolerance ±.005	AL-40	64-211
X-ray Equip.	Mercer Tube	100/130 v. 60 cy-XRD- w/D4010A CA6 crystal analysis tube	1492	65-201
		I. M. SPATULA		
Microscope	See Corp.	w/paired 10x20 widefield eye pieces	M-430	63-119

SOURCE: James A. McFadden, Jr., "Industrial Research Has Accounting Problems," *N.A.A. Bulletin,* Section 1, June, 1953, p. 1336.

FIG. 16–3. Equipment Records

control reports which provide top management with objective comparisons covering the performance of each operating division. The research and development division, however, does not fit into this pattern. The nonstandard character of the work militates against an outside control agency, and the technical nature of the work militates against the exercise of top managerial judgment. As has been noted, top management appropriates total funds, based largely on its confidence in its research division, and generally feels incompetent either to guide or to appraise the division's work.

In spite of this, top management must take the responsibility for the expenditures and for the adoption of a successful research program, and it must provide the funds. Its role, therefore, must be clearly defined. It seems to this author that its obligations are:

1. To clearly define the long-range objectives as they relate to research and development.
2. To employ the best research administrator possible under the circumstances.
3. To develop through him the best possible communications relating to the objectives, costs, and results of the division's work.

CHAPTER 17

CAPITAL EXPENDITURES

	Page		Page
Purpose of chapter	303	Standards of acceptability	312
Capital expenditures defined	303	Computing the rate of return	312
Types of capital expenditures	304	The capital expenditure budget	314
Methods of expenditure	305	**Controlling Capital Expenditures**	
Budgeting Capital Expenditures		Reporting progress in expenditures	314
Long-range and short-range planning	306	Control of costs	317
Approval procedure	307	Post-completion audits	317

Purpose of Chapter. Capital budgeting is one of the most important areas of managerial decision. The size of the funds commonly involved and the fact that the expenditures are designed to be recovered over several (or many) rather than only one operating period require a high order of analysis and judgment. Current operating decisions commit the company to a line of action for only a few months and, if wrong, can soon be changed. Capital expenditure decisions, however, represent much longer commitments, and mistakes are more costly for this reason.

But capital budgeting is also one of the most difficult areas of decision. Because of the longer-term nature of the commitments, the decisions involve more extended estimation and prediction of things to come. In addition, the economic analysis of opportunities for capital expenditures requires a high order of intellectual ability. The selection of factors for consideration and the measurement of alternatives are extremely difficult.

Both the importance and the difficulty of capital expenditure decisions warrant the setting aside of a full chapter for this purpose. Even so, the subject is so broad and difficult that only the surface can be scratched in outline form. The chapter begins with a discussion of the nature of capital expenditures and then treats them in accordance with the pattern followed throughout this work—budgeting and controlling.

Capital Expenditures Defined. A capital expenditure is an expenditure intended to benefit future periods. Normally, in accounting, it is associated with the acquisition or improvement of fixed assets. Accounting usage of the term, however, may at times be too narrow since, from a financial viewpoint, the real distinction between a capital expenditure and a revenue expenditure is not the immediate charging of the expenditure to income, as opposed to its gradual amortization, but the length of time required for its recovery in cash. Revenue expenditures such as product costs are expected to be recovered in a matter of weeks or, at the most, months. Capital expenditure recoveries, however, are measured in years.

In view of this distinction, research expenditures and costs of advertising campaigns directed toward new products or to expansion of the firm's market may be considered capital expenditures equally with the acquisition of fixed property. However, since these items have been discussed in earlier chapters, the present chapter will treat capital expenditures as being primarily in the category of fixed asset expenditures, as normally defined.

Types of Capital Expenditures. The evaluation of capital investment opportunities depends in part on the purpose of the investment. As to purpose, different classifications may be used, but that of Joel Dean seems quite appropriate for the present purpose. His classification is as follows:

1. Replacement investments
   a) Like-for-like replacement
   b) Obsolescence replacement
2. Expansion investments
3. Product investments
   a) Product improvement investments
   b) New product investments
4. Strategic investments
   a) Risk-reducing investments
   b) Welfare investments [1]

The two types of replacement investments are of the cost-reduction type. Expenditures for like-for-like investments are designed to achieve cost savings simply because of the effect of age of equipment on cost of its operation. Expenditures for obsolescence replacement, on the other hand, are designed to reduce costs through technical improvements in the equipment.

Expansion investments are designed to increase the capacity of the existing facilities, without change in the nature of production.

Product investments may take two forms, that of merely improving a present product or that of developing a new product. It is particularly true of product investments that capital expenditures may encompass

[1] Joel Dean, *Capital Budgeting* (New York: Columbia University Press, 1951), chaps. v–ix.

far more than mere acquisition of fixed assets. It is here that research, engineering, product development, and special advertising costs are incurred.

Finally, there are strategic investments of either the risk-reducing or welfare type. The former relate to such activities as industrial integration and pure research. The latter deal with developments in the field of employee safety and welfare, personnel relations, and public relations.

The importance of the foregoing classification is in the light which it throws on the nature of the project evaluation problem. The nature of the cost estimates, of the assumptions and estimates and predictions, and the profit objectives depends on the purpose and type of the investment. Obviously, a welfare investment cannot be evaluated as precisely or in the same manner as another type of investment. Moreover, a cost-saving replacement investment can be evaluated more readily than a product investment.

These differences also result in another difference—the level of management at which investment proposals originate. Cost reduction proposals, for example, may be initiated in the operating levels of management, whereas strategic investment proposals tend to be initiated only at top management levels. Wherever they originate, however, the ultimate authority for the spending of company funds must rest with top management. Consequently, the nature of the investment also affects the procedures for communicating and evaluating the ideas. This latter point is of great importance in large companies where channels of communication pose a major problem.

Methods of Expenditure. Given the decision to make a capital expenditure, there frequently arises a question as to how it shall be made. Should the property be acquired from outside suppliers, or should it be self-constructed? This question may be settled automatically by the nature of the company's facilities in relation to the nature of the property to be acquired. In other cases, however, a close analysis of the make-or-buy variety may be called for.

Related to the make-or-buy question is that of own-or-lease. This question is not one of whether or not to make an expenditure, but rather of whether the expenditure should take the form of a capital expenditure or a revenue expenditure. This problem, too, requires careful analysis of various factors.

There will be no further discussion in this work of either the make-or-buy or own-or-lease questions, since they are subsidiary to the major question of spending versus nonspending. Reference has been made to them, however, because they are important and arise very frequently.

BUDGETING CAPITAL EXPENDITURES

Long-Range and Short-Range Planning. The time factor is very important in capital budgeting for two reasons. First, both the planning and execution of capital expenditures are time-consuming. A year or more may be consumed in planning large-scale capital developments and an even longer period in accomplishing them. Then, too, the raising of the needed funds requires time, depending on the source.

Where the funds are to be obtained by external financing through the sale of bonds or capital stock, months may elapse before all arrangements are completed and the securities sold. If, on the other hand, internal financing is involved, years may be required to raise large amounts of funds. Here, dependence is on funds provided by depreciation and by net profits not needed for dividends or other current purposes.

Not only is time a factor, but timing is also important. Planning the expenditures so as to achieve the most profitable results in terms of the market and the state of business and so as to achieve the lowest financing costs requires careful timing of the transactions.

With all these factors in mind, it is obvious that both long-range and short-range planning are needed. The fact that short-range budgets rarely exceed a year's duration and frequently are of even shorter duration makes it clear that major capital expenditures commonly extend over several short-range budget periods. Consequently, both types of planning are involved.

Aside from the physical requirements in time, a separation of long-range and short-range capital planning is essential because of the difference in accuracy of forecasts. The longer the projection is in time, the less reliable are the forecasts. Consequently, capital budgeting practice generally falls into two categories, as to the nature of the planning. The long-range plan states objectives in rather general terms and does not spell out in detail the exact costs and timing of the transactions, or even the exact nature of the transactions. For example, the decision to build a plant in a new territory four or five years hence is necessarily a tentative one. It reflects management's *present* thinking about the desirability of such action and guides its financial planning, but the decision may be modified as time progresses. Relevant developments simply cannot be forecasted accurately that far in advance. Long-range decisions of this type affect the current period's financial budget only with respect to management's dividend policy. The gradual accumulation of the funds is made an objective of the current year's financial planning, but it does not represent an incurred liability at this time. The commitment is not a legal one, but only a matter of corporate policy.

CAPITAL EXPENDITURES

On the other hand, projects that are determined to be started in the current year, or to be continued, represent firm commitments to the extent of the current year's expenditures. The construction of a plant started the previous year normally must be continued or completed during the current year. The related expenditures are a "must" which have to be provided for in the budget. Similarly, new projects, once started in the current year, represent a commitment of current year's funds.

In effect, therefore, the real distinction between long-range and short-range capital budgeting lies in the degree of urgency of the need for cash. The former involves cash accumulation for expected future use; the latter involves current spending. Accumulation versus spending —this is the real difference. This difference is demonstrated in the Illustrative Company budget reports. There the current capital requirements are reflected in budgeted expenditures; the future capital requirements are reflected in dividend policy in relation to net earnings.

While different in the foregoing aspects, nevertheless long-range and short-range planning also are related. This is obviously true in those cases where current year's expenditures are the result of long-range planning in the past. But the relation also exists with regard to projects to be undertaken currently. Proposals for new, current-year expenditures must be evaluated for their effect on the availability of funds in the future. Thus, the decision to obtain new machinery during the current year must meet not only the current year's test of economic worth, but must also be viewed as a claim for funds that may be needed later on for some project in the long-range category. Should the money be spent now for an immediately desired project or saved for the projected plant expansion four or five years hence? Actually, short-range capital budgeting must be done within the framework of long-range plans.

Approval Procedure. The requests for capital equipment funds may come from many sources within the company. All must be carefully evaluated and a proper selection made of the most desirable projects. Approval procedures must be designed to:

1. Generate ideas
2. Ensure their communication to top management
3. Ensure wise selection

Ideas for capital improvements or changes may come from the research and development division, operating men at all levels, and top management. It is important that ideas be forthcoming.

The starting point of a capital program might be labelled the idea stage. The idea might start with a plant operator, a supervisor, a research man, a general manager, or the president himself. Ideas are the stuff that has made American business what it is and they are the thing which will make a country prosperous even when its natural resources diminish. They are the spark of life of a company and should not be lost or buried under any circumstances. The failure to put a good idea in the capital program may be as costly to a company as the inclusion of a bad one.[2]

To ensure the development of new ideas, management cannot take a passive attitude. It must adopt the attitude of a *search* for ideas. The encouragement of lower management levels and even of workers to do creative thinking concerning their jobs is necessary. This obviously requires, in turn, the development of channels of communication so that ideas, once born, can readily be communicated to those responsible for their evaluation. Many good ideas have been lost, as well as the urge to develop them, through cavalier treatment somewhere down the line of management of an employee's suggestion.

Once the ideas are generated and communicated, however, they must be screened, tested, and compared for relative worth. If idea generation is successful, there will be far more demands for funds than can be supplied. The selection procedure thus takes on great significance. Figures 17–1 and 17–2 illustrate what happens to them in two well-known companies, Sylvania Electric Products, Inc., and Bigelow-Sanford Carpet Company, Inc., respectively.

In considering approval procedures, it must be observed that the procedures vary, depending on the amount of money involved. Most companies set different levels of authorization for different amounts of spending. For example, expenditures of less than $1,000 may be authorized by a division or plant superintendent; from $1,000 to $10,000, by the president; and over $10,000, by the board of directors. Understanding this fact gives insight in the timing of requests.

Major expenditures of the type requiring board authorization generally are studied and proposals prepared well in advance of the submission of the annual budget. In fact, they may constitute the bulk of the capital spending included in the annual budget. On the other hand, smaller expenditures may be authorized from time to time by lower management levels, but from a blanket authorization included in the annual budget approved by the board. In this case, the board and top management are not concerned with detailed projects involving small sums, but they still are concerned with the total expenditure.

Regardless of the level of management at which expenditures are authorized, the committee system of selection is commonly used. In

[2] John M. Schultz, "Planning Capital Expenditures for Future Earnings," *N.A.A. Bulletin*, Section 1, Mar., 1955, p. 918.

CAPITAL EXPENDITURES

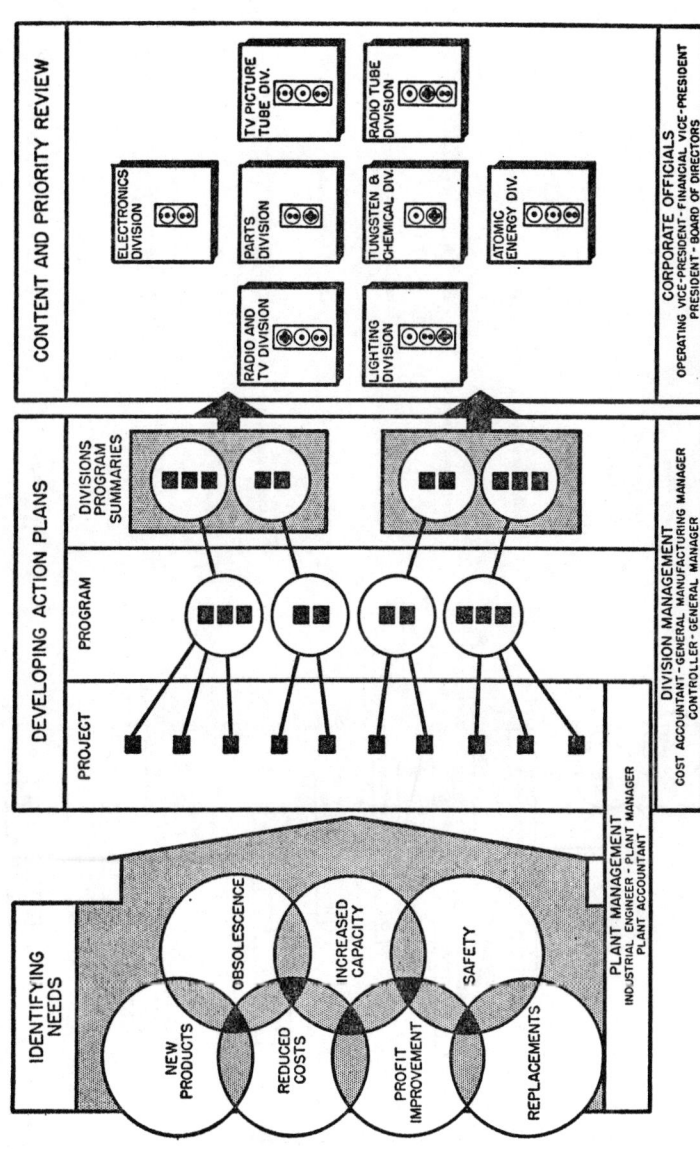

Fig. 17-1. Sylvania Capital Expenditures Control

Source: John E. Rhodes, "How to Make Capital Controls Work," *N.A.A. Bulletin*, Section 1, Sept., 1955, p. 6.

310 BUDGETING AND CONTROLLING TECHNIQUES

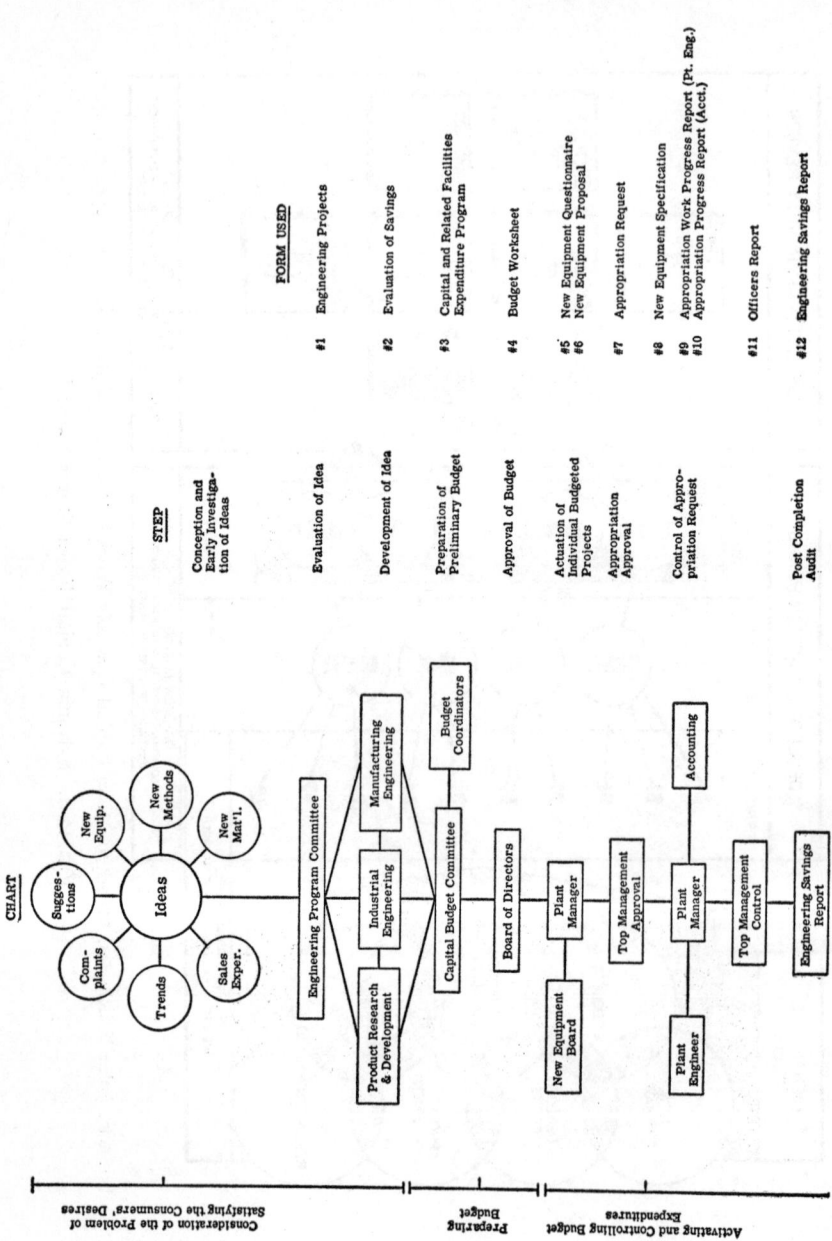

SOURCE: Elliott I. Petersen, "The Competitive-Demand System of Capital Budget Preparation," *Tested Approaches to Capital Equipment Replacement*, American Management Association, Special Report No. 1, 1954. p. 56.

small expenditures, committees of operating management are used; in large expenditures these committees are supplemented by other committees comprising top management personnel and members of the board.

There are three principal steps in authorizing a capital expenditure. They are:

1. Tentative approval of the idea
2. Gathering the essential information
3. Decision and authorization

Since some project suggestions require a large amount of fact-finding and study, they should receive a preliminary screening before the time and effort required for a thorough analysis are spent on them. It is imperative that the screeners be well qualified for the task. A high order of judgment and general background knowledge is essential to maintain a proper balance between nebulous hopes and sound practicality. The committee that does this preliminary screening must include personnel who are expert in the activity area involved, whether it be sales, production, or other activity.

Once the investigation is authorized, intensive effort should be directed toward exploring every facet of the project. Costs, anticipated results, financial requirements, legality, tax considerations, personnel considerations, market reactions—all must be explored. The problem here is twofold. First, there must be wise selection of the factors or issues to be studied, and their proper weighting. Second, the facts concerning each factor or issue must be gathered and classified. Both these problems may be difficult. With reference to the first, broad background knowledge and experience are essential to understanding what questions to raise concerning a project and the relative importance of the questions. As to the second, some of the desired information simply may not be available or, if it is, may take the form of estimates. Other information, particularly that pertaining to costs, may be available but only after considerable investigation and analysis. Frequently the costs desirable for this purpose are not the costs commonly recorded in the accounting records. The fact-finding generally is done by technicians.

Once the questions raised have been answered to the extent possible with the available data, a final decision concerning the proposed expenditure must be made. The decision will be in the negative if the project clearly does not meet the company's investment requirements. On the other hand, if it does meet the minimum requirements, it ordinarily will not immediately be approved but rather will be thrown in the pool of acceptable projects for a final comparative evaluation to determine which present the best investment opportunities. This final selection, again, usually rests with a committee of either high or lower levels of management, depending on the size of the projects.

In making the various evaluations, there obviously must be standards of acceptability, as a policy matter, and measures of relative worth. Such standards and measures should be carefully formulated beforehand. This is necessary, not only as a means of avoiding the necessity of fresh analysis of the basic problem every time a project comes up for consideration, but also to enable the evaluations to be delegated to various groups, a particularly important point in a large company.

Standards of Acceptability. There obviously are some capital expenditure projects which are "musts." An integral piece of equipment in a production line which is not functioning properly simply must be replaced without consideration of its merits as a separate equipment item. Its benefits are so related to the entire production process that normal measures of benefit cannot be applied.

Similarly, strategic investments frequently cannot be subjected to normal measures of usefulness. Yet they, too, may be considered as "musts." In such cases, acceptability and relative worth are matters of judgment and generally at a high management level. Appropriations of funds for this type of investment frequently are on a lump-sum basis.

For the most part, however, the investment opportunities which must be evaluated are susceptible of more precise evaluation. For these, the standards both of acceptability and of comparative worth are frequently stated as some percentage rate of return on the investment. After all, investment in a capital asset has the same purpose as investment in securities. The purpose is to produce net income commensurate with the amount expended. For example, a minimum rate of return may be established by top management, to set the standard of rejection or acceptability. Comparison of rates of return is a sound basis for final selection.

Computing the Rate of Return. Space considerations do not permit other than a cursory treatment of the calculation of comparative rates of return. A considerable body of literature is devoted to the subject, and the author's purpose here is simply to state the basic principles.

The return on the investment is the increased net profit resulting to the company from the expenditure. This increase may come about as a result of cost savings, as in the case of replacement investments. Or it may result from a change in both costs and sales, as in the case of expansion and product investments. In either case, it is important that the change in net income be estimated as accurately as possible. These estimates frequently are difficult to make.

Of the several types of investments, the replacement investments present the easier problems of estimation because they begin with an established cost and volume pattern. Even here, however, difficulties arise. The exact costs of operating present equipment may not be known since, commonly, the chart of accounts is not designed for this purpose. Moreover, the costs of new equipment cannot be fully known until the equipment has been tried out. Nevertheless, the analysis is restricted primarily to costs.

In the other two types of investment, however, both costs and sales have to be forecast. Large-scale production costs may not follow the pattern established by the pilot operation, and the changed or new product may not meet the test of consumer preference. Regardless of the type of investment, however, estimated return, by whatever method computed, is a good starting point in the determination of rate of return.

In a comparison of rates of return on competitive proposals, the factor of time is important since capital replacements and additions will be destined for various periods of usefulness. Some will have a use value of only a few years, while others will be useful for many years. While the time factor automatically is considered in determining rates of return through the normal recognition of cost recovery (depreciation), it has additional significance for two reasons.

First, the longer the expected use of the asset, the greater is the difficulty of forecasting. Hence, there is a risk factor which tends to increase as the time projections lengthen. An estimated annual return of 15 per cent over a ten-year period appears better than a 12 per cent return over five years, but the latter may be a more accurate estimate than the former. In choosing between one or the other of these proposed projects, judgment must be applied to the risk element in the estimates.

Second, since the present value of a dollar, determined so as to give effect to interest, varies inversely with the length of time over which the project is to be useful, interest calculations must be included in the analysis. These calculations must apply not only to the useful term of the assets, but also to the period of their construction, if significant.

Various methods have been devised for recognizing all these factors in rate-of-return comparisons. Some of them give the appearance of great precision. It must be recognized constantly, however, that the basic data used in the calculations contain numerous estimates. The calculations, in the final analysis, are no better than the estimates. Consequently, judgment is important in all investment decisions and the chief managerial problem in this regard, particularly in larger companies where there are many investment decisions to be made, is that of securing uniform bases for judgment to the extent possible throughout the various decision-making centers.

314   BUDGETING AND CONTROLLING TECHNIQUES

The Capital Expenditure Budget. Having determined the most profitable, or otherwise useful, projects for adoption, and having related them to the available funds, the capital expenditure budget finally can be prepared. Because some projects may require more than one year for completion, and since expenditures may be required in the current year for projects already under way, the budget commonly is prepared for a period of several years but with provision for analysis by years. Figure 17-3 illustrates such a budget. Once this budget schedule is approved, the financial and balance sheet data for the current year are incorporated in the cash schedule and the balance sheet schedule of the master forecast budget for the current year. There then remains only the requirement of issuing the individual project authorizations. Figure 17-4 illustrates such authorization.

CONTROLLING CAPITAL EXPENDITURES

The control of capital expenditures should be designed to:

1. Prevent unauthorized expenditures
2. Measure performance in estimating and making capital expenditures
3. Make post-completion audits of value of the expenditures

The first of these is basic to budgeting and needs no more comment, and only the last two items are discussed in this final section of the chapter.

Reporting Progress in Expenditures. Major capital expenditures cannot be accomplished overnight. The preparation of detailed plans and instructions, the issuance of work orders and purchase orders, the acquisition of needed materials and labor supply, and the actual construction and erection of the assets are time-consuming. Moreover, all sorts of unexpected delays may be encountered. Control of progress is essential for at least two reasons. First, changes in the timing of expenditures may disarrange the related financial plans and cause unexpected drains on available funds or create excessive interest costs, depending on the circumstances, and secondly, to control costs.

An example of the relation of variation from time schedules to financing costs is found in connection with building construction. Where a building is under construction with an estimated eighteen-month completion period, cash requirements normally are budgeted on the basis of the architects' forecast schedule of monthly construction billings. These, in turn, usually cover the actual construction costs and inventories of building materials accumulated on the site during the month, the total cost being reduced by the agreed withholding percentage. Variations in construction progress because of weather and other

TWO-YEAR CAPITAL EXPENDITURE PROGRAMS
SUMMARY
($000's Omitted)

Division _____   Years: _____

Priority Rating	Program Number	Title or Description of Program	Open Requisitions, Already Approved for Programs	Amounts Already Spent on Open Requisitions[1]	To Complete Open P P R's	195__ New Money	195__ Total	195__[2]	Working Capital Required for Program	Total Cost of Program (Inc. Working Capital)	Current Savings or Profit Improvement from Program[3]	Return on Investment[3]

[1] Including work-in-process, unfinished plant, and any partial capitalizations against requisitions still open.
[2] Any amounts to be spent subsequent to the second year should be shown in a footnote.
[3] A footnote should indicate whether savings and return on investment are based on one or two years' property expenditures.

SOURCE: L. C. Guest, Jr., "An Over-all System of Capital Controls," *Tested Approaches to Capital Equipment Replacement*, American Management Association, Special Report No. 1, 1954, p. 22.

FIG. 17-3. Capital Expenditure Budget

```
┌─────────────────────────────────────────────────────────────────────┐
│                                                      NO. _____   │
│              AUTHORIZATION FOR CAPITAL EXPENDITURE                  │
├─────────────────────────────────────────────────────────────────────┤
│ DEPARTMENT                    │ DIVISION                            │
├───────────────────────────────┴──────────────────┬──────────────────┤
│ PROJECT:                                         │ ☐ ADDITION       │
│                                                  │ ☐ REPLACEMENT    │
│                                                  │ ☐ BETTERMENT     │
├──────────────┬──────────────┬──────────────┬─────┴──────────────────┤
│    TOTAL     │ EXPENDITURES │ EXPENDITURES │                        │
│  ESTIMATED   │    TO BE     │    TO BE     │                        │
│ EXPENDITURES │  CAPITALIZED │   EXPENSED   │ UNDEPRECIATED COST OF PROPERTY RETIRED $ │
│ $            │ $            │ $            │ SCRAP VALUE OF PROPERTY RETIRED $        │
├──────────────┴──────────────┴──────────────┴────────────────────────┤
│ DESCRIPTION:                                                        │
│                                                                     │
├─────────────────────────────────────────────────────────────────────┤
│ PRODUCTS AFFECTED:                                                  │
├─────────────────────────────────────────────────────────────────────┤
│ PURPOSE:                                                            │
│                                                                     │
├──────────────────────────────────┬──────────────────────────────────┤
│ DATE WORK TO BE STARTED      19  │ ESTIMATED COMPLETION DATE    19  │
├──────────────────────────────────┴──────────────────────────────────┤
│ REQUESTED BY_____ TITLE _____ DATE _____ 19__ │
├──────────┬──────────────────────────────────────────────┬───────────┤
│          │ BY_____        │ _____ 19_│
│          │        Plant Superintendent                  │           │
│ APPROVAL:│ BY_____        │ _____ 19_│
│          │        Divisional Executive                  │           │
│          │ BY_____        │ _____ 19_│
│          │        Executive Committee                   │           │
├──────────┴──────────────────────────────────────────────┴───────────┤
│ SPECIAL ACCOUNTING INSTRUCTIONS                                     │
├─────────────────────────────────────────────────────────────────────┤
│ Date _____ 19                              _____ │
│                                                       Comptroller   │
└─────────────────────────────────────────────────────────────────────┘
```

SOURCE: Arthur H. Wernecke, "Control of Capital Outlay Authorizations," *N.A.A. Bulletin,* Section 1, Nov., 1951, p. 358.

FIG. 17-4. Authorization for Capital Expenditure

conditions and changes in the rate of receipt of materials because of supply and transportation factors may greatly affect the monthly billings. Thus, the actual monthly cash requirements may vary considerably with the forecast monthly requirements. If, in the same situation, financing has been arranged for on a scheduled monthly basis, variations in billings can be embarrassing. Excessive billings may require dipping into current working capital, thus creating additional working capital costs. On the other hand, low billings result in borrowed funds coming in faster than required, with resultant excess interest costs.

But a more serious result of schedule variations is their effect on related projects and operations and on the estimates of benefits to be received from the expenditure. Where the asset in process of acquisition is to be an integral part of a sequential procedure, delay will affect the entire procedure with, perhaps, untold results. But, in addition, the failure to complete a capital improvement in time to meet a market situation may completely negate all the estimates upon which authorization of the project was based. Timing, particularly in the case of product capital expenditures, can be extremely important. In view of these considerations, close control and reporting of progress are necessary.

Control of Costs. With reference to the costs actually incurred on the project, the principal budgetary requirement is to keep the costs in line with the budget, to the extent possible, and where they cannot be kept in line, to analyze the cost variations as a means of testing the estimates that were used. This is done by comparison of the actual costs with the official estimates prepared by those responsible for the work.

One of the detailed steps in capital budgeting is the preparation of cost estimates. Normally they should be reported on special forms, as these estimates are essential both for budgeting and control. On a month-to-month basis, the comparison may not be too significant, but once the project approaches completion, it should be useful. Granted that once the variations have occurred, nothing can be done with them, the information is useful in the preparation of estimates for projects in the future. Figure 17–5 illustrates a progress report showing both the progress achieved to date and the gain or loss on completed projects.

Post-Completion Audits. An important phase of the control of capital expenditures is the making of post-completion audits of projects to determine whether their actual value is in line with that determined at the time of authorization. In the case of a replacement investment, are the estimated cost savings being realized? In the case of expansion and product investments, are both the cost and income estimates proving realistic? In the case of strategic investments, do they appear to have been sound?

Periodic audit and review of prior decisions at intervals of one or two years, depending on the original useful-time estimates of the projects, can be very helpful to management. First, they aid in determining whether the operation should be continued. Second, and of great significance, they aid in bringing to light faulty estimation procedures, the correction of which may be invaluable in the consideration of future projects. Are significant factors commonly being overlooked? Should cost data be refined further? Should a greater risk factor be built into long-term calculations?

FIG. 17-5. Appropriations Progress Report

SOURCE: Elliott I. Petersen, "The Competitive-Demand System of Capital Budget Preparation," *Tested Approaches to Capital Equipment Replacement*, American Management Association, Special Report No. 1, 1954, p. 68.

CAPITAL EXPENDITURES 319

Another essential control for modern management of capital expenditures is a post-completion audit of actual earnings of the project compared with the earnings forecasted in the rate of return estimate. The prime purpose of this post mortem is to keep the project earnings estimates honest. A secondary purpose is to find out how to improve the company's techniques for projecting sales volumes, profit margins, cost behavior, and the other ingredients of project earnings. To preserve the integrity of the estimates of project earnings and prevent them from being inflated to the point of making a joke of the entire capital-rationing system, the organization needs to know in advance that actual earnings will be compared with estimated earnings for each project.

Precise comparability of reported and estimated earnings is, however, difficult to achieve for several reasons. First, the earnings of the early years do not represent a valid or long enough test period for sampling the entire economic life of a project. Sometimes adjustment factors have cyclical conditions, and other distortions may develop. It is always desirable to take soundings several years later as well as in the early years. Second, the concepts and measurement of project earnings that are economically correct for the capital expenditure decision do not conform to the conventions of accountancy. Consequently, actual earnings which are comparable with estimated earnings cannot be mechanically taken off from the books of account. But they can be derived from reported results with the right kind of economic analysis.[3]

The foregoing quotation shows both the purposes and the problems of post-completion audits. A method used by one company in its review after the fact is described as follows:

Conditions tend to change and basic assumptions used in the original estimate are often found to be in error to a greater or less degree. These changes are not always within the control of the operating people, so that it is often difficult to judge the adequacy of the original statement and the competence of those responsible for its preparation. To overcome these difficulties we prepare our audit of savings statements in three columns. The first column is a repetition of the original savings estimate. The second is the original estimate modified to reflect changes in noncontrollable conditions, such as sales price (but not volume), labor rates (but not labor hours), fuel costs (but not steam or power consumed), etc. The third column reflects the actual savings based on actual conditions.[4]

While, as was pointed out earlier, such reviews do not correct earlier mistakes, they do point the way to sounder capital expenditure decisions in the future. This is their real value to budgeting and budgetary control.

---

[3] Joel Dean, "Controls for Capital Expenditures," *Modern Management of Capital Expenditures,* American Management Association, Financial Management Series, No. 105, p. 12.

[4] Franklin L. Mettler, "Before-the-Fact Control of Capital Outlay," *N.A.A. Bulletin,* Section 1, June, 1951, p. 1249.

CHAPTER 18

FINANCIAL POSITION

	Page		Page
Purpose of chapter	320	Budgeting fixed assets	332
Requirements for financial well-being	321	Budgeting accounts payable	333
Source of funds	321	Budgeting accrued wages and payroll taxes	334
Use of funds	324		
Budgeting cash	326	Budgeting other accruals	334
Budgeting accounts receivable	328	Budgeting other liabilities	334
Budgeting inventories	331	Budgeting capital	334
Budgeting prepaid expenses and deferred charges	332		

Purpose of Chapter. The financial position (or condition) of a company relates to its financial well-being—the amount and composition of its assets in relation to the amount and composition of its liabilities, and both, in turn, related to the nature, scope, and size of the company's operations. It is portrayed by the balance sheet and its several analyses. Financial position is both an objective and a result of operations. While earning a profit is the number one objective, the year's plans must also be laid with a view to achieving a sound position financially, and this latter objective may seriously modify steps planned solely with the first objective in mind. A too-hasty expansion of production schedules, for example, designed to cash in on a sudden boom in the market, may strain the company's resources and leave it extremely vulnerable to the financial dangers inherent in a volatile market. Adequate financing of operations is as important a consideration in planning as the profit objective.

It is in the study of this phase of budgeting that the real significance of double-entry bookkeeping is brought out. The duality of business transactions in their effect on (1) the income account and (2) the balance sheet, must be fully comprehended in budgeting. The fact that profits may not be immediately realizable in the form of cash and the fact that so many of the assets of a company are recoverable in cash only over a period of time give this duality added significance. Operational planning and financial planning must go hand in hand. The best matching, for example, of sales and sales effort from the profit viewpoint may not be possible (in the short run) from the financial viewpoint.

Because financial position is both an objective and a result of operations, over-all budgeting involves a series of interdependent analyses, as

Another essential control for modern management of capital expenditures is a post-completion audit of actual earnings of the project compared with the earnings forecasted in the rate of return estimate. The prime purpose of this post mortem is to keep the project earnings estimates honest. A secondary purpose is to find out how to improve the company's techniques for projecting sales volumes, profit margins, cost behavior, and the other ingredients of project earnings. To preserve the integrity of the estimates of project earnings and prevent them from being inflated to the point of making a joke of the entire capital-rationing system, the organization needs to know in advance that actual earnings will be compared with estimated earnings for each project.

Precise comparability of reported and estimated earnings is, however, difficult to achieve for several reasons. First, the earnings of the early years do not represent a valid or long enough test period for sampling the entire economic life of a project. Sometimes adjustment factors have cyclical conditions, and other distortions may develop. It is always desirable to take soundings several years later as well as in the early years. Second, the concepts and measurement of project earnings that are economically correct for the capital expenditure decision do not conform to the conventions of accountancy. Consequently, actual earnings which are comparable with estimated earnings cannot be mechanically taken off from the books of account. But they can be derived from reported results with the right kind of economic analysis.[3]

The foregoing quotation shows both the purposes and the problems of post-completion audits. A method used by one company in its review after the fact is described as follows:

Conditions tend to change and basic assumptions used in the original estimate are often found to be in error to a greater or less degree. These changes are not always within the control of the operating people, so that it is often difficult to judge the adequacy of the original statement and the competence of those responsible for its preparation. To overcome these difficulties we prepare our audit of savings statements in three columns. The first column is a repetition of the original savings estimate. The second is the original estimate modified to reflect changes in noncontrollable conditions, such as sales price (but not volume), labor rates (but not labor hours), fuel costs (but not steam or power consumed), etc. The third column reflects the actual savings based on actual conditions.[4]

While, as was pointed out earlier, such reviews do not correct earlier mistakes, they do point the way to sounder capital expenditure decisions in the future. This is their real value to budgeting and budgetary control.

[3] Joel Dean, "Controls for Capital Expenditures," *Modern Management of Capital Expenditures,* American Management Association, Financial Management Series, No. 105, p. 12.
[4] Franklin L. Mettler, "Before-the-Fact Control of Capital Outlay," *N.A.A. Bulletin,* Section 1, June, 1951, p. 1249.

CHAPTER 18

FINANCIAL POSITION

	Page		Page
Purpose of chapter	320	Budgeting fixed assets	332
Requirements for financial well-being	321	Budgeting accounts payable	333
Source of funds	321	Budgeting accrued wages and payroll taxes	334
Use of funds	324	Budgeting other accruals	334
Budgeting cash	326	Budgeting other liabilities	334
Budgeting accounts receivable	328	Budgeting capital	334
Budgeting inventories	331		
Budgeting prepaid expenses and deferred charges	332		

Purpose of Chapter. The financial position (or condition) of a company relates to its financial well-being—the amount and composition of its assets in relation to the amount and composition of its liabilities, and both, in turn, related to the nature, scope, and size of the company's operations. It is portrayed by the balance sheet and its several analyses. Financial position is both an objective and a result of operations. While earning a profit is the number one objective, the year's plans must also be laid with a view to achieving a sound position financially, and this latter objective may seriously modify steps planned solely with the first objective in mind. A too-hasty expansion of production schedules, for example, designed to cash in on a sudden boom in the market, may strain the company's resources and leave it extremely vulnerable to the financial dangers inherent in a volatile market. Adequate financing of operations is as important a consideration in planning as the profit objective.

It is in the study of this phase of budgeting that the real significance of double-entry bookkeeping is brought out. The duality of business transactions in their effect on (1) the income account and (2) the balance sheet, must be fully comprehended in budgeting. The fact that profits may not be immediately realizable in the form of cash and the fact that so many of the assets of a company are recoverable in cash only over a period of time give this duality added significance. Operational planning and financial planning must go hand in hand. The best matching, for example, of sales and sales effort from the profit viewpoint may not be possible (in the short run) from the financial viewpoint.

Because financial position is both an objective and a result of operations, over-all budgeting involves a series of interdependent analyses, as

FINANCIAL POSITION

was pointed out in Chapter 2. An operating plan designed to produce the desired profit may prove impractical when translated to a forecast balance sheet. Similarly, a satisfactory forecast financial position may not yield a satisfactory profit for the period. Plans have to be reworked for the best possible integration of the two objectives.

It is the purpose of this chapter to review the requirements of a sound financial position and to discuss the problems of relating operations to financial position. Unlike other chapters in this Part of the book, this chapter does not treat the control phase of budgeting separately. Once the budget is established, financial position automatically results from operations, and control of the balance sheet items is provided by the control of the operating transactions already discussed in preceding chapters.

Requirements for Financial Well-Being. There are many measures of financial position that frequently are used, but the position should be analyzed with three basic factors in mind:

1. Source of the funds
2. Use of the funds
3. Safety

The funds should be acquired economically. They should be used to good advantage. The over-all arrangement should provide financial safety. It is around these three principles that various balance sheet and operating ratios are constructed, and it should be recognized that, for their use, the balance sheet data are basic. While the factor of safety is listed separately, it is so intertwined with the other two that it will not be separately discussed.

Source of Funds. The forecast balance sheet of Illustrative Company as of March 31, shown in Chapter 5, may be condensed as follows:

Current Assets	$1,564,550	Current Liabilities	$ 622,800
Fixed Assets	1,664,000	Long-term Debt	216,000
		Capital Stock	2,000,000
		Retained Earnings	389,750
Total	$3,228,550		$3,228,550

Of the $3,228,550 funds expected to be available on that date, creditors will provide $838,800, and owners, $2,389,750 through original investment and reinvested earnings. The owners will have provided 74 per cent of the funds on that date, and creditors, 26 per cent. Whether this is a good proportion depends on circumstances, but should be judged in the light of three basic principles, as follows:

1. Use of borrowed funds pyramids the return on owners' investment so long as the interest rate is less than the profit rate per dollar of capital employed.

2. The burden of repayment, particularly in the case of long-term credits, is affected by price level changes.
3. Both debts and interest charges have to be paid and represent commitments of funds.

With reference to the first principle, it is obvious that debt is not a burden on a company's owners if, during the period of the debt, all available funds can be fully employed at a rate of return in excess of the interest rate on the debt. Actually, it would pay to apply this principle under that circumstance. The danger, however, lies in the fact that one cannot be sure that the foregoing conditions will prevail throughout the period of the debt. If they do not, the adverse effect on profits can be as great as the benefit realized under favorable conditions. Hence, the desire for maximization of rate of return must be tempered with caution and the use of debt funds restricted, depending on the degree of stability of the industry's market.

As to the second principle, the effect of major changes in price levels over a period of time can be equally significant. Debt incurred at the start of a price rise becomes less burdensome, and more profitable, as the rise continues. But the reverse is also true. Again, the degree of predictability is important.

Concerning the third principle, the essence of debt is the obligation to pay principal and interest under all circumstances. Dependence on borrowed funds involves loss of managerial flexibility. This is particularly true where specific assets have to be pledged or mortgaged.

All of these factors must be considered in formulating policy with reference to the source of company funds. The problem is one for top management only, but it is so significant that major debt financing steps are taken only with the greatest care.

Thus far, we have discussed the sources of total funds, but now attention must be given the breakdown of funds into current and fixed. This analysis is important since short-term debt should not be used to finance long-term investments. The following rearrangement of Illustrative Company's balance sheet data serves to facilitate an understanding of the dependence on the several sources of funds.

Current Assets	$1,564,550	
Current Liabilities	622,800	
Working Capital		$ 941,750
Fixed Assets	1,664,000	
Long-term Debt	216,000	
Permanent Capital		1,448,000
Capital Stock	2,000,000	
Retained Earnings	389,750	
Total Capital		$2,389,750

Whereas owners have supplied 74 per cent of the total funds, this arrangement of the data shows that they have supplied 60 per cent of the working capital and 87 per cent of the permanent capital. While the financing of working capital generally is less costly than that of fixed capital and while, normally, there will always be some dependence on creditors for working capital, if for no other reason than the time required to process and pay invoices, nevertheless, the importance of a large owner investment in working capital cannot be overemphasized. Factors affecting the need for and amount of current funds are so volatile that management needs the greatest possible freedom of action in the administration of these funds. Hence, the advisability of obtaining them largely from either owners or long-term creditors. Too great dependence on short-term creditors is dangerous.

The reference to the volatile character of the current funds leads to a further analysis of the source of funds—the breakdown of owners' investment into capital stock (original investment) and retained or reinvested earnings. The fact that profits themselves change from day to day with the state of the company's operations has a significant effect on working capital and is the primary reason for not obtaining this capital in too large amount from creditors. A change in profits is felt first in the current funds.

While the sources of total funds are three:

1. Creditors
2. Owners' investment in capital stock
3. Retained earnings

a different analysis is required when total funds are analyzed into current and permanent funds. This is due to the fact that there may be shifts between the two funds. Current funds may be used temporarily for financing fixed assets, or fixed assets may be sold and the proceeds added to the current funds. Moreover, in the case of depreciation charges, this latter shift tends to take place as a normal matter if the recovered depreciation is not funded or immediately reinvested in new fixed assets. Consequently, changes in working *capital* may be created as follows:

Decrease	*Increase*
Losses	Profits retained in current form
Investment in fixed assets or in reduction of long-term debt	Depreciation not funded or reinvested in fixed assets
Payment of dividends	Long-term financing
	Liquidation of fixed assets, proceeds left in current form

The foregoing changes in working capital, together with changes in permanent capital, should be planned. Actually, they are planned in the sense that the originating transactions are planned, but the point is that the originating transactions should be planned with full knowledge of their effect on the financial structure. This is one reason for requiring a forecast balance sheet and forecast statement of sources and uses of funds as an integral part of a complete budget.

Use of Funds. Analysis of the use of funds should be based solely on their contribution to the profit goals of the company. This analysis is applicable to every single asset. That is, every product brought into the line should be selected only after giving effect to the rate of return on the needed investment. And this investment includes not only the cost of the fixed facilities involved, but also the working capital required to be invested in cash, inventories of materials, work in process, and finished product, and receivables. Thus, the amount of each asset planned for is determined indirectly as a result of other decisions, but those other decisions are not made without regard to their effect on asset position. Figure 18–1 demonstrates how product selection involves a study of the cost of investment needed for each product. It is apparent, therefore, that the selection of products to be produced, together with the determined volume, automatically establishes standard assets investments.

The required investment in fixed facilities to produce a given product and the related investment costs normally are computed as an integral part of the product study. Frequently, however, less attention is given the other investments, but they should also be analyzed. The investment in receivables resulting from the sale of a given product, for example, may, or may not, follow the normal collection pattern for other products. A special product designed for sale to one large customer, such as the government, may involve a larger or smaller running investment in accounts receivable than do other products designed for the general market. Similarly, investments in inventories may differ among products, depending on all the circumstances surrounding the procurement of materials, the manufacture of the product, and its sale and delivery. In the example shown in Figure 18–1, the several products do vary as to inventory requirements, but it is assumed that the cash and receivable requirements are the same. In that illustration the following standards are used:

1. The standard for cash should be set as the ratio of the desired base-date over-all operating balance to the annual over-all operating disbursements.
2. The standard for receivables should be established as the normal ratio of base-date receivables to annual sales.
3. Inventory standards should be determined through a combination of inventory policy with respect to general levels as of the base-date and the conditions imposed by the requirements of the various products.

COMPARATIVE INVESTMENT

Data	Product A	B	C	D	E
1. Selling Price	$9.00	$9.00	$9.00	$9.00	$9.00
2. Total Cost Excluding Depreciation	6.70	6.69	6.71	6.67	6.71
3. Total Manufacturing Cost	6.50	6.49	6.51	6.50	6.50
4. Cash Requirement—% of Cash Costs	10%	10%	10%	10%	10%
5. Receivables % of Sales	10%	10%	10%	10%	10%
6. Materials % of Year	16.67%	8.33%	25.00%	16.67%	16.67%
7. Material Cost	2.50	2.49	2.51	2.05	2.86
8. Work in Process Inventory % of Year Required at 85% to adjust to percent to be applied to total cost	10.5%	5.25%	15.7%	10.5%	10.5%
9. Finished Goods Inventory % of year required	12.5%	6.25%	18.8%	12.5%	12.5%
10. Fixed Plant Investment	$350,000	$350,000	$350,000	$350,000	$350,000
11. Annual Units	100,000	100,000	100,000	90,000	110,000
Investment Per Unit					
Cash—4 × 2	$ .67	$ .67	$ .67	$ .67	$ .67
Receivables—5 × 1	.90	.90	.90	.90	.90
Materials Inventory—6 × 7	.42	.21	.63	.34	.47
Work in Process Inventory—8 × 3	.68	.34	1.02	.68	.68
Finished Goods Inventory—9 × 3	.81	.41	1.22	.81	.81
Working Capital	3.48	2.53	4.44	3.40	3.53
Fixed Plant—10 ÷ 11	3.50	3.50	3.50	3.89	3.18
12. Total Investment	6.98	6.03	7.94	7.29	6.71

SOURCE: J. E. Zwisler, "Standard Product Investment," *The Controller*, Oct., 1953, p. 472.

FIG. 18–1. Comparative Investment

4. Fixed plant investment should be departmentalized and the amount of investment per processing hour should be determined on a normal capacity basis.[1]

The investment in receivables for a given product is determined by the nature of the market and the customs of the trade. These must be analyzed to set the standards. In the case of inventories, the factors to be analyzed have already been discussed in Chapter 11. Cost of facilities is a matter for the cost accountant to determine. Cash costs, on the other hand, depend on the free cash balances which the company determines should be available, on deposit, at all times. This is a matter of financial policy and is governed by such factors as interest rates, good bank relations, the stability and predictability of cash requirements, and the factor of safety. Obviously, cash which is being accumulated for a non-operating purpose should not be included in these determinations.

[1] J. E. Zwisler, "Standard Product Investment," *The Controller*, Oct., 1953, pp. 472–73.

Once the over-all budget is determined and put into effect, with full consideration for its estimated balance sheet results, the periodic balance sheets during the period of the budget should conform to all the other segments of the budget to the exent that the budget itself is made effective. The remaining sections of the chapter deal with the calculation of the various account balances on the forecast balance sheet and are based on the data used in Chapter 5.

Budgeting Cash. If business firms operated strictly on a cash basis, the scheduling of cash receipts and disbursements would be a simple matter once the operating plans were completed. Actually, however, this is rarely the case. Depreciation accounting, credit sales and purchases, inventory changes, accruals and prepayments all result in a flow of cash which on a month-to-month basis does not match the firm's income and expenditures. Short-term scheduling of receipts and disbursements requires that close attention be paid the time factor. The tighter the cash position is, the greater must be the consideration of the time factor. In the case of Illustrative Company (see Chapter 5), the month is the unit of time.

In the case of most companies, cash comes from only a few sources, as follows:

Cash sales
Collection of receivables
Interest and dividends
Miscellaneous—sale of capital assets, tax refunds, etc.
Loans

The last-named item generally is scheduled only after a matching of scheduled receipts and disbursements leads to a decision concerning the need for and timing of borrowing.

The most significant of the foregoing items, as to both size and difficulty of forecasting, is collection of receivables. This is a function of a number of factors, as follows:

Cash sales
Account sales
Sales returns
Sales discounts for prompt payment
Bad debts
Time of payment—prompt, slow, very slow, etc.

These factors must be estimated from past experience, modified by current and expected changes.

In the case of Illustrative Company, collections were believed to follow the pattern:

60 per cent in month of sale, less 2 per cent cash discount
30 per cent in first succeeding month
8 per cent in second succeeding month
2 per cent uncollectible

On this basis, and after careful review of the accounts on hand at the beginning of the budget period, and after scheduling sales, cash collections were scheduled as follows:

	January	February	March
From last year's sales	$374,500	$115,000	–
From January sales	364,560	186,000	$ 49,600
From February sales	–	370,440	189,000
From March sales	–	–	517,440
Total	$739,060	$671,440	$756,040

Since this was the only source of Illustrative Company's receipts, other than loans, the foregoing table completes this company's study of cash receipts. Before proceeding with the discussion of disbursements, however, it should be pointed out that the experience with reference to the foregoing collection factors frequently can be determined only by considerable analysis of available data. Where, for example, sales are uniform throughout prior months and month-end receivable balances do not fluctuate greatly, it is a simple matter to determine a monthly ratio of receipts to sales. Such ratios, however, would be meaningless in the case of wide fluctuations in monthly sales and in the month-end balances of receivables. In such case, a complete analysis of the type used in calculating the provision for doubtful accounts is required.

The scheduling of cash disbursements normally is a more difficult task than that of cash receipts. The disbursements are more varied in nature than the receipts and involve different time patterns. Normally, the disbursements are in payment of the following items:

Accounts payable—for purchased materials, supplies, and services
Accrued payroll—for salaries and wages
Accrued taxes—income taxes, tax withholdings, social security taxes, real estate taxes, etc.
Accrued interest—on notes, bonds, etc.
Dividends
Capital improvements—for purchased facilities
Debt reduction—payment on mortgages, bonds, notes, etc.

Some of the foregoing items can easily be scheduled since the amount and time of payment are known beforehand. Examples of these are amortization payments on a mortage, real estate taxes, and last year's income tax liability. Other items, such as accrued interest and capital improvements, depend in part on top management decisions arrived at in the preparation of the current budget. But the greatest difficulty is found in the accounts payable, payroll accruals, and current income and social security tax accruals. The amounts can be determined only after assembling information from a number of sources. And, while the timing of tax payments is regulated by law, and that of payrolls by both law and company practice, the timing of payments of accounts payable is definite or indefinite depending on the company's ability and practice with respect to taking allowed discounts. In any event, most of the foregoing types of disbursements can be scheduled only after many other decisions have been made and other schedules have been prepared.

Some companies which do not do complete budgeting attempt to forecast cash requirements by short-cut methods. Such methods are deceptive, however, and can be dangerous where the cash position is critical. Month-to-month variations in purchases, production, and other activities tend to make cash spending ratios of little value unless a wide margin of error is provided for, and, obviously, the larger this provision, the less useful the data.

Figure 18–2 shows the schedule of monthly cash disbursements of Illustrative Company. The classification of disbursements is made different from that shown above in order to promote a more comprehensive understanding of the ramifications of the data needed in building the schedule of payments. The noncash expenses referred to in that figure relate to depreciation, accruals, and prepayment expirations.

Once the receipts and disbursements are scheduled, it then is possible to view the cash picture as a whole to determine the amount and timing of any needed financing. The following data summarize the expected monthly receipts and disbursements and show the expected month-end cash positions without resort to external financing.

	January	February	March
Scheduled disbursements	$743,700	$727,870	$1,003,220
Scheduled receipts	739,060	671,440	756,040
Excess of disbursements over receipts	4,640	56,430	247,180
Balance, beginning of month	250,000	245,360	188,930
Balance, end of month	$245,360	$188,930	($ 58,250)

External financing obviously is required. It was decided, at the time the budget was prepared, that $200,000 should be borrowed in March on a time loan. Figure 18–3 presents the complete cash schedule of Illustrative Company for the three months of the first quarter, the period for which the budget was drafted.

Budgeting Accounts Receivable. This subject has already been partially covered in connection with the discussion of cash receipts. It

ILLUSTRATIVE COMPANY
ESTIMATED MONTHLY CASH DISBURSEMENTS
First Quarter, 19—

	January	February	March
Accounts payable, balance January 1	$300,000	–	–
Accounts payable, direct material purchases, less purchase discounts:			
January purchases	–	$266,070	–
February purchases	–	–	$ 214,620
Payroll, direct labor	190,000	190,000	190,000
Accounts payable and payroll, factory burden, excluding noncash expenses	129,600	129,600	129,600
Accounts payable and payroll, selling expenses, less commissions and noncash expenses	74,500	75,000	87,500
Payroll, sales commissions:			
Accrued as of January 1	15,000	–	–
On January sales	–	18,600	–
On February sales	–	–	18,900
Accounts payable and payroll, general and administrative expenses, less noncash expenses	19,600	24,600	24,600
Dividends payable	15,000	–	–
Federal income tax payable	–	–	220,000
Interest on mortgage	–	–	6,000
Mortgage reduction	–	–	12,000
Prepaid insurance	–	24,000	–
Capital improvement	–	–	100,000
	$743,700	$727,870	$1,003,220

FIG. 18-2. Illustrative Company, Estimated Monthly Cash Disbursements

ILLUSTRATIVE COMPANY
SCHEDULE OF CASH RECEIPTS AND DISBURSEMENTS
First Quarter, 19—

	January	February	March
Receipts:			
Accounts receivable collections	$739,060	$671,440	$ 756,040
Bank loan	–	–	200,000
Total	$739,060	$671,440	$ 956,040
Disbursements:			
Accounts payable, payroll, etc.	$728,700	$727,870	$ 665,220
Mortgage reduction	–	–	12,000
Interest	–	–	6,000
Dividends	15,000	–	–
Income taxes	–	–	220,000
Capital improvements	–	–	100,000
Total	$743,700	$727,870	$1,003,220
Summary:			
Excess of receipts over disbursements	($ 4,640)	($ 56,430)	($ 47,180)
Balance, beginning of month	250,000	245,360	188,930
Balance, end of month	$245,360	$188,930	$ 141,750

FIG. 18-3. Illustrative Company, Schedule of Cash Receipts and Disbursements

was pointed out there that the estimated collections are determined by applying the returns, discounts, bad debts, and time of payment factors to the receivables created during the month and the receivables on hand at the beginning of the month. The scheduled end-of-month receivables are arrived at simply by subtracting estimated receipts plus discounts from the total receivables. The estimated amount of bad debts is not subtracted from the receivables, but is added to the account "provision for doubtful accounts." The forecast balance sheet of Illustrative Company presented in Chapter 5 shows the estimated receivables at February 28 and March 31 as follows:

	February 28	March 31
Accounts receivable	$324,000	$437,400
Provision for doubtful accounts	(35,000)	(52,600)
Book value	289,000	384,800

The increase of $113,400 in the gross receivables is accounted for as follows:

Sales in March (from Chapter 5)		$880,000
Collections in March (from Fig. 18–3)	$756,040	
Discounts allowed in March, 2 per cent of 60 per cent of sales (from p. 327)	10,560	766,600
Increase in receivables		$113,400

The increase of $17,600 in the provision for doubtful accounts equals 2 per cent of the month's sales. With reference to this item, the Illustrative Company illustration in Chapter 5 makes no provision for the writing off of receivables proved to be worthless. While from an accounting viewpoint such write-offs should be made when worthlessness finally is established, failure to provide for them in the illustration does not affect any of the forecasted results of operation. The provision of the allowance for doubtful accounts satisfies all the budgetary requirements. Budget authorization is not essential to these write-offs.

Budgeting Inventories. An entire chapter (Chapter 11) is devoted to budgeting and controlling inventories. Emphasis in that chapter, however, is on quantitative requirements. Now we are concerned with dollars of inventory as reported on the balance sheet of the company. Where standard costs are used, as is the case with Illustrative Company, balance sheet values (at standard cost) can readily be obtained merely by applying the unit standards to the budgeted quantities in inventory. However, if actual costs are used on a Fifo, Lifo, moving average, or some other basis, balance sheet values can be determined only by the accounting method of following the charges and credits through the inventory accounts.

Budgeting Prepaid Expenses and Deferred Charges. In this category the balance sheet of Illustrative Company shows prepaid insurance, excess of standard cost in finished product inventory over the current standard cost, and deferred advertising. Since insurance payments cover premium costs amortizable monthly over the period covered by the premium, they are charged, when paid, to a prepaid expense account and then amortized. This is a common accounting procedure; the only justification for even referring to it here is that it represents one of those items which, once provided for in the cash schedule, can easily be overlooked in preparing monthly forecast financial and operating statements. The information for the amortization should come from the schedule of monthly journal entries prepared in advance for the year.

The second of the items referred to, excess of standard cost in finished product inventory over current standard cost, results from the fact that the reduction in the value of the inventory at January 1, following a reduction in unit standard costs, was not immediately charged off, but was set up on the books as a deferred charge. This procedure was designed to charge cost of sales with the several standard costs applicable to the several lots of goods sold. This is not necessarily the only procedure available where standards are changed, but again it illustrates the close relation of budgeting and accounting.

The item of deferred advertising is another example of the part accounting plays in the preparation of a complete budget. For the purpose of scheduling cash disbursements, only the amount and time of payment are important. But in order to prepare monthly forecast operating and financial statements, amortization procedure must be followed, if applicable under the circumstances.

Budgeting Fixed Assets. Here again, the problem is solely one of *pro forma* accounting, giving effect to budgeted transactions in all of their budgetary and accounting aspects. With respect to the asset accounts alone, the only transaction of the Illustrative Company is the budgeted acquisition of new machinery and equipment in the third month of the budget period. But there must also be an accounting for depreciation taken to date on all assets. This information normally is obtained from the schedule of monthly journal entries, and involves decisions concerning both the type of depreciation method to be used and the expected useful life of the assets.

One transaction frequently encountered but which is not included in the Illustrative Company illustration is that of disposal of fixed assets either by sale, trade-in, or abandonment. Where such transactions are budgeted, appropriate accounting involves both the asset and depreciation accounts, together with the operating and/or capital accounts.

While the calculation of the depreciation taken to date for the forecast balance sheet is a simple matter from the accounting viewpoint, it does present an important question of financial policy. The question also arises in connection with the cash budget schedule, but originates with consideration of the depreciation provision accounts. Assuming the company is not operating at a loss, the recording of depreciation as a cost has the effect of recovering, through sales, of a portion of the cost of the depreciated asset, in cash or its equivalent. Hence, fixed assets tend to be converted to current assets. Where companies are operating on a close working capital position, the depreciation funds serve as an aid in financing working capital requirements. In the long run, however, this should not be allowed to happen. The author does not suggest that these funds be segregated in special investment accounts, since managements ordinarily should not restrict the total earnings of their companies by investing some funds at an interest rate far below the rate of return expected from operations. He does suggest, however, that the depreciation funds not be lost sight of and that they be related in some manner to the future capital needs of the company.

Depreciation funds should be the first source of funds for new capital facilities. Expenditures in excess of these funds represent an expansion and not a replacement of facilities, except insofar as the excess is occasioned only by a rise in prices of capital equipment.

Budgeting Accounts Payable. The expected accounts payable at the end of a month are the function of purchases, payments, discounts taken, and the time factor. As pointed out earlier in this chapter in connection with the discussion of cash disbursements, the expected credits to accounts payable arise from a variety of transactions which have to be gathered together from a number of budget schedules. Effect then must be given to the planned payments, together with the discounts to be taken. These are dependent on the availability of cash and involve financial planning.

In the case of accounts payable arising from purchases of direct factory materials and regularly scheduled services, the amounts to be budgeted are determined by reference to other budget schedules prepared in the course of the budget-making process. Miscellaneous supplies and materials, however, frequently present a more difficult problem because of lack of complete accounting controls. In the aggregate, these purchases may be substantial. Therefore, care should be taken to estimate them as accurately as is possible under the circumstances, granting, of course, that refined control accounting procedures may not be expedient to the extent deemed necessary in the case of direct factory materials.

In applying the factor of purchase discounts to accounts payable, estimation may be necessary, even though prompt payment is company practice. Not all invoices carry discounts. Consequently, an experience ratio of discounts to expenditures should be computed. This is necessary in budgeting cash payments as well as in forecasting end-of-month liabilities.

Budgeting Accrued Wages and Payroll Taxes. Payroll accounting is one of the major routine operations of the accounting department. Accordingly, it also presents a problem in short-term budgeting. Because payroll dates do not always coincide with the end of the month and because of the nature of the various deductions and payroll charges, there are always month-end liabilities for payroll, payroll taxes, bond purchases, and other commitments of employer and employees. The gross pay, of course, is budgeted in relation to all budgeted operations, but the determination of month-end liabilities requires analysis of all the relevant data.

Budgeting Other Accruals. Accruals of interest, income taxes, real estate taxes, and so forth, also follow conventional accounting practices applicable under the circumstances. Interest accruals, of course, are related to decisions already made relative to amount and method of external financing. Budgeting income taxes, on the other hand, involves the computation, on an estimated basis, of the taxes that will be due if the budgeted income is realized. This problem has already been discussed in an earlier chapter from the viewpoint of costs. It should be recognized, however, that the problem at times goes beyond that of current operating charges. Prior years' adjustments, carry-backs and carry-forwards, and other factors may have a special effect on the balance sheet showing of this item.

Budgeting Other Liabilities. The budgeting of dividends payable, notes payable, and long-term debt depends on top-level decisions concerning the need for and amount of external financing and distributions to shareholders. Short-term financing tends to approach the area of routine administration within the general policy framework of the company. Long-term financing, however, and dividend declarations are top policy matters. Moreover, long-term financing is in a class by itself simply because it is long term in nature. The decisions with regard to this item affect future periods. Once such commitments are made, they present no significant technical budget problems in the affected periods.

Budgeting Capital. Here we are concerned with the three common items of the capital section of the balance sheet, capital stock, retained earnings, and surplus reserves. In assembling the budget data required for the forecast balance sheet, capital stock presents no technical problems. As a matter of long-term financing, however, management must give careful attention to the adequacy of this figure. How should the firm's growth be financed? Only three sources are available—earnings, debt, and new investment. A wise decision in this regard is imperative.

The retained earnings at a given date are a function of the initial balance at the start of the period, the period's net income, and dividends (and special charges and credits, if any). In budgeting the period's net income, the entire budgetary process applicable to revenue and expenses is involved. It is in this connection that the forecast profit and loss statement is prepared, and it is largely on the basis of this statement, together with the view of the financial condition, that the entire budget is either approved or returned for modification.

Given the initial balance of retained earnings and the expected net income of the period, management must then make a decision as to dividends. The problem essentially is that of balancing the demands of stockholders against the financial needs of the company. As pointed out above, net income is one of the three sources of growth funds, and historically it has been the most important source. It is not the purpose of this work to serve as a treatise in corporation finance, but it may properly be suggested that dividend decisions should be made only in the light of long-range plans, both operational and financial.

Surplus reserves are in the same category, and policy in this regard is decided only by top management. Where such accounts are established (they are not required as an accounting matter) the amount and purpose are determined by the president and/or the board of directors. Once having been established, their eventual disposition is also a matter for top management alone to decide.

Aside from the financial requirements associated with growth, top management, either through the creation of surplus reserve accounts or simply through a conservative dividend policy, should make provision for (1) losses and (2) the effects of price changes. Since over the years profits tend to be unstable, prudent managerial action should be taken so that when losses occur the financial position of the firm is not jeopardized. As to price level changes, management's concern is to be in a position to finance the resultant increased working capital requirements and also the higher costs of asset replacement. In this latter connection, so long as it is not a generally accepted accounting practice to relate depreciation to price level changes, managements must provide for them in another manner.

This chapter completes the series on the technical aspects of budgeting the various items which ultimately find their way into the profit and loss statement and balance sheet. As is pointed out in the introduction to the chapter, the preparation of these two statements is largely an exercise in accounting, once the detailed decisions have been made. However, the results reflected in these statements in turn serve as a basis for judging the adequacy of those detailed decisions for the company's purposes. As was pointed out much earlier in this work, budget-making involves a series of interdependent steps, each step being taken only after anticipating its effect on the following steps.

This chapter is concerned primarily with translating the details of the previous chapters to the balance sheet. But in practice this is the final budget-making step only with respect to the formalities of statement preparation. Each step along the way is made only with full knowledge of its effect on the balance sheet.

CHAPTER 19

BUDGET REVISIONS

	Page		Page
Purpose of chapter	337	New managerial decisions in other areas	342
The nature of budget deviations	337	Significance of budget deviations	343
Cost reduction programs	339	Authorizing partial budget changes	344
Changes in amount or direction of sales effort	341	Recording partial changes	346
		Complete revision of budget	348
Cutback or expansion of production schedules	342	The budget as a business model	350

Purpose of Chapter. The budgeting process discussed in the preceding chapters of this work is wholly integrated. Consequently, a deviation from any part of the budgetary plan will have repercussions elsewhere in the plan, and management must be alert to the necessity of reviewing the plan and revising it whenever the deviations become significant. Such review, looking to the need for revision, should be based on an understanding of (1) the nature and cause of deviations, and (2) when they become significant. The significance of the deviations determines whether they can be treated merely as variances from the plan, the plan itself being considered basically unchanged, or whether the plan as a whole has been changed and accordingly should be restated in all its phases.

The chapter, therefore, has three purposes. They are:

1. To discuss the nature of deviations from the original plan
2. To promote an understanding of the significance of deviations
3. To discuss the methods of revising the budget

This chapter, like the preceding one, relates ultimately to the budgeted balance sheet, and accordingly attention is focused on the financial effects of deviations and changes in operating results. Whereas the preceding chapter is devoted to the budgeting of balance sheet items, this chapter deals essentially with their control through vigilant concern with the results of operations.

The Nature of Budget Deviations. The possible sources of budget variances can best be understood by reviewing the various detail plans which make up the over-all budget. A list of the detailed plans to be considered follows.

Sales
Marketing and distribution costs
Inventories and production
Production costs
  Direct labor
  Direct material
  Factory expenses
General and administrative costs
Research and development
Capital expenditures
Cash
Other assets, liabilities, and capital (including profit)

In connection with any one of these detail plans, variations may result from either unexpected and uncontrolled causes or controlled changes after the over-all plan has been promulgated.

Illustrations of the first reason for variations include:

1. Variations in sales, in total or by products, territories, or other sales categories
2. Cost efficiency variances
   a) In the factory
   b) In the sales organization
   c) In other segments of the organization
3. Variations in planned flow of production
4. Variations in the acquisition of inventories of direct material and supplies
5. Variations in collection of receivables and payment of invoices
6. Variations in the rate of capital and research and developmental expenditures

Each of these represents a common source of unplanned budget variations resulting either from variations in managerial efficiency or from the fact that the budget is not entirely realistic.

Illustrations of controlled changes in the budget after its promulgation include:

1. Changes in costs resulting from a cost reduction program
2. Changes in direction or amount of sales effort to meet unexpected requirements of a specific market situation
3. Cutback or expansion of production schedules
4. New managerial decisions in regard to capital or research expenditures, or any other activity of the firm

The unplanned and unexpected variations of the types presented in the first of the foregoing two lists have been discussed in preceding chapters. They result from either internal or external causes and may or may not be controllable. If controllable, organizational inefficiencies

BUDGET REVISIONS

are at the root of the matter; if noncontrollable, the budget is not realistic. Variations in sales may result from variations in performance of the sales organization, or from unexpected market conditions. Cost efficiency variances may result from lack of adequate internal cost control procedures, or from improperly established cost standards. Variations from the planned flow of production may result from breakdowns, improper scheduling, or other internal controllable causes; or from external factors not anticipated at the time of preparing the budget. Illustrations of the latter include material shortages resulting from strikes in plants of suppliers, unauthorized walkouts in the company's own plants, acts of God, political disturbances, and so on.

In the case of controlled changes of plan after the over-all budget has been promulgated, these changes may be required by the unexpected variations referred to above or may represent either improvements in method or changes in short-run objectives. These require further discussion.

Cost Reduction Programs. Cost reduction and cost control, while related, have somewhat different purposes. Cost control, as the term is used here, denotes efforts to keep costs in line with predetermined standards. Cost reduction, on the other hand, is concerned with the improvement of the standards.

When the budget of Illustrative Company was prepared, no cost variations were provided for. This implies that, for the time being, the management accepted the standards as of the first of the year as being satisfactory. For the purposes of the over-all budget it was considered that the objective, as it related to costs, was to concentrate on cost control in order to make them conform to scheduled operations. For this purpose both the fixed and variable costs were predetermined for scheduled operations and flexible cost budgets were prepared for guidance in those instances where the amount of work accomplished differed from the budget.

All managements, however, must constantly be alert to the potentialities for cost reduction which lead to lower cost standards. A continuous program of cost reduction is a prerequisite in a competitive economy. Whether cost reduction should be scheduled as an integral part of the over-all budget or treated separately and the accomplishments given effect to in the over-all budget for the next budget period depends on circumstances. In either case, however, efforts toward cost reduction should be carefully organized and fully supported by all ranks of management.

Pressure needs to be applied all along the line to overcome the inertia of those who feel complacent with a job reasonably well done. This can best be done by establishing cost reduction goals on a departmental basis. Such goals must be meaningful and, once established, should earnestly be sought. In the case of Illustrative Company, the need for a cost reduction program is evidenced by the failure of the current budget to earn the desired rate of return on capital employed. Only two principal avenues of attack are open, increased volume and greater efficiency. Given a budgeted volume of business, it is a simple matter to compute the total cost reduction necessary to achieve management's goal as to rate of return on capital. Judgment is then needed to determine the best sources of cost savings and to establish goals for the several departments and divisions.

The wide range of potentialities for cost reduction is illustrated by the following classified check list:

Products:
1. Have standard parts and materials been used wherever possible?
2. Has the amount of special deep-draw die work and special dies and tools been held to a minimum?
3. Are tolerances as wide as can be allowed?
4. Have parts been designed from the standpoint of production by the cheapest method, either on available equipment within the plant or by outside suppliers?
5. Has due regard been given to ease and speed in assembly?

Materials and supplies:
1. Are bids being obtained from a representative number of good sources?
2. Other things being equal, is the low bidder getting the business?
3. What is the experience with vendors on reject materials and the cost of materials inspection to guard against poor vendor quality?
4. Are standard parts, standard materials, and standard supplies being purchased wherever possible?
5. Are standard quantities ordered?
6. Is there a better way vendors could pack to reduce their cost or the plant's cost of handling to storage and to production floors?

Direct labor:
1. Can efficiency be improved by better housekeeping?
2. Are tools, jigs, and fixtures properly maintained?
3. Is machine down time minimized through adequate maintenance?
4. Can layout and methods be improved?
5. Are time standards kept up to date?
6. Is there a smooth flow of materials to and from the work stations, thus eliminating interruptions in operating cycles?
7. Is manual work eliminated wherever it is economical to do so?
8. Is obsolete equipment replaced?

Quality of production:
1. Is scrap excessive? Why?
2. Are rejects excessive? Why?
3. **Is excessive rework required?** Why?

Factory overhead:
1. Is there a proper ratio of indirect to direct labor?
2. Can material handling methods be improved?
3. Are the most economical transportation methods being used? Are there delays in loading and unloading?
4. Is the operating organization effective? Are there too many layers of supervisory men between the plant manager and the foremen? Is there too fine a breakdown of functions, so that responsibility cannot be easily placed or quick action taken to implement changes?

Sales:
1. Can returns and allowances be reduced?
2. Is packaging economical?
3. Can costs of servicing be reduced?
4. Can product lines be simplified profitably?
5. Is selling properly selective?

All nonfactory departments:
1. What does each group contribute to earning a profit?
2. Is the contribution adequate?
3. What would happen if a group were eliminated or reduced in size or scope?[1]

Either the beforehand selection of projects for study or the "brute force" approach of assigning percentage reduction goals will be used, depending on the urgency of the need for lower costs. Where the operations are already at an efficient level and where time permits careful study of long-range improvements, the first method will be used. Where, however, the profit position is in jeopardy, the "brute force" method may have to be used, but this type of pressure cannot long be maintained.

The choice of method is of concern in preparing the over-all budget. In the case of the first method, the cost savings will normally appear as favorable variances in the period they are first achieved, but will be reflected in lower cost standards in subsequent budgets. In the case of the second method, however, they may be incorporated immediately in the master budget since the savings *must* be realized.

Changes in Amount or Direction of Sales Effort. We are not concerned here with inefficiency of sales effort, but with decisions of the sales management, consciously arrived at, to meet unexpected market situations. The development of unexpected resistance to sales may require a quick decision to spend more for sales effort. Or, the unexpected development of a new market may suggest added efforts toward its fullest possible exploitation. One type of sales effort may quickly prove ineffective, and a new method, with changed costs, may be warranted for tryout.

[1] Arranged from Charles H. Gleason, "An Organized Profit Improvement Program," *N.A.A. Bulletin,* Oct., 1950, pp. 128–31.

Decisions of this character frequently have to be made quickly. They cannot wait for a careful working out of their effect on the budget, and, even if it is known approximately that the results may not measure up to the budget standards of profitability, there is no choice but to take the necessary steps to keep sales moving. The administration of sales efforts involves a certain amount of trial and error. Sales are the first requirement for the operation of the plan for the period. These decisions tend to create variances in selling costs, both in total and as a percentage of sales. When these variances become too large, revision and review of the entire operating plan are called for.

Cutback or Expansion of Production Schedules. One of the most important decisions to depart from the master plan of operations relates to factory production schedules. Production schedules are designed to satisfy both shipping and inventory requirements. If shipments exceed the amounts budgeted, the increase must come from inventory of finished product or from current production. Similarly, if shipments are less than expected, current production must be curtailed or the inventory permitted to increase.

In either case, the effect on the financial position of the company is quickly felt because of the fact that production costs represent a significant portion of the total operating expenditures. If the production schedule is revised upwards to meet increased sales, there is an added drain on the company's cash because of the lag between the incurrence of production costs and the collection of the resulting receivables. If, on the other hand, production finds its way into inventory of finished product instead of sales, the lag between payments and reimbursements is further enlarged, with the added risks attendant upon inventory accumulation.

Changes in production schedules are also important because of their many ramifications. Production must be integrated with recruitment and training of personnel and procurement of materials and supplies. If the schedules are revised, steps must be taken quickly to regulate in accordance therewith the inflow of all the factors of production. In addition, care must be taken so as not to interrupt the flow of production within the plant. Across-the-board adjustments of production schedules are not practical. Revisions must be worked out in detail.

Whereas unplanned production changes create budget variances which may, or may not, lead to formal revision of the master budget, planned changes commonly lead to budget revisions because of their far-reaching effect.

New Managerial Decisions in Other Areas. Since business operates in a dynamic world where events and changes are not geared to the budget period, it follows that managements frequently have to make decisions not contemplated in the original budget. While many decisions cannot be implemented overnight because of the detailed planning required, there are others which on occasion must be made and put into effect immediately. A serious fire loss may necessitate immediate steps and financial outlays; a new discovery may call immediately for cessation of a developmental or construction project; the actions of a competitor may force an immediate change of direction or an accelerated adoption of plans intended to be put into effect next year. These are examples of top management decisions to depart from the original budget.

Significance of Budget Deviations. As noted in the preceding pages, budget deviations may be planned or unplanned. In either case the question arises as to when the deviations are so significant in the aggregate as to call for a completely new budget, prepared in the same manner as the original master budget. Obviously, this is a matter of judgment, but the judgment can be an informed one only through understanding the relation of all the parts to the whole.

	Profit and Loss	Cash	Finished Goods and Work in Process Inventories		Materials Inventories	
			$	Quantity	$	Quantity
Cost reduction savings *	X	X				
Excess direct labor costs	X	X				
Reduction in production schedule	X†	X	X	X	X	X
Variation in sales—price	X	X				
Variation in sales—quantity	X	X	X	X		
Changed capital expenditures		X				
Slow collections		X				

* Assumed not to be budgeted.
† Because of effect on over-/underabsorption of overhead.

FIG. 19–1. Relation of Typical Budget Deviations to Key Accounts

Some deviations affect net income, some affect only balance sheet accounts, but all of them tend to affect cash. Since cash position is always important, the significance of deviations frequently is viewed first in relation to the company's finances. Figure 19–1 illustrates the effect of certain typical deviations on certain important accounts.

Referring to the items in Figure 19–1, cost reduction savings, which result from surpassing the standards, have a direct beneficial effect both on net income and on cash. The figure does not indicate it, but it must be recognized that if the cost savings are in the use of materials, the effect will be on materials inventories rather than cash, unless material purchases are immediately cut back in conformity with the reduced usage.

The incurrence of excess direct labor costs (labor costs in excess of the standard cost of the actual production) will reduce both net income and cash. The reduction of the production schedule, however, will affect all the accounts listed. It might at first be assumed that this change would not affect profit and loss, but it actually would do so because of the reduced absorption of factory overhead into product costs and the resulting increased underabsorption of the fixed overhead costs.

Variations in sales will have different effects depending on whether the variations are in price or quantity. Price variations will affect only profit and loss and cash, but quantity variations will affect both of these and, in addition, the inventory of finished stock. On the other hand, slow collection of accounts receivable and deviations in planned capital expenditures will affect only one of the accounts indicated, namely, cash.

The foregoing illustration and accompanying comments show the accounts affected by certain types of deviations and thus aid in understanding the several effects of deviations. The significance of the deviations, however, for testing the validity of the present budget, depends on their size relative to profit and loss or cash, or whatever factor happens to be of most importance at the moment to management. A slowing down of sales and shipments may require an immediate curtailment of production and related transactions in the case of a company with a poor financial position. A richer company, however, is better able to accumulate inventories where it believes the slow-down is only temporary.

Authorizing Partial Budget Changes. If details of the original master plan are to be changed during the budget period, the changes should be approved and adjustments made to the budget schedules; otherwise they will show up subsequently as budget variations and lead to erroneous interpretations of the performance record. Changes may be of two principal types: first, those that affect the total revenue or total costs of the several budget schedules, and, second, those which do not affect the totals, but consist only of shifts of revenue or cost or expenditure items within the schedules. Examples of the first type of change are:

Changes in budgeted total sales, with or without shifts among the several products
Changes in total production costs
Changes in total selling expenses
Changes in total general and administrative expenses
Changes in total research expenditures

Examples of the second type are:

Shift in emphasis between product A and product B, but with no change in total budgeted sales
Increase in production of one product and decrease in that of another product, with no change in total productive effort
Substitution of increased personal sales effort for advertising, with no change in total selling costs
Shifts between routine and administrative work in the general offices, with no change in total costs
Change of direction of research effort, with no change in total outlay

The fact that budget changes fall into these two categories raises an important question concerning the source of authority for the changes. The first type of change affects financial position. Consequently, it is obvious that management personnel other than the head of the particular division or department in which the change is initiated are involved in the decision. The second type of change, however, is internal only—within the division or department. Should the head of that department or division have full authority to make changes of this type, or should all budget changes require top level approval?

There are two schools of thought concerning this question, and the basic issue is that of centralization versus decentralization of authority and responsibility. In practice, the issue must be resolved in each company in the light of its size, competence of managerial personnel, and the presence or absence of well-defined company policies.

The size of the company and of its various budget divisions obviously affects the manner in which budgetary changes are authorized. In a small company where there is close contact among all management personnel, the issue of centralization versus decentralization is not so important since, in either case, decisions can be communicated and agreed to with relative ease. As size increases, however, the obstacles to communication and the weight of responsibility at the top tend to require more and more delegation of authority and responsibility, and managerial decentralization is the natural result.

Willingness on the part of top management to decentralize the organization also depends in part on the confidence which it has in the general body of managerial personnel. Management plans must be designed to fit the particular organization. Internal changes which may appear desirable in the immediate future may have long-run implications which are less desirable. Willingness on the part of the chief executive to delegate authority may depend on his confidence in the ability of lower executives to take all factors into account in arriving at their decisions. An example of this is found in that situation where a sales manager believes results can be improved through raising the level of compensation to salesmen and obtaining the necessary funds by economizing elsewhere in his expenditures. From the viewpoint of sales alone, his judgment may be sound. The action, however, may be undesirable from the viewpoint of company-wide morale because it would seem to change the relative levels of compensation among different groups of employees. In other words, the decision, while directed towards improving the work of the particular division, has certain company-wide implications, thus requiring higher authority for its approval.

The problem just referred to tends to disappear where company policies are well-defined and well-known. A sound plan of job evaluation and related compensation is one example of a policy definition. Given clear-cut policies on all important matters of a company-wide nature, a policy framework is provided within which a departmental or divisional executive may freely make those decisions which seem to him to be necessary for the proper functioning of his segment of the company.

In concluding this section, it must, of course, be recognized that even where decisions can properly be made internally within a department or division, they still may have to be communicated to others. For example, even though the factory management has the authority to revise its standard costs as a result of a successful cost-reduction program, knowledge of the revision is important to the sales people because of its possible impact on product pricing. A plan of decentralization cannot ignore the company-wide or interdepartmental significance of certain actions.

Recording Partial Changes. Knowledge of budget changes must be communicated to all those who have anything to do with either the execution or the control of the affected operations. The changes must be reflected both in the detail budget schedules and in the master budget. This requires that a notification procedure be established and that provision be made in this procedure for incorporating the changes in the budget schedules. It is particularly important, too, that all information recording changes be available in one place—the office of the budget executive. It is here that full effect of the changes is given to all parts of the integrated budget, including the forecast income statement and balance sheet. Figures 19–2 and 19–3 illustrate a form for recording

GENERAL & ADMINISTRATIVE DEPARTMENT BUDGET CHANGE CONTROL													
	Jan.	Feb.	Mar.	Apr.	May	June	July	Aug.	Sept.	Oct.	Nov.	Dec.	TOTAL
Original Annual Budget Jan.													133,200
Rent	1000	1000	(200) 1000	(200) 1000	(200) 1000	(200) 1000	(200) 1000	(200) 1000	(200) 1000	(200) 1000	(200) 1000	(200) 1000	(2000) 12000
Deprec. on Furniture Mo. Yr. to date	1000 1000	1000 1000	800 800	800 800	800 800	800 800	800 800	800 800	800 800	800 800	800 800	800 800	10000 123200

NEW YORK SALES OFFICE BUDGET CHANGE CONTROL													
Original Annual Budget Jan.													775,800
Salaries		1750 (22000)	1750 2000	1750 2000	1750 2000	1750 2000	1750 2000	1750 2000	1750 2000	1750 2000	1750 2000	1750 2000	19000 —
Newspaper Adv.	(250) 2000													
Deprec. of Furniture	(1000)	(1000)	(1000)	(1000)	(1000)	(1000)	(1000)	(1000)	(1000)	(1000)	(1000)	(1000)	(12000)
Mo. Yr. to date	750 750	(21250) (21250)	2750 2750	2750 2750	2750 2750	2750 2750	2750 2750	2750 2750	2750 2750	2750 2750	2750 2750	2750 2750	7000 768800

CHICAGO SALES OFFICE BUDGET CHANGE CONTROL													
Original Annual Budget Jan.													258,600
Salaries—Mo. Yr. to date		(1500) (1500)	(1500) (1500)	(1500) (1500)	(1500) (1500)	(1500) (1500)	(1500) (1500)	(1500) (1500)	(1500) (1500)	(1500) (1500)	(1500) (1500)	(1500) (1500)	(16500) 273100

SOURCE: H. G. Oberlander, "Working Papers for the Operating Budget," *N.A.A. Bulletin*, Oct., 1951, p. 194.

FIG. 19-2. Record of Departmental Budget Changes

Annual Profit and Loss Summary Budget

	Original annual budget	January* Annual change	January* Revised annual budget	February* Annual change	February* Revised annual budget
Sales	5,400,000		5,400,000		5,400,000
Deduct: Cost of sales	2,400,000		2,400,000		2,400,000
Gross profit on sales	3,000,000		3,000,000		3,000,000
Deduct:					
Selling expenses—					
New York office	775,800	7,000	768,800		768,800
Chicago office	258,600	(16,500)	275,100		275,100
Total	1,034,400	(9,500)	1,043,900		1,043,900
General and administrative expenses	133,200	10,000	123,200		123,200
Total selling and general and administrative expenses	1,167,600	500	1,167,100		1,167,100
Net operating profit	1,832,400	500	1,832,900		1,832,900
Add: Other income (Net)	18,000		18,000		18,000
Net profit before taxes	1,850,400	500	1,850,900		1,850,900

* Similar columns for all months of the year.

SOURCE: H. G. Oberlander, "Working Papers for the Operating Budget," *N.A.A. Bulletin,* Oct., 1951, p. 196.

FIG. 19-3. Budget Changes Reflected in Forecast Annual Operating Statement

departmental changes and a method for reporting changes in relation to the forecast annual profit and loss statement.

In order to simplify the preparation of revised schedules of the integrated budget, it is necessary that there be a regular procedure for accumulating changes. One method is to use a special budget journal designed only for budget changes. Figure 19-4 shows a journal form designed for one company. The form can be adapted to the needs of any company and, of course, is actually a budget work sheet and not a formal book of account.

Complete Revision of Budget. When partial changes in the aggregate serve to alter materially the original master plan, it is time to re-examine the entire plan. The balance between the various parts in the budget cannot be seriously altered without destroying the validity of the plan. A new course must be charted in all its details. This involves a repetition of the original budget-making steps and a close re-examination of all phases of the plan. It cannot be overemphasized that successful budgeting and budgetary control depend on integration. No short cuts are available.

Granting that management has established useful criteria for determining when to drop partial changes and embark on a full-scale revision

BUDGET CHANGE JOURNAL
(Annual Changes)

NAME	DEPT.	Effective Date	Change Amount	Change Period	Termination Pay	Explanation	Sales	Cost of goods sold	N.Y. sales office	Chicago sales office	General and administrative department	Other income (net)	PROFIT AND LOSS
January Rent	Genl.	3/1/50	(200)	Mo.		Rate increased					(2000)		(2000)
Smith, J. H.	Sales—N.Y.	1/31/50	250	Mo.	(250)	Termination			2500				2500
Newspaper— Advert.	Sales—N.Y.	1/1/50	[2000]	Mo.		Redistribute year total			Within dept.				—
Deprec. of Furniture	Genl. Sales— N.Y.	1/1/50	[1000]	Mo.		Transfer from Gen. to Sales			(12000)		12000		—
Smith, J. V.	Sales—N.Y. & Chicago	2/1/50	[1500]	Mo.		Transfer from N.Y. to Chicago			16500	(16500)			—
									7000	(16500)	10000		500

SOURCE: H. G. Oberlander, "Working Papers for the Operating Budget," *N.A.A. Bulletin*, Oct., 1951, p. 199.

FIG. 19-4. Illustration of Budget Change Journal

of its operating plan, the frequency of need for such revision depends in part on the nature of the industry and in part on economic conditions. The degree of economic stability is an important factor for most companies. Where annual budgets commonly are satisfactory in long periods of stable economic activity, frequent revisions may be necessary in periods of economic change. In such periods, management must constantly be alert to the need for complete revision and may find it expedient to adopt formally a shorter budget period.

The Budget as a Business Model. As developments in the field of "operations research" progress and are implemented by the use of electronic data processing equipment, it can be expected that the power and sophistication of this equipment will be utilized to perform the complex and voluminous computations required in the preparation and revision of budgets. It should become evident to the student of budgeting that a properly designed budget is a model of the business system of the enterprise and, consequently, could be used to simulate the effect of managerial decisions *before* they are made. The use of an electronic computer with its logical abilities and operating at electronic speeds may make it feasible to employ simulation techniques extensively in the company of the future to improve its decision-making function.

CHAPTER 20

ALTERNATIVE BUDGETING PRACTICES

	Page		Page
Purpose of chapter	351	**Direct Costing and Budgeting**	
Partial Budget Methods		Cost variability the key factor	360
Examples of partial budgeting	352	Direct costing defined	360
Partial budgeting applied to cash	353	**Product Profit and Loss Measurements**	
Partial budgeting applied to sales and sales costs	355	Practices in reporting product profit and loss	362
Partial budgeting applied to financing of capital expenditures	356	The contribution theory of profit	364
		Effect of decentralization	364
Standard Costs Versus Actual Costs		**Time Factor in Budgeting**	
Costing problems in budget preparation	356	The natural business year	365
Costing problems in budgetary control	358	Equal budget periods within the year	366

Purpose of Chapter. This work is dedicated to the idea that budgeting is a complete, integrated set of procedures designed for effective management. The discussion and the illustrations presuppose a willingness and an ability fully to implement budgetary principles. Certain conditions are essential. They include a well-developed managerial organization embodying the principles of fixed authority and responsibility, the recognition of the need for clearly defined goals, and an adequate accounting system for both financial and cost accounting.

In the interest of clarity, the discussion has followed one single line, that of discussing budgetary procedures in a step-by-step fashion in the order in which a budget should be formulated and applied. In the main, alternative piecemeal procedures and variations in underlying conditions have been ignored. The purpose has been to develop a basic set of principles and procedures for those managements which wish seriously to put them to full use. There are, however, alternative practices and variations in circumstances which should be considered, and they constitute the subject of this final chapter.

First, it is recognized that not all companies possess the managerial maturity and professional competence to embark on a full-scale budgetary program. They have to proceed more cautiously—a tentative step here and another step there—until they realize that partial measures bring only partial results and until they acquire the necessary competence and the confidence which goes with it. For such organizations, and in the hope that some undertaking is better than none and may eventually lead to greater accomplishment, there is a brief discussion of partial budget methods.

Following this, attention is directed to a series of technical matters. The first relates to the role of standard cost accounting in budgeting and the problems presented by the use of "actual" cost accounting rather than standard cost accounting. The second relates to the recent developments of direct or marginal costing theory as they impinge on budgeting. The third concerns the various ways in which the final periodic reckoning can be reported to management. All three are important because they deal with the gathering and interpretation of data. Managerial decisions are not arrived at automatically. Neither are the essential data easy to obtain. Good basic data, informative reporting, and clear interpretation are prime essentials to successful judgments.

Finally, attention is directed to the time factor in budgeting. In the introductory pages, attention is paid to the length of the budget period, but here we are concerned with the natural business year and comparable budget periods.

PARTIAL BUDGET METHODS

The underlying thesis of this work is that, to be fully effective, budgeting must be done on a complete basis, covering all phases of the firm's activity. However, since partial planning may be better than no planning, and since partial budgeting is frequently practiced, some attention must be given partial budgeting methods.

Examples of Partial Budgeting. If complete budgeting is a mark of an intelligent, progressive, and seasoned management, as the author believes, then partial budgeting is the sign of a growing-up, of a gradual awakening to the need for careful planning. It is readily understood how partial budget methods come to be adopted first, instead of full-fledged methods. First, budgeting is not easy, and many managements apparently prefer to progress by easy stages, starting with those areas which present the most urgent, immediate needs. Second, the comprehensive nature of complete budgeting calls for an equally comprehensive knowledge of the refinements of profit planning and control, and this knowledge does not come readily but must be acquired through long observation and study. Much of this knowledge is highly technical in nature, and unless the management staff is large enough to provide both depth and broadness of experience and training, the human resources needed for selling *and* implementing a complete planning procedure may not be available to the company.

Observation of partial budget methods and analysis of practice in this regard tend to confirm the belief that budgeting starts frequently on a partial basis because of recognized needs in particular segments of the business, and because partial budgets in those segments have some chance of successful operation. An outstanding example of this type of initial, partial budgeting is found in the flexible manufacturing expense budget designed for cost control purposes. Not only is the control of production costs quickly recognized as a fertile field for the application of budgetary methods, but also it can be initiated without reference to the other activities of the business. Since the flexible expense budget is designed to establish expense controls for any level of activity, it is useful in the control of production efficiency even though production schedules are not coordinated with other company activities and plans.

Similarly, the control of expenses in a department, whose activities are thought of as being primarily of a fixed nature, provides an easy place to apply partial budget methods. General administrative departments and some company service departments fall in this category. These budgets tend to be in the nature of fixed appropriation budgets, although as managerial comprehension advances, they, too, tend to be moved in the direction of the flexible budget for cost control purposes.

Partial budgets of the foregoing types are designed for purposes of control, but not for the purposes of planning and coordination. An example of partial budgeting which results from an urgent need, and which is related to planning and coordination but not control, is the cash "budget." The company's treasurer soon learns that some method must be designed to facilitate an orderly planning of receipts and disbursements. Consequently, a cash "budget" frequently is prepared even though there are no other budget applications within the firm. This type of partial budgeting is discussed below, in detail. Aside from its importance in serving a practical requirement, it also serves to indicate the need for more complete planning.

Partial Budgeting Applied to Cash. The flow of cash receipts and disbursements is governed by all the activities of the company. Consequently, the preparation of this "budget" or "budgets" calls for knowledge of the company's plans for the period. In the absence of complete budgeting, the treasurer (or equivalent officer) must obtain, on a piecemeal basis, knowledge of individual plans affecting cash, recognizing that those plans are not coordinated in formal fashion. Instead of translating the operating and other budget schedules in terms of cash receipts and disbursements, he must first take the initiative in obtaining and assembling available data concerning operations and activities as a preliminary to preparing his cash forecasts. In the absence of coordinated plans, and perhaps even of clear-cut uncoordinated plans, he obviously must make many estimates and assumptions on his own initiative.

Several methods are available for forecasting cash position. One of these is illustrated in Chapter 18. In this method receipts and disbursements are directly scheduled by nature of item. This method is wholly consistent with the idea of a complete, integrated budget.

A second method, not heretofore discussed, is known as the adjusted earnings method. The form and method of calculation is illustrated as follows:

Estimated net profit (for month or quarter)
Add:
    Depreciation
    Prepaid expenses amortized
    Excess collections over sales
    Reductions in inventories
    Increase in accounts payable
    Sale of investment securities
    Sale of capital assets
    Increase in expense accruals
Deduct:
    Excess sales over collections
    Payment of accrued taxes and other accruals
    Increase in inventories
    Decrease in accounts payable
    Purchase of investments
    Purchase of capital assets for cash
    Payments to sinking funds
Net increase or decrease in cash balance
Add: Cash on hand at beginning of period
Add or subtract: New loans or repayments
Balance at end of period

This method, philosophically, is more closely associated than the first method with the broad estimates necessary in a plan of partial budgeting. Where the operational pattern remains fairly constant, the method is reasonably practical. On the other hand, it is obvious from a study of the preceding illustration that even this method provides no easy road to a successful cash forecast. An accurate determination of all the items making up this method requires the same detailed knowledge of plans as is called for in the first method. Moreover, the estimated net profit for the period can be a very misleading point of departure. Net profits may be affected by accounting decisions and, in any event, cannot readily be forecasted in relation to random or individual operating factors. In addition, inventory changes and changes in receivables and payables, particularly, result from so many diverse factors that this method of forecasting can give little comfort to the treasurer during periods of change.

A third method is sometimes known as the balance sheet projection method. According to it, if all other balance sheet items can be forecasted for the end of the period, the projected cash balance is determined merely by completing the balance sheet. Comparison of this balance with the cash balance at the beginning of the period indicates any need for financing. It does not, however, provide information concerning total receipts and disbursements, or their timing. Even with this limitation, the method obviously is no better than the underlying estimates.

In conclusion, it should be pointed out that where the pattern of operations tends to remain unchanged, an analysis of prior years' receipts and disbursements, and the timing thereof, can be quite helpful in scheduling future cash flows. When conditions are changing, however, past experience loses its significance and the treasurer frequently is hard put to account for a change in cash position. In the absence of a complete budget as a means of interpreting the nature of the underlying changes, he must, on his own initiative, attempt to discover and interpret the changes as they relate to his work. Of even graver consequence is the fact that he frequently is put in a position of having to rationalize changes already accomplished instead of being able to predict changes in cash flows. It is primarily because of this fact that, as was noted above, partial cash budgeting is related to the planning and coordinating aspects of budgeting, but not to the control aspects. The treasurer must endeavor to relate all known plans in his cash forecast, but obviously, since his forecasts have little predictive value during changing times, he exercises little control even in his own work area and merely attempts to cope with requirements as they develop.

Partial Budgeting Applied to Sales and Sales Costs. Even where companies do not do complete budgeting, there is frequently some attempt to plan sales and sales efforts. Most managements are more conscious of sales than of any other single operating factor. The effort, as it relates to sales, may comprise little more than using last year's data as a guide or setting sales quotas. Or, it may take the form of a careful determination of sales budget data by products, territories, and other classifications. Good sales management can hardly do less than this.

Equal care may, and should, be used in scheduling costs of sales efforts and in relating these efforts to the expected results. As in the case of the flexible manufacturing expense budget, a really effective application of partial budgeting may be achieved *within* the department. Much of the benefit to the company as a whole, however, is lost if the sales and sales effort budgets are not related to production, general administration, purchasing, and other activities.

Partial Budgeting Applied to Financing of Capital Expenditures. Occasionally, companies which get along successfully year after year without formal budgeting first discover the need for careful financial planning when they inaugurate a construction program. For the first time, the normal flow of cash is seriously altered and serious planning must be done. The construction may extend over a period of a year or two and will involve a long series of monthly payments of construction invoices. These will vary greatly in amount from month to month. Construction progress is erratic depending on the weather, the availability of materials and labor, and the stage of completion. The monthly invoices must be paid. On the other hand, and particularly if funds are acquired through a construction loan, care must be taken to avoid a too rapid advancement of funds and corresponding excessive interest costs. With the architects' progress forecasts as a starting point, and allowing for the percentage withholding of payments pending completion, a financial plan must be prepared. The procedure is elementary, but it frequently serves as a first lesson in partial budgeting.

STANDARD COSTS VERSUS ACTUAL COSTS

The discussion up to this point has been based on the use of an accounting system based on cost standards. Accounting for standard costs is common practice among progressive firms. Nevertheless, since it is not universal practice, some attention must be given the problems in budgeting which arise where standard cost accounting is not in use. For this purpose it first is necessary to review the part which the accounting system plays in budget preparation. For convenience, and also because it is the most important and common application of standard cost accounting, the discussion will be limited to manufacturing.

Costing Problems in Budget Preparation. As stated in Chapter 1, "Knowledge of unit product costs, for all products, is needed not only in pricing, but also for facilitating the preparation of cost forecasts under varying conditions of volume and sales mix, and also for the prompt analysis of alternative courses of action, consideration of which is an integral part of budgeting." The need for cost accounting tends to vary in importance with the number of products manufactured by the firm.

In order to understand the complexities of product cost determination, let us review the component costs of a unit of product. They may be listed as follows:

Direct labor
  Department A
    Operation A1
    Operation A2
    Etc.
  Department B
    Operation B1
    Operation B2
    Etc.
  Etc.

Direct material
  Material A—from stock
  Material B—from stock
  Etc.

Finished parts
  Sub-assembly C—from stock
  Sub-assembly D—from stock

Other direct charges
  Engineering service
  Purchased services and materials

Factory burden—representing an allocation, on the basis of predetermined burden rates, of all indirect factory costs
  Supervision
  Indirect labor
  Indirect materials and supplies
  Depreciation
  Heat, light, and power
  Service department expenses
  Etc.

All of these, when aggregated, give product cost.

In budgeting the production costs of a given production schedule covering varying quantities of different products, the foregoing component costs must be computed for each of the products involved. In the case of Illustrative Company, these computations were facilitated by the use of previously determined cost standards established for labor, inventoried materials and parts, and for burden. In such case, the only complications which may arise are those related to variations from standard costs and over- or underabsorption of burden. With reference to the cost variations, these may or may not be budgeted depending on their significance and the manner in which the standards are established. On the other hand, scheduled over- or underabsorption of burden is a natural result of plant operations at a level different from the normal level used in setting the burden rates.

In the case of Illustrative Company, not only did the standards facilitate the computation of budgeted production costs, but they also served to facilitate scheduling costs of materials procurement.

If standard costs are not used, the computations are far more burdensome, although they still can be made. Detailed unit costs must now be computed either from product specifications or from past experience, or both. Where there is a variety of products, and particularly where numerous products utilize joint facilities, the determinations can be quite difficult. Moreover, in the absence of standard inventory costs, the budgeted flow of costs through the accounts is further complicated by the need either to identify lots of material as to acquisition cost or to use some special method of inventory costing, such as the moving average method, Fifo, and so on.

None of the foregoing is intended to imply that the setting of standard costs is easy. Actually, a scientifically set cost standard may involve far more study and analysis than an estimated "actual" cost. The advantage of standard costs to budgeting, aside from their greater accuracy, is in the fact that a well-organized standards department is constantly reviewing and revising standards so that the standards are readily available for use in budgeting. When cost standards are used, the initial attempt at budgeting is relatively simple—the basic cost data are already at hand. Where standard costs are not used, however, basic cost determinations become an added burden at the time of budget preparation.

In addition to costing scheduled production and procurement, the ease of budgeting cost of sales and finished product inventories also depends on the cost accounting method in use. Again referring to Illustrative Company, the allocation of production cost to cost of sales and inventories was quite easily accomplished with standard costs. From the viewpoint of the forecast financial and operating statements, this allocation is very important. In the absence of standard costs, the allocation is more laborious.

In essence, the budget-making requirements as to cost data do not differ essentially from those needed for the various other purposes of management. Budget-making does not require standard cost accounting per se, but it does require adequate knowledge concerning costs of production and sales under the conditions surrounding the operations of the firm. If this information is available through other means, budgeting can be accomplished; otherwise it cannot.

Costing Problems in Budgetary Control. The control of costs against the budget is an important phase of budgetary procedure. Where the budget is an accurate reflection of attainable goals, it establishes the standards for cost control purposes. However, as has been noted throughout this work, conditions are liable to change. Cost variances, consequently, must be differentiated as between those which are the result of changing level of operations and those which result from inefficiencies. It is in this connection that cost standards are especially useful.

A good example of their need is found in the use of direct materials in a job order system. Where materials are requisitioned at actual cost and charged to the job, the job record will show the actual material cost incurred on the job, but without any indication as to the efficiency of the material usage. Hence, the information is of little or no use either in determining the propriety of the cost of this particular job when completed, or for the purposes of planning future production of the same type. Furthermore, even if upon completion it becomes apparent that the material cost was excessive, what of the situation where, at the end of an accounting period, the job is still in progress? Cost bench marks are needed as the job progresses.

Similar observations may be made concerning direct labor costs. Actual costs to date, even though accurately reported through a system of cost accounting, have little use either for cost control or forward planning unless accompanied by some system of comparison with target data.

Moreover, in accounting for factory burden, the most complete system for allocating and recording costs serves only the purpose of balance sheet accounting if not related to some form of standard cost. Cost control and future planning require a measure of efficiency of performance.

But, again, standard cost accounting per se is not a prerequisite, provided there are other means of measuring performance. For the purposes of cost control, however, there must be some form of standard, regardless of whether it is recognized formally in the books of account. Whatever the form or manner in which recorded, the cost data, if they are adequate for control purposes, will serve the purposes of budgetary control. On the other hand, if the data are not adequate for cost control, then one of the principal purposes of budgeting cannot be served.

DIRECT COSTING AND BUDGETING

The purposes of budgeting are planning, coordination, and control. Planning consists of the preliminary weighing of alternative courses of action and charting the selected course. In the selection of this course, analysis of the various cost-volume-profit relationships is the primary managerial tool. In both the selection and the setting of the course and in the subsequent measurement of performance, knowledge of how costs should behave under various conditions of operation is a major prerequisite. To the extent that pricing is involved in the selection and plotting of a course, the cost data are also essential for this purpose.

Cost Variability the Key Factor. The behavior of costs under various conditions of operation relates principally to their variability. The concepts of break-even analysis, marginal costing, differential costing, and flexible budgeting are based on the fact that some costs tend to be fixed while others tend to vary more or less directly with volume. The search for a proper variability classification of all costs and study of their behavior are required in all phases of budgetary work. As previously noted, this search and study take the form of account inspection, or statistical analysis of the records, or engineering surveys, or a combination of these. In all three methods it is implicit that the accounts themselves do not directly provide the necessary information.

The importance of variability data and the difficulties encountered in their determination have resulted, in recent years, in an intensive search by industrial accountants for better reporting and analytical methods. The technique known as "direct costing" is one of the results of this search.

Direct Costing Defined. The term "direct costing" appears to have different meanings for different persons. For some, it signifies a form of product costing in which products are charged only with variable costs while the fixed costs are pooled. This interpretation has led to much controversy concerning the accounting treatment of these pooled costs. Are they to be treated as period costs and not inventoried, or are they to be allocated finally between cost of sales and inventories? For some, the term implies a method of cost bookkeeping, while for others it means a method of reporting results in periodic statements.

This author believes that the purposes of direct costing, if adopted, should be (1) centered around internal management rather than public reporting and (2) directed not only to product costing but to all cost record-keeping. The discussion of the method in a book on budgeting is applicable only if the method serves to improve the collection of cost variability data, and in the author's opinion this implies a recording technique by which fixed and variable costs are separated in the accounts, and that this separation is applied not only to product costs, but also to costs chargeable to departments or operations.

The author wishes to make it clear that he is not here concerned with the question of marginal costing versus full costing, nor with the questions related to public reporting. Alternative actions in both these areas may be possible even with conventional cost bookkeeping methods —if supported by adequate off-the-record cost analyses. He is concerned only with direct costing as an alternative technique for obtaining cost variability data.

For this purpose, the method essentially is one of devising a chart of accounts based on a different (or additional) classification—that of fixed and variable costs. In the case of direct labor and direct material, no change is needed, for under any cost system they follow their natural classification of variable costs. It is in the area of overhead costs that changes would be required.

In applying direct costing to overhead items, the first change is in the account classification. Indirect costs must now be classified, upon incurrence, not only by the primary nature of the expense, but also by variability. The latter classification can most readily be obtained by separate groupings of the two categories of expenses in the expense ledgers, with separate control accounts. This procedure can easily be applied in dealing with expenses that are clearly fixed or constant, or clearly variable. It is more difficult, however, where an expense item is of mixed nature. Ideally, in this case, the expense should be accounted for in both classifications, one classification for the constant portion of the expense and the other for the variable portion.

The second change, necessitated by the first, relates to the application of costs to product. The application of all overhead costs must now be achieved through two application procedures, one for the variable costs and one for the constant costs. The first application would be made on the basis of a predetermined variable expense rate per unit of production multiplied by the number produced. Under- or overabsorption would measure efficiency in the control of these costs.

The second application would be on the basis of normal volume. Constant costs have no relation to actual volume. They are the costs of capacity availability and, hence, must be allocated on an availability basis; this can best be done by reference to the normal level of output. In the case of these expenses, under- or overabsorption may result from both efficiency variation in the control of costs and volume variations.

Whether the constant expenses are applied to individual products or groups of products, or merely treated as period expenses, is not of interest in this discussion. From a budgetary viewpoint, the purpose of the procedure is to provide management with adequate knowledge of its costs to ensure:

1. Intelligent selection from among alternative courses of action (with reference to pricing, additional volume, new products, etc.)
2. Accurate budgeting in line with selected course of action
3. Accurate comparison of actual costs and budgeted costs, and interpretation of variances

Again, it should be emphasized that the subject of direct costing is discussed here only in relation to its budgeting aspects. The only question raised here concerns the advantages of formal recording over informal determination of cost variability behavior for budgetary purposes. Only time will disclose whether the new procedure is the best. Formal recording on the basis of variability classifications may prove superior to other methods, but it must be recognized that the difficulties inherent in such classification preclude easy solution. Where judgment is such an important factor in a classification, there can be no assurance that adoption of a formal classification procedure will automatically produce better results.

PRODUCT PROFIT AND LOSS MEASUREMENTS

The profit and loss statement is the final representation of the results of the period's operations and serves both as the basis for appraising management's efforts and as a starting point in shaping policy for the future. Where numerous products are produced and sold, the comparative reporting of results by products becomes very important. It is through this type of information that product selection is made and sales mixes are planned. Because of the presence of joint costs, however, the form and method of reporting has many variations in practice. Practice ranges from a complete classification of all revenue and costs by products to a classification by products of only direct or out-of-pocket costs, followed by a pooling of all other costs.

Practices in Reporting Product Profit and Loss. For the typical practices, see Figure 20–1.

Detailed product profit and loss reports obviously are the most desirable if they can be prepared accurately and reliably. The joint nature of many of the expenses, however, present difficult problems of expense allocation. The artificiality of many of these allocations had led, in many cases, to the use of the second type of statement. Note that in this statement allocations are still present (in the cost of sales data), since joint costs are present in the factory as well as in other segments of the operation. The adoption of this type of statement presumes a confidence in factory cost accounting procedures along with a distrust of allocations of nonfactory costs.

The third type of statement is of recent adoption and reflects the growing concern with the need for a sharper distinction between joint and direct costs in all operations whether in the factory or elsewhere in the organization. It embodies the most realistic appraisal of the accounting difficulties inherent in joint costs, but, like the second statement, it

COMPLETE PRODUCT CLASSIFICATION	Product A	Product B	Product C	Total
Sales	$ –	$ –	$ –	$ –
Cost of sales	–	–	–	–
Gross margin	$ –	$ –	$ –	$ –
Selling expenses	$ –	$ –	$ –	$ –
Administrative expenses	–	–	–	–
Other expenses	–	–	–	–
Total expenses	$ –	$ –	$ –	$ –
Net profit	$ –	$ –	$ –	$ –
PARTIAL PRODUCT CLASSIFICATION				
Sales	$ –	$ –	$ –	$ –
Cost of sales	–	–	–	–
Gross margin	$ –	$ –	$ –	$ –
Selling expenses				$ –
Administrative expenses				–
Other expenses				–
Total expenses				$ –
Net profit				$ –
PRODUCT CLASSIFICATION OF DIRECT COSTS				
Sales	$ –	$ –	$ –	$ –
Direct cost of sales	$ –	$ –	$ –	$ –
Direct selling expenses	–	–	–	–
Total direct costs	$ –	$ –	$ –	$ –
Operating margin	$ –	$ –	$ –	$ –
Fixed production expenses				$ –
Fixed selling expenses				–
Administrative expenses				–
Other expenses				–
Total pooled expenses				$ –
Net profit				$ –

Fig. 20–1. Examples of Product Profit and Loss Reports.

tends to transfer the responsibility for evaluating the incidence of cost allocations from accountants to management. This, however, need not necessarily be construed to be a disadvantage since management may prefer to exercise judgment in this area.

The Contribution Theory of Profit. The fact that companies are tending toward greater multiplicity of products, together with the growing realization of the difficulties involved in allocating joint costs, gives impetus to the adoption of the contribution theory of profit. This is based on the principle that every product must contribute something toward the recovery of joint costs and that all the products, in the aggregate, must serve to recover all costs and earn a profit. Ideally, every product should earn a fair profit, but, practically, it seems to be accepted that, at least in the short run, companies cannot afford to be that selective. Otherwise idle facilities should help to pay for themselves if they cannot be operated at full profit. It is this philosophy which has given use to the concept of direct or marginal costing in managerial thinking.

Effect of Decentralization. As firms take on more and more operations and products, the allocation of full cost to the several products, and the measurement of net profits by products, becomes an increasingly formidable task. There is a countervailing development, however, in many companies which serves to lessen the problem—the move towards decentralization of operations.

Where size of operations permits or requires separate plants for specific products, cost allocations become easier, since joint costs give way to single-purpose costs. Where not only a separate plant but also a separate complete operating division is established for a product or family of products, and where the division is responsible for sales as well as production, the cost accounting problems are greatly simplified. In cases of extreme decentralization, the area of joint costs may be reduced so as to include only home office administrative and corporate expenses. In such cases the division operates as a separate company, but then the problem of joint facilities arises as to the products of that division.

TIME FACTOR IN BUDGETING

The duration of the budget period has been discussed earlier in this work. The time factor has added significance in budgeting, however, in two respects. The first concerns the relation of the budget period to the normal operating cycle, and the second relates to the need for comparability of periods. These are matters respectively of planning and control. The first is embodied in the idea of a natural business year, while the second deals with the division of the year into equal parts as represented by periods of thirteen weeks, or similar practices. Each is discussed in turn.

The Natural Business Year. It has long been argued that the problems of periodic profit determination would be simplified if companies adopted the so-called natural business year instead of the calendar year for accounting purposes. It is suggested that this would also be beneficial in the area of budgeting.

The natural business year is a fiscal year ending with the annual low point of a firm's activity. In many companies business activity is not at the same level throughout the year, but is subject to marked fluctuations. In this case there generally is one characteristic period when the bulk of the annual business is completed and inventories, receivables and payables, and operations are at a low level. Such a period is generally a favorable time for the annual closings because of the ease of adjustments and inventory taking and because it permits more time for the accounting work.

While the close of the period is important for accounting purposes, it is the opening of the new year that is important in budget preparation. Consequently, the low level of activity preceding a new rush of business is a favorable time for planning the forthcoming period's operations. It is difficult to lay plans for a period which begins at the middle of the annual high volume activity. The idea of the natural business year, therefore, is useful both in accounting and in budgeting.

It must be recognized, of course, that many companies do not have a natural business year for the reason that they deal in many products whose annual fluctuations do not coincide one with the other. In such cases, in the aggregate, there may be no marked fluctuations. For these there may be no good reason for departing from the calendar year basis of budgeting and accounting. In still other cases, the natural business year may be the same as the calendar year. Where there is a natural business year, however, which differs from the calendar year, the use of such fiscal period may be advantageous.

In such case, a proper selection of opening and closing dates is important. In some industries, the selection may be quite obvious, while in others study may be required to determine the best dates with respect to both volume of activity and nature of operations.

In considering the adoption of a natural business year, consideration must be given to tax requirements and any other requirements inherent in the geographical location of the firm. Assuming such considerations are not controlling and that there is a natural business year for the firm, its adoption should prove advantageous.

New policies are usually introduced at the beginning of the natural business year. Financial statements prepared at the end of such a period, because they reflect the results of these policies over one complete cycle of operations, provide management with a check on their effectiveness.[1]

While in the foregoing discussion the emphasis has been on the annual period, it must be recognized that a budget period may be of less than a year's duration. It may be a season rather than a year. Where this is the case, the idea of the natural business season obviously becomes appropriate.

Equal Budget Periods Within the Year. Where budgets are prepared and/or evaluated for periods of less than a year (months or quarters, for example), difficulties arise from the fact that these periods commonly are not equal. This is due to the fact that calendar months and quarters are not uniform in length of time, and also to the existence of holidays, legal or otherwise. Thus a budget prepared for February will differ from that prepared for January or March or December, even though the same daily level of operations is contemplated in all three months. Moreover, comparisons of results as between the several months will be meaningless unless adjusted for time variations.

To overcome these difficulties many companies use a thirteen-period year. Under this plan the calendar year is divided into thirteen periods of four weeks each, with each period having twenty-eight days. Obviously, the close of the final period would not always coincide with the end of the year, but the periods themselves would be uniform in length and would always begin and end on the same days.

The principal defect of this method is the irregularity introduced by the presence of holidays. Not all weeks would be uniform as to number of work days. To overcome this irregularity, some companies do not use periods of uniform calendar duration, but of uniform numbers of work days.

One company's practice is described by Lawrence P. Jennings in the *N.A.A. Bulletin* (Section 1, Mar., 1951, pp. 805–7) under the title "Thirty Days Hath September" and from which the following comments are extracted.

The twenty-one work-day accounting month, based on a five-day week Mondays through Fridays, is both simple in operation and sound in approach. In any ordinary year, after allowances are made for Saturdays, Sundays, and six legal holidays, there are 255 working days which must be allocated over twelve working months. Thus there are 21.25 working days in each working month. Hence twenty-one days will

---

[1] R. Carson Cox, "Another Look at the Natural Business Year," *N.A.A. Bulletin*, Section 1, Jan., 1952, p. 612.

constitute an average work month provided that the extra one-fourth of a day is included in the vacation month. This will be distorted in any event because of the plant-wide shutdown.

By application of the above principle to the year 1951, accounting cutoff dates for each month are established as follows:

Month	Cutoff Date	Number of Working Days
January	January 30	21
February	February 28	21
March	March 29	21
April	April 27	21
May	May 28	21
June	June 27	21
July	July 27	21
August	August 30	14 (Vacation)
September	October 1	21
October	October 30	21
November	November 29	21
December	December 31	21
		245

The referenced article concludes with the observation that based upon the experience of the past few years, the twenty-one work-day accounting month offers significant possibilities to the accounting department of going concerns. The standardization of all compilations of facts and figures results in operating reports which may be compared to prior months' reports without adjustment and also compared to each other in every instance where the factors of production and merchandising may be related.

APPENDIXES

APPENDIXES

APPENDIX A

SUPPORTING INFORMATION AND JOURNAL ENTRIES FOR ILLUSTRATIVE COMPANY BUDGET REPORT

This section is designed only for the reader who wishes to explore further the mechanics of budget-building and to verify the figures appearing in the budget report shown in Figure 5-1. Following are detailed data supporting certain items on the December 31 balance sheet shown in Exhibit V of Figure 5-1.

ACCOUNTS RECEIVABLE. It is estimated that 5 per cent will be paid in January less 2 per cent discount; 70 per cent will be paid in January with no discount; 23 per cent, in February; and the remaining 2 per cent will prove uncollectible.

INVENTORY OF DIRECT MATERIALS. The direct material inventory comprises the following:

Material A1, 3,000 units @ $20.00	$ 60,000
Material A3, 7,000 units @ 5.00	35,000
Material B1, 1,500 units @ 15.00	22,500
Material B2, 500 units @ 4.00	2,000
Material B3, 1,000 units @ 3.00	3,000
Material C1, 6,000 units @ 6.00	36,000
Material C3, 4,000 units @ 2.00	8,000
Inventory, per balance sheet	$166,500

INVENTORY OF FINISHED PARTS. This consists of 3,000 units of Product B completely processed through Department 1 only (referred to as B1 parts) and stored.

INVENTORY OF WORK IN PROCESS. This is the cost of 3,000 units of Product A in process in Department 1 (referred to as A1 parts), complete as to material A1, but only half finished as to labor and burden.

INVENTORY OF FINISHED PRODUCTS. This inventory is made up as follows:

1,000 units of Product A	$ 52,000
3,000 units of Product B	204,000
6,000 units of Product C	170,400
Inventory, per balance sheet	$426,400

PREPAID INSURANCE. This represents the unexpired portion of an annual premium of $24,000. Renewal of the policy will be made as of February 1.

DEPRECIATION TAKEN TO DATE. The depreciation rates, based on cost, are:

Machinery and equipment	1 per cent per month
Buildings	¼ per cent per month

DIVIDEND PAYABLE. The dividend, declared in December, is payable January 15.

FEDERAL INCOME TAX ACCRUED. The December 31 liability will be paid in March.

MORTGAGE PAYABLE—CURRENT INSTALMENT. This instalment is payable March 1.

LONG-TERM DEBT—MORTGAGE PAYABLE. Interest on the mortgage is payable March 1 and September 1 at the rate of 5 per cent per annum.

The following *pro forma* entries bring together all the data used in the preparation of the budget report. Attention is called to the following considerations adopted in the interest of simplicity. First, all purchases of materials are paid and discounted in the month following the purchase. Second, all labor costs are paid in the month of incurrence, except salesmen's commissions, which are paid in the following month. Third, to avoid the necessity of classifying in too great detail miscellaneous purchases of supplies, services, and labor, the purchase discounts are related solely to direct materials purchased.

ILLUSTRATIVE COMPANY
PRO FORMA JOURNAL ENTRIES FOR THE BUDGET REPORT

Entry No.		January		February		March	
		Dr.	Cr.	Dr.	Cr.	Dr.	Cr.
1.	Accounts Receivable	$620,000		$630,000		$880,000	
	Sales		$620,000		$630,000		$880,000
	To record sales of units shown in Schedule I-a of Fig. 5-1 at prices of $80, $90, and $35, respectively.						
2.	Cash - on December 31 accounts	374,500		115,000		49,600	
	" " January "	364,560		186,000		189,000	
	" " February 28 "			370,440		517,440	
	" " March 31 "						
	Sales Discounts - on December 31 accounts	500					
	" " January "	7,440		7,560			
	" " February 28 "					10,560	
	" " March "						
	Accounts Receivable		747,000		679,000		766,600
	To record collections on accounts receivable. Of the December 31 accounts 5 per cent are estimated to be paid in January, less 2 per cent discount; 70 per cent are to be paid in January, gross; 23 per cent in February, gross; and the balance will prove uncollectible. Of current sales, 60 per cent are expected to be paid in month of sale, less 2 per cent discount; 30 per cent in the first succeeding month, gross; 8 per cent in the second succeeding month, gross; and the remainder uncollectible.						

APPENDIX A 373

ILLUSTRATIVE COMPANY
PRO FORMA JOURNAL ENTRIES FOR THE BUDGET REPORT (Cont'd)

Entry No.		January Dr.	January Cr.	February Dr.	February Cr.	March Dr.	March Cr.
3.	Cash					$200,000	
	Note Payable						$200,000
	To record planned loan on March 1.						
4.	Direct Materials	$271,500		$219,000		265,000	
	Accounts Payable		$271,500		$219,000		265,000
	To record purchases of direct materials using unit data from Fig. 4-5 and standard cost data shown in Entry #6.						
5.	Factory Burden	18,700		18,700		18,700	
	Selling Expenses	20,600		20,900		28,400	
	General and Administrative Expenses	400		400		400	
	Other Charges to Income	26,530		33,735		68,235	
	Depreciation taken to date on Machinery and Equipment		10,000		10,000		10,000
	Depreciation taken to date on Buildings		2,000		2,000		2,000
	Accrued Real Estate Taxes		7,100		7,100		7,100
	Accrued Salesmen's Commissions		18,600		18,900		26,400
	Prepaid Insurance		2,000		2,000		2,000
	Accrued Interest on Note Payable						500
	Accrued Interest on Mortgage Payable		1,000		1,000		950
	Allowance for Doubtful Accounts		12,400		12,600		17,600
	Accrued Federal Income Tax		13,130		20,135		49,185
	To record monthly accruals and amortization as per Fig. 4-6.						

APPENDIX A

ILLUSTRATIVE COMPANY
PRO FORMA JOURNAL ENTRIES FOR THE BUDGET REPORT (Cont'd)

Entry No.		January Dr.	January Cr.	February Dr.	February Cr.	March Dr.	March Cr.
6.	Work in Process	$597,500		$597,500		$597,500	
	Accounts Payable (Direct Labor Payroll)		$190,000		$190,000		$190,000
	Stores (Direct Materials)		219,000		219,000		219,000
	Applied Factory Burden		155,500		155,500		155,500
	Finished Parts		33,000		33,000		33,000

To record costs of production of units called for in Fig. 4–4, based on standard costs as follows:

	Product A	Product B	Product C
Department 1:			
Material – A1	$20.00	–	–
B1	–	$15.00	$ 6.00
C1	–	–	5.00
Labor	8.00	10.00	4.00
Burden (80%)	6.40	8.00	
Total	$34.40	$33.00	$15.00
Department 2:			
Material – B2	–	4.00	–
Labor	5.00	8.00	–
Burden (100%)	5.00	8.00	–
Total	$10.00	$20.00	–
Department 3:			
Material – A3	5.00	–	–
B3	–	3.00	2.00
C3	–	–	7.00
Labor	2.00	5.00	2.00
Burden (70%)	1.40	3.50	4.90
Total	$8.40	$11.50	$13.90
Total Product: Standard Cost	$52.80	$64.50	$28.90

With regard to the material consumption, reference is made to the effect of material in process, as shown in Fig. 4–5. Note also from Fig. 4–4 that each month 1,000 of part B1 are to be withdrawn from stock to be used in production.

ILLUSTRATIVE COMPANY
PRO FORMA JOURNAL ENTRIES FOR THE BUDGET REPORT (Cont'd)

Entry No.		January Dr.	January Cr.	February Dr.	February Cr.	March Dr.	March Cr.
7.	Deferred Inventory Adjustment	$ 6,700					
	Finished Product		$ 6,700				
	To adjust December 31 finished product inventory to the new standard costs as follows:						
	Increase in standard cost of A, 1,000 @ $.80 = ($ 800)						
	Increase in standard cost of C, 6,000 @ .50 = (3,000)						
	Decrease in standard cost of B, 3,000 @ 3.50 = 10,500						
	Net Decrease $6,700						
8.	Finished Parts	34,400		$ 34,400		$ 34,400	
	Work in Process	590,300		590,300		590,300	
	Finished Product		624,700		$624,700		$624,700
	To record standard cost of monthly finished stock completions and increase in A1 parts.						
9.	Cost of Sales	465,800		460,800		614,200	
	Profit and Loss	3,200		3,500			
	Finished Product		465,800		460,800		614,200
	Deferred Inventory Adjustment		3,200		3,500		
	To record unit shipments as shown in Schedule I-a of Fig. 5-1, at standard costs as per schedule in Entry #6, and to write off inventory adjustment applicable to first of year inventories, as disposed of.						
10.	Factory Burden	129,600		129,600		129,600	
	Accounts Payable (indirect labor and purchased services and supplies)		129,600		129,600		129,600
	To record planned burden incurrence of $148,300 based on anticipated production, less burden already accounted for in Entry #5.						

ILLUSTRATIVE COMPANY
PRO FORMA JOURNAL ENTRIES FOR THE BUDGET REPORT (Cont'd)

Entry No.	January Dr.	January Cr.	February Dr.	February Cr.	March Dr.	March Cr.
11. Selling Expenses	$70,000		$71,000		$96,000	
Deferred Advertising	4,500		4,000			$8,500
Accounts Payable		$74,500		$75,000		87,500
To record selling expenses per Schedule I-b, not accounted for in Entry #5.						
12. General and Administrative Expenses	19,600		24,600		24,600	
Accounts Payable		19,600		24,600		24,600
To record General and Administrative expenses per Schedule I-c, not accounted for in Entry #5.						
13. Accrued Commissions	15,000		18,600		18,900	
Dividend Payable	15,000					
Federal Income Tax Accrued					220,000	
Mortgage Payable -- Current Instalment					12,000	
Interest Accrued on Mortgage					6,000	
Machinery and Equipment					100,000	
Prepaid Insurance			24,000			
Cash		30,000		42,600		356,900
To record miscellaneous cash payments.						
14. Accounts Payable	713,700		690,700		650,700	
Purchase Discounts				5,430		4,380
Cash		713,700		685,270		646,320
To record payment of accounts payable.						

APPENDIX B

ILLUSTRATIVE COMPANY'S BUDGET DEVIATIONS IN JANUARY

As Reflected in Journal Entries

Chapter 6 presents Illustrative Company's budget comparisons for the first month of the quarter. In further support of the discussion there presented and for the purpose of illustrating more fully the full effect of the deviations, the following *pro forma* journal entries compare the January *pro forma* journal entries included in Appendix A to support the original budget in Chapter 5, and the January entries to reflect actual operations.

APPENDIX B 379

ILLUSTRATIVE COMPANY
PRO FORMA JOURNAL ENTRIES FOR BUDGET DEVIATIONS IN JANUARY

Entry No.		January Pro Forma Dr.	January Pro Forma Cr.	January Actual Dr.	January Actual Cr.	Deviations in Profit and Loss Dr.	Deviations in Profit and Loss Cr.	Increase (Decrease) in Cash	Increase (Decrease) in Inventories
1.	Accounts Receivable	$620,000		$589,400		$30,600			
	Sales		$620,000		$589,400				
2.	Cash – December accounts	374,500		368,500				($6,000)	
	– January accounts	364,560		355,000				(9,560)	
	Sales Discounts – Dec. accounts	500		300			$200		
	– Jan. accounts	7,440		7,300			140		
	Accounts Receivable		747,000		731,100				
3.	None in January								
4.	Direct Materials	271,500		291,500					$20,000
	Material Price Variance				4,000		4,000		
	Accounts Payable		271,500		287,500				
5.	Factory Burden	18,700		18,700					
	Selling Expenses	20,600		19,682			918		
	General & Administrative Expenses	400		400					
	Other Charges to Income	26,530		20,783			5,747		
	Depreciation Taken to Date								
	Machinery & Equipment		10,000		10,000				
	Buildings		2,000		2,000				
	Accrued Real Estate Taxes		7,100		7,100				
	Accrued Salesmen's Commissions		18,600		17,682				
	Prepaid Insurance		2,000		2,000				
	Accrued Interest on Mortgage Payable		1,000		1,000				
	Allowance for Doubtful Accounts		12,400		11,788				
	Accrued Federal Income Taxes		13,130		7,995				
6.	Work in Process	597,500		597,500					
	Material Usage Variance			400		400			(400)
	Accounts Payable (D. L. payroll)		190,000		190,000				
	Direct Materials		219,000		219,400				
	Applied Factory Burden		155,500		155,500				
	Finished Parts		33,000		33,000				

ILLUSTRATIVE COMPANY
PRO FORMA JOURNAL ENTRIES FOR BUDGET DEVIATIONS IN JANUARY (Cont'd)

Entry No.		January Pro Forma Dr.	January Pro Forma Cr.	January Actual Dr.	January Actual Cr.	Deviations in Profit and Loss Dr.	Deviations in Profit and Loss Cr.	Increase (Decrease) in Cash	Increase (Decrease) in Inventories
7.	Deferred Inventory Adjustment	$ 6,700		$ 6,700					
	Finished Product		$ 6,700		$ 6,700				
8.	Finished Parts	34,400		34,400					
	Finished Product	590,300		590,300					
	Work in Process		624,700		624,700				
9.	Cost of Sales	465,800		450,130					
		3,200		3,550					
	Profit and Loss						$15,670		$15,670
	Finished Product		465,800		450,130				
	Deferred Inventory Adjustment		3,200		3,550	$350			
10.	Factory Burden	129,600		129,800		200			
	Accounts Payable (Indirect labor and purchased services and supplies)		129,600		129,800				
11.	Selling Expenses	70,000		69,900			100		
	Deferred Advertising	4,500		4,500					
	Accounts Payable		74,500		74,400				
12.	General & Administrative Expenses	19,600		19,960		360			
	Accounts Payable		19,600		19,960				
13.	Accrued Commissions	15,000		15,000					
	Dividends Payable	15,000		15,000					
	Cash		30,000		30,000				
14.	Accounts Payable	713,700		714,160					
	Cash		713,700		714,160			($ 460)	
						31,910	26,775		
	Decrease in Net Income, per Fig. 6-1, Exhibit I.						5,135		
						$31,910	$31,910		
	Decrease in Cash, per Fig. 6-1, Exhibit II.							($16,020)	
	Increase in Inventories, per Fig. 6-1, Exhibit II.								$35,270

APPENDIX C

A CASE STUDY

In the following paragraphs are discussed the methods used in constructing the budgets in an actual case.

The company which has been chosen as an example is a manufacturer of household heating systems. The company operated about four hundred factory branches throughout the United States. It manufactured five types of furnaces, each in a variety of sizes, and also marketed several accessories such as regulators. There was also a substantial repair business, as well as income from cleaning chimneys, furnaces, flues, and so on.

The first step in the development of the budget was the preparation of a sales forecast. Division managers with the assistance of their branch managers estimated by branches the amount of sales for the coming year. In making their estimates, the division managers were asked to take into consideration three factors and to estimate each factor separately. The three factors were:

1. Estimated sales, taking into consideration no changes in product or organization; that is, it was to be assumed that the existing line would remain unchanged, as would also the personnel at the branches and the plan of branch operation.
2. Estimated increased sales which might result through the introduction of a new design cast-iron furnace to be sold at a price competitive with the lowest prices quoted by mail-order houses; also to consider in the added products, a steel furnace and an oil burner at a competitive price.
3. Estimated potential sales volume existing in certain branches, provided the manpower in those branches was increased to a point where such potential sales volume could be solicited effectively.

The individual estimates of the division managers were reviewed by the sales manager and his staff and further discussed with the division managers until a point was reached where the sales department felt that it had arrived at a reasonable and conservative estimate of sales for the coming year. The sales in units reflected in the estimate were allocated to the various classes of furnaces and other products, percentagewise, on the basis of recent experience and after considering the effect on probable customer demand of the introduction of the new products. The apportionment of anticipated sales to the months of the fiscal year was made on the basis of average experience during the preceding five years.

Using the sales forecast as a basis, each operating department was required to prepare a forecast of its activities in relation to the sales program.

The production department prepared a schedule of the numbers of the various classes of furnaces to be manufactured each month to meet the anticipated sales requirements and to maintain satisfactory inventories of finished product as well as to maintain as smooth a production curve as conditions in the industry permitted. With the production schedules as a basis, the cost department scheduled the direct labor and direct material requirements for each month. The various factory departments were furnished schedules showing their expenses during the preceding period and were asked to furnish estimates of their expenses for the coming year in relation to the anticipated manufacturing activity, and giving appropriate consideration to the variability of the various expenses from month to month with fluctuations of volume.

The purchasing department prepared a schedule of raw material purchases based on the schedules of monthly requirements furnished by the cost department. The purchase schedule took into consideration the maintenance of proper raw material inventories and purchasing in such volume and at such times as would result in the most favorable prices. Expense material was considered as being purchased when required.

The various office departments were furnished schedules of expenses for the preceding period and were asked to prepare estimates of their expenses at the anticipated sales volume.

Certain items of administrative expense as well as book charges, such as depreciation, amortization of deferred charges, and so forth, were calculated by the accounting executives. Expenditures which were a matter of management policy, such as advertising and additions to plant, were naturally determined by the major executives.

The treasurer, in addition to preparing schedules of expenses for the cashiers' and collection departments, was required to furnish a forecast of accounts receivable and allowances for doubtful accounts, which showed monthly, estimated collections, cash discounts, removals, cancellations, and uncollectible accounts.

In this particular company the estimating of branch selling expenses was especially difficult. It should be recalled that the company operated about four hundred branches. Each branch, because of variations in size and local conditions, presented a different problem with respect to personal selling by the manager, compensation of salesmen, supervision by salesmen of installation work, and so on. In spite of the detail involved, the budget for each branch was separately prepared. In this case the branch budgets were compiled by the home office sales department. This was necessary since the preparation of the individual forecasts was influenced by company policies of branch management and operation, as well as certain features of branch managers' and salesmen's contracts.

Finally, all of the schedules, submitted by department heads and officials directly responsible for or most conversant with the various operations, were reviewed, discussed, and revised by the controller and his immediate assistants, having in mind at all times the reasonableness of the estimates in view of the anticipated volume of activity, past experience, and future requirements and plans.

To review the several steps in the preparation of the budget: Based on the sales forecast, the production department had estimated its manufacturing activity in units. Predicated on these two basic forecasts, each manufacturing, selling, and administrative department had in turn forecast its own activities. The controller had before him a file of separate but related schedules, and with them he was to compile the budget by months. The controller naturally prescribed the form and contents of the various schedules, to ensure uniformity, conformity with the classification of accounts, and an arrangement which would lend itself to subsequent accounting treatment.

The first task was one of summarization. The sales department's forecasts of sales and expenses by branches had been summarized prior to submission to the controller. The manufacturing, selling, and administrative expenses were next summarized. The controller now had reduced the working schedules to about a dozen, all of them presenting forecasts for each of the ensuing twelve months. The schedules were:

Sales	Purchases
Direct material and direct labor	Manufacturing expenses

APPENDIX C 383

Home office selling expenses
Branch selling expenses
Administrative expenses

Other deductions and other income
Accounts receivable
Plant additions and betterments

The assembly of the above summary schedules into monthly forecasted balance sheets and income accounts was resolved into a purely mechanical task. A journal sheet was set up consisting of twenty-six columns and a name space. The twenty-six columns consisted of a debit and credit column for each of the twelve months and total for the year. The name space was used to write in the names of the accounts affected by the budgeted transactions.

A set of journal entries was then prepared to give effect to each of the items in the various schedules. For example, sales represented a debit to accounts receivable and credit to sales. The estimated collections each month were reflected as debits to cash and credits to accounts receivable. Direct material used in production was recorded as a debit to work in process and credit to raw materials. Purchases were debited to inventory accounts and credited to accounts payable, which were liquidated according to purchase terms by credits to cash. A similar procedure was followed for all of the items in the schedules. When journalizing expense schedules the debits were naturally made to controlling accounts only, with related credits to cash, allowance for depreciation, prepaid expenses, and so on.

The next step consisted of posting the journal entries. For this purpose sheets were lined up similar to the usual form of working trial balance. The accounts were listed along the left side of the sheet. The first money column contained the balances of real accounts at the beginning of the year. There followed two columns for adjustments as indicated by the first month's journal entries and a fourth column for the balances at the end of the first month. The sheet was continued toward the right for each of the twelve months, ending with the forecasted trial balance at the close of the year.

Before preparing the balance sheets and income accounts, a statement of estimated cash receipts and disbursements was compiled from an analysis of the monthly postings to the cash account in the work sheets. The statement of cash receipts and disbursements and resulting cash balances at the end of each month disclosed the months in which it would be necessary to resort to bank loans to provide adequate cash balances and the months when these loans could be repaid. Journal entries were then made to give effect to anticipated borrowings and liquidation as well as resultant interest expense. After these entries had been posted to the work sheets, the final step was the preparation of monthly balance sheets and income accounts, and the budget was finished.

The procedure which has been outlined is, as stated before, taken from an actual case. It may sound somewhat formidable and may become pretty badly involved unless preceded by painstaking planning. The controller or other officer responsible for the budget must possess enough imagination and vision to see the finished picture behind a mass of detail. He must know what he wants and what to do with it when he gets it. Each step must be laid out in advance and reduced to elemental accounting operations which fit into each other. There must be no question as to who is responsible for each of the schedules, and a time schedule for their submission, review, and revision should be established. Cooperation throughout the organization is, of course, essential. The reader may be assured that, with proper foresight, preparation, and planning, the time and expense of doing a thorough job of budgeting should be entirely commensurate with benefits to be obtained.

There are annexed a number of typical forecasts and statements illustrative of the data developed in the course of constructing the budgets in this case.

STATEMENT OF IN-

	Year	April	May	June	July
INCOME:					
Sales:					
Furnaces, fittings, etc.	$5,860,155	$214,593	$426,753	$697,817	$626,412
Repairs and parts	1,239,840	29,716	55,429	92,926	98,158
Cleaner	641,655	8,470	50,819	106,643	93,489
	7,741,650	252,779	533,001	897,386	818,059
Less, Cancellations and allowances	368,650	12,037	25,381	42,733	38,955
	7,373,000	240,742	507,620	854,653	779,104
Less, Cash discounts	24,000	888	1,608	1,296	1,560
	7,349,000	239,854	506,012	853,357	777,544
Cost of sales:					
Factory cost	1,925,700	69,529	129,186	209,873	192,391
Installation cost	1,290,000	44,400	87,500	143,800	131,800
Cost of cleaner service	318,885	30,650	39,639	48,781	41,042
	3,534,585	144,579	256,325	402,454	365,233
Gross profit	3,814,415	95,275	249,687	450,903	412,311
EXPENSES					
Selling and advertising:					
Branch	2,294,467	126,611	188,414	262,277	249,085
General office	768,578	48,587	56,668	66,453	75,408
General and administrative	402,694	29,796	31,301	33,506	40,446
	3,465,739	204,994	276,383	362,236	364,939
Operating profit	348,676	109,719*	26,696*	88,667	47,372
Other deductions:					
Bond interest	135,140	11,355	11,355	11,355	11,355
Other interest	17,000	37	38	75	75
Provision for doubtful accounts	146,980	4,797	10,120	17,067	15,551
Sundry	10,000	833	833	834	833
Maintenance--idle plants	50,000	4,167	4,167	4,166	4,167
Bond discount and amortization	10,230	875	875	875	875
Life insurance premiums	12,000	1,000	1,000	1,000	1,000
	381,350	23,064	28,388	35,372	33,856
Other income:					
Interest earned	7,500	625	625	625	625
Discount earned	9,300	400	800	1,000	1,150
Earned finance income	168,381	13,120	11,953	12,049	12,772
	185,181	14,145	13,378	13,674	14,547
Net deductions	196,169	8,919	15,010	21,698	19,309
Net profit before provision for contingencies	152,507	118,638*	41,706*	66,969	28,063
Provision for contingencies	80,000	6,667	6,667	6,666	6,667
Net profit	$ 72,507	$125,305*	$ 48,373*	$ 60,303	$ 21,396

* Indicates red figures.

APPENDIX C

COME AND EXPENSES

	August	September	October	November	December	January	February	March
	$ 884,152	$ 889,668	$ 748,172	$422,536	$358,581	$177,279	$177,391	$236,801
	165,269	200,132	215,539	131,104	113,132	49,577	42,791	46,067
	107,156	137,892	99,072	20,020	7,764	3,914	3,208	3,208
	1,156,577	1,227,692	1,062,783	573,660	479,477	230,770	223,390	286,076
	55,075	58,462	50,609	27,318	22,832	10,989	10,636	13,623
	1,101,502	1,169,230	1,012,174	546,342	456,645	219,781	212,754	272,453
	1,512	1,896	2,700	2,472	2,616	2,748	2,112	2,592
	1,099,990	1,167,334	1,009,474	543,870	454,029	217,033	210,642	269,861
	273,639	288,315	256,050	152,535	135,138	67,512	66,866	84,666
	190,800	197,800	174,800	100,800	85,600	41,300	40,000	51,400
	45,903	55,417	41,886	7,235	3,166	2,070	1,546	1,550
	510,342	541,532	472,736	260,570	223,904	110,882	108,412	137,616
	589,648	625,802	536,738	283,300	230,125	106,151	102,230	132,245
	323,261	339,685	308,722	141,332	111,062	83,884	83,276	76,858
	79,190	83,316	82,064	72,227	56,554	49,894	47,745	50,472
	34,306	36,461	36,121	34,236	32,976	31,681	30,301	31,563
	436,757	459,462	426,907	247,795	200,592	165,459	161,322	158,893
	152,891	166,340	109,831	35,505	29,533	59,308*	59,092*	26,648*
	11,355	11,315	11,275	11,235	11,195	11,155	11,115	11,075
	1,074	2,888	3,825	3,450	2,700	1,763	1,000	75
	22,000	23,347	20,189	10,877	9,081	4,341	4,213	5,397
	833	834	833	833	834	833	833	834
	4,167	4,166	4,167	4,167	4,166	4,167	4,167	4,166
	875	875	875	875	875	785	785	785
	1,000	1,000	1,000	1,000	1,000	1,000	1,000	1,000
	41,304	44,425	42,164	32,437	29,851	24,044	23,113	23,332
	625	625	625	625	625	625	625	625
	1,150	1,150	1,150	750	650	400	300	400
	13,317	14,696	15,931	16,498	16,198	15,169	13,963	12,715
	15,092	16,471	17,706	17,873	17,473	16,194	14,888	13,740
	26,212	27,954	24,458	14,564	12,378	7,850	8,225	9,592
	126,679	138,386	85,373	20,941	17,155	67,158*	67,317*	36,240*
	6,667	6,666	6,667	6,667	6,666	6,667	6,667	6,666
	$ 120,012	$ 131,720	$ 78,706	$ 14,274	$ 10,489	$ 73,825*	$ 73,984*	$ 42,906*

APPENDIX C

FORECAST OF COST OF

	Year	April	May	June	July
Variable:					
Materials purchased	$1,259,460	$ 91,429	$160,675	$153,704	$162,347
Salvage, furnaces removed	25,000	650	2,575	3,450	3,275
Freight to branches	162,323	11,991	20,824	19,876	20,907
Direct labor	206,310	15,338	26,243	25,095	26,505
Manufacturing expenses:					
Indirect labor	58,671	4,342	7,510	7,158	7,569
Compensation insurance	5,300	391	678	647	684
Factory supplies	31,500	2,331	4,032	3,843	4,064
Water	1,500	-	-	450	-
Power	17,500	1,300	1,900	1,850	1,900
Sand	8,000	592	1,024	976	1,032
Coke	18,000	1,332	2,304	2,196	2,322
Perishable tools	2,000	148	256	244	258
Sundry supplies	3,000	222	384	366	387
Freight, express and cartage	7,500	555	960	915	968
Sundry expense	750	56	96	91	97
	1,806,814	130,677	229,461	220,861	232,315
Fixed:					
Supervision	27,150	2,250	2,288	2,250	2,250
Indirect labor	3,120	260	260	260	260
Clerical	10,049	828	875	828	828
Depreciation	25,944	2,162	2,162	2,162	2,162
Insurance, miscellaneous	960	80	80	80	80
Taxes	38,000	3,166	3,167	3,167	3,166
Coal	2,000	100	-	-	-
Telephone and telegraph	1,200	100	100	100	100
Subscriptions	125	25	-	-	-
Rent	5,700	475	475	475	475
Repairs	3,000	250	250	250	250
Stationery and office supplies	1,100	100	100	100	100
Traveling	1,000	83	83	84	83
Patent expense	7,500	625	625	625	625
Experimental	10,000	833	833	834	833
Inventory reserve charge	40,000	3,333	3,333	3,334	3,333
	176,848	14,670	14,631	14,549	14,545
	1,983,662	145,347	244,092	235,410	246,860
Deduct, Increase or add decrease of raw material in process and finished goods inventory	57,962*	75,818*	114,906*	25,537*	54,469*
Total	$1,925,700	$ 69,529	$129,186	$209,873	$192,391
Production, furnaces	19,893	1,470	2,552	2,436	2,562

* Indicates red figures.

APPENDIX C 387

GOODS SOLD--FACTORY

August	September	October	November	December	January	February	March
$184,567	$160,080	$ 71,752	$ 62,274	$ 56,825	$55,255	$50,307	$50,245
3,200	2,175	2,175	1,625	875	1,675	1,175	2,150
23,650	20,561	8,874	8,076	7,343	7,176	6,522	6,523
30,194	26,173	11,858	10,176	9,274	9,036	8,210	8,208
8,566	7,451	3,227	2,934	2,640	2,580	2,347	2,347
776	673	291	265	238	233	212	212
4,599	4,000	1,733	1,575	1,417	1,386	1,260	1,260
-	500	-	-	300	-	-	250
2,300	1,900	1,100	1,050	1,050	1,050	1,050	1,050
1,168	1,016	440	400	360	352	320	320
2,628	2,286	990	900	810	792	720	720
292	254	110	100	90	88	80	80
438	381	165	150	135	132	120	120
1,095	952	413	375	337	330	300	300
110	95	41	37	34	33	30	30
263,583	228,497	103,169	89,937	81,728	80,118	72,653	73,815
2,287	2,250	2,250	2,288	2,250	2,287	2,250	2,250
260	260	260	260	260	260	260	260
850	828	828	850	828	850	828	828
2,162	2,162	2,162	2,162	2,162	2,162	2,162	2,162
80	80	80	80	80	80	80	80
3,167	3,167	3,166	3,167	3,167	3,166	3,167	3,167
-	-	150	250	375	375	375	375
100	100	100	100	100	100	100	100
-	-	-	-	-	20	15	65
475	475	475	475	475	475	475	475
250	250	250	250	250	250	250	250
100	100	100	100	100	100	50	50
83	84	83	83	84	83	83	84
625	625	625	625	625	625	625	625
033	034	033	033	034	033	033	034
3,333	3,334	3,333	3,333	3,334	3,333	3,333	3,334
14,605	14,549	14,695	14,856	14,924	14,999	14,886	14,939
278,188	243,046	117,864	104,793	96,652	95,117	87,539	88,754
4,549*	45,269	138,186	47,742	38,486	27,605*	20,673*	4,088*
$273,639	$288,315	$256,050	$152,535	$135,138	$67,512	$66,866	$84,666
2,898	2,520	1,085	990	900	880	800	800

APPENDIX C

INSTALLATION COST AND

	Year	April	May	June
Installation cost:				
Labor	$ 986,317	$29,417	$37,900	$ 86,200
Drayage	132,638	4,633	9,045	15,300
Outside material	156,045	5,350	10,555	17,300
Adjustment - labor reserve	15,000	5,000	30,000	25,000
Total	$1,290,000	$44,400	$87,500	$143,800
Cost of cleaner service:				
Labor, gas, and oil	$ 213,885	$ 2,830	$16,950	$ 35,500
Repairs and supplies	60,000	27,820	15,189	5,781
Depreciation - motors and trucks	45,000	-	7,500	7,500
Total	$ 318,885	$30,650	$39,639	$ 48,781

* Indicates red figures.

COST OF CLEANER SERVICE

	July	August	September	October	November	December	January	February	March
	$ 92,600	$138,500	$144,000	$156,500	$ 98,500	$75,000	$47,000	$36,900	$43,800
	13,300	19,300	19,660	17,200	10,200	10,000	4,300	4,300	5,400
	15,900	23,000	24,140	21,100	12,100	10,600	5,000	4,800	6,200
	10,000	10,000	10,000	20,000*	20,000*	10,000*	15,000*	6,000*	4,000*
	$131,800	$190,800	$197,800	$174,800	$100,800	$85,600	$41,300	$40,000	$51,400
	$ 31,200	$ 35,700	$ 46,000	$ 33,000	$ 6,670	$ 2,600	$ 1,305	$ 1,065	$ 1,065
	2,342	2,703	1,917	1,386	565	566	765	481	485
	7,500	7,500	7,500	7,500	-	-	-	-	-
	$ 41,042	$ 45,903	$ 55,417	$ 41,886	$ 7,235	$ 3,166	$ 2,070	$ 1,546	$ 1,550

APPENDIX C

BRANCH SELLING AND

	Year	April	May	June
Direct branch expenses:				
Variable:				
Branch managers' sales commissions	$ 266,190	$ 8,252	$ 18,557	$ 31,994
Heating engineers' sales commissions	727,717	22,702	50,655	87,095
Bonuses	100,000	8,000	24,000	38,000
Credit reports and permits	43,500	2,175	3,480	3,480
Miscellaneous	50,000	2,000	3,500	6,000
	1,187,407	43,129	100,192	166,569
Fixed:				
Branch managers' drawing accounts	506,610	42,217	42,218	42,217
Heating engineers' drawing accounts	118,311	4,500	10,000	16,650
Warehouse	56,785	4,731	4,733	4,733
Clerical	138,738	11,561	11,562	11,561
Rent	144,997	12,083	12,083	12,083
Free service labor	67,619	4,057	3,043	3,381
Financing expense - auto	7,000	583	583	583
Collection commissions	67,000	3,750	4,000	4,500
	1,107,060	83,482	88,222	95,708
Total	$2,294,467	$126,611	$188,414	$262,277

* Indicates red figures.

APPENDIX C

ADVERTISING EXPENSES

July	August	September	October	November	December	January	February	March
$ 29,039	$ 40,163	$ 43,482	$ 36,920	$ 18,764	$ 15,357	$ 7,412	$ 7,141	$.9,109
79,096	109,669	118,458	100,808	51,614	42,348	20,438	19,699	25,135
35,000	70,000	70,000	60,000	37,000*	43,000*	40,000*	35,000*	50,000*
3,915	5,220	4,785	5,220	6,525	2,393	2,392	1,740	2,175
5,000	5,000	8,000	6,000	3,500	3,000	2,500	2,500	3,000
152,050	230,052	244,725	208,948	43,403	20,098	7,258*	3,920*	10,581*
42,218	42,217	42,218	42,217	42,218	42,217	42,218	42,217	42,218
18,150	12,650	12,650	14,600	9,111	5,000	5,000	5,000	5,000
4,733	4,733	4,732	4,732	4,732	4,732	4,732	4,731	4,731
11,562	11,561	11,562	11,561	11,562	11,561	11,562	11,561	11,562
12,083	12,083	12,083	12,084	12,083	12,083	12,083	12,083	12,083
2,705	3,381	3,381	5,746	10,140	8,788	9,464	6,771	6,762
584	584	584	584	583	583	583	583	583
5,000	6,000	7,750	8,250	7,500	6,000	5,500	4,250	4,500
97,035	93,209	94,960	99,774	97,929	90,964	91,142	87,196	87,439
$249,085	$323,261	$339,685	$308,722	$141,332	$111,062	$83,884	$83,276	$76,858
12,083	12,083	12,083	12,084	12,083	12,083	12,083	12,083	12,083

APPENDIX C

		GENERAL OFFICE SELLIN		
	Year	April	May	June
Selling:				
Variable:				
Divisional management:				
Division assistants - salaries	$ 6,240	-	-	-
Provision for division bonus	12,000	-	-	-
Insurance:				
Compensation	43,410	$ 2,184	$ 2,730	$ 3,510
Pub. liability - property damage and products	11,590	616	770	990
Other insurance	700	58	58	59
Freight, express and cartage	45,000	2,500	3,000	3,500
Fixed:				
Divisional management:				
Drawings	52,520	4,376	4,376	4,376
Expenses	53,300	4,441	4,441	4,442
Division assistants - salaries	13,000	1,083	1,083	1,083
Division assistants - expenses	13,000	1,083	1,083	1,083
Sales management:				
Salaries	40,000	3,000	3,000	3,400
Clerical	42,776	3,463	3,459	3,640
Insurance:				
Losses on agent's insurance - autos	21,000	1,750	1,750	1,750
Cleaner trucks and equipment	9,000	-	1,500	1,500
Surety bonds	13,000	1,083	1,083	1,084
Losses not covered by surety bonds	14,000	1,166	1,167	1,167
Stationery and office supplies	38,000	3,500	4,000	3,000
Traveling	20,000	2,000	2,000	2,000
Taxes	21,500	1,700	1,700	1,000
Prizes and gifts	10,000	100	250	1,000
Gratis and guarantee material	40,000	2,400	1,800	2,000
Moving expenses	7,000	1,000	750	275
Sales meetings	8,000	800	1,200	1,200
Depreciation	58,500	4,875	4,875	4,875
Telephone and telegraph	4,500	375	375	375
Inventory taking	3,500	475	275	275
Sundry sales supplies	1,250	50	75	150
Power, water, and coal	2,750	150	150	400
Subscriptions and periodicals	500	23	22	23
Janitors' salaries	1,272	106	106	106
Miscellaneous	7,500	625	625	625
Advertising:				
Fixed:				
Newspapers	95,000	250	3,000	10,000
Magazines	2,500	200	200	200
Advertising materials	40,000	2,500	5,000	4,500
Direct mail	7,920	235	235	2,035
Art work, engraving, etc.	4,500	200	200	500
Publicity	350	20	30	30
Branch advertising - uncontrollable	3,500	200	300	300
Total	**$768,578**	**$48,587**	**$56,668**	**$66,453**

APPENDIX C

393

AND ADVERTISING EXPENSES

July	August	September	October	November	December	January	February	March
$ 1,560	$ 1,560	$ 1,560	$ 1,560	-	-	-	-	-
3,000	3,000	3,000	3,000	-	-	-	-	-
3,510	4,875	6,960	5,460	$ 4,056	$ 2,730	$ 2,145	$ 1,950	$ 3,300
990	1,375	1,540	1,540	1,144	770	605	550	700
58	58	59	58	58	59	58	58	59
4,000	4,500	5,250	6,000	5,250	3,500	2,500	2,000	3,000
4,376	4,377	4,377	4,377	4,377	4,377	4,377	4,377	4,377
4,442	4,442	4,442	4,442	4,442	4,442	4,442	4,441	4,441
1,083	1,084	1,084	1,084	1,084	1,083	1,083	1,083	1,083
1,083	1,084	1,084	1,084	1,084	1,083	1,083	1,083	1,083
3,400	3,400	3,400	3,400	3,400	3,400	3,400	3,400	3,400
3,639	3,639	3,640	3,639	3,639	3,640	3,459	3,459	3,460
1,750	1,750	1,750	1,750	1,750	1,750	1,750	1,750	1,750
1,500	1,500	1,500	1,500	-	-	-	-	-
1,083	1,083	1,084	1,083	1,083	1,084	1,083	1,083	1,084
1,166	1,167	1,167	1,166	1,167	1,167	1,166	1,167	1,167
3,000	3,500	3,500	3,500	3,000	3,000	2,500	2,500	3,000
2,000	2,000	2,000	2,000	1,000	1,000	1,000	1,000	2,000
1,300	900	2,100	2,400	1,800	2,300	2,200	2,000	2,100
1,500	1,500	1,500	1,500	1,500	500	250	200	200
1,600	2,000	2,000	3,400	6,000	5,200	5,600	4,000	4,000
275	275	275	275	275	275	1,000	1,000	1,325
1,200	1,200	1,200	1,200	-	-	-	-	-
4,875	4,875	4,875	4,875	4,875	4,875	4,875	4,875	4,875
375	375	375	375	375	375	375	375	375
275	275	275	275	275	275	275	275	275
150	150	150	150	150	150	25	25	25
100	100	450	150	225	300	225	225	275
22	150	23	125	22	23	22	23	22
106	106	106	106	106	106	106	106	106
625	625	625	625	625	625	625	625	625
15,250	15,250	15,000	15,000	15,000	5,000	500	500	250
250	250	200	200	200	200	200	200	200
3,000	5,500	5,500	3,500	3,000	2,000	2,000	2,500	1,000
2,035	435	435	435	435	435	435	385	385
500	500	500	500	500	500	200	200	200
30	30	30	30	30	30	30	30	30
300	300	300	300	300	300	300	300	300
$75,408	$79,190	$83,316	$82,064	$72,227	$56,554	$49,894	$47,745	$50,472

APPENDIX C

GENERAL AND ADM

	Year	April	May	June	July
Fixed:					
Management salaries	$ 68,500.00	$ 5,708.00	$ 5,708.00	$ 5,709.00	$ 5,708.00
Clerical	105,700.00	8,995.00	8,860.00	8,330.00	8,875.00
Taxes	22,850.00	1,700.00	1,700.00	2,500.00	1,700.00
Postage	30,000.00	2,100.00	2,500.00	2,750.00	2,700.00
Depreciation	14,500.00	1,208.00	1,208.00	1,208.00	1,208.00
Stationery and office supplies	20,000.00	1,300.00	1,550.00	1,900.00	1,800.00
Traveling	12,000.00	1,000.00	1,000.00	1,000.00	1,000.00
Legal and professional	15,000.00	1,000.00	500.00	500.00	8,000.00
Charitable contributions	5,500.00	350.00	375.00	450.00	500.00
Insurance	3,500.00	291.00	291.00	291.00	291.00
Telephone and telegraph	4,000.00	333.00	333.00	334.00	333.00
Subscriptions and dues	3,500.00	291.00	291.00	293.00	291.00
Stock fees	4,000.00	333.00	333.00	334.00	333.00
Janitors' salaries	2,544.00	212.00	212.00	212.00	212.00
Power	2,900.00	225.00	225.00	225.00	175.00
Water	1,500.00	-	-	500.00	-
Coal	700.00	60.00	25.00	5.00	5.00
Sundry supplies	750.00	62.50	62.50	62.50	62.50
Bond fees	1,000.00	-	-	-	-
Repairs	750.00	62.50	62.50	62.50	62.50
Freight, express and cartage	750.00	62.50	62.50	62.50	62.50
Gratuities	1,000.00	25.00	25.00	25.00	25.00
Entertainment	1,000.00	82.50	82.50	82.50	82.50
Sundry	250.00	20.00	20.00	20.00	20.00
Collection fees	5,500.00	375.00	375.00	450.00	500.00
Salaries and traveling expenses - field collection org.	75,000.00	4,000.00	5,500.00	6,200.00	6,500.00
Total	$402,694.00	$29,796.00	$31,301.00	$33,506.00	$40,446.00

APPENDIX C

ISTRATIVE EXPENSES

	August	September	October	November	December	January	February	March
	$ 5,708.00	$ 5,709.00	$ 5,708.00	$ 5,708.00	$ 5,709.00	$ 5,708.00	$ 5,708.00	$ 5,709.00
	9,560.00	10,060.00	9,720.00	9,165.00	8,515.00	7,970.00	7,825.00	7,825.00
	1,700.00	1,700.00	3,000.00	1,700.00	2,000.00	1,700.00	1,700.00	1,750.00
	2,950.00	3,000.00	2,850.00	2,550.00	2,400.00	2,000.00	2,000.00	2,200.00
	1,208.00	1,208.00	1,208.00	1,208.00	1,208.00	1,208.00	1,208.00	1,212.00
	2,150.00	2,150.00	2,100.00	1,650.00	1,600.00	1,200.00	1,200.00	1,400.00
	1,000.00	1,000.00	1,000.00	1,000.00	1,000.00	1,000.00	1,000.00	1,000.00
	500.00	500.00	500.00	500.00	500.00	1,500.00	500.00	500.00
	500.00	600.00	600.00	600.00	450.00	425.00	325.00	325.00
	291.00	291.00	291.00	291.00	291.00	291.00	291.00	299.00
	333.00	334.00	333.00	333.00	334.00	333.00	333.00	334.00
	291.00	293.00	291.00	291.00	293.00	291.00	291.00	293.00
	333.00	334.00	333.00	333.00	334.00	333.00	333.00	334.00
	212.00	212.00	212.00	212.00	212.00	212.00	212.00	212.00
	175.00	200.00	225.00	300.00	300.00	300.00	275.00	275.00
	-	650.00	-	-	175.00	-	-	175.00
	5.00	30.00	60.00	80.00	90.00	120.00	110.00	110.00
	62.50	62.50	62.50	62.50	62.50	62.50	62.50	62.50
	-	500.00	-	-	-	-	-	500.00
	62.50	62.50	62.50	62.50	62.50	62.50	62.50	62.50
	62.50	62.50	62.50	62.50	62.50	62.50	62.50	62.50
	25.00	25.00	25.00	725.00	25.00	25.00	25.00	25.00
	82.50	82.50	82.50	82.50	82.50	82.50	82.50	92.50
	20.00	20.00	20.00	20.00	20.00	20.00	20.00	30.00
	575.00	575.00	575.00	500.00	450.00	375.00	375.00	375.00
	6,500.00	6,800.00	6,800.00	6,800.00	6,800.00	6,400.00	6,300.00	6,400.00
	$34,306.00	$36,461.00	$36,121.00	$34,236.00	$32,976.00	$31,681.00	$30,301.00	$31,563.00

STATEMENT OF SOURCES AND APPLICATION OF FUNDS

Sources of funds:
  Net income per forecast of income account $ 72,507
  Add, Losses not requiring expenditure
    of funds:
      Depreciation credited to allowance
        for depreciation   149,097
      Depreciation credited to allowance
        for agents' accounts   25,000
      Amortization of bond discount   10,230 $256,834
  Collections from agents' accounts   40,000
  Deferred finance income   669
                                                                  $297,503

Application of above funds:
  Additions to fixed assets $ 30,000
  Debentures retired   65,000
  Increase in cash surrender value of life
    insurance   44,836
  Increase in working capital (per schedule
    annexed)   157,667
                                                                  $297,503

SCHEDULE OF CHANGES IN WORKING CAPITAL

	Increase in Working Capital	Decrease in Working Capital
Cash and U.S. Treasury Bills		$409,365
Accounts receivable (net of allowance for doubtful accounts)	$666,070	
Inventories	17,962	
Bonuses payable and accrued liabilities		117,000
	$684,032	$526,365
Net increase in working capital	$157,667	

FORECAST OF CASH RECEIPTS AND DISBURSEMENTS

Receipts:
  Collections on accounts receivable $6,700,000
  Collections on employees' accounts   40,000
  Maturity of U.S. Treasury Bills   671,328
  Money borrowed   500,000
  Miscellaneous collections   16,800 $7,928,128

Disbursements:
  Accounts payable, payrolls, etc.   7,071,165
  Repayment of money borrowed   500,000
  Retirement of debentures   65,000
  Additions to fixed assets   30,000   7,666,165
                                                          $ 261,963

APPENDIX C

FORECAST OF ACCOUNTS RECEIVABLE

	Gross Sales	Finance Charges and Sales Tax	Cash Collections	Cancellations and Allowances	Cash Discounts	Removals	Bad Debts and All Changes	Other Credits	Total Credits
April 30	$ 252,779	$ 7,583	$ 375,000	$ 12,037	$ 888	$ 6,500	$ 4,800	$ 1,590	$ 400,815
May 31	533,001	15,008	400,000	25,381	1,608	25,750	46,400	4,680	503,819
June 30	897,386	24,709	450,000	42,733	1,296	34,500	52,000	3,090	583,619
July 31	818,059	22,585	500,000	38,955	1,560	32,750	40,000	3,270	616,535
August 31	1,156,577	32,205	600,000	55,075	1,512	32,000	29,200	1,230	719,017
September 30	1,227,692	33,783	775,000	58,462	1,896	21,750	23,200	2,460	882,768
October 31	1,062,783	29,490	825,000	50,609	2,700	21,750	29,600	1,320	930,979
November 30	573,660	16,840	750,000	27,318	2,472	16,250	29,600	2,670	828,310
December 31	479,477	14,512	600,000	22,832	2,616	8,750	22,400	1,710	658,308
January 31	230,770	6,388	550,000	10,989	2,748	16,750	24,000	2,490	606,977
February 28	223,390	6,728	425,000	10,636	2,112	11,750	32,400	2,130	484,028
March 31	286,076	8,719	450,000	13,623	2,592	21,500	66,400	3,360	557,475
Total	$7,741,650	$219,050	$6,700,000	$368,650	$24,000	$250,000	$400,000	$30,000	$7,772,650

APPENDIX C

FORECAST OF ALLOWANCE FOR DOUBTFUL ACCOUNTS

	Provision Charged to Operations	Removals Less Estimated Salvage	Bad Debts and Allowances	Total Debits
April 30	$ 4,797	$ 5,850	$ 4,800	$ 10,650
May 31	10,120	23,175	46,400	69,575
June 30	17,067	31,050	52,000	83,050
July 31	15,551	29,475	40,000	69,475
August 31	22,000	28,800	29,200	58,000
September 30	23,347	19,575	23,200	42,775
October 31	20,189	19,575	29,600	49,175
November 30	10,877	14,625	29,600	44,225
December 31	9,081	7,875	22,400	30,275
January 31	4,341	15,075	24,000	39,075
February 28	4,213	10,575	32,400	42,975
March 31	5,397	19,350	66,400	85,750
Total	$146,980	$225,000	$400,000	$625,000

INDEX

A

Accountants', Part in budgetary control, 51–52
Accounting, 36–37
  Budgetary control rests on system of, 51–52
  Burden, unabsorbed, 159–61
  Chart of accounts, 157
  Cost (See "Cost Accounting")
  Financial, 9
  Functions of, 9–13
    Alternative actions, analysis of, 10, 351–67
    Cost data a prerequisite, 12–13
    Income and financial accounting, 9
    Measurement of performance, 10
    Provision and pricing of data, 9–10
  Income, 9
  Natural business year, 365–66
  Pro forma entries, 9
  Promptness in collecting and analyzing data, 157
  Requirements, 10–12
    Controlling sales, 191–93
    Sales chart of accounts, 192–93
  Services, 273
  Time periods, 364–67
Accounting Department,
  Basic information, supplying of, to other departments, 77–78
  Budget planning, 77–79
  Budgeting, role in, 77–79
  Controls to ensure integration of budget plan, 78
  Estimation of accruals, 78–79
  Estimation of prepayments, 78–79
Accounts,
  Chart of, 157
    Sales, 192–93
  Classification of, 10–12, 37, 87, 270
Accounts Payable, Budgeting, 333–34
Accounts Receivable,
  Budgeting, 328–31
  Cost of, 198
Accruals,
  Budgeting, 334
  Estimation of, 78–79
  Interest, 334
  Monthly accruals and amortization charges, 78–79
  Payroll taxes and wages, 334

Action-taking,
  Budgetary control, 129–30
  Sales budgets, 191
Activities,
  Departmentalization of, 155–56
  Rate of, 157–59
Activity Levels,
  Activity range, need for determination of, 135–36
  Costs, changing behavior of, 136
  Costs for each, determination of, 139–53
  Measurement of, 269
  Range, determination of, 135–39
  Range of analysis, factors influencing, 136
Activity Measures,
  Determination of appropriate, 132–35
  Ease of application, 134
  Nonmonetary terms, 157
  Understandability of, 135
  Validity of, 132–34
Administrative Expenses, 270–84 (See also "General and Administrative Expenses")
  Budgeting, 271–79
  Controlling, 279–84
  Nature of, 271–72
Advertising,
  Accounting for, 214
  Allocation of expenditures to various media and localities, 205
  Amount to spend, factors determining, 203–4
  Budget performance report, 215
  Budgeting costs of, 203–6
  Costs, 69
    Controlling, 214–17
    Treated as capital expenditures, 304
  Deferred, 332
  Effectiveness of, measuring, 214–17
Allowances for Cost Control, 131–53
  Approval of, 153
  Changing behavior of some costs, 136
  Comparison of actual and allowed expenses, 157–61
  Cost behavior, danger of preconceived ideas of, 139
  Cost variances, due to quantity or price, 139–40
  Determination of costs for each activity level, 139–53
  Determination of known fully variable costs, 140–41
  Determination of range of activity levels, 135–39

399

INDEX

Allowances for Cost Control—*Continued*
  Determination of range of activity levels—*Continued*
    Factors influencing, 137–39
  Fixed costs, determination of known, 141
  Measures of activity, 132–35
    Capacity of plant, 134–35
    Ease of application, 134–35
    Understandability of measure, 135
    Validity of measure, 132–34
  Operating supplies, 146–50
  Predetermined, 135–36
    Utility of, 131
  Prior experience used in determining, 142–53
  Promulgation of, 153
  Purpose of, 139
  Schedules of flexible cost, 131–53
  Statistical analyses of prior experience, 142–53
    Record, plotting the, 143–47
  Variability studies of other cost items, 141
    Engineering studies, 141–42
    Prior experience, statistical analyses of, 142–53
    Trend line, determining the, 147–53
Alternative Budgeting Practices, 351–67
  Analysis of, 10
  Differential method of analysis, 33–35
  Direct costing and budgeting, 359–62
    Cost variability, the key factor, 360
    Definition, 360–62
  Partial budget methods, 352–56
    Applied to cash, 353–55
    Applied to financing capital expenditures, 356
    Applied to sales and sales costs, 355–56
    Examples of, 352–53
  Product profit and loss measurements, 362–64
  Standard costs versus actual costs, 356–59
    Budget preparation, 356–58
    Budgetary control, 358–59
  Study of, 37
  Time factor in budgeting, 364–67
Amortization,
  Charges, schedule of, 78–79
  Prepaid expenses, 332
Analysis,
  Cost performance, promptness in analyzing, 157
  Differential method of, 33–35
  Operations, 108, 122
  Sales performance, 108
Approval of the Budget, 83–84
  Budget changes, partial, 344–46
  Capital expenditures, 307–12
Assets,
  Capital employed includes, 20–21
  Fixed,
    Budgeting, 332–33
    Expenditures for, 303–4
    Return on investment method, 22–24
    Valuation of, 22–24

Assets—*Continued*
  Fixed—*Continued*
    Valuation of—*Continued*
      Depreciated, 22–24
      Gross book value, 23–24
    Working, 21–22
      Cash, 21
      Inventories, 22
      Receivables, 22
Assumptions,
  Amendment of plans and, 79–82
  List of, prepared by department heads, 66–79
Audits, Capital expenditures, 317–19
Authority,
  Coordination of responsibiilty and, 155
  Delegation of, by management, 345–46
Authorization of the Budget, 83–84
  Budget changes, partial, 344–46
  Signaling, 47
Automobiles, Expenses, Measure of activity, 135

B

Bad Debts, 270
  Allowances for, 140–41, 277
  Analysis of, 281
  Control of, 281
  Doubtful accounts, provision for, 331
Balance Sheets,
  Accounts payable, budgeting, 333–34
  Accounts receivable, budgeting, 328–31
  Accruals, budgeting,
    Income taxes, 334
    Interest, 334
    Real estate taxes, 334
    Wages and payroll taxes, 334
  Capital, budgeting, 334–35
    Capital stock, 335
    Retained earnings, 334–35
    Surplus reserves, 335
  Cash, budgeting, 326–28
  Fixed assets, budgeting, 332–33
  Forecasts, 86, 99
    Data for, 334–35
    Source of funds, 321–24
  Inventories, budgeting, 221–29, 331
  Liabilities, budgeting, 334
  Prepaid expenses and deferred charges, budgeting, 332
  Use of funds, 324–26
Bigelow-Sanford, Capital expenditures control, 310
Billing Costs, 198
Board of Directors, Budget approved by, 83
Break-even Point,
  Calculations, 28–29
  Chart, 26
  Distribution costs and gross margins, 187
  Formula, 28
  Stability of basic data, 31
  Terms of plant capacity and, 29
Brokers, Sales, 172

INDEX

401

Budget Department, 40
Budget Period, 364–67
  Fiscal or calendar year, 57
  Length of budget, 57
  Natural business year, 365–66
Budget Schedules, 4 (See also "Schedules")
Budgeting,
  Accounting functions of, 9–13
  Accounts payable, 333–34
  Accounts receivable, 328–31
  Accruals, other, 334
  Accrued wages and payroll taxes, 334
  Capital, 334
  Capital expenditures, 306–14
  Cash, 326–28
  Completeness, importance of, 351–52
  Control aspects, 107 (See also "Control, Budgetary")
  Costing problems, 356–58
  Definition, 4
  Direct labor costs, 248–52
  Direct material costs, 237–43
  Fixed assets, 332–33
  Historical background, 3
  Internal control procedures, and good, 13
  Inventories, 221–29, 331
  Liabilities, other, 334
  Prepaid expenses and deferred charges, 332
  Purpose of, 3
  Research and development costs, 287–96
  Sales, 169–84
  Variances, 297
Budgeting and Controlling Techniques,
  Alternative budget practices, 351–66
  Budget revisions, 337–50
  Capital expenditures, 303–19
  Direct labor costs, 247–57
  Direct material cost, 236–46
  Factory expense, 258–69
  Financial position, 320–36
  General and administrative expenses, 270–84
  Inventories, 220–35
  Marketing and distribution costs, 194–219
  Research and development costs, 285–302
  Sales, 169–193
Budgets,
  Approval of, 47
  Budget consciousness, promotion of, 129–30
  Definition, 3
  Illustration of, 86–104
  Master plan, 7
    Presenting to management, 82–83
    Recording changes in, 346–48
    Revisions, 348–50
    Preparation (See "Preparation of Budget")
  Purpose and nature of, 8, 85
  Schedules, detailed, 8
Building Construction Costs, 314–17
Burden,
  Absorption, 12, 63, 74, 124

Burden—*Continued*
  Accounting for, 159–61
  Allowance, 158
  Basis for absorbing factory, determining the, 62
  Factory, 72, 258–69 (See also "Factory Expense")
  Overabsorption of, 124
  Scheduling, 74
  Fixing responsibility for, 159–61
  Unabsorbed, 159–61
  Variability with production, 159

C

Call Reports, Salesmen, 218
Capacity-to-Make-and-Sell Concept, 63
Capital,
  Budgeting (See "Capital Expenditures, Budgeting")
  Employed,
    Definition, 20–21
    Desired return on, 24–25
    Forecast statement of return on, 86
    Profits based on, 17–25
    Relationship between sales volume and, 18
  Working (See "Working Capital")
Capital Expenditures, 303–19
  Appropriations progress report, 318
  Authorization for, 314, 316
  Budget, 314–15
    Sample, 92–93
  Budgeting, 46–47, 306–14, 334–36
    Approval procedure, 307–12
    Authorization of, 311–12
    Bigelow-Sanford capital expenditures control, 310
    Long-range and short-range planning, 306–7
    Projects, 307–12
    Rate of return, computation of the, 312–13
    Standards of acceptability, 312
    Sylvania capital expenditures control, 309
  Control of, 314–19
    Appropriations Progress Report, 318
    Costs, 317–18
    Earnings, comparison of reported and estimated, 319
    Expenditures, reporting progress in, 314–17
    Post-completion audits, 317–19
  Decisions concerning, 303, 305
  Definition, 303–4
  Evaluation of, 311–12
  Investments in, 65
  Long-term commitments, 303
  Methods of expenditure, 305
  Organization for, 46–47
  Partial budgeting methods, 356
  Replacement investments, 313, 317
  Revenue expenditures differ from, 304

INDEX

Capital Expenditures—*Continued*
  Timing, 314-17
  Types of, 304-5
Capital Stock, 335
Cash,
  Accounting for, 21
  Adjusted earnings method, 354
  Balances, treated in budget report, 91
  Budget deviations, relation of, to, 343-44
  Budgeting, 277, 326-28
  Cash and noncash transactions, distinguishing between, 78
  Collection of receivables, 326
  Costs of, 325
  Disbursements, 327-28
    Schedule of monthly, 329
  Method of forecasting cash position, 354
  Partial budget methods, 353-55
    Adjusted earnings methods, 354-55
    Analysis of prior year's receipts and disbursements, 355
    Balance sheet projection method, 355
  Receipts, 326-27
    Budgeting, 277
    Forecasting, 12-13
  Schedule of cash receipts and disbursements, 330
  Sources of, 326
  Treatment of, 21, 91
Changes in Budget,
  Budget change journal, 349
  Effect of, on financial position, 344-45
  Partial,
    Authorization of, 344-46
    Recording, 346-48
    Shift of income or cost within the schedules, 344-45
    Types of, 344-45
Charts,
  Accounts, 157
    Sales, 192-93
  Internal budget reports, 113
  Use of, 113
Chemical Industry, Quantity standards, 239
Clerical Costs,
  Control of, 282
  Variable,
    Budgeting, 202
    Marketing and distribution, 202, 214
Clothing Industry, Quantity standards, 240
Committees,
  Budget, 40
  Budget policy, 42
  Forecasting, 42
Compensation,
  Budgeting variable sales costs, 199-200
  Controlling the variable costs of order-filling, 209-10
  Payroll costs, 272-73
Competition,
  Principal forms, 32-33
  Volume-price relationship, 32-33
Construction Program, 314-17
  Partial budgeting method, 356

Control, Budgetary, 107-66
  Accountants' part in, 51-52
  Analyzing and interpreting the results, 122-29
  Budget performance reports, 112-21
  Capital expenditures, 314-19
  Cost accounting separate from, 266
  Cost control. (See "Cost Control")
  Costing problems, 358-59
  Definition, 107-8
    Executory stage of operations, 107-8
    Planning stage, 107-8
  Direct labor costs, 252-57
  Direct material costs, 243-46
  Factory expenses, 266-69
  Function of, 7-8
  General and administrative expenses, 279-84
  Internal reports, 112-21
    Comparison of actual and planned results, 114
  Manufacturing expenses, 8
  Marketing and distribution costs, 207-19
  Organization for, 48-52
    Line and staff functions, distinction between, 52
  Performance, reviewing and analyzing, 49-51
  Procedures improved by, 13
  Reporting the results, 48-49, 112-21
    Internal reports, 112-21
    Nature of budget reports, 112-21
  Research and development costs, 297-302
  Sales, 184-93
  Steps in, 111-12
  Taking action, 49-51, 129-30
    Budget consciousness, promotion of, 129-30
    Budget revisions, 130
    Individual performance, improvement of, 130
    Persons responsible for, 130
  Variations (See also "Variations")
    Analysis and reporting of, 107-30, 154-66
    Efficiency measured by, 108-9
Controllable vs. Noncontrollable Costs, 156-57
Controller, 39-40, 52
Cooperation,
  Importance in planning, 6-7
  Preparation of the budget, 57
Coordination,
  Detailed plans of, 79
  Need for, 65
  Organization for budget making, 39-41
Cost Accounting, 9-10
  Budgetary control separate from, 266
  classification of costs, 36-37
  Different costs for different purposes, 173
  Nonmanufacturing costs, 60
  Periodic studies, 60
  Procedures, improvement of, 173
  Standard costs, 9-10
  Unit product costs, 12

INDEX

Cost Control, 108-9
  Activity levels, determination of costs for, 139-53
  Authority and responsibility for, 155
  Changing behavior of some costs, 136
  Cost variances, 154-66
    Analysis of, 154-61
    Reports, 161-66
  Flexible budget allowances for, 131-53
    Activity, determination of appropriate measures of, 132-135
    Activity levels,
      Costs for, determination of, 139-53
      Determination of, 135-39
    Promulgation of, 153
    Interpolation, method of, 137-38
    Measures of activity,
      Determination of, 132-35
      Ease of application, 134-35
      Expenses grouped according to, 135
      Understandability of, 135
      Validity of, 132-34
    Plans, 7-8
    Predetermined allowances, uses of,
      Applying cost control procedures, 136
      Revising the budget, 135-36
    Program of, 339-41
    Quantity and price, costs a function of, 139-40
    Reports, 164
      Departmental, 268
    Semivariable costs, 136-37
    Stepped, 136-37
Cost Reduction Programs, 339-41
  Goals, establishing, 340
Costing,
  Direct, 359-62
  Marginal, 360-61
Costs,
  Allowances (See "Allowances")
  Alternative budgeting practices, 356-59
  Behavior of, danger of preconceived ideas concerning, 139
  Comparative, study of, 34
  Control (See "Cost Control")
  Controllable vs. noncontrollable, 156-57
  Cost reduction program, 339-41
  Costing problem in budget preparation, 356-58
  Different costs for different purposes, 36-37, 173
  Direct costing and budgeting, 359-62
    Cost variability the key factor, 360
    Definition, 360-62
  Direct material, 236-46
  Estimates, preparation of, 317-18
  Factory expense, 258-69 (See also "Factory Expense")
  Fixed (See "Fixed Costs")
  Fixed and variable, volume-cost-price-profit relationship, 27-28
  Forecasts, variations in, 110-11
  Joint, 362-64
  Laws of, 30-31
  Managed, 198

Costs—*Continued*
  Marketing and distribution, 194-219
  Nonmanufacturing, 60
  Period, 36
  Product, 36
  Quantity and price, a function of, 139-40
  Responsibility for various classes of, 155
  Sales, analysis of variations in, 124-26
  Standard, 9-10
    Versus actual, 356-59
  Stepped, 136-37
  Unit, 35
  Unit product, 356-57
  Variable (See also "Variances, Cost")
    Analysis and reporting of, 154-66
    Determination of known, 140-41
    Studies of, 141-53
  Variations, 357, 361
  Volume-cost-price-profit relationships, 25-32
Customers, Relative profitability of, 187

D

Data,
  Electronic processing machines, 274-75, 350
  Promptness in collecting and analyzing, 37, 157
  Sound use of, 111
Deductions, Forecasts, 104
Deferred Charges, Budgeting, 332
Definition of Terms, 3-4
Departments (See also names of departments)
  Budget plans and departments affected, 67
  Budgetary plans, amendment of, 79-81
  Budgets, 40
  Cost control reports, 268
  Responsibility for costs incurred in one department and used by another, 155
Depreciation,
  Budgeting, 265
  Controlling costs, 267
  Funds, 333
  Office equipment, 274-75
  Recorded as a cost, 333
Deviations (See also "Variations")
  Nature of, 337-39
  Significance of, 343-44
Differential Method of Analysis, Planning for profit, 33-35
Direct Costing and Budgeting, 359-62
  Cost variability the key factor, 360
  Definition, 360-62
  Purposes of, 360
Direct Labor Costs, 247-57
  Budgeting, 248-52
  Controlling, 252-57
  Definition, 247-48
Direct Material Cost, 236-46
  Budgeting, 237-43
  Controlling, 243-46

INDEX

Directives,
  Alterations of, 81–82
  Budget, 65–66
  Budget report of Illustrative Company, 90–93
  Formalizing, 81–82
  Illustrative Company, 90–93
  Reconsideration of, 83
  Wording of, 269
Directors,
  Board of, budget approved by, 83
  Budget, 40
    Budget plan submitted to, 82–83
    Statistical forecasting by, 182–83
Discounts,
  Purchase, 64, 270, 334
    Budgeting, 278–79
    Controlling, 283–84
  Sales, 270
    Budgeting, 276–77
    Controlling, 281
    Variations in, analysis of, 127
  Taking of, directive concerning, 91
Distribution,
  Costs (See also "Marketing and Distribution Costs")
  Sales method, selection of, 171–72
  Standard order size, determination of, 187–88
Dividends,
  Management's decision concerning, 335
  Payable, 334
Donations, Corporate, 272, 276
  Controlling, 279
Doubtful Accounts, 277, 331
Down-time and Set-up Requirements, 134
Dues, Budgeting costs of, 276

E

Earnings, Adjusted earnings method of forecasting cash position, 354
Economic Lot Calculation, 226–28
Efficiency, Budget variations as a measure of, 108–9
Electronic Data Processing, 274–75
  Use in preparation of budgets, 350
Employees,
  Individual performance, improvement of, 130
  Safety and welfare expenditures, 305
Engineering Department, Budget planning, 76–77
Engineering Studies of Variability, 141–42
Equipment,
  Availability and utilization of, 108
  Costs, 272, 274–75
  Down-time and set-up, determination of proper allowances for, 134
  Electronic data processing, 274–75
  Interchangeable machine test classification system, 133–34

Equipment—*Continued*
  Machine tool classification system, 133–34
  Office, 274–75
  Physical check of, 133
  Records of, 133, 301
  Research, 300
  Tabulation of all productive, 133–34
Equity, Ratio of profit to owners', 21
Estimates, Cost, 317–18
Exception Items, Internal reports, 113
Executives,
  Budget officer, 39
  Jury of executive opinion method of forecasting sales, 176–77
Exhibits, Illustrative Company Budget Report, 94–99, 115–18
Expansion Investments, 304–5
Expenditures,
  Capital, 303–19 (See also "Capital Expenditures")
  Revenue, 304
Expenses (See also "Costs")
  Comparison of actual and allowed, 157
  Factory, 258–69 (See also "Factory Expense")
  General and administrative, 270–84 (See also "General Administrative Expenses")
  Grouped according to measures of activity, 135
  Manufacturing,
    Budget, 138
    Control of, 8
    Plant manager's responsibility for, 44–46
  Other,
    Bad debts, 277, 281
    Budgetery, 276–77
    Controlling, 281–83
      Bad debts, 281
      Interest expense, 281–83
      Sales discounts, 281
      Variations in income taxes, 283
    Income taxes, 277–78, 283
    Interest expense, 277, 281–83
    Sales discounts, 276–77, 281
  Prepaid, 332
  Pro forma expense distribution sheet, 266–67
  Selling (See "Selling Costs")
  Stepped, 139
  Traveling (See "Travel Expenses")
Experience, Statistical analyses of prior, 142–53

F

Factory Expense, 258–69
  Budgeting, 260–65
    Fringe benefits, 264–65
    Idle time, 263–64
    Indirect labor, 260–63
      Producing department, 260–62
      Service departments, 262–63
    Indirect materials, 265
    Time charges, 265

INDEX

Factory Expense—*Continued*
  Controlling, 266–69
    Departmentalization of, 266
    Measurements, 268–69
    Point of control, 266–68
  List of cost items, 258–59
  Nature of, 258–59
  Proration of costs, 268–69
  Proration of general expenses, 268
Factory Overhead, Cost reduction program, 341
Faulty Procedures, 111
Field Office Organization, Budgeting cost of, 206–7
Financial Plans, Analysis of variations from, 128–29
Financial Position, 320–36
  Balance sheet data, use of, 321
  Budgeting,
    Accounts payable, 333–34
    Accounts receivable, 328–29
    Accrued wages and payroll taxes, 334
    Capital, 334–36
    Cash, 326–28
    Fixed assets, 332–33
    Inventories, 331
    Other accruals, 334
    Other liabilities, 334
    Prepaid expenses and deferred charges, 332
  Changes in budget that affect, 344–45
  Definition, 320–21
  Measuring, 321–25
  Relating operations to, problem of, 321
  Requirements for financial well-being, 321
  Source of funds, 321–24
  Use of funds, 324–26
Financing, Long- and short-term, 334
Finished Products, Inventories of, 221
Fiscal Year, 57
Fixed Assets,
  Budgeting, 332–33
  Disposal of, 332–33
  Expenditures for, 303–4
Fixed Costs,
  Changing behavior of, 136
  Known, determination of, 141
  Marketing and distribution, 197, 198
  Controlling, 209
Flexible Cost Allowances for Cost Control, 131–53
Flexible Expenses, General and administrative, 280
Forecasting,
  Annual operating statement, budget changes reflected in, 348
  Cash position, 354
  Cash receipts, 12–13
  Committees, 42
  Data,
    Availability of, 111
    Sound use of, 111
  Faulty methods, 111
  Income taxes, 277–78
  Sales, 175–83

Forecasting—*Continued*
  Sales—*Continued*
    Accounting requirements, 191–92
    Averaging-in the budget director's statistical forecasts, 182–83
    Combination of methods, 179–83
    Importance of, 225
    Jury of executive opinion method, 176–77
      Advantages and disadvantages, 176–77
      Example of, 177
    Market conditions, based on, 109–10
    Organization for, 42–44
    Over-all economic adjustment by top management, 183
    Sales force composite method, 178, 180–82
    "Share of the market," 175
    Statistical analyses, 179
  Scientific method in, 111
Forecasts,
  Approving, 47
  Balance sheet, 86, 99
  Data for, 334–35
  Budget plans and departments affected, 67
  Changes in working capital, 86, 98
  Cost, 12
  General and administrative expenses, 103
  Illustrative Company, 95–104
  Market conditions, 109
  Monthly statements, financial and operating, 332
  Operating statement, 86, 95
  Other income and deductions, 104
  Profit and loss statement, 335
  Return on capital employed, 96
  Sales (See "Forecasting, Sales")
  Sales and factory cost of sales, 101
  Selling expenses, 102
  Source and application of funds, 86, 97
  Statement of return on capital employed, 86
Foremen,
  Manpower budget for, 254
  Participation in determination of expense budget schedules, 268
  Weekly labor cost report, 162–63
Forms, Budget, 54, 85–104, 115–22
  Budget performance reports, 114–21
  Illustrations of, 86–104, 115–22
  Internal reports, 114–21
Fringe Benefits, Budgeting, 264–65
Funds,
  Source of, 321–24 (See also "Source and Application of Funds")
  Use of, 324–26

G

General and Administrative Expenses, 270–84
  Budgeting, 271–76
  Controlling, 279–84
    Clerical costs, 282
    Departmentalization of, 280–81

406　INDEX

General and Administrative Expenses—
Continued
　Controlling—*Continued*
　　Fixed and appropriated expenses, 279–80
　　Flexible expenses, 280
　　Standards for, 280
　Equipment costs, 274–75
　Forecasts, 103
　Nature of, 271–72
　Professional services, 273
　Salaries and wages, 271, 272–73
　Space costs, 275
　Subscriptions, dues, and memberships, 276
　Supplies, 274
　Telephone, telegraph, and postage, 275
　Travel costs, 275–76
　Variations in, analysis of, 126–27
General Foods Corporation, 290–91

H

Handling Costs,
　Controlling variable, 210
　Standard order size, determining, 187–88

I

Ideas, Development of new, 307–8
Idle Time, 259
　Budgeting, 263–64
　Common causes of, 263
Illustration of Budget, 86–104
Illustrative Company,
　Budget deviations, 378–80
　Budget performance reports, 115–21
　Budget report first quarter, 90–104
　　Directives and conformity therewith, 90–93
　　Exhibits,
　　　Forecast balance sheet, 99, 321
　　　Forecast changes in working capital, 98
　　　Forecast operating statement, 95
　　　Forecast sources and application of funds, 97
　　　Forecast statement of return on capital employed, 96
　　Schedules,
　　　Forecast general and administrative expenses, 103
　　　Forecast other income and deductions, 104
　　　Forecast sales and factory cost of sales, 101
　　　Forecast selling expenses, 102
　Budget report for January,
　　Exhibits,
　　　Balance sheet, 116
　　　Changes in working capital, 118
　　　Operating statement and return on capital employed, 115
　　　Sources and applications of funds, 117

Illustrative Company—*Continued*
　Budget report for January—*Continued*
　　Schedules,
　　　General and administrative expenses, 121
　　　Other income and deductions, 122
　　　Sales and cost of sales, 119
　　　Selling expenses, 120
　Budgeting fixed assets, 332–33
　Budgeting prepaid expense and deferred charges, 332
　Cash receipts, 326–27
　Cash receipts and disbursements, schedule of, 330
　Company and its operations, 58–59
　Estimated monthly cash disbursements, 329
　Form of budget report, 86–104, 115–22
　Interest expense, 277, 281
　Journal entries and supporting data, 371–72
　Long- and short-range planning, 306–7
　Objectives of the budget, 59–65
　Preparation of budget, 58–84 (See also "Preparation of Budget")
　Product profit and loss statement, 363
　Sources of funds statement, 322–23
Improvements, Capital (See "Capital Expenditures")
Incentive Systems, 134, 251
Income,
　Forecasts, 104
　Interest earned, 279
　Investment, 270, 279
　　Control of, 284
　Marginal income ratio, 30–31
　Miscellaneous,
　　Budgeting, 278–79
　　Controlling, 283–84
　　　Interest earned and investment income, 284
　　　Purchase discounts, 283–84
　　Interest earned and investment income, 279, 284
　　Purchase discounts, 278–79, 283–84
　Net, vs. net operating, 20
　Variation in, analysis of, 127–28
　Variations in net, analysis of, 127–28
Income Taxes,
　Budgeting, 334
　Net income subject to tax, forecasting, 277
　Rates of tax, forecasting, 277
　State, 283
　Variations in, control of, 283
Indirect Materials, 265
Insurance,
　Budgeting, 265, 332
　Costs, control of, 267
　Prepaid expenses, budgeting, 332
Integration, Need for, 65, 66
Interest,
　Accruals, 334
　Earned, 279
　　Control of, 284
　Expense, 270
　　Budgeting, 277
　　Control of, 281–83

INDEX 407

Interest—*Continued*
  Payments, scheduling, 277
Interpolation, 269
  Method of, 137–38
Inventories,
  Accounting for, 22
  Amount of each product to be carried, 70–71
  Budgeting, 221–29
    Balance sheet treatment, 331
    Delays, prevention of, 224–26
    Economy of acquisition, 226–28
    Financial limits on, 228–29
    Quantitative inventories, interrelation of, 221–22
    Requirements, measuring the, 224–28
  Budgets, and improvement of balance in, 64
  Computation of,
    Monthly purchase and inventories of direct materials in units, 76
    Uniform monthly production requirements in units of product, 73
  Control of, 229–35
    Amount of inventory, 229–31
    Deviations from the budget, problem of, 231–32
    Quantitative data, use of, 231
    Records, importance of, 234–35
    Reports, 234–35
    Standard inventory ratios, use of, 232–34
      Surplus items report, 234
    Standards and the budget, 231
  Direct materials, 222
  Economic lot calculation, 226–28
  Financial aspects, 228–29
  Finished product, 81, 221
    Completions scheduled, computation of, 71
    Ending inventories under level production in units of product, calculation of, 72
    Sales department planning, 68–70
  Minimum, maintenance of, 226
  Nature of, 221
  Production schedules influenced by, 221
  Reasons for, 222–23
    Anticipation of price increases and/or shortages, 223
    Economy of acquisition, 223
    Prevention of delays, 22–23
    Stabilization of production, 223
  Reserve factor, calculation of, 224
  Standards, 64, 81
    Treatment in budget report, 91–92
  Treatment in financial statements, 221
  Valuing, 22
  Work in process and finished parts, 81, 221–22
Investments,
  Capital improvements, 65
  Income from, 270, 279
Invoices,
  Discounting, 278–79

Invoices—*Continued*
  Payment dates, 64
Issuance of the Budget, 84

J

Jury of Executive Opinion Method of Forecasting Sales, 176–77

L

Labor,
  Budgeting of, 45–46
  Direct labor costs, 247–57
    Budgeting, 247–52
      Elements of cost, 248
      Labor price standards, 250–51
      Labor time standards, 248–50
      Variances, 252
    Classification of, 247–48
    Controlling, 252–57
      Control action of the standards, 252–53
      Price variances, 253
      Time variances, 254–55
    Cost reduction programs, 340
    Definition of, 247–48
    Deviations in, 343–44
    Direct materials cost contrasted with, 236–37
    Performance report, 165
  Expenses, measure of activity, 135
  Foreman's weekly labor cost report, 162–63
  Fringe benefits, 264–65
  Indirect, 259, 260–63
    Producing departments, 260–62
  Manning tables, 141–42
  Manpower budget, 254, 261
  Pay plan, 250
  Performance reports, 255–57
  Price standards,
    Incentive pay plan, 251
    Output per worker, 251
  Rework, 262
  Supplementary costs, 264–65
  Time standards, 248–50
    Advance estimate, 249–50
    Average of past performance, 249
    Service departments, 263
    Time and motion studies, 249
Liabilities, Budgeting, 334
Losses, Provision for, 335

M

Machine Tool Classification System, 133–34
Machines (See "Equipment")
Maintenance,
  Costs,
    Apportioning, 155–56
    Controlling, 266–67
    Labor, problem of budgeting, 262

INDEX

Managed Costs, 198
Management,
  Authority and responsibility, delegation of, 164, 345–46
  Budget performance reports, 114
  Budget plan, presenting to, 82–83
  Choice of alternatives by, 37
  Deviations from budget, concern with, 86
  Function of, 4
  Improvement of individual performances, 130
  Partial budget changes, authorizing, 345–46
  Philosophy of, 268, 269
  Top level,
    Budget performance reports, 114
    Budgeting capital by, 334–35
    Capital expenditures, proposals for, 305
    Cost allowances approved by, 153
    Decisions to depart from budget, 342–43
    Forecasts, over-all economic adjustment to, 183
    Research and development expenditures, role in controlling, 300–302
Manning Table, 141–42
Manpower,
  Availability and utilization of, 108
  Budget, 254, 261, 269
Manuals of Procedure, 46, 52–55
  Accuracy in, 54
  Advantages of, 53
  Authorship, 54
  Budget forms, 54
  Contents of, 53–54
  Form and distribution of, 54–55
  Importance of, 52–53
Manufacturing,
  Cycles, 225
  Expense budget, 138
  Expenses,
    Indirect (See "Burden, Factory"; "Factory Expenses")
    Organization for budgeting, 44–46
Market Conditions, Forecasts of, 109
Marketing and Distribution Costs, 194–219
  Administration costs, controlling, 218
  Budgeting, 196–207
    Administration costs, 207
    Advertising and sales promotion costs, 203–6
    Fixed costs, 197, 198
    Managed costs of obtaining sales, 202–3
    Marketing administration costs, 207
    Sales budgeting, relation to, 196
    Selling costs, 206–7
    Variable costs,
      Clerical, 202
      Resulting from sales, 198–99
      Sales compensation, 199–200
      Transportation, 201–2
    Warehousing costs, 200–201

Marketing and Distribution Costs—Continued
  Classification of, 194–96, 219
  Controlling, 207–19
    Advertising and sales promotion costs, 214–17
    Direction of sales efforts, 218–19
    Fixed costs, 209
    Marketing administration costs, 208, 218
    Nature of costs, procedures affected by, 207–9
    Selling costs, 217–18
    Variable costs,
      Clerical, 214
      Order-filling, 209–10
      Transportation, 210–14
      Warehousing, 210
  Nature of costs, 197–98
Master Budget, 7
  Changes in, recording, 346–48
  Presenting to management, 82–83
  Revisions, complete, 348–50
Material Handling Expenses, 135
Materials,
  Budgeting of, 45–46
  Cost reduction program, 340
  Direct,
    Consumption, 141–42
    Definition, 236
    Direct labor contrasted with, 236–37
    Inventories, 76, 222
      Estimating size of, 225
    Purchase and use of, 237
  Direct material costs, 236–46
    Controlling, 243–46
      Price variances, 244–45
      Usage variances, 245–46
    Elements of, 237
    Fabricated materials and parts, 241
    Quantity standards, 238–40
      Determination of, 238–39
      Methods of setting, 239–40
    Standard purchase price, establishment of, 240–42
    Standards, control function of, 243–44
    Variances, treatment of, 243
  Excess material requisitions, 245
  Forecasts of prices, 110
  Indirect, 260, 265
  Miscellaneous, estimating, 333
  Price standards, 240–42
  Scrap, 245–46
  Variability, engineering studies of, 141–42
Measurements,
  Controlling factory expense, 268–69
  Cost control allowances, validity of, 132–34
  Quantitative, 269
  Ratio of profits to sales, 15
Meetings, Staff, 49
Memberships, Costs of, 276
Method and Time Study, 249
  Budgeting costs, 268
  Clerical operations, 272–73
  Idle time, 263–64

INDEX

409

N

National Industrial Conference Board, 177
Natural Business Year, 365–66
New Products, Introduction of, 304
Nonfactory Departments, Budget planning by, 77
Nonmanufacturing Costs, 60
Notes Payable, 334

O

Objectives,
  Determining, 59–65
  Reconsideration of, 83
Office Expenses (See "General and Administrative Expenses")
Officer, Budget, Performance report comments by, 122
Offices,
  Budget, 39
  Management, 272–73
  Sales, budgeting cost of, 206–7
  Space costs, 275
Operating Data, Analysis of, 123
Operating Statement,
  Charges to income, 276
  Forecast, 95
Operations,
  Analysis of, 108
  Control of, 130
  Financial position related to, 321
  Method of performing, study of, 34–35
Operations Research, Use of, in budgeting, 350
Orders,
  Analysis of profit by size of orders, 188
  Assembling, cost of, 198, 207–10
  Minimum, 187
  Order-filling costs, 207–10
    Controlling, 209–10
    Standards, 199
  Order-getting costs, 207–9
    Controlling, 218–19
  Shipping time, 225
  Standard order size, determination of 187–88
Organization,
  Budget department, 40
  Budget director, 40
  Budget making, 38–48
    Basic assumptions, 41–42
    Capital expenditures, 46–47
    Coordination, 39–41
    Detailed planning, 42
    "Go ahead" signal, giving, 47–48
    Manufacturing expenses, 44–46
    Requirements, 38–39
    Sales forecasts, 42–44
  Budgetary control, 48–52
    Accountants' part in, 51–52
    Action function, 49–51
    Control function, 48
    Reporting function, 48–49

Organization—*Continued*
  Centralization vs. decentralization, 345–46
  Manuals of procedure, 52–55
Overhead Costs,
  Cost reduction program, 341
  Direct costing, 361
  Research and development projects, 295–96
Overtime, 157, 264
Owners' Equity, Ratio of profit to, 21

P

Packing Costs, 198
Partial Budget Methods, 352–56
Payroll Accounting, 334
Payroll Taxes, Budgeting, 334
Performance,
  Control of costs and, 164
  Direct labor performance report, 165
  Indexes, 154, 166
  Individual, improvement of, 130
  Measuring, budget report as means of, 85
  Reports of, 48–49, 112–21, 165
  Reviewing and analyzing, staff meetings for, 49–51
Personnel, Clerical and supervisory, 136
Personnel Department, Planning budget for, 76
Personnel Relations, Expenditures for, 305
Planning,
  Amendment of plans and assumptions, 79–82
  Budgetary control, 107
  Choice of alternatives, 37
  Comparison of plan and result of operations, 7–8
  Control and, 7–8
  Cooperation required, 7
  Coordination, 6–7
  Detailed plans or schedules, 7
  External forces influencing, 5
  Good planning, essence of, 111
  Importance of, 4–8
  Integrated plans required, 66
  Internal forces influencing, 5
  Length of period for, 6
  Long-range and short-range, 5–6, 57
  Management, presenting plan to, 82–83
  Master plan, 7 (See also "Master Budget")
  Need for, 5
  Profit, 14–37
  Purpose and nature of, 4–7
  Techniques, 33–37
    Differential method of analysis, 33–35
Plans, Budget,
  Budget variations as a measure of validity of, 109–11
  Management, presenting to, 82–83
  Summary of results, 82–83
Plant Capacity, 133–34
  Break-even point, 29
  Sales based on, 175
Postage Costs, 275

INDEX

Power Costs,
  Apportioning, 155-56
  Controlling, 266-67
Prepaid Expenses, 332
  Budgeting, 332
Preparation of Budget, 56-84
  Costing problem, 356-58
  1st step: specifying objectives, 58-66
    Budget directives, 65-66
    Capital improvements, investment in, 65
    Inventory balance, improvement of, 64
    Product costs, obtaining better, 62-65
    Production schedules, greater uniformity in, 64-65
    Purchase discounts, greater realization of, 64
    Return on investment, improvement of, 59-65
    Sales and sales costs, obtaining better relationship between, 64
  2nd step: formlating of plans and assumptions by department heads, 66-79
    Accounting department, 77-79
    Engineering department, 76-77
    Integrated plans required, 66
    Nonfactory departments, budgeting administration of, 77
    Outline of budget plans and departments affected, 67
    Personnel department, 76
    Production department, 72-74
    Purchasing department, 74-76
    Sales department, 68-70
      Decisions, 70-72
    Treasury department, 77
  3rd step: amendment of plans and assumptions, 79-83
    Amendments of departmental plans, 79-81
    Budget directives, alterations of, 81-82
    Coordination of detailed plans, 79
    Relationship of budget schedules, 80
  4th step: presenting plans to management, 82-83
    Reconsideration of objectives and directives, 83
    Summary of results of plan, 82-83
  5th step: approval of the budget, 83-84
  6th step: issuance of the budget, 84
Prepayments, Estimation of, 78-79
President of the Company,
  Budget plan approved by, 83-84
  Budget plan submitted to, 82-83
Prices and Pricing,
  Controlling variances, 244-45
  Cost a function of price and quantity, 139-40
  Cost-plus method, 15, 172-73
  Determination of, 172-75
  Flexible market pricing, 173
  Following price structure of the principal producer, 173

Prices and Pricing—*Continued*
  Labor price standards, 250-51
    Controlling price variances, 253-54
    Incentive pay plan and, 251
  Policy, 172
    Predetermined burden absorption rate effects, 62-63
  Price trends, estimating, 240
  Standard purchase price, establishment of, 240-42
  Volume-cost-price-profit relationships, 25-33
Prior Experience, Used in determining cost allowances, 142-53
Pro Forma Entries, 9, 266-67
Pro Forma Expense Distribution Sheet, 266-67
Production,
  Budgeting for more uniform schedules, 64-65
  Budgeting of, 45-46
  Burden absorption rate, 63
  Change-overs, 226-27
    Norton formula, 226
  Control of physical operations, 108
  Cost reduction program, 340
  Cycle, 224
  Department,
    Expense schedule, 259
    Expenses, departmentalization of, 266-67
    Indirect labor, 260-62
    Planning, 72-74
    Pro forma expense distribution sheet, 266-67
  Direct labor requirements, 72
  Direct materials requirements, 72
  Economic lot calculation, 226-28
  Factory burden, 72
  Inventory schedules important in achieving, 221
  Run, finding most economical, 226
  Schedules, 64-65, 72
    Budget directive, 92
    Completions, of, 72
    Cutback or expansion of, 342
  Variations from plan, 110
  Work in process inventory, 72
Products,
  Budgets, use of in obtaining better cost, 62-65
  Cost reduction program, 340
  Costing procedure, 62-64, 269
  Costs, obtaining better, 62-65
  Development (See "Research and Development Costs")
  Finished, inventories, 221
  Investments in, 324-26
  New,
    Cost and income, comparative, study of, 34-35
    Development of, 170
    Expenditures for, 304-5
    Planning, short- and long-range, 171
  Profit and loss, 362-64

INDEX

Products—*Continued*
  Profit and loss—*Continued*
    Measurements,
      Contribution theory of profits, 364
      Decentralization, effect of, 364
      Reporting, practices in, 362–64
    Profit contribution reports, 219
    Profitableness, variation in, 170–71
    Rate of return analysis, 324
    Sales mix, determination of, 185
    Selecting product to be sold, 170–71, 324
    Standard order size, determination of, 187–88
    Unit costs, 12, 356–57
Professional Services, 271
  Budgeting, 273
Profit and Loss,
  Alternative budgeting practices, 362–64
  Budget deviations, relation to, 343–44
  Contribution theory of profit, 364
  Reporting, practices in, 362–64
Profit and Loss Statement, 362–64
  Decentralization, effect of, 364
  Forecast, 335
  Preparation of, 335–36
Profit Planning, 14–37
  Analysis of profit by size of orders, 188
  Objective and measurements in, 14–17
  Standard sales mix, determination of, 185–86
  Techniques, 33–37
    Differences must be real, 35–36
    Different costs of or different purposes, concept of, 36–37
    Differential analyses, method of, 33–35
    Principles, use of, 37
    Volume-cost-price-profit relationships, 25–32
Profits,
  Basis for,
    Capital employed, 17
    Sales, 17
  Contribution theory of, 364
  Estimated net, 354
  Laws of, 30–31
  Net operating, vs. net income, 20
  Profit planning, objective of, 14–17
  "Pure," 16
  Ratio of profit to owners' equity, 21
  Ratio of profits to sales, 15
  Return on investment method, 16, 17–25
    Capital employed, meaning of, 20–21
    Desired return on capital employed, 24–25
    Factors affecting, relationship of, 19
    Fixed assets, 22–24
    Net operating profit vs. net income, 20
    Time as a factor in analysis, 17–20
    Working assets, 21–22
  Volume-cost-price-profit relationships, 25–32
    Break-even calculations, 28–29
    Break-even chart, 26
    Fixed and variable costs, 27–28
    Laws of costs and profits, 30–31

Profits—*Continued*
  Volume-cost-price-profit relationship—*Continued*
    Limitations of analyses, 31–32
    Required volume to earn a profit, 29–30
    Volume-price relationship, 32–33
Property, Acquisition of fixed, 304
Public Relations, Expenditures for, 305
Purchase Discounts,
  Budgeting, 278–79
  Control of, 283–84
  Taking advantage of, 64
Purchases,
  Research and development, 299–300
  Standard purchase price, establishing, 240–42
Purchasing Department,
  Planning budget for, 74–76
  Schedules, 74–76

Q

Quantities,
  Cost a function of price and, 139–40
  Determination of, 175
  Price and volume relationship, 175
Quantity Standards, 238–40
  Determination, 238
    Analysis of past experience, 238
    Engineering studies, 238
    Test runs under controlled conditions, 238
  Methods of setting, 239–40

R

Rate of Return on Capital Employed, 17–25
  Budgets used to improve, 59–65
  Comparisons of, computing, 312–13
  Forecast statement, 96
  Variations in, analysis of, 128
Ratios,
  Cash receipts to sales, 327
  Discounts to expenditures, 334
  Inventory, 232–34
  Marginal income, 30–31
  Profit to owners' equity, 21
  Profits to sales, 15
Receivables,
  Account (See also "Accounts Receivable")
  Accounting for, 22
  Collection of, 326–27
  Investment in, 325
Records,
  Equipment, 301
  Inventories, 234–35
  Partial budget changes, 346–48
Repairs,
  Apportioning costs of, 156
  Office equipment, 274–75
Replacements, Expenditures for, 304, 313, 317
Reports,
  Advertising budget performance, 215
  Background information included, 86

Reports—*Continued*
  Budget (See also "Illustrative Company, Budget reports")
    Distribution of, 48
    Exhibits section, 82, 86, 94–99, 115–18
    Final form, 86–104
    Form of, 85–104 (See also "Form of Budget")
    Narrative section, 82, 86, 90–93
    Schedules section, 86, 100–104, 119–22
  Budget performance, 112–21
  Cost control, 164
    Departmental, 268
  Cost variances, 161–66
    Contents of, 164
    Direct labor performance, 165
    Examples of, 164–66
    Foreman's weekly labor cost report, 162–63
    Performance indexes, 164, 166
  Illustrative Company, 89–104 (See also "Illustrative Company, Budget reports")
  Internal, 112–21
    Charts and schedules, 113
    Comparison of actual and planned results, 114
    "Exception items," 113
    Form of, 114
    Nature of, 112–13
    Purpose of, 112–13
  Inventory control, 234–35
  Labor performance, 255–57
  Performance, 48–49, 164, 166, 255–57
  Preparation of, by controller's division, 48–49
  Presentation of, to management, 82–83
  Purposes of, 85
  Research projects, 298–99
  Sales performance, 189–90
  Schedules, 95–104, 119–22
  Scrap, 246
  Statement of objectives, 86
  Transportation expense statistical, 212–13
Research and Development Costs, 285–302
  Basic research, 286
  Budgeting, 287–96
    Definition of project, 292
    Financial accounting for costs, 296
    Form of project request, 291–93
      Experimental work order request, 294
    Individual projects, 295
    Nature of costs, 293–96
    Overhead costs, 295–96
    Planning the total expenditure, 287–89
    Selection of projects, 289–91
  Control of, 293, 297–302
    Equipment costs, 300
      Records, 301
    Form and use of reports, 298–99
    Over-all costs, 297
    Periodic review of all projects, 299
    Project costs, 297
    Purchases, 299–300
    Supplies, 300
    Top management, role of, 300–302

Research and Development Costs—*Continued*
    Funds, allocation of, within the division, 295–97
    Process development, 286
    Product development, 285, 286
    Scientific research departments, growth of, 285–86
    Types of research, 286–87
  Research Director, Duties of, 297
  Reserves, Surplus, 335
  Responsibility,
    Costs incurred in one department but used by another, 155–56
    Delegation of authority and, 164
  Retained Earnings, 323, 334–35
  Return on Investment Method of Measuring Profits, 17–25
    Capital employed, 24–25
    Definition of, 20–21
    Desired return on capital employed, 24–25
    Fixed assets, 22–24
    Forecasts, 86, 96
    Improvement of company's, 59–65
    Net operating profit vs. net income, 20
    Relationship of factors affecting, 19
    Time as a factor in the analysis, 17–20
    Working assets, 21–22
      Cash, 21
      Inventories, 22
      Other assets, 22
      Receivables, 22
  Revisions, Budget, 130, 337–50
    Budget as a business model, 350
    Budget deviations, nature of, 337–39
    Changes in amount or direction of sales effort, 341–42
    Complete, 348–50
    Cost reduction programs, 339–41
    Deviations, significance of, 343–44
    Economic conditions, effect of, on, 350
    New managerial decisions in other areas, 342–43
    Partial budget changes,
      Authorization of, 344–46
      Recording, 346–48
    Production schedules, 342
  Rework Budget, 262

S

Salaries and Wages, 271–73
  Accrued wages and payroll taxes, budgeting, 334
  Control of, 279
  Time standards, use of, 272–73
Sales,
  Accounts, classification of, 12, 192–93
  Actual and planned sales, comparison of, 189–90
  Branch offices, 172
  Brokers, 172
  Budget, deviation in, 344
  Budgeting, 169–84
    Marketing and distribution cost related to, 196

INDEX 413

Sales—*Continued*
  Budgeting—*Continued*
    Methods of forecasting sales, 175–83
    Price, determination of, 172–75
    Product to be sold, selection of, 170–71
    Quantities, determination of, 175
    Sales method, selection of, 171–72
    Sales policy, determination of, 169–70
  Budgeting variable costs resulting from, 198–99
  Control of, 184–93
    Accounting, requirements, 191–93
    Budgeting and, interrelationship of, 184–85
    Definition, 184–85
    Interpretation and action, 190–91
    Sales standards reviewed, 189
    Standard order size, determination of, 187–88
    Standard sales mix, determination of, 185–87
    Standard territorial distribution, 188–89
    Standards, 185
    Taking action, 191
  Cost reduction program, 341
  Department,
    Decisions, 70–72
    Planning, 68–70
  Discounts, 276–77
    Control of, 281
  Efforts, 169
    Changes in amount or direction of, 218–19, 341–42
    Controlling direction of, 218–19
    Cost of, 198, 202–3 (See also "Selling Costs")
  Expenses, in budget report, 90–91, 119–20
  Forecasts, 175–83 (See also "Forecasting, Sales")
    Based on market conditions, 109–10
    Factory cost of sales, 101
    Foundation of budget, 109
    Methods, selection of, 171–72
  Mix, determination of standard, 185–86
    Activity, measure of, 135
    Budgeting costs of, 206–7
  Partial budget methods, 355–56
  Performance,
    Analysis of, 123–25
    Reports, 189–90
  Planning, 66–68
  Plans, 7
    Budget report includes, 90
    Cornerstone of operating budget, 169
  Policy, determination of, 169–70
  Price determination, 172–75
  Promotion,
    Allocation of expenditures, 205
    Budgeting costs of, 203–6
    Costs, control of, 214–17
  Ratio of profits to sales, 15
  Relationship between capital employed and volume of, 18
  Relationship between sales effort and, 64
  Schedules, 4, 189

Sales—*Continued*
  Standard, comparison of actual and, 189–90
  Standards, review of, 189
  Variations, cost of, 124–26
    Material usage variance, 126
    Overabsorption of factory burden, 124
    Purchase variance, 126
    Result of quantities of product sold, 124
Salesmen,
  Budgeting selling costs, 206–7
  Call reports, 218
  Compensation of, 35, 69
  Evaluating effort of, 217–18
  Overhead cost of selling, 217–18
  Profit contribution reports, 219
  Territories, 188–89
  Travel expenses (See "Travel Costs")
Schedules, Budget,
  Changes in, recording, 346–48
  Cost allowances, 153
  Definition, 4
  Detail in, extent of, 86
  Illustrative Company, 100–104, 119–22
  Inclusion of, in budget report, 82
  Relationship of, 80
  Sales, 189
  Time periods, 189
Scrap Materials, 245–46
  Report, 246
Selling Costs,
  Analysis of, 12
  Budgeting, 206–7
  Forecast, 102
  Marketing and distribution, 217
  Sales department planning, 68–70
  Sales efforts, 169
  Variations in, analysis of, 126
Service Departments,
  Expense schedule, 259
  Expenses, departmentalization of, 266–67
  Indirect labor, budgeting, 262–63
  Manning tables, 263
  Pro forma expense distribution sheet, 266–67
  Types of, 262
Shipping Costs, 198, 225
Social Security Tax Accruals, 328
Sources and Applications of Funds, 117
  Forecast, 86, 97
Sources of Funds, 321–24
  Creditors, 323
  Debt financing decisions, 321–23
  Forecasts, 86, 97
  Owners' investment in capital stock, 323
  Retained earnings, 323
Space,
  Costs of,
    Apportioning, 155–56
    Budgeting, 268, 272, 275
  Utilization, 210
Standards,
  General and administrative expenses, 280

Standards—*Continued*
  Labor price, 250–51
  Labor time, 248–50
  Material price, 240–42
  Quantity, 238–40
Statistics,
  Analyses of prior experience, 142–53
    Arrangement of data, 144
    Plotting the record, 143–47
    "Least-squares" method, 147–50
    Sales, forecasting, 175, 179
    Scatter diagram, 144–45
    Trend line, determination of, 147–53
      High-low method of, 150–53
      Mathematical approach, 147–50
Steel Industry, Quantity standards, 239–40
Stock, Capital, 335
Storage Costs, 200–201
Subscriptions, Dues, and Memberships, 272, 276
Supervisors (See "Foremen")
Supplies, 271, 274
  Budgeting, 274
  Cost reduction program, 340
  Estimating miscellaneous, 333
  Forecasts of prices of, 110
  Indirect materials, 265
  Operating,
    Relationship of work force to cost of, 146–50
    Statistical study of, 146–47
  Research and development, 300
Surplus Items Report, 234
Surplus Reserves, Policy decided by top management, 335
Sylvania Capital Expenditures Control, 309

T

Taking Action, 129–30
  Budget consciousness, promotion of, 129–30
  Control, as a method of, 129
  Individual performance, improvement of, 130
  Persons responsible for, 130
  Revisions, budget, 130
  Sales budgets, 191
Taxes,
  Budgeting, 265
  Controlling costs of, 267
  Payroll, 334
  Social security tax accruals, 328
Technical Services, 268
Telephone, Telegraph, and Postage, 272, 275
Territories, Sales,
  Profit contribution reports, 219
  Territorial distribution of sales, 188–89
Time,
  Factor in analysis, 17–20
  Idle, 259, 263–64
Time Charges, Control of, 267

Time Factor in Budgeting, 17–20
  Alternative practices, 364–67
  Equal budget periods within the year, 366–67
  Natural business year, 365–66
  Thirteen-week periods, 365
  Twenty-one work-day month, 366–67
Time-keeping Costs, 268
Time Standards,
  Advance estimate, 249–50
  Clerical employees, 272–73
  Incentive systems and, 134
  Labor, 248
  Past performance, average of, 249
  Time and motion studies, 249, 263–64
  Variances, 254–55
Transportation Costs, 198
  Variable,
    Budgeting, 201–2
    Control of, 210–14
      Expense statistical report, 212–13
      Report and interpretations of, 210–14
Travel Costs, 272, 275–76
  Control of, 279
  Cost control allowance, 132–33, 140–41, 146
  General and administrative, 275–76
  Record of, plotting, 143–47
  Scatter diagram of, 145
Treasury Department, Budget planning, 77
Trends,
  Determining trend line, 147–53
    Mathematical approach, 147–50
  High-low method of trend determination, 150–53
  Sales, 192
Turnover, Capital investment, 16

U

Usage Variances, Materials, 245–46
Utilization Studies, Electronic equipment, 275

V

Validity of Measure, Cost control allowances, 132–34
Valuation,
  Depreciated value, 22–24
  Gross book value, 22–24
Variability,
  Engineering studies of, 141–42
  Prior experience, statistical analyses of, 142–53
  Trend line, determination of, 147–53
Variances, Cost
  Activity and responsibility, departmentalization of, 155–57
  Actual and allowed expenses, comparison of, 157–61
    Data, collection of, 157
    Rate of activity, 157–59
    Unabsorbed burden, problem of, 159–61

Variances, Cost—*Continued*
  Analysis and reporting of, 154–66
  Budget deviations, nature of, 337–39
  Controllable vs. noncontrollable costs, 156–57
  Engineering studies of, 141–42
  Known, determination of, 140–41
  Marketing and distribution, 197
  Reports, 161–66
    Contents of, restricting, 164
    Examples of, 164–66
    Foreman's weekly labor cost report, 162–63
    Requirements summarized, 161
  Stepped, 137–38
  Studies of, 141–53
Variations,
  Analysis and reporting of, 107–30
    Cost of sales, 124–26
    Efficiency, measure of, 108–9
    Financial plan used for, 128–29
    General and administrative expenses, 126–27
    Net income and rate of return, 128
    Operating data, 122
    Other income and deductions, 127–28
    Sales mix, change in, 122–23, 125
    Selling expenses, 126
    Validity of plan, measure of, 109–11
  Direct labor costs, 252
  Direct material costs, 243
  Inventory, 231–32
  Price, 244–45
  Reports of, 112–21
    Charts and schedules, 113
    Form of, 114–21
    Illustrative Company, 115–21

Variations—*Continued*
  Reports of—*Continued*
    Purpose of, 112–13
    Unrealistic budget, a cause of 110–11
Volume,
  Burden absorption rate, 63
  Relationship between cost, price, profit and, 25–32
    Break-even calculations, 28–29
    Fixed and variable costs, 27–28
    Laws of costs and profits, 30–31
    Limitations of analyses, 31–32
    Required volume to earn a profit, 29–30

W

Wage Plans, 250–51 (See also "Salaries and Wages")
Warehousing, Variable costs of,
  Budgeting, 201
  Control of, 210
Wholesalers, 172
Wire Cost Standards, 239
Work in Process Inventories, 221–22, 225
Working Capital,
  Changes in, 323–24
  Depreciation funds used to finance, 333
  Forecasts, 86, 98
  Sales discounts, effect of, on, 277
Working Shift Schedule, 133

Y

Year,
  Calendar, 57
  Fiscal, 57
  Natural business, 365–66

RET'D APR 28 1986

MAY 27 1992